This book belongs to:

# THE BOOK OF JEZEBEL

*An Illustrated Encyclopedia of*
*Lady Things*

**Edited by ANNA HOLMES**

**Written by: KATE HARDING, AMANDA HESS**

**Contributing Writers:** Chloe Angyal, Katie J. M. Baker, Gabrielle Birkner, Irin Carmon, Megan Carpentier, Pixie Casey, Jessica Coen, Madeleine Davies, Michelle Dean, Sady Doyle, Rana Emerson, Ann Friedman, Jessica Grose, Katie Halper, Mikki Halpin, Margaret Hartmann, Anna Holmes, Elisa Kreisinger, Amanda Marcotte, Marisa Meltzer, Tracie Egan Morrissey, Anna North, Latoya Peterson, Kartina Richardson, Alyssa Rosenberg, Erin Ryan, Jenna Sauers, Becky Sharper, Lizzie Skurnick, Sadie Stein, Dodai Stewart, Rachel Syme, Moe Tkacik, Rebecca Traister, Jennifer Gerson Uffalussy, Lindy West, Jess Zimmerman, Claire Zulkey

**Graphics & Illustrations:** Julie Teninbaum, Susie Cagle, Domitille Collardey, Molly Crabapple, Eleanor Davis, Vanessa Davis, Tatyana Fazlalizadeh, Sarah Glidden, Lisa Hanawalt, Rachel Herrick, Wendy MacNaughton, Kris Mukai, Elizabeth Carey Smith, Jen Sorensen, Esther Werdiger, Christie Young, Ping Zhu

**Endpaper Illustrations:** Craig Bostick

**Interns (Research & Writing):** Alexis Chaney, Kate Dries, Catherine Garcia

**Photo Editing & Research:** Anna Holmes, Bethany Mezick, Lorenna Gomez-Sanchez

**Production Editor:** Erica Warren

**Researchers:** Hilary Elkins, Kyla Jones, Alysha Webb, Elizabeth Whitman

**GRAND CENTRAL**
PUBLISHING

NEW YORK • BOSTON

Grand Central Publishing
Hachette Book Group
237 Park Avenue
New York, NY 10017

www.HachetteBookGroup.com

Cover Illustration by Patric King/House of Pretty
Interior Design by BTDNYC

Printed in the United States of America

Q-MA

First Edition: October 2013

10 9 8 7 6 5 4 3 2

Grand Central Publishing is a division of Hachette Book Group, Inc.
The Grand Central Publishing name and logo is a trademark of Hachette Book Group, Inc.

The Hachette Speakers Bureau provides a wide range of authors for speaking events.
To find out more, go to www.hachettespeakersbureau.com or call (866) 376-6591.
The publisher is not responsible for websites (or their content) that are not owned by the publisher.

Library of Congress Control Number: 2013939252

ISBN 978-1-4555-0280-6

FOR ALL THE JEZEBELS,
biblical and otherwise

# INTRODUCTION

**DEAR READERS:**

The volume you are about to peruse is a work of fact and opinion. Or perhaps, opinion and fact. Regardless, within these pages you will find over one thousand encyclopedic entries on everything from abortion rights and the beloved YA author Judy Blume to the problematic elitism of *Vogue* magazine and euphemisms for the word "vagina"—many accompanied by beautiful, provocative photographs, graphics and illustrations. What you will also find: A seemingly pathological obsession with pop culture characters, bodily functions, and political heroines. Mockery of Scott Baio. Pro-choice, feminist politics. A flowchart on how to respond to a marriage proposal. Caterwauling about the patriarchy. And perhaps the most disgusting illustrated taxonomy of clogged pores and pimples ever committed to paper.

**You may be thinking: okay, but why?** (Also: Ew!) The answer is pretty straightforward: because we thought it might be fun to collect our various observations, fascinations, annoyances, and inspirations into one easy-to-use, attractive-looking volume. Because signing on for a book project of this size and scope always sounds a lot easier in theory than it is in reality. But most importantly, because we love and are in awe of our readers' diversity, intellect, and exuberance.

**How to use this book:** Buy it. Laugh with it...or at it. Give copies as gifts. React to it. (Unfortunately, due to space limitations and general forgetfulness, some people and subjects are missing altogether; give us your thoughts and suggestions by emailing bookofjezebel@jezebel.com.) Most importantly: Enjoy it.

**YOUR EDITOR,**

**ANNA**

### Aaliyah (1979–2001)

Talented nineties R&B singer who died at the age of twenty-two in a particularly celebrity way after her plane crashed coming back from a music video shoot in the Bahamas because it was weighted down with luggage. Her legacy lives on through the work of contemporaries like Missy Elliott and her producer Timbaland, in scandalous Drake remixes, and in the memory of her brief, illicit, and annulled marriage to R. Kelly (and the song "Age Ain't Nothing But A Number," which he wrote and she recorded).

### Abakanowicz, Magdalena (1930–)

Polish-born sculptor who spent much of her early life under Soviet domination and learned to make do with the materials she could cobble together. In the 1960s, Abakanowicz created three-dimensional *Abakans* forms with materials she wove herself. In the eighties, she moved on to bronze, stone, wood, and iron sculptures. Her work is installed around the world. In 2006, *Agora*, a large permanent project for Chicago's Grant Park consisting of more than a hundred nine-foot-tall iron cast figures, was installed.

### Abercrombie & Fitch

Venerable retailer of safari gear loved by Theodore Roosevelt that was acquired and transformed in 1988 by Ohio-based Limited Brands into a suburban prep staple known as much for its cologne-drenched mall stores and shirtless catalog models as for its questionable employee "look policy" and its history of releasing sexist and racist T-shirts. Nineties boy band LFO once sang the refrain "I like girls who wear Abercrombie & Fitch," but when the company began selling T-shirts with slogans such as "Show the Twins" and "Who Needs Brains When You Have These?," it was hard not to believe the store felt the same way about its female customers.

### abortifacient

A chemical agent or drug used to terminate a pregnancy, usually either by hormonally inducing a miscarriage, by activating contractions, or by some combination of the two. Mifepristone, the drug commonly known as RU-486, works hormonally; misoprostol (Cytotec) and most early abortifacients like ergot and cotton root bark promote contractions and are also used during childbirth for that reason. More than a century before the French chemist Georges Teutsch synthesized mifepristone, cotton root and ergot were often advertised as "French renovating pills." The term *abortifacient* is also regularly and deliberately misused by right-wingers to describe the "morning-after pill," Plan B, which is a contraceptive.

### abortion

A safe and legal way to end an unwanted pregnancy.

### Abramović, Marina (1946–)

Belgrade-born, New York–based performance artist, considered one of the pioneers of the genre. Abramović's work revolves around the human body, particularly its physical limits and tolerance for pain: she's particularly well known for a six-hour 1974 performance, *Rhythm 0*, during which she provided the gallery audience with seventy-two objects—including a gun and a bullet, a rose, a scalpel, a whip, and honey—that they were permitted to use on her body in any way they chose. Video of the work shows gallery-goers removing Abramović's clothing, writing on her body with lipstick, and scratching her with the rose's thorns; one person aimed the gun at her head. Abramović's 2010 retrospective at the Museum of Modern Art brought her more acclaim for her piece *The Artist Is Present*, in which she sat on a wooden chair across from a member of the public every day for three months. The piece was enormously popular—celebrities like Björk, James Franco, and Sharon Stone even attended—with many moved to tears.

### Abramson, Jill (1954–)

The first-ever female to become executive editor of the *New York Times*. Before she took over the position in 2011, she gained experience (and respect) by weathering some of the paper's most trying times—including the Jayson Blair and Judith Miller scandals—as Washington bureau chief and managing editor. Has also written a book about raising a puppy.

### *Absolutely Fabulous*

British comedy series also known as *Ab Fab* that ran from 1992 to 1995 starring Joanna Lumley and Jennifer Saunders, who also created it. Back in the early nineties, the boozy, pill-popping, acid-tongued, credit-wrecking, gleefully narcissistic exploits of publicist Edina Monsoon (Jennifer Saunders) and fashion editor Patsy Stone (Joanna Lumley) were

as shocking as they were hilarious. Not to mention, you'll notice that on that list of current envelope pushers, you don't see any revolving around two middle-aged women and their mostly female comrades. More than twenty years later, there is still, truly, no other show like it—which is kind of depressing if you think about it. Where are our pills?

### abstinence

Purposely refraining from having sex, often because of religious objections to premarital sex and/or in an effort to avoid pregnancy and/or sexually transmitted infections (STIs). Though eliminating all contact with another person's genitals and bodily fluids is a fully effective, if frustrating, method for avoiding pregnancy and all STIs, many people nonetheless consider themselves abstinent if they only avoid vaginal penetration. (This method of abstinence, though modeled by Bill Clinton, can still transmit infections or, more rarely, viable sperm to the vagina.) Despite the fact that full, informed abstinence is increasingly rare, religious conservatives have fought for years to make it the focus of sex ed in primary and secondary schools, though this has been correlated with higher rates of teen pregnancy and STIs.

### Abzug, Bella Savitsky (1920–1998)

Civil rights lawyer, feminist, peace activist, three-term congresswoman, and famous hat-wearer. A first-generation American born in the Bronx to Russian Jewish immigrants and a graduate of Hunter College and Columbia Law School, Abzug first entered politics when she raised money for the Jewish National Fund by making speeches in New York subway stations. Abzug began her law practice with cases supporting "bypassed peoples," represented Willie McGee in his appeals to the Supreme Court after his conviction for raping a white woman in Mississippi in a racially motivated trial, and took on cases of McCarthyite accusations of citizens. In 1961, Abzug and a group of friends and colleagues founded Women Strike for Peace, which advocated for a ban on nuclear testing, an end to the Vietnam War, and Eugene McCarthy's 1968 presidential campaign. In 1970, she jumped into the political fray herself, primarying against Leonard Farbstein, the longtime Democratic representative of New York's Nineteenth Congressional District. Abzug rallied her supporters under the slogan "This woman's place is in the house… the House of Representatives!" and, after her win, her uncompromising advocacy (on issues including Vietnam, child-care services for working women, her introduction of the Equality Act of 1974, and the first federal gay rights bill) led Senate Minority Leader Hugh Scott to declare Abzug "the only man in the House." Other criticisms were similarly sexist: Norman Mailer famously wrote that her voice could "boil the fat off a taxicab driver's neck."

### Accused, The

Unsparing 1988 drama based on the real-life case of Cheryl Araujo, starring Jodie Foster as the victim of a brutal gang rape who discovers and cultivates her own inner strength and sense of empowerment as the criminal trial against her attackers commences. Though the film was conceived and produced by capital-H Hollywood—whose idea of justice for rape victims oscillates

between straight-up revenge (*The Last House on the Left, I Spit on Your Grave*) and a stage on which white-guy defenders can strut their righteous stuff (*A Time to Kill*)—its (male) director and screenwriter were able to create a narrative that skewers ye olde "She Was Asking for It" myth.

work of having too much of an "abstract and cerebral resonance" and no heart, which is just what some dudes *would* say, isn't it?

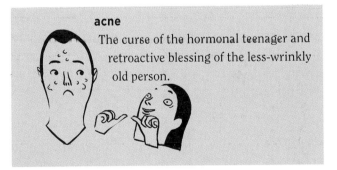

**acne**
The curse of the hormonal teenager and retroactive blessing of the less-wrinkly old person.

### Acker, Kathy (1947-1997)

American postmodern novelist who was tattooed and sex-positive by the late 1970s, before being tattooed and sex-positive was a big thing. Her 1984 book *Blood and Guts in High School*, which arguably presaged the LiveJournal style, concerned a girl named Janey Smith who is sold into prostitution by her father. Acker, said British novelist Michael Bracewell approvingly, was a courageous risk-taker as a writer, a purveyor of "a kind of reckless give-a-shit determination to be contrary—even when the celebrity and applause with which her work had first been greeted had long since died down." Others were not so kind. David Foster Wallace panned her early books in the *Harvard Review*, accusing her

### A cups

Small-size breasts, commonly defined by a half- to one-inch difference in the circumference around a woman's actual breasts and that around her upper chest. For some, these mini mammaries are the locus of a certain amount of angst, so persistent and loud is the ambient culture's demand for breasts that are perky, symmetrical, and big. For others, A cups come with certain advantages, like finding clothing that fits well—most labels' pattern blocks aren't designed with larger breasts in mind—and ease of use while jogging. Those who really are gunning for president of the Itty-Bitty Titty Committee may even realize their busts are too modestly sized to benefit from bras at all. Freedom!

## Adam

Inchoately sexed mud-person. Seriously. In the second account in Genesis of the creation of humanity, 'adham ("earth creature") is the human progenitor made out of dirt and divine breath. It is out of 'adham that both man and woman are taken, by being separated into sexate humanity, so the whole "first man, then woman" thing doesn't exactly hold up. Phyllis Trible, feminist biblical scholar and general superstar, wrote a watershed 1973 article about this, causing those who argue for male supremacy based on primordial male precedence to look even more daft than they did previously. Of course, then there's the fossil record, but whatevs.

## Adams, Abigail (1744-1818)

The baller behind President John Adams who was the real brains behind the American Revolution, Abigail Adams also

wrote a good letter, especially when she famously told husband John to get his shit together while writing the Constitution and "remember the ladies." In the made-for-TV movie *1776*, her husband was played by Mr. Feeny (William Daniels) from *Boy Meets World*.

## Adams, Carol J. (1951-)

Author and activist whose 1990 book *The Sexual Politics of Meat: A Feminist-Vegetarian Critical Theory* linked carnivorism to patriarchy by highlighting sexual imagery in meat advertising and who was mocked a bit at the time. A little bit militant about the necessity of being a vegetarian in order to be properly antisexist. Hates PETA. (*See also* GAGA, LADY; PETA)

## *Adam's Rib*

1949 film about married lawyers (Katharine Hepburn and Spencer Tracy) who oppose each other in court over a case involving a married woman accused of shooting her husband. Its delightful subversion of traditional gender roles earned the movie a spot on AFI's list of 100 Funniest American Movies of All Time. (*See* HEPBURN, KATHARINE)

## Addams, Jane (1860-1935)

Philosopher, activist, and suffragette who, alongside Theodore Roosevelt, was one of the most prolific reformers of the Progressive Era. The first woman to be awarded the Nobel Peace Prize. With Ellen Gates Starr, Addams founded Chicago's Hull House—America's first settlement house—in 1889. It eventually became a facility where women in need could live, take

night classes, cultivate hobbies, and care for their children. At its peak, the settlement house was also a center for philanthropy where women would research and tackle social issues such as overcrowding, children's illiteracy, and disease. In 1910, Addams became the first female recipient of an honorary degree awarded by Yale University. In 1915, she was elected national chairman of the Women's Peace Party and, that same year, elected president of the Women's International League for Peace and Freedom.

## Adderall

Miracle drug used to treat ADHD and narcolepsy that enables users to sit at their desks getting Tiger Mom–approved quantities of work accomplished and losing five to ten pounds *at the same time*. (So long as they don't mind the accompanying hand tremors, dramatic gum erosion, sometime compulsion to masturbate, occasional bloody shits, hopeless addiction, and moderate to severe acne eruptions on highly improbable areas of the body, like eyelids.)

## adoption

Formal process of becoming parent to a child not biologically your own. If you're pregnant and cannot raise the child yourself, antichoicers would have you believe this is a relatively easy process and a morally superior alternative to abortion, even though it means enduring forty weeks of pregnancy, labor, and any complications that might arise from those, then handing the baby over to strangers while you're physically exhausted and maximally hormonal.

## adventuress

Woman with a love of travel and a curiosity about the world. To men, an unscrupulous seeker of wealth, social position, and, most threateningly, opportunity, usually by means of sexual wiles; to unsympathetic women, a gender traitor; to the rest of us, a rebel and sometimes pioneer. Gold diggers are distinct from adventuresses in that, for the former, financial security is the point, while for the latter it's a temporary respite. "What more am I, when every act of my life is a venture? What else am I, when adventure or misadventure form the whole ensemble of my existence?" wrote the anonymous author of "My Experiences as an Adventuress" in the 1888 July–December edition of *Lippincott's Monthly* magazine. "The ordinary adventuress adventures to gain by others' loss. An extraordinary adventuress, such as I am, adventures to benefit herself in spite of fate and to nobody's loss save the waste of prophecy to the knowing ones who declare she will yet come to grief." Famous adventuresses include literary actress Irene Adler, lady pirate Anne Bonney, the multicareered Moll Flanders, and aviatrix Beryl Markham. (*See also* EARHART, AMELIA; PERÓN, EVA)

## advertising

**1.** Simple means of informing the public about goods and services that has become a relentless global flood of symbols of commercialization so pervasive that it is now part of our culture's entertainment. **2.** Industry in which Don Draper, Peggy Olson, and most of the *Mad Men* cast toil. **3.** Unavoidable media constructed to make you feel so bad about yourself you'll have to buy something you don't need.

## age of consent

More or less self-explanatory concept but one that apparently confuses and concerns a certain kind of man because he "can't help it" if he is attracted to "younger women." (Look at that poor Polanski fellow, after all, entrapped by the cleverness of a thirteen-year-old!)

## AIDS

Disease of the human immune system. Affects 15.9 million women around the world, most in sub-Saharan Africa. Very much misunderstood: in Botswana, one minister of health publicly blamed women for its spread, and a US study found that 59 percent of Americans are uncomfortable with an HIV-positive female child-care provider.

## airbrushing

Apparel detailing popular in the 1980s among young women who embellished pieces of clothing—usually tops—with swirly script lettering, unicorns and palm trees and names of lovers whose relationships rarely lasted longer than the fabric on which they were immortalized. (*For airbrushing of photographs, see* PHOTOSHOP; PHOTOSHOP OF HORRORS)

## Akhmatova, Anna (1889–1966)

Writer, poet. Publicly, Akhmatova wrote on love. Privately, Stalin. Early in her career, Akhmatova established herself as Russia's siren ("lifting his dry hand / He lightly touched the flowers: / 'Tell me how you kiss men.' / And his lusterless eyes / Did not move from my ring"). When Stalin's regime killed her husband, threw her son in a Siberian prison camp, and began obsessively surveilling her every move, she took on the role of Russia's mother. "This woman's absolutely ill, / This woman's absolutely single," she wrote in *Requiem*, her elegiac condemnation of Stalin's terrors. "Her man is dead, son—in a jail, / Oh, pray for me—a poor female!" Akhmatova distributed the poem orally among fellow artists, who ritualistically memorized the text before destroying any copies. Meanwhile, she churned out written texts in praise of the regime, hoping it would help her free her son. When he was free, and Stalin dead, she published *Requiem* in her native USSR.

### Albanian sworn virgins

Also known as "Burrnesha" or "Virginesha," women who are able to avoid arranged marriages, wear men's clothing, own and inherit property, smoke, and participate in business where all of the above have historically been prohibited (especially in remote mountain communities of northern Albania), all in exchange for a promise of lifelong celibacy. It's estimated that there are fewer than forty Burrnesha in existence today. (Related: Alice Munro's short story "The Albanian Virgin" is an excellent read.)

### Albright, Madeleine (1937–)

First female secretary of state of the United States (1997–2001). Czech-born Wellesley grad and Columbia PhD. Fluent or damn close in six languages. Mother. Author. *Gilmore Girls* guest star. Collector of fancy brooches. Capable of leg-pressing four hundred pounds at age sixty-nine.

### Alcott, Louisa May (1832–1888)

Writer of books including the much-beloved *Little Women*. Alcott based the novel's headstrong Jo March on herself. In real life, the author's upbringing was more colorful: her father, Bronson Alcott, was a noted transcendentalist and impractical crank who dragged the family between ill-fated utopian communities and instilled an appreciation for progressive causes. (The Alcotts housed a fugitive slave for a week during Louisa's early adolesence.) It's no wonder, then, that her narratives championed independent women. One nineteenth-century critic called her oeuvre, which featured freethinkers and early feminist themes, "among the decided 'signs of the times.'" Alcott's novels were major bestsellers, yes, but her heroines—including progressive heiress Rose Campbell and independent music teacher Polly Milton—did more than make money:

they created a new model for young women. As Alcott famously wrote in her childhood journal, "I want to do something splendid…Something heroic or wonderful that won't be forgotten after I'm dead…I think I shall write books."

### Alexander, Jane (1939–)

Actor (*The Great White Hope*, *All the President's Men*, *Kramer vs. Kramer*), writer, producer, former chairwoman of the National Endowment for the Arts.

### Ali, Laylah (1968–)

American artist best known for her *Greenheads* paintings, which feature androgynous figures that wouldn't be out of place in a comic book.

### *Alice's Adventures in Wonderland*

1865 novel by Lewis Carroll starring a seven-year-old girl who escapes her dull seventh birthday party by falling down a rabbit hole into a world of infinite roles, including a psychedelic obstacle course of womanhood, where she confronts the forces of objectification, claustrophobia, body dysmorphia, and food issues.

### Allen, Debbie (1950–)

Actress, choreographer, director, dancer, and sister to *The Cosby Show*'s Phylicia Rashad. Alongside the dubious honor of being the only performer to appear in all three versions of *Fame* ("You got big dreams? You want fame? Well, fame costs. And right here is where you start paying—in sweat!"), Allen has won ten NAACP Image Awards and three Emmys, has released one solo album, directed an all African American production of *Cat on a Hot Tin Roof* on Broadway, created choreography for five Academy Awards shows plus every recording artist whose moves you tried to copy as a kid, and served as a judge on *So You Think You Can Dance*. Also the founder of the Debbie Allen Dance Academy in L.A. and has made major contributions to Paula Abdul's career. (*See also* Huxtable, Clair)

### Allen, Joan (1956–)

American actress. In the 2000 film *The Contender*, for which she was nominated for a Best Actress Oscar, Allen's vice presidential candidate Senator Laine Hanson faces pundits who say that "the people of this nation can stomach quite a bit. But the one thing they can't stomach is the image of a vice president with a mouthful of cock." She proves them wrong.

### Allende, Isabel (1942–)

Chilean American author of nineteen books (*The House of the Spirits*, *Daughter of Fortune*), philanthropist, and international speaker on women's rights and politics. "In reality," she writes, "the most important things about my life happened in the secret chambers of my heart and have no place in a biography." All right, then.

### Alley, Kirstie (1951–)

American actress who burst onto the scene as the superhot and feisty Rebecca Howe on *Cheers* back in the day, making us forget all about that prissy Shelly Long. Also, she was married to a Hardy Boy, which: awesome. Then, in some order, there was *Look Who's Talking* and addiction and Scientology and the aging process, and at some point she gained weight, so then there was *Fat Actress*—terribly promising; terribly disappointing. Since then she's alternated between losing weight for money and gracing tabloid covers after the inevitable regain.

### Alloy

Mind-bogglingly crowded entertainment and style website for teen girls that comes with a convenient built-in shop hocking cute, trendy, semidisposable clothing and accessories. Or wait, is it more of a shop with a built-in website? Tough to say! Especially when you're being assaulted by Kotex ads, horoscopes, quizzes, and AlloyTV fashion advice—on autoplay, natch—all at once. Points for carrying some clothes up to a junior size 3X, though.

### *Allure*

American women's magazine that provides crucial information on the beauty products ladies must use to make themselves look presentable. Roundly mocked in June 2008 for an illustrated step-by-step guide to taking a shower, which taught millions of American women how to use that big spigot in their bathrooms.

### Almodóvar, Pedro (1949–)

Spanish screenwriter and filmmaker for whom theatricality replaces subtext to explain intricate intersections of sexuality, death, and identity. Women are nearly always central—Almodóvar has said they are "more spectacular as dramatic subjects, they have a greater range of registers"—but gender is never stable or fixed in his films. Performance is the one constant; in the words of Agrado in Almodóvar's most acclaimed film, *Todo sobre mi madre* (*All About My Mother*), "The more you become like what you have dreamed for yourself, the more authentic you are."

### Always

Feminine hygiene product that can be enjoyed with or without wings. (*See also* WINGS)

### Amanpour, Christiane (1958–)

Highly respected and tenacious Iranian-English news anchor and foreign correspondent. In her decades at CNN, including her decades-long tenure as CNN's chief international correspondent, Amanpour waded into war zones and confronted despots and dictators, perpetrators of genocide and their victims, all with that sonorous voice. Amanpour has consistently refused to bow to Americans' habitual indifference to foreign news, even after being named host of *This Week on ABC* to a chorus of inside-the-Beltway sniping. (We're talking to you, Tom Shales.) She has said, "I'm so identified with war and disaster these days that wherever I go, people say jokingly, or maybe not so jokingly, that they shudder when they see me…And I calculated that I have spent more time at the front than most normal military units."

### Amazon

According to myth, any member of a tribe of supertall all-female warriors who supposedly kicked a ton of ass and had straight sex once or twice a year to keep the race going, then abandoned any male children who came along. According to insecure twenty-first-century men, any woman over five six.

### *Amélie*

From the 2001 film of the same name, the whimsical French gamine who launched a thousand haircuts.

### American Apparel

Manufacturer of "sweatshop free" hoodies and T-shirts turned manic recycler of 1980s fashion trends. Best known for sometimes cartoonishly pornographic advertisements featuring its own (often underage) retail employees that blanketed alternative newsweeklies. Gained early media plaudits for high wages and humane working conditions inside factories, but upon frenzied expansion into retail stores the brand came quickly to embody all the excesses and predatory Ponzinomics of millennial late capitalism. Pioneered the inimitable "deep V" V-necked T-shirt that became perhaps the most absurd fashion trend adopted by heterosexual American males en masse in our nation's history; also popularized leotards, metallic lamé bikinis worn in lieu of bras, basic neon in lieu of basic black. (*See also* CHARNEY, DOV)

### American Girl

Line of dolls, books, and accessories sold via catalog and in mega American Girl Place shopping centers, based on young female characters that originally focused on various periods of American history and eventually expanded to include contemporary girls. To some, American Girl is an example of all that is wrong with America; to others, an example of girl power. To most: just another one of those crazy things little girls like. (*See also* DOLLS)

# How Is Your American Apparel Model Feeling Today?

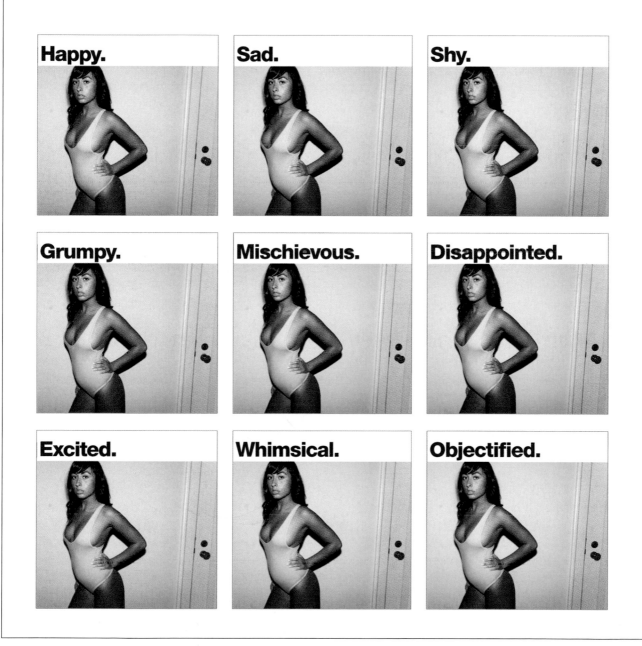

## America's Next Top Model

Competitive reality show that premiered in 2003 on UPN and now airs on the CW. Sixteen cycles later, *ANTM* is a grandaddy of reality TV, yet no more realistic than most scripted shows (the wannabe models rarely go on to make a significant impact in the fashion world and are fed reality TV girl-power clichés that have nothing to do with the fashion world). But realism is not what the show is selling. What has become evident, over the years, is that what the show is selling is Tyra Banks, who is not just a personality but a brand, and sometimes more a brand than a person. (*See also* BANKS, TYRA) Now replayed in syndication on various networks.

## Amos, Tori (1963–)

Artist. Writes, sings, plays piano, changes hair color, hangs with author Neil Gaiman. Beloved for such albums as *Little Earthquakes* and *Under the Pink*.

> "If they keep crashing stuff into the moon, the moon's gonna get pissed off, and the tides'll change, and all the women'll start PMSing together. Then you guys are going to fucking regret it."
>
> —AMOS to *Rolling Stone*, 1999

## anchor baby

Offensive suggestion made by xenophobes that some women are more entitled to deliver children on American soil than others. (The implication, you see, is that undocumented immigrants purposely and cynically conceive or bear children within the borders of the United States simply to secure citizenship for themselves and their offspring.) (*See also* ANGLE, SHARRON)

## Anders, Allison (1954–)

Kentucky-raised director of women-centric films such as *Gas Food Lodging* and *Mi Vida Loca*.

## Anderson, Gillian (1968–)

Actress who has played Lily Bart and Lady Dedlock and Ahab's wife, but let's be real: Fuck yeah, Scully. (*See also* SCULLY, DANA)

## Anderson, Laurie (1947–)

American singer, musician, composer, and career weirdo (otherwise known as a "performance artist"). The studiously androgynous Anderson has managed to bridge the gap between the avant-garde and the mainstream, most notably by having one of her music videos, "O Superman," land in MTV's rotation in the 1980s, and has worked with everybody who's anybody in the counterculture like William Burroughs, Frank Zappa, Andy Kaufman, Spalding Gray, Timothy Leary, and her partner, Lou Reed. Her art often touches on feminist themes, as in a 1973 series of text and black-and-white photos in which she pointed her Nikon camera at men in her downtown New York City neighborhood after they catcalled or harassed her.

## Andrews, V. C. (1923–1986)

Author of the Flowers in the Attic series and numerous follow-ups, all featuring stifling families in which sexual deviance is mixed with murderous impulses mixed with emotional gas-lighting. Frightening, appalling, and delightfully filthy, the books not uncommonly contain such twisted familiarity as a female character beaten naked with a hairbrush by a family member, leaving red, stinging welts on youthful flesh. (Also: lots of incest.) The iconic black covers feature a beautiful heroine's face in a center oval, then open to an illustration of the spooky clan. (Think *Dallas* meets the *Addams Family*.) This facade allowed the books to pass muster with parents at the supermarket checkout line, leading to years of uncensored reading.

## Angelou, Maya (1928–)

American poet and writer born Marguerite Annie Johnson. Became a mother at seventeen. Once danced with Alvin Ailey, put out a calypso album, and was a major force in the civil rights movement before publishing her autobiography *I Know Why the Caged Bird Sings* in 1970 at the age of forty-one. Early mentor to Oprah; presented with the Presidential Medal of Freedom by President Barack Obama in 2011. Came from nothing, in other words, to live one of the most interesting lives of the twentieth century.

## Angle, Sharron (1949–)

Nevada representative who opposes same-sex marriage, believes that women should remain in the home, feels that Harry Reid lacks adequate masculinity to preside over the Senate, and compares teen girls delivering the child of rape to a refreshing summer drink ("I think that two wrongs don't make a right. And I have been in the situation of counseling young girls, not 13 but 15, who have had very at-risk, difficult pregnancies. And my counsel was to look for some alternatives, which they did. And they found that they had made what was really a lemon situation into lemonade."). (*See also* ANCHOR BABY)

## Aniston, Jennifer (1969–)

Actress and unwitting homecoming queen of tabloid culture. Aniston is best known for having a popular haircut while starring in the long-running and unexceptional sitcom *Friends* and later "losing" her then husband Brad Pitt to Angelina Jolie. Most people refer to Aniston as Jen, presumably because we feel like we *know* her. Her depiction in popular media goes something like this: Jennifer Aniston has great hair. Jennifer Aniston was married to Brad Pitt. Jennifer Aniston misses her ex-husband, Brad Pitt. Jennifer Aniston is totally over Brad Pitt. Jennifer Aniston hates Angelina Jolie. Jennifer Aniston has great hair. Jennifer Aniston is lonely. Jennifer Aniston is happy alone. Jennifer Aniston wishes she could have a baby. Jennifer Aniston is pregnant. Jennifer Aniston is not pregnant. Jennifer Aniston has great hair. Jennifer Aniston has finally found love. Jennifer Aniston is miserable. Jennifer Aniston does not take fashion risks. Jennifer Aniston is very fashionable. Jennifer Aniston is happier than ever. Jennifer Aniston will never be happy. Jennifer Aniston has finally found love. Jennifer Aniston has great hair. Jennifer Aniston contains multitudes.

## Ann-Margret (1941–)

Actress and famous redhead (given surname: Olsson) who pegs her on-screen persona along the Little Miss Lollipop–Sexpot–Banshee continuum. "People who saw the performer astride a motorcycle on stage, hair wild, body contorting, could not have envisioned the shy woman inside," the Stockholm-born performer wrote in her autobiography. "The outside world…figured I was a seductress, an extrovert with few inhibitions, and who could blame them?" But Ann-Margret's greatest trick wasn't in landing those good girl–bad girl acrobatics. It was in continuing to turn up on screens after those sex kitten roles dried up. "It is true that Hollywood is still obsessed with age, but who cares?" Ann-Margret said in 2001, a few months after she turned sixty. "Who really cares?"

## Ann Taylor

Named for a dress, not a woman.

## *Anne of Green Gables*

Internationally beloved Canadian children's book written by Lucy Maud Montgomery, first published in 1908 and still a mainstay of Prince Edward Island tourism. Protagonist Anne Shirley is a chatty, strong-willed, redheaded orphan in search of a bosom friend, and Canadian women love her as much as American women love Laura Ingalls, Jo March, and Caddie Woodlawn combined. A recent Canadian TV movie, *Anne of Green Gables: A New Beginning*, apparently killed off Anne's childhood sweetheart and eventual husband, Gilbert Blythe, which is almost as appalling as spelling "Anne" without the *E*. Besides which, Megan Follows, who portrayed her in the 1980s miniseries, is and always will be the one true Anne. Fact.

## *Annie Hall*

What can we say? Woody Allen's a kook, but we need the eggs. In this 1977 romantic comedy, Allen plays Alvy Singer, a television gag writer who falls for Annie Hall (Diane Keaton), an aspiring photographer and singer who is so inhibited and alienated from herself and her own desires at the film's outset that she can't even tell Alvy whether she's going uptown or downtown—she wants to give him a ride, but she doesn't want it to seem like she's going out of her way, or else then he might think she wants to give him a ride, or maybe she doesn't know what she wants, and anyway, she's just embarrassed. Although Alvy has most of the best lines, Allen is extremely generous to Keaton's character. The real story of the film is Annie's awakening, and her gradual realization that she is a person of worth and sufficient unto herself. We don't just love this demented romantic comedy, we *lurve* it. We *luff* it. More coherent than *The Curse of the Jade Scorpion* and less abject than *Manhattan*, *Annie Hall* is quite possibly Allen's best work. Also, Keaton's wardrobe—she favors men's shirts, vests, bowler hats, and a killer sisal tote bag—in the film is deservedly famous.

## Anthony, Susan B. (1820–1906)

Women's rights activist. Immortalized on a beautiful one-dollar US coin and in debates that are still ongoing. Take the Susan B. Anthony List, an antiabortion rights lobbying group that has resurrected the suffragist's ghost in its branding and that claims, "Courageous women leaders like Susan B. Anthony and Elizabeth Cady Stanton recognized that authentic women's rights could never be built upon the broken rights of innocent unborn children. They believed that abortion was just a tool of oppression used against women." Counters Lynn Sher, author of Anthony biography *Failure Is Impossible: Susan B. Anthony in Her Own Words*: "We've pointed this out zillions of times…I don't know what her position on abortion is, and for them to pretend that they do is simply flat-out wrong." (*See also* SUFFRAGETTE)

## Anthropologie

The go-to shopping destination for twee, ultrafeminine, over-priced crafty goods you never knew you needed but suddenly can't live without. Identified by its abundance of scented candles, "ethnic" prints, piles of "one of a kind" objects sourced in distant lands, shipped to the US, and marked up, and quirky romantic dresses.

## antifeminists

People who object to feminism's goals, i.e., people who (often willfully) misunderstand feminism and/or are huge assholes. Notable examples include Phyllis Schlafly, Camille Paglia, Caitlin Flanagan, the entire "men's rights" movement, proponents of wifely "surrender," hard-core religious fundamentalists, teenagers who just discovered Andrea Dworkin, Bart Stupak, Mike Pence, and the pope. Not to be confused with thoughtful people who believe in women's equality but object to the mainstream feminist movement's tendency to focus on middle-class, white, heterosexual women to the exclusion of everyone else. (*See also* DWORKIN, ANDREA; FLANAGAN, CAITLIN; PAGLIA, CAMILLE; SCHLAFLY, PHYLLIS)

## antiheroine

Type of lady we don't see very often. While the lovable asshole male is a staple in the fiction of everyone from Philip Roth to Jonathan Franzen, ladies are often either the virtuous

## antichoice

Term that the antichoice movement would prefer you eschew in favor of the cozy-sounding "pro-life," even though it's objectively bogus. "Pro-life" simply cannot describe a movement that objects to vaccinating young women against HPV to save them from cervical cancer. Or that objects to distributing condoms in communities in which HIV is rampant. Or that objects to stem cell research that could potentially save millions of lives.

In lieu of "pro-life," antichoicers will often begrudgingly accept "antiabortion," but again, this term fails a basic accuracy test. After all, antichoicers work hard at increasing the main cause of abortion, unwanted pregnancy, which can't help but increase the abortion rate. They do this by fighting contraception education in schools, by defunding family plan-

ning programs that provide contraception here and abroad, by supporting laws that allow pharmacists to deny women contraception, and by spreading misinformation about the safety and efficacy of the pill.

*Antichoice* is the inverse of *pro-choice*, a perfectly accurate, if limited, term to describe the people who think women should have choices when it comes to reproduction. But "antichoice" does fail to reflect the breadth and depth of the fear and loathing experienced by antichoice activists when it comes to the subject of women having sex without paying a terrible price, either at the end of a coat hanger or in being marched down the aisle to marry a guy whose sole husbandly qualification is that he turned you on after a few rounds one Saturday night.

At a recent event at the Manhattan Institute, conservative Kay Hymowitz nostalgically recalled the halcyon days before feminism, when "a 20-year-old woman would have been a wife and a mother." (You know, instead of doing pointless things that women find so enticing these days, such as getting educations and careers, and avoiding having your first divorce and remarriage before you're thirty.) For the antichoice movement, visions of twenty-year-old brides do not have to be relegated to the world of fifties' sitcom fantasy but can become a twenty-first-century reality. All they need is to apply a little force. An abortion ban here, the end of birth control pill distribution there, and next thing you know, all the gains women have made in the past few decades have crumbled into a pile of dirty diapers. And it's the force part of the equation that makes the term *antichoice* an apt description feminists return to time and again.

princess or the evil witch with weird horns on her hat—the virgin or the whore. Antiheroines—women you sort of root for even though they are fucked-up or just plain bad—are thinner on the ground. You could call Emma Bovary one, but it seems so clear that Flaubert thinks she is dumb that it's sort of hard to get behind her. Readers looking for a contemporary example should look for Marcy Dermansky's *Bad Marie*, which opens with the line "Sometimes, Marie got a little drunk at work." (Work turns out to be taking care of a two-year-old, whom Marie later kidnaps after she has an affair with the child's dad.) It's hard not to root for her, though, because she almost never does something women are told they must always do: apologize.

## anxiety

Unpleasant and/or debilitating mental state that all marketing and culture aspire to create in women. Subjects about which one is meant to be anxious: your hair, your weight, your face, your skin, your age, your hair (armpit and/or leg), your babies, your lack of babies, your husband, your lack of husband, whether you are sexually generous enough, whether you are too sexually generous, your hair (pubic), your personal cleanliness, your home's cleanliness, whether or not the germs in your toilet are about to become little animated cartoons and kill everything you love—seriously though, you should scrub your toilet more often—and your face, and then moisturize, and get Botox, and also buy a Swiffer. (*See also* Xanax)

## Apatow, Judd (1967–)

Writer-producer of beloved but often short-lived nineties TV shows (*The Ben Stiller Show, The Larry Sanders Show, The Critic, Freaks and Geeks*) who went on to make increasingly off-putting comedy films for dudebros and the women who go to movies with them (*The 40-Year-Old Virgin, Knocked Up, Forgetting Sarah Marshall*). Famously (and accurately) criticized by *Knocked Up* star Katherine Heigl for depicting women as "shrews, as humorless and uptight," which naturally resulted in Heigl developing a reputation as a humorless, uptight shrew. Both directly and indirectly responsible for the early twenty-first century's glut of comedies about underemployed, casually homophobic, white twenty-something stoner guys who magically attract gorgeous (if just a wee bit shrewish) overachieving women. Former Apatow collaborator Mike White pretty much nailed the disappointment early fans have about later Apatovian works when he told the *New York Times* in 2007: "My sense of it is that because those guys are idiosyncratic-looking, their perception is that they're still the underdogs. But…at some point it starts feeling like comedy of the bullies, rather than the bullied." (*See also* BRIDESMAIDS; KNOCKED UP)

## Aphrodite

Greek goddess of love and beauty who rose from the sea, had a lot of sex, and eventually had a Kylie Minogue album and song named after her.

## Apple, Fiona (1977–)

Singer-songwriter whose ambivalence about the media-fame machine means she's destined to get all straight male reporters' issues from that "crazy bitch" they dated projected onto her. Her first album went triple platinum, but her frankness about being unimpressed by an MTV Music Award got her called "ungrateful" by various critics, and she has never quite managed to get out from under that image despite putting out two more great albums. Oh, well: as Fiona herself says, "Nothing wrong when a song ends in a minor key."

## Aqua Net

The ultrapowerful aerosol hairspray responsible for holding together everything from bouffants to mall bangs, Aqua Net powered many a big do back in the day. You know that eighties Whitesnake video where Tawny Kitaen sticks her head out a car window and gets her hair blown all over the place and then comes back into

the car and her hair doesn't look like it moved at all? Some might say that was the result of editing. Those of us who lived through the eighties, however, know an Aqua Net hold when we see one.

## Arbus, Diane (1923–1971)

American photographer for whom nothing was off-limits. Arbus's subjects included everything from transgender people to giants to the handicapped. Her career began with taking photos for her family's department store ads, and her work eventually wound up in *Glamour, Vogue,* and *Harper's BAZAAR*. Arbus's focus switched to inhabitants of New York City who usually went unnoticed, like the cross-dressing young man in one of her most famous portraits, *A Naked Man Being a Woman*. "I really believe there are things nobody would see if I didn't photograph them," she said. After a battle with depression, Arbus committed suicide in 1971.

### Arendt, Hannah (1906-1975)

Writer widely acknowledged to be one of the major political theorists of the twentieth century, and so one of the few who can be said to have penetrated the boys' club in the ivory tower. Her writings often have the same ballbusting, troublemaking spirit we associate with suffragettes, riot grrls, and other female revolutionaries. But she seems to have disliked feminism in the capital F, movement sense, which apparently made her a disappointment to many. Per Adrienne Rich: "To read such a book [Arendt's *The Human Condition*], by a woman of large spirit and great erudition, can be painful, because it embodies the tragedy of a female mind nourished on male ideology." Yikes. But Arendt was never much for any party line, lady-centric or otherwise, as it happened. She wrote a book called *Eichmann in Jerusalem*, using the trial of a Nazi bureaucrat to illustrate what she calls the "banality of evil." Thinking she was trying to excuse Eichmann, and the Nazis more generally, from responsibility for their crimes—she meant something more like "unthinkable acts can be made to seem normal, and that is itself unthinkable"—everyone promptly went berserk. She also criticized the reasoning of *Brown v. Board of Education* and integrationist strategies in the South more generally, although she said she was just concerned that they would lead Southern whites to the kind of full-scale systematic violence associated with the Nazis. If you disagree with her, of course, it might be hard to separate the courage from the convictions. But then that's always the rub with the firecrackers of all kinds, the grandes dames of political theory or any other sphere. You can't trust that just because they've managed to locate their voices you're going to like what they have to say.

### *Are You There God? It's Me, Margaret*

I must, I must, I must increase my bust! (*See also* BLUME, JUDY)

### Arnold, Eve (1912-2012)

Groundbreaking American photojournalist, one of the few female ones of her time, best known for her photographs of Marilyn Monroe on the set of the 1961 movie *The Misfits*. She also traveled the world capturing images of far less sparkly subjects, like disabled Vietnam veterans and Apartheid-era South Africa, and she's also well known for her series of photographs of American First Ladies and an iconic photograph of Malcolm X. (*See also* MONROE, MARILYN)

### Arthur, Bea (1922-2009)

American actress. Although she was a staff sergeant in the Marine Corps in her twenties and a Tony Award–winning Broadway star in her forties, Arthur's career didn't really take off until her fifties, when she starred as the feminist title character in Norman Lear's TV series *Maude*. She won her first Best Lead Actress in a Comedy Emmy for that role in 1977, and her second for playing wisecracking realist Dorothy Zbornak in *The Golden Girls* in 1988. Post–*Golden Girls*, she performed at the Metropolitan Opera, played Larry David's mom in *Curb Your Enthusiasm*, and, in 2001, returned to Broadway in her late seventies with a one-woman show.

### as if

(*See also* CLUELESS)

### ass

Human buttocks, or an example of a recent paradigm shift in terms of physical ideals in the American white woman. Up through the eighties, the preferred shape was nearly nonexistent, the taut frame of a Cheryl Tiegs or Farrah Fawcett; to be cursed with an ample ass would require a shirt around the waist. Then in the early nineties, as hip-hop washed over mainstream culture, young men and women became privy to music and videos praising the big butt, and a popular show called *In Living Color* happened to feature the fly-girl talents of one Jennifer Lopez. By the turn of the millennium, J.Lo was mainstream and so was her can, an ass that walked her onto the covers of high-fashion magazines. In one generation the ass has gone from pancake to pop, which of course has shifted the low-self-esteem pendulum from ass-hiders to ass-enhancers. (*See also* LOPEZ, JENNIFER; T&A)

## Astroglide

Brand of personal lubricant, which can result in an immediate and positive difference in the sex lives of most women, making penetration easier, and fun to apply for partners as well. But while we're at it, can we recommend you try Pjur Original Bodyglide Super Concentrated instead?

**astrology**
Pseudoscientific practice of using the position of the planets and stars at one's birth to explain why one has a shitty personality. Though its popularity possibly peaked in the 1970s, ladymags keep printing horoscope pages, and *Cosmo* even publishes a "Bedside Astrologer" that helps women seduce men using zodiac sign compatibility. Linda Goodman's *Love Signs* is considered the astrology bible; many a copy has been earmarked, underlined, and shared by high school girls with questions only the constellations can answer.

## Athena

Greek goddess of wisdom. Frequently referred to as "gray-eyed" or "flashing-eyed," and associated with the owl. In *The Odyssey*, she is Odysseus's guardian, guiding him on his journey home, governing strategy in war, and, at the end, stops the men battling it out on Ithaca. In Robert Fitzgerald's translation:

> *Their faces paled with dread before Athena,*
> *and swords dropped from their hands unnerved, to lie*
> *strewing the ground, at the great voice of the goddess.*

Pretty badass.

## Atkins Diet

Most famous embodiment of the principle that eating a high-protein, low-carbohydrate diet will, like many other food plans, cause almost invariably temporary weight loss.

### Atlas Shrugged

Novel by writer, philosopher-king, and amphetamine enthusiast Ayn Rand, published in 1957. Tells the inspirational story of a woman who runs a successful corporation, is smarter than everyone, sleeps with all the hot dudes, and is finally rewarded for her virtue by being raped by a maintenance worker in a railway tunnel. She's into it, though, because he's also a genocidal dictator who is about to give a seventy-page speech about how everyone is a Communist and should die. Has sold over seven million copies. (*See also* RAND, AYN)

### Atonement

Very beautiful book (and film) about a false rape accusation. It is a delicate subject if you believe, as a lot of feminists do, that too many women are disbelieved when they say they've been raped. And in less skillful and beautiful hands than Ian McEwan's, this whole book could have been a disastrous male-centric cri de coeur about the wiles of women who wield the alleged taboo of rape against the righteous male. (Imagine it as authored by late-career Roth or Mailer, for example, and shudder away.) Instead it is a meditation about how a single false impression can ruin an entire life, whether anyone meant the harm or not. About how the suffering that can be caused by this kind of thing when it happens—and it does, of course, happen, no one denies that mistakes are sometimes made—touches everyone involved. A tip: when you get to the fourth and final section of the book, make sure you're alone, because you're about to have an ugly cry.

### Atwood, Margaret (1939–)

Canadian novelist, poet, and essayist. Still sometimes referred to as Peggy by friends. Perhaps the only literary figure of our time who regularly and properly uses the term *cosplay*. Her first major novel, *The Edible Woman*, was about a woman who anthropomorphizes food to the point where she finds she can no longer eat and uses self-starvation as a way to ward off adulthood. It was published in 1969, just as the second wave of the women's movement was beginning. Her subsequent novels have evinced similar interests: women and Canada tangled with bizarre and oppressive twists of science. (*See also* HANDMAID'S TALE, THE)

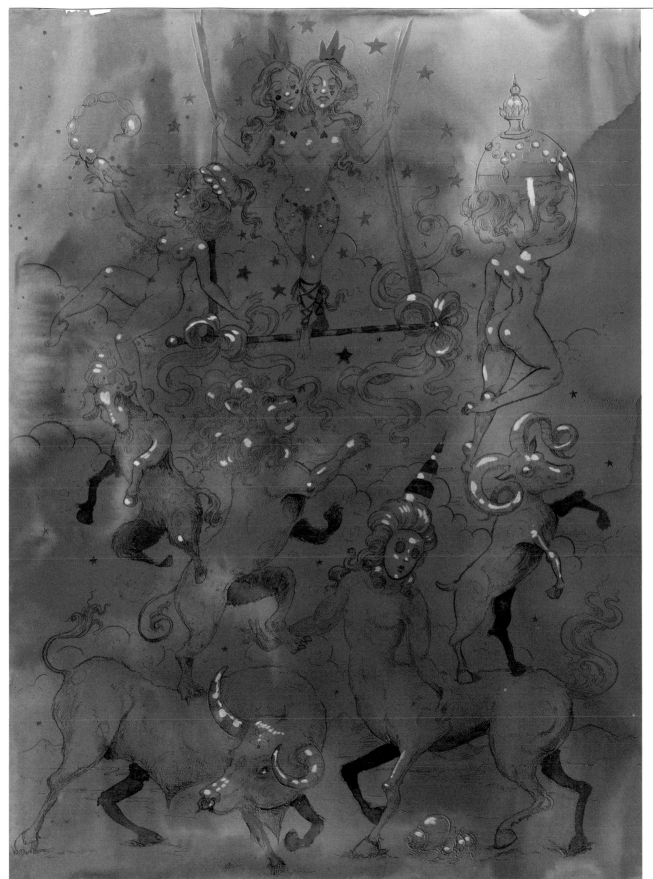

### Aunt Jemima

Brand of pancake-related foodstuffs and the most recognizable Mammy caricature in American advertising history. Portrayed by a woman named Nancy Green, who was born a slave, until her death in 1923. To some extent, white housewives lost their taste for that crap as time went on, but Aunt Jemima—first introduced in 1889 and now owned by Quaker Oats—remains, even if she's finally lost her kerchief and about two hundred pounds.

### au pair

Fancypants European nanny who, if television has taught us anything, will almost certainly neglect your kids and sleep with your husband.

### Austen, Jane (1775–1817)

English novelist who inspired a rash of late-nineties period films, popular contemporary knockoffs like *Clueless* and *Bridget Jones's Diary*, and the got-old-real-fast public domain literature + monsters publishing trend of 2009–2011. Best known today as the only pre-1900 female writer most people can name off the top of their head.

### autism

Neural and developmental disorder. Psychologist Bruno Bettelheim, Holocaust survivor and pioneering autism researcher, attributed the condition to frigid women who neglect their children into neurodevelopmental disorder. Like the SS, but for babies: "When one is forced to drink black milk from dawn to dusk, whether in the death camps of Nazi Germany or while lying in a possibly luxurious crib, but there subjected to the unconscious death wishes of what overtly may be a conscientious mother—in either situation a living soul has death for a master," Bettelheim wrote of autism's roots. After the psychologist's suicide in 1990, the bulk of his work was discredited as made-up—and bizarrely anti-Semitic.

### Avon

Seller of cosmetics, giver of makeovers, supporter of Breast Cancer Research, home of the iconic Avon Lady, this company has been going strong since 1886. And back in 1989—when Lauren Conrad was just a gleam in some MTV exec's eye—it became the first major cosmetics peddler to ban animal testing. Incidentally, their Smooth Minerals Eyeshadow has something of a cult following.

### Awesome

Like, totally. We are never giving this word up.

### ax wound

Horrible euphemism for human vulva.

## babies

Tiny, dependent human beings believed to cause ovarian explosions among young women and commitment phobia among young men. Conclusively proven to cause endless fucking drama in the feminist blogosphere. (*See also* EMBRYO; FETUS; LABOR; PREGNANCY)

### Baby Boom

1987 film and step-by-step blueprint for every overworked, undersexed romantic comedy heroine to come, in which J.C. (Diane Keaton) is punished for loving her demanding job by being saddled with a fully realized human baby (spontaneously inherited from her long-lost dead cousin). While J.C. takes stabs at adopting her off, she carts the kid in her underarm, driving away her investment banker boyfriend and her high-powered gig. Only when she morphs into a good mommy, moves to the Vermont countryside, and begins canning baby applesauce for a living is she rewarded with the loving embrace of a handsome local veterinarian.

### baby bump

Any abdominal protrusion or imagined abdominal protrusion in a female, particularly a female celebrity. Syndrome can be caused by inhalation of air, overly loose clothing, overly tight clothing, a love of fine wines and beers, bad posture, a fetus, and/or those tacos really acting up on you. Will be reported as a pregnancy-related event regardless. Depending on the relevance and marketability of the female celebrity, she may be called upon to release a formal statement clarifying whether she does/does not have a fetus lodged up her bits.

### Baby Doll

1956 Elia Kazan film so filthy the Catholic Legion of Decency fought to ban it. Granted, in 1956 that didn't take much (no openmouthed on-screen kisses were allowed), but *Baby Doll* is the sexiest movie you will ever see. Based on a Tennessee Williams screenplay, the film stars Carroll Baker as Baby Doll, the sleepy-eyed nineteen-year-old wife of broke, middle-aged, damp Archie Lee Meighan (Karl Malden). In order to marry Baby Doll, Archie Lee, a poor cotton gin owner, promised her father that they wouldn't consummate the marriage until Baby Doll's twentieth birthday. That fateful birthday is now only two days away, and Archie Lee's about to implode. Sexual desperation does not appeal to Baby Doll, however, and she guards her vagina well. After all, it's the only power she has. Pitiful, sex-starved, and broke, Archie Lee sets fire to the gin of Silva Vaccaro, his main competitor in the cotton trade, played by a studly Eli Wallach. Vaccaro vows to make Archie Lee pay and soon realizes there's no sweeter revenge than seducing your enemy's virgin bride.

### baby mama

Semiderogatory and often possessive title used by a man to describe an unmarried woman who has a child. *Disambiguation:* 2008 comedy in which single yuppie supermarket executive Tina Fey hires Amy Poehler to be her surrogate (NB: Poehler pees in a sink at one point, which may be the funniest use of urination on film to date).

### Baby-Sitters Club, The

213 novels that were all the rage among middle schoolers in the 1980s and 1990s. Each book, which came in a different color from the one before it, focused on a different member of the club's quartet. The four original characters were Kristy Thomas (the sporty one), Claudia Kishi (the fashionable one), Mary Anne Spier (the nerdy one), and Stacey McGill (the New Yorky one). An inspiration to aspiring small businesswomen everywhere from the days before the career dreams of the American teenager were whittled down to reality superstardom and a fashion line.

### Bachelor, The

Long-running ABC reality TV franchise that includes the spin-off shows *The Bachelorette* and *Bachelor Pad*; hosted by Chris Harrison, who broke viewers' hearts in 2012 when he announced he was divorcing his wife of eighteen years. Highlight "bachelors" from the flagship show include Brad (seasons 11 *and* 15, who couldn't pick a girl the first round), Jake (season 14, who has mutual acrimony with his chosen mate, Vienna), and Jason (season 13, who changed his mind after picking his final girl). The only "real" success story of the franchise is Trista and Ryan, who married on television in 2003 and remain together. While *The Bachelor* and *-ette* center around forced polyamory that leads to a proposal and commitment to one singular person, *Bachelor Pad* is basically an orgy for money and whatever love looks like on television. As Jennifer Pozner wrote in her 2010 book *Reality Bites Back*, the

entire franchise has been rightly criticized for being racially discriminatory and "emphasiz[ing] women's matrimonial motivations with a nearly endless stream of marriage-minded femmes professing some variation of the belief that being the last girl standing at a network altar—even though they'd be standing there with a virtual stranger—will make all their dreams come true."

### Bachmann, Michele (1956–)

American politician, onetime presidential candidate, member of the unreality-based community. In Bachmann World, slave owners worked tirelessly to abolish slavery at the same time

the human beings they owned were working tirelessly to take care of their homes and land. Not coincidentally, Bachmann World is also the only location on earth where accusing Secretary of State Hillary Clinton's Deputy Chief of Staff Huma Abedin of having ties to a terrorist organization (because: she's Muslim) is somehow *not* understood to be screamingly racist bullshit. (Among those from her own party who called Bachmann out on the latter outrage was her former campaign manager Ed Rollins, who wrote in a Fox News op-ed, "I am fully aware that she sometimes has difficulty with her facts.") When *Newsweek* ran a cover photo of Bachmann staring straight at the camera with what could only be called "crazy eyes," American feminists toggled between empathy/outrage (they'd never do that to a man!) and schadenfreude. Between her proud ignorance and her extrapuritanical vision for America, Bachmann can be a difficult lady to defend—unless you're a white Evangelical Christian who believes wives should submit to their husbands, even when they're running for president. In that case, she's the bee's knees.

### bacon

A smoky, delicious breakfast treat. A fine accompaniment to salads, scallops, dates, and baked potatoes. An internet meme grown so tiresome, we *almost* don't even want to eat bacon anymore. Almost.

### Baez, Joan (1941–)

American singer-songwriter. "If I had been able to write the songs like that, that would have been what I would have written," the Staten Island–born Baez said of first encountering Bob Dylan. Instead, she wrote her most acclaimed tune "Diamonds&Rust"—*about* him. Baez's real contribution to music lies in turning the words of others with her voice, one she's lent to dozens of Dylan songs. "I was fortunate to have been born with this voice, to use it in ways that lend credibility to traditional music and beyond," she wrote. "In my mind's eye I can see the black children leaving a church to knowingly be arrested, singing at the top of their lungs, 'I ain't gonna let nobody turn me around…' I'm proud to have sung with them."

### Bair, Sheila (1954–)

Former chair of the Federal Deposit Insurance Corporation (FDIC) who was the sole woman of any repute to witness (or attempt, mostly in vain, to exert any influence over) the 2008–2009 Wall Street bailout; summarized the experience with a trenchant observation from Margaret Thatcher, of all people: "If you want something said, ask a man; if you want something done, ask a woman."

### Baker, Ella Jo (1903–1986)

Civil rights activist. The Virginia-born Baker began her work as an advocate for social justice and human rights during college at Raleigh's Shaw University, where she was valedictorian. When she moved to New York City, she joined and cofounded several social justice organizations and then spent significant time working against Jim Crow laws in the Deep South with the NAACP from the late 1930s through the 1950s. After the success of the Montgomery Bus Boycott in the mid-1950s, Baker helped organize the Southern Christian Leadership Conference (SCLC) along with Dr. Martin Luther King Jr. By 1960, inspired by student-led sit-ins at Woolworth's lunch counters in North Carolina, Baker decided to leave the SCLC in order to collaborate with activists in forming the Student Nonviolent Coordinating Committee (SNCC). Baker and the SNCC helped organize the 1961 Freedom Rides and the 1964 Freedom Summer, which continued the fight against segregation and black voter suppression. Baker believed in building racially diverse justice movements utilizing the collectivist leadership model of participatory democracy. ("My theory is, strong people don't need strong leaders," she said.) During her later years back in New York, Baker's activism focused more specifically on women's issues, Puerto Rican independence, and civil rights around the world.

### Baio, Scott (1960–)

Actor, has-been. (Alternate definition, per Urban Dictionary: "Thick, sticky brown discharge from the vagina of a woman who is on the last couple of days of her menstrual period.") In the teen-idol menu of either melting into obscurity or living in ignominy, Scott Baio chose the modern forms of the latter: serial reality shows and Twitter beef. Dim, possibly fond memories of his roles on *Happy Days*, *Joanie Loves Chachi*, *Charles in Charge* (or as Bob Loblaw on *Arrested Development*) have long since given way to "Scott Baio Is 45…and Single" and "Scott Baio Is 46…and Pregnant." And Twitter beef. In 2010, he mocked First Lady Michelle Obama and then defended himself by announcing that his wife's best friend is black, providing photographic evidence in support. After his announcement that his taxes would go to "lazy non working people [*sic*]" did not meet with favor, he waged an inexplicable war with a Jezebel writer. His wife Renee dealt the next blow: "You

bunch of FAR LEFT Lesbian shitasses…No wonder you're all lesbos because what man in his right mind could put up with your cuntness? Scott Baio has more class in his piss than all of you all!!!" It was also learned that Renee Baio has lesbian friends. No photographic evidence was provided in support.

## Baker, Josephine (1906–1975)

Singer. Dancer. Bon vivant. Provocateuse. Civil rights activist. Actress. La Baker, destitute, dropped out of school in the slums of St. Louis at the age of twelve and went on to become the first African American to star in a major motion picture—and the first black woman to be internationally famous. Ernest Hemingway called her "the most sensational woman anyone ever saw." Known for performing the infamous banana dance—hypnotic, magnetic, sensual, racially charged—Baker was also a gorgeous pinup, a World War II correspondent, and the mother of twelve adopted children. Though she often performed nude, she never seemed vulnerable, victimized, or exploited. Photographs reveal defiance, elegance, a winking self-awareness, and a playful charm. Baker is the rare heroine who teaches us all that it doesn't matter where you come from: it's what you do with what you've got.

## Ball, Lucille (1911–1989)

Actress, comedienne, businesswoman, iconic (if fake) redhead. The title of the show may have been *I Love Lucy*, but when it came to Lucille Ball's performance as the dizzy, fame-hungry housewife who happened to be half of a groundbreaking interracial television couple with her real-life husband, Desi Arnaz, we all did. A failed Broadway performer and a contract movie actress in the Hollywood studio system, Ball got her first breakout in radio with the CBS program *My Favorite Husband* and then on television, where she developed *I Love Lucy*.

Lucy's brilliant physical comedy, domestic mishaps, and relationship with both her husband and her older neighbors, the Mertzes, made *I Love Lucy* a smash hit that produced a ratings-record-breaking episode of television, the birth story "Lucy Goes to the Hospital," and the highest-rated TV show of all time. After her divorce from Arnaz, she starred as a widow in *The Lucy Show* (the show was the first to feature a regular character who was a divorced mom) and *Here's Lucy*, about the generation gap between a single mother and her children, which was more markedly political than her previous efforts. But Ball was as important behind the camera as she was in front of it. She was the first female head of a major television production company, buying out Arnaz's share of Desilu Productions after their split and greenlighting and backing *Star Trek* with NBC brass.

## Bancroft, Anne (1931–2005)

Mrs. Robinson. Annie Sullivan. Emmy, Golden Globe, Tony, and Oscar winner, beloved wife of Mel Brooks. *Miracle Worker* director Arthur Penn once said of Bancroft, "More happens in her face in ten seconds than happens in most women's faces in ten years."

## Bangles, The

All-female band formed in the early eighties, originally called The Supersonic Bangs and then The Bangs. Band, as in, they all played instruments! One of their first hits, "Manic Mon-

day," was written by Prince, but their most popular song was the Liam Sternberg–composed "Walk Like an Egyptian," which received nearly incessant radio play the fall of 1986. In 1987, they released a cover of Simon and Garfunkel's "Hazy Shade of Winter," recorded for the soundtrack for the film *Less Than Zero*. After internal disputes over artistic direction and credit led to a breakup in the late 1980s, lead singer Susanna Hoffs went on to be a part of Ming Tea, a band known for the song "BBC," which played in the end credits of the movie *Austin Powers: International Man of Mystery*. (Hoffs's husband, Jay Roach, directed the film.)

### Banks, Tyra (1973–)

Former model, current lunatic, Tyra is a successful businesswoman and failed singer who has achieved an elevated status as a prominent media personality on the shoulders and crushed spirits of exploited, aspiring models turned reality TV show contestants. Her most notable contribution to society has been familiarizing the masses with weaves. (*See also* AMERICA'S NEXT TOP MODEL)

### Bara, Theda (ca. 1885–1955)

Silent film actress. In a different time, Elton John would have written a song about Bara, born Theodosia Burr Goodman. Hollywood dyed her hair black, changed her name, spun her a concubine-artist lineage, and made her into the first on-screen vamp. "Since Miss Bara is so well fitted by looks to act this sort of creature before the camera, it would be squandering her resources to cast her in a Mary Pickford sort of role," the *New York Times* wrote of Bara in 1916. Bara disagreed. She gunned for heroine roles but eventually found that her only way to evade typecasting was not to be cast at all. Her final film was a 1926 comedic send-up of her vamp persona.

### *Barbarella*

1968 comic-based sci-fi flick starring young Jane Fonda and her mind-boggling legs and featuring a mad scientist named Dr. Durand Durand, whose name Nick Rhodes and John Taylor would later appropriate, minus a *D* or two, when they put a band together a decade later. A critical and commercial disaster turned camp classic.

## Barbie

Doll whose breasts are so big she'd fall over if she were real. (Her feet are also permanently flexed into a high-heeled position.) Barbie has been a doctor, an astronaut, an executive, and an engineer, but a talking version of her once complained that "Math class is tough!" Barbara Millicent Roberts was conceived in the mid-1950s by Mattel cofounder Ruth Handler to give little girls an alternative to baby dolls. (Giving them devastating body image issues and seriously mixed messages about women's roles in society was apparently an unexpected bonus.) More than fifty years and a zillion feminist critiques later, the Barbie doll remains a strong seller, a hot collectors' item, and a convenient shorthand for the white, thin, and utterly impossible American ideal of beauty.

## BAD-IDEA BARBIES

### I Can Be a Bride Barbie

**DESCRIPTION:** The Barbie "I Can Be" series inspires girls ages three and up to realize their career aspirations: Barbie can be a Zoo Doctor, a Pizza Chef, the President (party affiliation: "B"), or even Ken's wife. Barbie may be the plastic-molded image of feminine perfection, but she hasn't reached her full potential until she locks down a man.
**Released**: in 2009. Still on shelves.

### Slumber Party Barbie

**DESCRIPTION:** Barbie's slumber party accessories include a tiny fuzzy pink scale permanently set to 110 pounds and a diet book with some no-nonsense advice: "DON'T EAT!" Since Barbie's estimated real-life weight is 101 pounds, Slumber Party Barbie could use the tip to drop those last nine from her seven-foot two-inch frame.
**Released:** in 1965. Discontinued.

### Oreo Fun Barbie

**DESCRIPTION:** In 1997, Mattel turned Barbie into a Nabisco sandwich cookie ad, complete with Oreo purse, plate of cookies, and cups of milk for dipping. (I Can Be a mass-produced food item!) It also churned out a black "version" of the doll, not knowing that *Oreo* is a hostile and racially problematic term for a person who, like the cookie, is "black on the outside, white on the inside." The black doll was quickly recalled, though it lives on in a collector's edition, offering a commentary on Mattel's skin-color-swapping diversity initiative.
**Released** in 1997. White Oreo Barbie was still having fun with Oreos at the time of this printing.

### Barbie Forever Barbie Doll with Tanner the Dog

**DESCRIPTION:** This nearly $100 specimen comes complete with pet dog, pooper-scooper, trash can, and a cycle of canine misery. Feed Tanner doggy biscuits. Wait for him to expel them into piles of feces. Then use the magnetic scooper to place them right back into his dog bowl.

## Bardot, Brigitte (1934–)

French model and actress who came to international prominence as the star of *And God Created Woman*. Now iconic photos of a young, bikini-clad Bardot popularized the bathing suit style and cemented her eternal "sex kitten" image in the public imagination. In 1973, she announced her retirement from acting and began to focus primarily on her work as an

Tanner then eats his own excrement, ensuring that the fun never ends.
**Released** in 2006. Still on shelves.

## Star Trek Barbie

**DESCRIPTION:** Mattel beamed up this *Star Trek*–themed Barbie and Ken in 1996 to celebrate the thirtieth anniversary of Gene Roddenberry's original sci-fi series. But Mattel's racial politics had yet to catch up to Stardate 1508.3. Ken makes a fine Kirk in his mustard captain's uniform, but beach-blonde Barbie bore little resemblance to the *Enterprise*'s lone female officer, Commander Uhura. A Barbie version of a young Uhura, based on Zoe Saldana's character in the film reboot, was released in 2009.
**Released:** in 1996. Limited edition.

## Teen Talk Barbie

**DESCRIPTION:** What teen girls talked about in 1991, according to Mattel: "Will we ever have enough clothes?"; "I love shopping"; and "Math class is tough!" The arithmetically challenged Barbie was pulled after criticism from the American Association of University Women, but the mall-based discussion topics survived.
**Released** in 1991. Discontinued.

## Palm Beach Sugar Daddy Ken

**DESCRIPTION:** Released in 2010 for "the adult collector," Palm Beach Sugar Daddy Ken exudes "cool sophistication in breezy Palm Beach!" with his itsy dog, jacquard jacket, and the implication that he subsidizes Barbie's affections using his engorged money clip.
**Slated for release** in 2010. Discontinued.

## Happy Family Pregnant Midge & Baby

**DESCRIPTION:** In 2002, Barbie's homely best friend welcomed a baby in the form of a plastic fetus wedged inside Midge's detachable stomach. Just pop off Midge's pregnant belly, excavate the accessory from her womb, discard her magnetic bump, and you've got a new baby and an instantly skinny yummy mummy.
**Released** in 2002. Still on shelves.

animal welfare activist, which would have been pretty cool if she'd left it there. Instead, she eventually became outspoken about her fear of Muslims "destroying" her country, and as of 2008, French courts had fined her no less than five times for inciting racial hatred.

## Barnard College

Notable alumnae of the New York women's college, in reverse order of Google hits as of this writing:

**ATOOSA RUBENSTEIN**, *magazine editor*: 24,300

**HELEN M. RANNEY**, *physician*: 69,400

**HELEN GAHAGAN DOUGLAS**, *actor and politician*: 180,000

**JHUMPA LAHIRI**, *novelist*: 187,000

**JOAN WHITNEY PAYSON**, *New York Mets owner*: 336,000

**NTOZAKE SHANGE**, *author*: 374,000

**EDWIDGE DANTICAT**, *novelist*: 436,000

**JEANE KIRKPATRICK**, *diplomat*: 463,000

**MAYA SOETORO-NG**, *teacher*: 675,000

**RACHEL MENKEN**, *fictional girlfriend of Don Draper*: 817,000

**ANN BRASHARES**, *novelist*: 889,000

**ANNA QUINDLEN**, *journalist*: 902,000

**CHRISTY CARLSON ROMANO**, *actress*: 908,000

**TWYLA THARP**, *choreographer*: 1.2 million

**FATIMA BHUTTO**, *activist, writer, poet*: 1.27 million

**IDA PAULINE ROLF**, *chemist*: 1.3 million

**PATRICIA HIGHSMITH**, *writer and comic book writer*: 1.4 million

**GRETA GERWIG**, *actress*: 1.6 million

**ZORA NEALE HURSTON**, *novelist*: 1.69 million

**JOAN VOLLMER**, *poet*: 1.7 million

**MARGARET MEAD**, *anthropologist*: 3.3 million

**JUDITH MILLER**, *journalist*: 5.19 million

**JUDITH KAYE**, *judge*: 5.66 million

**SUZANNE VEGA**, *musician*: 5.7 million

**KARLA JAY**, *LGBT scholar*: 6.7 million

**CYNTHIA NIXON**, *actor*: 7 million

**JOAN RIVERS**, *comedienne*: 10.9 million

**JOYCE JOHNSON**, *novelist*: 12 million

**LAUREN GRAHAM**, *actress*: 21 million

**MARTHA STEWART**, *living specialist*: 70 million

**LOUISE POST**, *musician*: 125 million

### Barr, Roseanne (1952–)

Comedienne, actress, businesswoman, and onetime presidential candidate. If you go back and watch her groundbreaking, top-rated, eponymous show from the 1980s and 1990s—in which working-class midwesterners, fat people, gay people, occasional people of color, and a young George Clooney all come across as basically normal and frequently hilarious—you can almost forget about the multiple personality/Tom Arnold/Native appropriation years. (*See also* CONNER, DARLENE; ROSEANNE)

### Bass, Chuck

Hedonistic young playboy from the YA series Gossip Girl with a penchant for villainous accessories, like ascots and monkeys for pets. When the WB adapted the books for television, it hoped to humanize this nihilist blowhard: kept the neckwear, ditched the monkey, and imbued Chuck with a soft spot for the preppy boarding school queen Blair Waldorf. The result? Chuck is a megalomaniacal abusive lover, the twenty-first-century reboot of the soap opera's rapist hero. Observe: *General Hospital*, Port Charles, 1979: Luke Spencer rapes Laura Webber in an abandoned disco to the tune of Herb Alpert. Two seasons later, wannabe rapist and victim wed in the daytime television event of the decade. Elizabeth Taylor shows up to curse the couple. *Gossip Girl*, New York, 2007: Chuck Bass attempts to rape Jenny Humphrey on an abandoned rooftop to the tune of Akon. Two seasons later, rapist claims victim's virginity, then shoos her from the bedroom to propose to Blair. Waldorf shows up to banish Humphrey from Manhattan forever; among fans, Chuck and Blair achieve Luke and Laura status.

### Bates, Kathy (1948–)

Memphis-born actress probably best known for her starring turn in 1990's *Misery*, Bates revolutionized the female nude scene when she slipped into a jacuzzi with Jack Nicholson in 2002's *About Schmidt*, blowing Nicholson out of the water and significantly expanding the role of a woman's body on film.

### Bath, wife of

One of Chaucer's pilgrims in *The Canterbury Tales*, she's had five husbands since the age of twelve—three good, two bad. The last one was twenty years her junior. She's combative, lusty, loquacious, and not afraid to use the word *queynte*. We would like to hang out with her, please.

### bat mitzvah

So what if she's yet to get her first period—in Jewish tradition, it's the bat mitzvah that marks a young girl's passage into womanhood. The event may begin with a twelve- or thirteen-year-old girl leading a synagogue service and end with a themed after-party—replete with a three-course meal, a five-tier chocolate fountain, and a ten-piece band that is decidedly well-versed in "Hava Nagila" and the collected works of Justin Bieber.

### battle-ax

**1.** Weapon, often made of iron, designed for hand-to-hand combat in warfare and meant to injure or sever limbs such as arms and legs. **2.** Pejorative term for a woman, usually an older woman, who displays aggression, dominance, combativeness, or a firm belief in her own opinions.

### Beale, Big Edie (1895–1977) and Little Edie (1917–2002)

Onetime socialites from a prominent New York family who gained notoriety as the eccentric, singing-and-dancing, highly stylized yet impoverished mother-and-daughter recluses in the 1975 cult-classic documentary *Grey Gardens*, named for

their dilapidated, twenty-eight-room East Hampton mansion that had become overrun with raccoons, cats, garbage, and human waste. As women of the aristocracy in the early twentieth century, the Edies, like most of their peers, were born and bred to be wives and mothers. But Big Edie and her husband divorced and Little Edie never married, and both women were totally unprepared—and financially unable—to navigate the lifestyle they were expected to inhabit.

### Beauvoir, Simone de (1908–1986)

French writer, philosopher, intellectual. When she died, *Le Nouvel Observateur* declared, "Women, you owe her everything!" And yet when *The Second Sex* was published, in 1949, at first she too declined to call herself a feminist. (It took de Beauvoir twenty-three years to come around.) For most of her adult life she was in a relationship with Jean-Paul Sartre, in which each partner allowed "contingent" affairs to balance out their "essential" love. For this she was rewarded with widespread dismissal by male philosophers who said she rode

Sartre's coattails. "In a way, Sartre felt he was immortal," she told the *Paris Review* in 1965. "He had staked everything on his literary work and on the hope that his work would survive, whereas for me, owing to the fact that my personal life will disappear, I'm not the least bit concerned about whether my work is likely to last."

### Bechdel, Alison (1960–)

Writer, artist, and originator of the comic *Dykes to Watch Out For* and author of the graphic memoirs *Fun Home* and *Are You My Mother?* Namesake of the Bechdel test, even though she claims she doesn't deserve credit. (*See also* BECHDEL TEST)

### Bechdel test

Ask yourself: does this movie/book/play have (a) at least two female characters who (b) speak to each other about (c) something other than a man? Alison Bechdel, who popularized the test in her comic *Dykes to Watch Out For,* credits her friend Liz Wallace with originating the deceptively simple measure of sexism in entertainment.

### bedazzler

A rhinestone stapler for your ass. Only $19.95.

### Bedelia, Amelia

Lovable but basically incompetent housekeeper at the center of a series of children's books by Peggy Parish (and more recently her nephew Herman Parish), beginning in 1963. Known for her delicious pies, hats that would make Princess Beatrice weep with envy, and painful literal-mindedness (you don't want to ask her to "babysit"), Amelia Bedelia, like all the best children's heroines, has a knack for saving the day, right after she fucks it up beyond recognition.

### Bee, Samantha (1969–)

Canadian comedienne, author (*I Know I Am, But What Are You?*), and very senior *Daily Show* correspondent. If we didn't already love her for her hilarious deadpan, feministy sensibilities and brass ovaries, then we'd love her for telling *Big Girls Don't Cry* author Rebecca Traister, "I'm always excited when something of mine ends up on Jezebel." (*See also* DAILY SHOW, THE)

### Beecher Stowe, Harriet (1811–1896)

New England–born author and abolitionist best known for her 1852 antislavery novel *Uncle Tom's Cabin,* which sold over three hundred thousand copies in its first year. Although the melodramatic story galvanized the abolitionist movement, it has since been widely criticized for its depiction of African American characters, especially the meekly suffering, subservient Uncle Tom himself, whom James Baldwin described as "robbed of his humanity and divested of his sex."

Feminist critics in the late twentieth century made an effort to rescue Beecher Stowe's intellectual reputation, but her most famous book's combination of purple prose and racist condescension is pretty tough to defend in contemporary terms.

### Behar, Joy (1942–)

Stand-up comedienne turned Emmy-winning TV host, known for feuding with *The View* cohost Star Jones, storming off set with other cohost Whoopi Goldberg after guest Bill O'Reilly started running his mouth about Muslim terrorists, and having zero patience with still other cohost Elisabeth Hasselbeck's gibberish. From 2009 to 2011 she hosted *The Joy Behar Show* on HLN.

### Behn, Aphra (1640–1689)

Novelist, playwright, and poet who was probably the first Englishwoman to make her living as an author. Her work fell out of favor during the nineteenth century for being too racy (she tackled women's sexuality a few hundred years before most of Western society was ready to admit there is such a thing) but has since become a staple of Restoration lit syllabi. Writing in the *Guardian* in 2007, novelist Belinda Webb explained Behn's enduring appeal: "Operating with striking success outside gender conventions, it was she who paved the way for other women to do the same. What's more, she included as much wit and bawdiness as she could muster, along with a sharp insight into both sex and politics. She was the Restoration's very own combination of Dorothy Parker and Mae West."

Also, she was a spy for King Charles II, who stiffed her for it and landed her in debtor's prison. Cool. Except for the debtor's prison part.

Like almost every female writer, Behn inspires fierce arguments about whether she truly deserves a place in the canon or has only been retroactively included for the sake of political correctness. Virginia Woolf put it this way in *A Room of One's Own*: "All women together ought to let flowers fall upon the tomb of Aphra Behn…for it was she who earned them the right to speak their minds. It is she—shady and amorous she was—who makes it not quite fantastic for me to say to you tonight: Earn five hundred a year by your wits."

### Bel Geddes, Barbara (1922–2005)

Actress with a decades-long career, including turns in Alfred Hitchcock's *Vertigo* and eighties' guilty pleasure *Dallas*. As the latter's matriarch, Ellie, Bel Geddes largely evaded the tabloid fascination visited upon the soap's younger cast members. Then she had her own ripped-from-the-headlines moment. "When the producer asked me if I would mind having Ellie discover a malignant lump on her breast, I thought, 'No, this time I won't mind,'" said Bel Geddes, who had undergone her own radical mastectomy less than a decade prior. "I think it's a good idea and in a funny, strange way it might help somebody. It might be useful to somebody going through the pain and anguish. It might cheer someone up to see me running around on a stage. One does get over it." She won an Emmy.

### *Beloved*

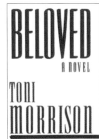

Pulitzer Prize–winning 1987 novel by Toni Morrison about a former slave named Sethe who murders her baby daughter rather than allow her to be enslaved. "Outside of its novelistic or literary merit, even outside of the reader confronting the transfiguration of the page, what is it for? It's almost as though the novel substitutes for something, that it exists instead of something else," wrote Toni Morrison two years after the book's publication.

> **"There is no place you or I can go, to think about or not think about, to summon the presences of, or recollect the absences of slaves; nothing that reminds us of the ones who made the journey and of those who did not make it. There is no suitable memorial or plaque or wreath or wall or park or skyscraper lobby. There's no three-hundred-foot tower. There's no small bench by the road. There is not even a tree scored, an initial that I can visit or you can visit in Charleston or Savannah or New York or Providence, or better still, on the banks of the Mississippi. And because such a place doesn't exist (that I know of), the book had to."**

### Benatar, Pat (1953–)

American singer, the first female solo artist to have her work played on MTV, and one of those late seventies–early eighties badass, trailblazing rock chicks whose success seems so inevitable in retrospect, it's hard to believe a bunch of sexist jerks tried to stop and/or tame them at every turn. A classically trained singer,

Benatar has won four Grammys, sold over twenty million records, produced nineteen Top 40 singles, and is still touring. Now please excuse us while we go watch Jennifer Garner rocking out to the "Love Is a Battlefield" video in *13 Going on 30* again.

### Benes, Elaine

Fictional character on the quintessential nineties sitcom *Seinfeld*. Played by Julia Louis-Dreyfus, who won numerous awards, including a Golden Globe and an Emmy, for her portrayal. A selfish, combative, jaded, and neurotic serial dater and the only fully employed character on the show, Benes was, in some ways, transgressive but played off lady stereotypes for laughs in others. (On one hand, she's an unabashed, enthusiastic user and hoarder of birth control sponges. On the other, she's a horrible driver.) Over the course of the series' nine seasons, Benes became the archetype of the sarcastic, single, urban, working woman. She favored loose, masculine-inspired clothing and declared that what she really wanted from a soul mate was "a barren, sterile existence that ends when you die." In a bizarro-world turn of fate, Elaine's character came to be because NBC executives ordered the show's creators, Jerry Seinfeld and Larry David, to add a woman to the cast to make the plot less male-centric.

### Benetton

Italian clothing conglomerate that pioneered and continues to (in its own inimitably European way) improve upon the otherwise tiresome practice whereby retail brands deploy ad campaigns to draw attention to humanitarian causes; following legal threats in 2011, the company officially apologized to the Vatican for its ad featuring a doctored photo of Pope Benedict XVI kissing prominent Egyptian cleric Mohammed Ahmed el-Tayeb.

### Benglis, Lynda (1941–)

American sculptor best known for using wax, polyurethane, aluminum, gold leaf, and zinc. She made waves in 1974 when, feeling underrepresented as a woman in the art world, she placed an ad in *Artforum* featuring herself naked and holding a large dildo between her legs.

### Bennet, Elizabeth

Beloved protagonist of Jane Austen's *Pride and Prejudice*. Every couple of years, someone decides to rank fictional heroines. But, like a life-dictator's sham elections, it's a farce: we all know Bennet will sweep. Seriously, does any other character in literature stand a chance against her wit, her charm, her incessant cinematic portrayal? On the face of it, she doesn't do that much: she's the second daughter of a gentleman in distressed circumstances, living a quiet life and engaged in a molasses-speed courtship with a reserved rich man. The genius is in the details: that Austen—and the character—make her world rich, endlessly entertaining, and, most of all, true to life. Lizzie is flawed, and that's her charm—the fact that, impetuous, judgmental, pert, and unconventional as she is, she still gets the guy (and the ultimate guy, at that) is endlessly affirming. And while we're on the subject: the best Elizabeth Bennet was Jennifer Ehle's 1995 BBC version. (*See also* AUSTEN, JANE)

### Bergman, Ingmar (1918–2007)

Film director who said of women: "They open up...I think women are more, perhaps from education, more used to enjoy[ing] this looking into the mirror that is the audience or the camera's eye...If a man stands in front of the mirror and looks at themselves, he can perhaps feel a little bit ashamed of it....a woman by education is not ashamed of looking at herself."

### Bergman, Ingrid (1915–1982)

Swedish actress best known for her portrayal of Ilsa Lund in the classic 1942 film *Casablanca*. In 1939, Bergman moved to Hollywood after signing a seven-year deal with producer David O. Selznick. This move launched a multi-decade acting career in which Bergman won three Oscars, two Emmys, and a Tony award. (Her other most famous films include *For Whom the Bell Tolls*, *Gaslight*, *Spellbound*, and *Joan of Arc*.) Gained notoriety when she left her first

husband, Petter Lindstrom, after having an affair and conceiving a child with film director Roberto Rossellini. (In 1950, a US Senator, Edwin C. Johnson, denounced Bergman—on the floor of the Senate, no less—as a "free-love cultist" and "a horrible example of womanhood and a powerful influence for evil.")

### Berlusconi, Silvio (1936–)

Former Italian prime minister and douche-bag-in-chief. Over the course of his long tenure, he's become notorious for his tasteless comments (he alleged, for instance, that the Chinese Communist Party under Mao boiled babies to use as fertilizer) and for his unceasing sexual harassment of pretty much every woman he encounters. In 2009, his infamy reached a new high with allegations that he'd hosted "bunga bunga parties" at which he and other dignitaries had sex with prostitutes and showgirls. The origin of *bunga bunga* is not completely clear, but the term is *not* believed to mean "sober foreign policy discussions." He's now accused of paying for sex with an underage girl named Karima el-Mahroug or "Ruby Heartstealer." Both swear they never had sex with each other, but only Berlusconi adds this interesting defense: "It's better to be fond of beautiful girls than to be gay."

### *Beverly Hills, 90210*

Popular 1990s television drama. The original version, which premiered in 1990, is perhaps the finest teen soap opera with practically middle-aged actors playing high school juniors in the history of television. It gave the world Tori Spelling, Luke Perry, Jason Priestley, Jennie Garth, and Shannen Doherty the Raging Bitch Diva—as opposed to Shannen Doherty the cute girl from *Little House* and first Heather-in-waiting—all of whom fictionally (at least) hooked up in every possible combination that wouldn't involve incest. There is also a newer version, but come on.

### Beyoncé

(*See* KNOWLES, BEYONCÉ)

### Bhutto, Benazir (1953–2007)

Former prime minister of Pakistan and first female leader of a Muslim state who, in December 2007, became the most famous woman assassinated since Indira Gandhi was killed by two of her bodyguards in 1984. Not the first in the family

to fall victim to political murder—her former prime minister father Zulfikar Ali Bhutto was hanged in 1979 following a military coup, and both of her younger brothers who were radicalized in response had been killed under sketchy politically motivated circumstances. Bhutto had spent the previous decade living in self-imposed exile in London while her husband faced extensive corruption charges. Lured back to Karachi in the fall by a promised power-sharing arrangement with General Pervez Musharraf brokered—somewhat dubiously—by the United States. Once she was back in Pakistan, however, the American embassy repeatedly rejected her pleas for help in hiring a security detail and, a little over two months after her arrival, Bhutto was killed at a rally in Rawalpindi, leaving a political legacy so consumed by assassination attempts, imprisonments, exiles, house arrests, terrorist attacks, border wars, and sundry dirty tricks campaigns it barely left time for the customary absurd gender stereotype–based attacks.

### Bialik, Mayim (1975–)

Actress and attachment parenting advocate. Though she will most likely always be remembered as the sunflower hat–wearing title character on the teen sitcom *Blossom*, Bialik avoided child star burnout and found both academic and acting success during her post–Blossom Russo years, earning a PhD in neuroscience from UCLA and landing the role of Amy Farrah Fowler, a brilliant but socially awkward neurobiologist on the CBS sitcom *The Big Bang Theory*.

### Bieber, Justin (1994–)

YouTube-discovered teenage Canadian pop singer best known for breaking nine-year-old hearts and rocking a modern-day Monkees hairdo. Chances are good that he'll be old news by the time this volume goes to press, but in 2010 your niece desperately wanted to make out with him. 'Member that? Good times.

### Bigelow, Kathryn (1951–)

Filmmaker. The first woman to win a Best Director Academy Award, for 2008's *The Hurt Locker*, but we would have given her one for *Point Break*.

### Big Love

Frustrating and occasionally amazing serial drama about a polygamous Mormon family in Utah. *Big Love*'s tragic flaw was that it tried to remain agnostic about its polygamist, empty cipher of a paterfamilias, Bill Paxton's Bill Henrickson. The best thing about it was its female characters, namely, Jeanne Tripplehorn's steadfast, long-suffering Barb; Chloë Sevigny's Nicki, so scheming, but incandescent when she wanted to be; and Ginnifer Goodwin's sweet, wayward Margene. And that's to say nothing of all the great female supporting roles: Nicki's imperious but often sweet mother, Adaleen (Mary Kay Place); Bill's addled and stubborn mom, Lois (Grace Zabriskie); or the entertainingly calculating child bride, Rhonda Volmer (Daveigh Chase). The list of all the great women who passed through the halls of this show while it was still standing could fill this book. But you kept wondering how it was that they all agreed to stay there, given how boring and conventional and fumbling and incapable their husbands and brothers and other assorted "handlers" were. Why didn't any of them follow the First Daughter, Amanda Seyfried's Sarah, right out the back door? Maybe that's the mystery of polygamy itself, at least the real fundamentalist kind.

### bikini

The most popular swimsuit style in the world. In 1946, a thoughtful Frenchman named Louis Réard came up with a novel idea: "Why not have bathing suits resemble women's underwear?" And so he invented the bikini, named after Bikini Atoll, a onetime testing site for atomic bombs, because a two-piece bathing suit that emancipated the torsos of women everywhere would be, you know, *the bomb*. (And here you thought French humor was inaccessible.) Now ladies were free to go swimming in garments that were just like their bras and underpants. Just imagine! There are now endless variations on the original style, with some bikinis little more than a discarded scrap of cheap fabric. Because even

the most modest of bikinis exposes most of a woman's body, bikinis have also become a source of female insecurity and despair; women's magazines and tabloids relentlessly push the idea of the perfect "bikini body," a totally subjective measurement of whether or not you look good in a bikini.

### Bikini Kill

Band. Formed in 1990 in Olympia, Washington, Bikini Kill became the most famous band to emerge from the feminist punk rock movement known as riot grrrl. While riot grrrl itself had a wide diversity of sound, Bikini Kill rose to prominence by playing hardcore, an abrasive and usually heavily masculine kind of punk rock, made more famous by bands like Minor Threat and Black Flag. Over a series of EPs and two albums, *Pussy Whipped* and *Reject All American*, lead singer Kathleen Hanna (who also published feminist zines including one titled *Revolution Girl Style Now*) and members Kathi Wilcox, Tobi Vail, and Billy Karren produced acerbic and often catchy songs denouncing condescending men and sexual violence and celebrating female displays of strength and resistance. The band helped coin the riot grrrl slogan "Girl power!" only to see it co-opted by mainstream bands such as the Spice Girls, who drained it of much of its feminist meaning. (Fun fact: Kurt Cobain of Nirvana came up with the title "Smells Like Teen Spirit" after reading graffiti Hanna had spray painted on the wall that said "Kurt smells like Teen Spirit.") (*See also* HANNA, KATHLEEN; ZINES)

### bikini wax

Also known as woman-on-woman violence. We could technically blame pornography for the landing-strip look, but even those who don't prefer the totally bare look still feel compelled to clean up the sides when swimsuits are involved. Still, how many among us have the

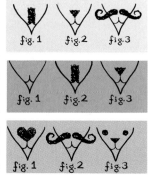

confidence to go to the beach completely ungroomed? The only way we can rebel against this most painful and ridiculous grooming habit is to bring back pantaloon-shaped swimsuits and undergarments, thus relegating the bikini wax to the "personal preference" and not "required swimming attire."

## binge drinking

Term to describe excessive consumption of alcohol. During the aughts, various studies showing that women self-report drinking more than they once did—kind of like men!—meant this time-honored method of alleviating disappointment and dampening social anxiety became the hot new Thing Young Women Are Doing to Fuck Up Their Lives Because of Feminism. "Does the sassy, self-confident girl-power generation feel it must show up guys everywhere, including at the bar?" asked Jodie Morse in *TIME* magazine. "This is the kind of equality nobody was fighting for," lamented Alex Morris in *New York Magazine*. "Exploding Bladders? Binge-Drinking Women Beware," warned an ABC News headline. According to the Centers for Disease Control, binge drinking overall has risen slightly over the past few years: the median number of American adults reporting having overindulged at least once in the past month ranged between 15.4 and 15.8 percent between 2006 and 2009. And though in 2010 it rose sharply, to 17.1 percent, it's possible that a higher prevalence of self-reported binges among the ladies just means contemporary women feel less self-conscious than previous generations about admitting that they got slaughtered in the past month.

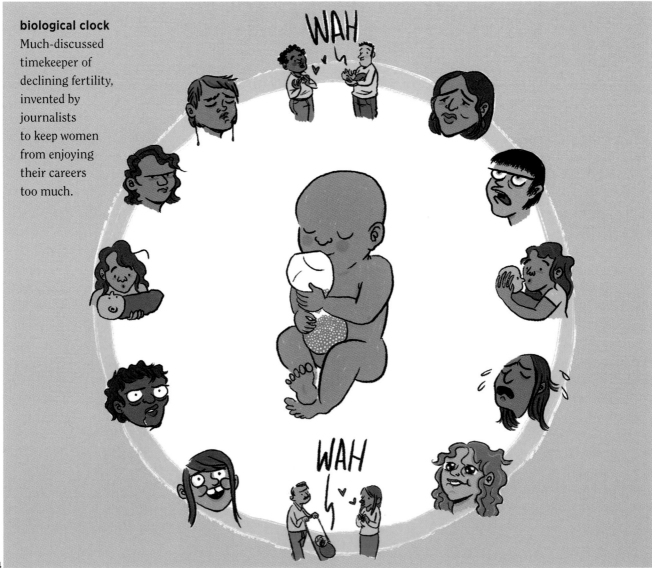

**biological clock**
Much-discussed timekeeper of declining fertility, invented by journalists to keep women from enjoying their careers too much.

But why would the press let obvious questions get in the way of a good panic about grown women making bad decisions? Exploding bladders, people! Date rape! (*See also* VICTIM BLAMING) Drunk teen sexting! Really bad karaoke! All these are the fault of hard-drinking women, who are the direct result of Betty Friedan. True facts.

### Bionic Woman, The

Television series spin-off of *The Six Million Dollar Man*, about an astronaut— Steve Austin, played by Lee Majors—whose body, after a near-fatal crash, was rebuilt with robotic parts that gave him superhuman powers. Starred Lindsay Wagner as Jaime Sommers, a onetime paramour of Austin and tennis pro severely injured in a skydiving accident and, like her boyfriend, rebuilt with bionic legs, one bionic arm, and a bionic ear. (In the show's third and final season, Jaime also had a bionic dog, named Max.) With her implants, Sommers led a double life as a schoolteacher and government agent, battling Fembots (seriously), kidnappers, smugglers, and other enemies of the state, while maintaining a flirty but professional relationship with her ex. In 1977, *TIME* magazine lauded the Sommers character as the year's Most Appealing Argument for Feminism, which, while totally patronizing, is also kind of rad. Many feminists applauded the show for showcasing a woman as an action hero; others pointed out that Sommers was frequently objectified and still took orders from men, much like on the other female action show at the time, *Charlie's Angels*. In later years, academic theorists have described Somers as the "first female cyborg." *The Bionic Woman* was canceled in 1978, but the character lived on in a series of TV movies until 1994, with the airing of *Bionic Ever After?*, in which Steve and Jaime took on yet more foes and finally, after twenty years, got married and lived happily ever after.

### birth

A highly politicized process involving the expelling of a newborn baby from its mother's womb.

### birth control

The medical advancement that allows you to avoid a life incubating human after human until your reproductive parts eventually fail.

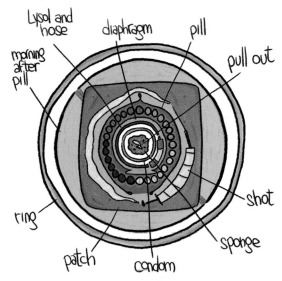

### bitch

An aggressive woman. A confident woman. A sexual woman. A woman. A female dog. A passive man. A gay man. A subordinate prisoner. Prefaced by "to," the act of complaining. With suffix *-ing*, something awesome. An openhanded slap. A nondriving motorcycle position. A losing poker hand. A heavy metal band. A feminist pop culture magazine. Elizabeth Taylor. Joan Collins. Elton John. Life. To Elizabeth Wurtzel, a position to aspire to. To Ludacris, someone who needs to get out of the way. To Meredith Brooks, several contradictory character traits present in a single woman. (*See also* CHILD; DREAM; HEALTH; LOVER; MOTHER; SAINT; SINNER)

### Bjelland, Kat (1963–)

Singer for the band Babes in Toyland who navigated child abuse, high school cheerleading, punk rock, schizophrenia, and Courtney Love.

> "I swear to God, I'm gonna tell you this one fucking time and I want a retraction…I did not steal the dress from Babes in Toyland. I loaned my dress to Kat and she went to England wearing it to every fucking show. I stole that dress from Christina Amphlett way back in 1981…fuck it, what do you think me and the band are having a huge feud about? She stole my dress, so I had to switch to the white dress, from that one dress I had to switch to the white dress because she pretty much pissed all over the first dress, so that's why I get annoyed about the white dress, because it took me about a year to figure out about the white dress. So I just want to clear that up. 'K? It's not a bad thing. It's not like I'm mad. I just want to make sure it's clear. Kat stole the dress from me. I started the dress."
>
> —COURTNEY LOVE slurring onto Muffs singer Kim Shattuck's voice mail, asserting her ownership over the kinderwhore look that defined early nineties lady grunge

### Björk (1965–)

Singer, artist. Björk released her first weird album, a collection of flute compositions and Icelandic covers of English-language songs (the Beatles' "Álfur út úr hól" makes an appearance) at age twelve. Almost a quarter century later, one dead swan's head hooked around her neck, she stepped out on the Oscars' red carpet as Iceland's biggest cultural export. Bigger than Leif Erickson. Bigger than the Blue Lagoon. Bigger than medieval wrestling. Bigger than ice. Only when Eyjafjallajökull spewed kilometers of volcanic ash across European airspace was Björk's cultural dominance rivaled.

### Blackwell, Elizabeth (1821–1910)

America's first female doctor. How did she do it? The staff at Geneva Medical College assumed her application to be a hoax and accepted her for the lulz. She graduated at the head of her class.

### Blanchett, Cate (1969–)

Australian actress, best known for *Elizabeth*, *The Lord of the Rings*, and *The Aviator*, for which she won an Oscar for Best Supporting Actress for her portrayal of Katharine Hepburn. Blanchett got her start in theater, and now she and her husband, playwright and director Andrew Upton, run the Sydney Theatre Company together. Eschews plastic surgery. "There's been a decade or probably more of people doing interventions on their faces and their bodies, and now people are seeing that [in the] long term, it's not so great," she said in a 2012 interview. "I'm not sitting on a soapbox telling women what they should and shouldn't do. I just know what works for me."

### Blige, Mary J. (1971–)

The most successful female R&B artist of the past twenty-five years, according to *Billboard* magazine, and the only performer with Grammys in pop, R&B, gospel, and rap. She definitely does not need no hateration in this dancery or any other.

### Bloomer, Amelia (1818–1894)

Crank, revolutionary, temperance advocate, and nineteenth-century feminist. Founding editor of *The Lily*, the first American publication for and by women, and an important early suffragette. Major advocate of rational dress. At a time when women were literally deforming themselves with whalebone corsets and bustled hobble-skirts, Bloomer encouraged loose trousers and tunics that encouraged free movement and healthy breathing. (The getup inspired such ridicule that even she dropped it after a while. But she was already immortalized.) Somewhere, she must be looking down at harem pants and smiling. (Cage heels? Maybe not so much.)

# BLACK BEST FRIEND

A tool used by writers and producers wanting to dazzle you with their open-mindedness and commitment to diversity. Although the inclusion of a "good" black character may seem like a positive thing, such pointed efforts at diversity often turn out to be manipulations that cleverly take advantage of the invisibility of black men and women and their historic subservient status to whites. (Latinas and Asian Americans are also deployed as supporting characters to similar effect.) As seen in the short list below, BBFs are used to perform one or more of the following functions: to provide humor; to serve as a sounding board for ideas; to support, guide, or even rescue; to add grit and sass; to emphasize the main character's essential decency.

## Ardelia from *Silence of the Lambs*

Fellow FBI trainee and sympathetic ear to Clarice Starling, who has been asked to conduct a psychological profile of a criminally insane murderer and cannibal.
**Known for:** Empathy, selflessness

## Cherie from *Punky Brewster*

Neighbor and best friend to Punky Brewster.
**Known for:** Faith in Punky, loyalty

## Chico from *Baby Face*

Coworker of protagonist Lily Powers at the latter's family speakeasy in a 1933 drama starring Barbara Stanwyck. Follows Lily to New York in search of fame and fortune, serving as maid and confidant and lending a nonjudgmental ear to her friend's scheming while washing her soiled delicates.
**Known for:** Quiet servitude, humble lack of judgment

## Elena from *Felicity*

Felicity's friend and fellow premed major at the University of New York. Supports Felicity through every heartache. Unlike the show's white female characters, not considered a serious contender for the romantic or sexual attention of any of the show's male characters, given that they are all white.
**Known for:** Telling it like it is, her sexuality

## Chastity from *10 Things I Hate About You*

The hotter best friend of Padua High School's Bianca. Tags along, standing invisibly by, as boys fight for her friend's affection.
**Known for:** Sticking by Bianca's side, her ongoing and devoted interest in Bianca's love life

## Dionne from *Clueless*

Cher's partner in crime and the second most popular girl at school. Adds color to Cher's Valley Girl existence and educates the audience about black things such as hair extensions and slang like "da bomb."
**Known for:** Adding drama, her sexuality

## Tara from *True Blood*

Sookie's finger-wagging longtime best friend with a troubled past and bad attitude. Takes a bullet meant for her friend. (To keep her from dying, Sookie turns her into a vampire.)
**Known for:** Fierce loyalty, hard-edgedness

---

## bloomers

Not just an endearingly old-timey word for underpants, it turns out! It is also a word for an endearingly old-timey set of Hammer or harem pants, popularized (though not invented) by women's rights activist Amelia Bloomer (see preceding entry). You may be familiar with said Hammer Pants of Justice from the time Sybil wore them on *Downton Abbey* to demonstrate that she was rebellious and forward thinking and would eventually marry an obnoxiously bossy chauffeur. And if Sybil had been caught by the press in this outfit, she would have been called a "Bloomer," which was the popular media insult for women who thought they could go around wearing pants like regular people. Nowadays, of course, the wearing of pants is undertaken by many ladies and has lost its political savor. To re-create the subversive thrill of bloomer wearing, we suggest maybe…jeggings? No, just kidding, nobody recommends that. (*See also* PANTS)

### *Blossom*

Nineties sitcom about a quirky teenage girl (played by Mayim Bialik) struggling to get through adolescence after being abandoned by her mother, *Blossom* took the "very special episode" concept and ran with it, tackling after-school-special type topics like pregnancy, periods, virginity, alcoholism, and eating disorders but filtering them through Blossom's humor, intelligence, and awkwardness in order to make them a bit more relatable. While the show could be heavy on the drama, the subject matter was usually lightened by the presence of

Blossom's fast-talking best friend, Six, and her dumb-but-sweet brother, Joey (Joey Lawrence), and his signature catchphrase, "Whoa!" (*See also* BIALIK, MAYIM)

### blow dry

### Blubber

Young adult novel. Long before the Heathers and the Plastics hit the mean girl scene, Judy Blume's *Blubber* explored the painful world of bullying among girls, giving an accurate and heartbreaking view of how easy it is to get caught up in teasing simply to ensure that you're not the one being laughed at.

(*See also* BLUME, JUDY; FAT SHAMING; HEATHERS; MEAN GIRLS)

### Blume, Judy (1938–)

Groundbreaking author whose young adult novels *Are You There God? It's Me, Margaret* and *Forever…*introduced girls

to menstruation, penises, and losing one's virginity, respectively. Though known (and challenged) most for their frank and humorous exploration of sex, Blume's twenty-plus novels, which include three works for adults, also broke ground in their depictions of friendship, school, divorce, sibling rivalry, adultery, puberty, racism, scoliosis, prejudice, masturbation, mortality, sexuality, and grief. (*See also* ARE YOU THERE GOD? IT'S ME, MARGARET; BLUBBER; DEENIE; WIFEY)

### Blythe

Alternately coy, shy, and snide wide-eyed doll with legions of obsessive fans—young and old—and a wardrobe to die for. If you think Barbie's measurements are unrealistic, take a tape measure to Blythe's head, and then compare the proportion to her arms and legs.

### Bobbitt, Lorena (1970–)

Domestic violence activist who inspired headlines and crass punch lines in 1993 after she severed her then husband's penis and subsequently threw it out the window of her car. Bobbitt later testified in court that husband John Wayne had abused her for years and raped her immediately prior to her attack. (He was eventually acquitted of spousal rape and denied the abuse allegations; Lorena was found not guilty by reason of insanity and went on to found domestic violence charity Lorena's Red Wagon.) "I admire the male body and prefer to find the penis attached to it rather than having to root around in vacant lots with Ziploc bag in hand," Barbara Ehrenreich wrote of Bobbitt's contribution to feminism in 1994. "But I'm not willing to wait another decade or two for gender peace to prevail. And if a fellow insists on using his penis as a weapon, I say that, one way or another, he ought to be swiftly disarmed." (*See also* EHRENREICH, BARBARA)

### Bodyguard, The

1992 romantic drama. Even an Oscars assassination attempt, a tearful tarmac good-bye, and the soaring finish of "I Will Always Love You" could not save the unexpected and interracial union of Whitney Houston and Kevin Costner, who inexplicably pressed their mouths together to become one of the biggest failed chemistry experiments in the history of on-screen couples. The film was panned; the sound track became an all-time bestseller.

### Boggs, Laney

Heroine of the nineties teen film *She's All That* and a prime example of Hollywood's ridiculous and condescending belief that putting glasses on a gorgeous girl will automatically make the audience view her as some sort of hideously ugly nerd in desperate need of a makeover.

### Boleyn, Anne (ca. 1501–1536)

Onetime Queen of England, later beheaded. According to a Venetian diplomat, "Not one of the handsomest women in the world…of middling stature, with a swarthy complexion, long neck, wide mouth, bosom not much raised, and in fact has nothing but the King's great appetite, and her eyes, which are black and beautiful…She lives like a queen, and the King accompanies her to Mass—and everywhere." But then Anne failed to have a son and the King grew tired of her, so she was falsely accused of adultery and incest and executed by a swordsman brought over from France for the job. She had the last laugh, though; her daughter, Elizabeth, outlived Henry VIII and his other children to become one of England's greatest monarchs.

### boner

Boner, hard-on, woody, chubby, pitched tent: there is no sexy slang term for "erection." A boner does not arise in the context of a sexual relationship. It is born in a pair of middle school gym shorts and dies nestled in a wad of toilet paper. A mature, adult erection may be expressed in a modification of the penis—a dick gets hard. A boner is its own thing. It is a spontaneous (boner alert!) display of individual male desire. It is aroused but never arousing. And it is more psychological than biological: see the co-opted term *lady boner.*

### bonerkiller

**1.** An unfortunate situation where a good but private time is interrupted accidentally by your mom walking in or unbidden thoughts about the current state of the nation and/ or memories of the plot points on *Jersey Shore.* **2.** How the douche bags of the world regard women who fancy themselves as rights-bearing persons and aren't afraid to say so. **3.** The main argument wielded by right-wing media against the possibility of Hillary Clinton holding high office. (*See also* PELOSI, NANCY)

### Bonham Carter, Helena (1966-)

English actress known for her pile of pre-Raphaelite curls, goth red carpet attire, and general weirdness—in a good, mostly noncreepy way. Has played several queens, a Harry Potter villain, Sweeney Todd's accomplice, a *Corpse Bride,* Ophelia, and a chimpanzee. That plus the fact that she's been cohabitating and procreating with Tim Burton for over a decade pretty much tells you what you need to know.

### Bonheur, Rosa (1822-1899)

Nineteenth-century French painter who may have anticipated the internet's obsession with animals. Her most famous subjects were horses, but she also did a fair amount of work on the rather less picturesque cattle and sheep. Kept her hair short, a cigarette in her mouth, and lions as pets. Thought by the art critic James Saslow to have painted herself in drag in her own most famous painting, *The Horse Fair.* Took up, at the end of her life, with a much younger woman, Anna Klumpke, and scandalized everyone. One of the first art stars to understand celebrity and successfully manipulate it and rise above it. "The epithets of imbeciles have never bothered me," she once said of her haters.

### Bonnie (1910-1934) and Clyde (1909-1934)

Depression-era outlaws (born Bonnie Elizabeth Parker and Clyde Chestnut Barrow) who spent a few years leading a gang that robbed banks and killed people before they were shot to death—at ages twenty-three and twenty-five, respectively— by police officers in Louisiana on May 23, 1934. A cache of photos discovered after they narrowly escaped capture in 1933—including one of Bonnie casually leaning on a car with a cigar in her mouth and a gun in her hand—helped turn the young, attractive couple into folk heroes. The 1967 movie *Bonnie and Clyde,* starring Faye Dunaway and Warren Beatty, solidified their legend in the public imagination.

### boob, boobie

Slang term for breast. Less offensive than tit but way too childish to be sexy. Especially popular among teenage boys, who enjoy writing the word on desks, bathroom walls, calculators, and sleeping friends' foreheads. Paradoxically, those most preoccupied with the word *boob* have had the least contact with one.

## Boop, Betty

Comic book character. In 1932, Boop became the world's first sexy cartoon character to run for president, paving the way for Olive Oyl's historic 1948 run. In "Betty Boop for President," Boop literally dances on that line between masculine authority and feminine allure that female major-party candidates would be forced to navigate decades later. Throughout her routine, Boop gets presidential by pulling her nose into a Hooveresque bulb and stuffing a cigar in her mouth. Then, she bends over a desk in front of the US Congress, shakes her booty, and purrs about chocolate ice cream. The episode loses touch with reality, however, when Boop wins the election.

## Boosler, Elayne (1952–)

Comedienne, actor, writer, and activist who in 1986 became the first woman to get her own cable comedy special—although she had to fund it herself. ("Not one to whine," says an official biography, "we won't dwell on how she was told TO HER cute little FACE that no one would watch a woman do an hour of comedy…") Since then, she's done six more, hosted TV and radio, written and directed films, guest starred on *Night Court*, become a staple of crossword editors everywhere, and rescued a whole bunch of animals. All female comics ought to let flowers fall upon the lap of Elayne Boosler, basically.

## Booty Bass

The official sound track of the high-waisted thong bikini. (*See also* BIKINI; THONG)

## Botox

Brand name of a popular cosmetic injectable and known poison. Because wrinkles are the undesirable mark of the completely natural process of aging, they must be warded off by all means. The most popular and famous of skin crease controls is to quite literally *paralyze* the muscle responsible for any offending creases by injecting it with poison, botulinum toxin. Of all the strange and exotic age-defying crap people can inject in their faces, Botox is still the go-to, the grande dame of injectables, the widely accessible go-to muscle paralyzer of choice. Overuse of Botox can leave one's face immobile and expressionless; it is thought to be responsible for the lifeless, vacant nonexpressions on the faces of well-to-do age-denying men and women everywhere.

## Boudreaux, Ouiser

Character created by Robert Harling for his play *Steel Magnolias* and cemented in pop culture legend by Shirley MacLaine in the 1989 film adaptation. (Other portrayals have been undertaken by actresses Alfre Woodard and Elaine Stritch.) A short-tempered, curmudgeonly woman who describes herself as "not crazy, I've just been in a bad mood for forty years." While often coming across as bitter and misanthropic, she secretly has a heart of gold, which never stops her from delivering lines like "You are a pig from hell."

## Bourgeois, Louise (1911–2010)

Sculptor whose thing for spiders culminated in a thirty-foot steel one she constructed toward the end of her career. She likened arachnopods to her mother, an image to which many

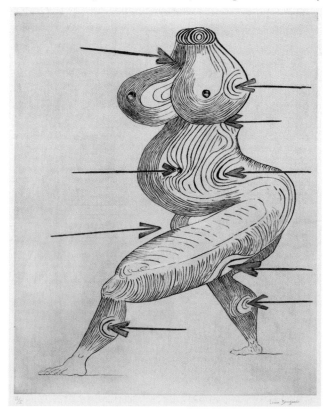

of us can relate. But her work was haunted by an idiosyncratic childhood that could have been written by a French Brontë, with an ailing mother and a father who philandered with the mistress-slash-governess. As a small act of protest, a tiny Bourgeois made a model of her father out of bread and then dismembered it. One of her most famous works, *Cell* (*Choisy*) (1990–1993), involves a guillotine poised over a marble model of her family's home. Effects lingered into her later life; she was germophobic and reclusive and had a habit of ironing her newspaper to destroy bacteria. Which doesn't make her crazy. "Art," she said, "is a guarantee of sanity."

### Bourke-White, Margaret (1904–1971)

New York City–born photojournalist, first female war correspondent, and photographer for *Life* magazine. (Her photo of Fort Peck Dam under construction was featured on the inaugural issue's cover.) Famed for capturing monumental moments in history such as the Great Depression and the

German invasion of Moscow during WWII. Bourke-White got her start photographing the interiors of steel mills before eventually moving on to capture the devastation caused by the Dust Bowl during the thirties and an iconic photo of Mahatma Gandhi at a spinning wheel.

**Bower, Angela**
The boss. Like it was ever really a question.

### Bowery Gals

Band of nineteenth-century working-class women who set the stage for gender equity in New York social spaces and whose peers laid the groundwork for modern-day victim blaming. Bowery gals staked out a new feminine persona in that ambiguous space between gentry women and prostitutes, hitting public spaces "not as street-walkers on the prowl but as members of a high-spirited peer group, reveling in their associations with each other," Christine Stansell wrote in *City of Women*. With a pastiche of high and low fashion and a heightened street visibility, the gals stomped on traditional class and gender divides. Some guys couldn't deal. "Bowery men saw public life…as a place where men were the main show and women the supporting cast," Stansell wrote. "The abuse of women, especially sexual abuse, remained a male prerogative; for some, it became a form of recreation. Group rapes, virtually unknown in the court records of the early nineteenth century, appear occasionally in court proceedings after 1830…Indeed, in a culture where women 'on the town' retained deep associations to prostitution, the working girl who made known her independence or even her aloneness could still be interpreted as issuing a sexual invitation."

### Boxer, Barbara (1940–)

Politician from California who was elected to the US Senate in 1992, bringing the body's female representation to a whopping six. Out of one hundred. The press called it the "year of the woman." George H. W. Bush said he hoped "a lot of them lose." She didn't, and became one of the Senate's most progressive voices, working for abortion rights and universal health care and against sexual harassment and the war in

Iraq. Eighteen years later, Boxer faced a new "year of the woman"—this time, backed by Republicans who had come around to the political benefits of a little bit of gender diversity. Boxer defeated Hewlett-Packard exec Carly Fiorina, and the "year of the woman" proved even less impressive than its first incarnation—women's representation in Congress failed to budge by a single rep.

## boyfriend

According to Liz Phair, a male provider of letters and sodas. (*See also* PHAIR, LIZ)

## bra, brassiere

Device worn under clothing for the purposes of breast support or sexual attractiveness, but rarely both at once. Breasts come in all shapes and sizes, but bras mainly come in band sizes 34 to 38 and cup sizes A to D. (The millions of women who don't fall into that range must buy bras from stores that specialize in what retailers delicately describe as "freak sizes." Or they can just squeeze themselves into a 34C and make the best of it, since Oprah has decreed that every woman is wearing the wrong bra size anyway.)

## bra burning

On September 7, 1968, feminists gathered outside the Miss America Pageant in Atlantic City chucked bras, cosmetics, and women's magazines into a trash can and threatened to light femininity on fire. The *New York Post* assigned reporter Lindsy van Gelder to mock the feminist action; instead, she drew parallels between the pageant protesters and Vietnam's draft card burners. A city official ultimately shut down the protest because organizers lacked a permit, but the mythic link between bra burning and militant feminism endured. Decades after van Gelder's draft card reference drifted away, *bra-burning feminists* remains entrenched in the antifeminist lexicon, ready to be employed whenever a legitimate women's issue is in need of a good belittling.

## Bradshaw, Carrie

Simultaneously beloved and annoyingly clueless protagonist of the *Sex and the City* books, television show, and movies, embodied in the latter two by Sarah Jessica Parker. Responsible for convincing the world that young writers in Manhattan can afford to buy $800 shoes, take cabs everywhere, and never wear the same cocktail dress twice. (But then, also responsible for making delicious cosmos and buttercream cupcakes widely available, so nothing's all bad.) (*See also* BUSHNELL, CANDACE; SEX AND THE CITY)

## Brady, Jan

Patron saint of awkward middle children everywhere, the middle daughter of the popular series *The Brady Bunch* was neither the pretty one nor the cute one out of the three girls in her family and in-

stead had to settle for being the angsty one. Whether she was complaining about the attention paid to her big sister, worrying that her glasses would make her look "positively goofy," or trying to convince everyone to believe in her imaginary boyfriend, George Glass, Jan had no shortage of anxiety or drama in her life, which is to be expected, really, when one is always being compared to "Marcia, Marcia, Marcia."

## Brangelina

**1.** Brad Pitt and Angelina Jolie.
**2.** A prime example of the supremely annoying early twenty-first-century trend of turning couples' names into snappy portmanteau words.

## Bratz

Extremely popular—like, sometimes-overtaking-Barbie popular—line of dolls for girls. The original four Bratz—Cloe, Jade, Sasha, and Yasmin—are meant to be a multicultural (i.e., identical but for hair and skin tone) group of stylish teenage girls who can miraculously stand upright despite having heads about seventeen times the size of their painfully skinny bodies, topped (of course) with knee-length hair. Like so many toys, Bratz dolls have stirred up controversy over

the abominable Chinese labor practices that produce them and the marketing of sexualized images to little girls. You can go ahead and guess how much either of those things have slowed them down.

## Bravo

NBC Universal network dedicated to the wealthy and the people who cook their food, manage their real estate, do their hair, and act as their gay sidekicks. Founded by a subdivision of Cablevision in 1980 as a fine arts channel, Bravo initially wooed high-end viewers with low-cost broadcasts of fine arts such as opera and ballet and independent movies. The rise of reality television and of a distinct gay market gave the network a new way forward in 2003 with the debut of *Queer Eye for the Straight Guy*, which sold gay men as the guardians of sophisticated living. Bravo has since dedicated its original programming to reality shows about lifestyle industries, ranging from cooking competition show *Top Chef* to the *Real Housewives* franchise, which follows wealthy women in communities from Orange County to New Jersey and is filming spin-offs in multiple countries, to shows chronicling the lives of publicist Kelly Cutrone, stylist Rachel Zoe, and actress Kathy Griffin.

## Brazilian wax

CARRIE: I got mugged. She took everything I got.
SAMANTHA: It's called the Brazilian wax.
MIRANDA: Why didn't you tell her to stop?
CARRIE: I tried. I feel like one of those freaking hairless dogs.
SAMANTHA: It's an aesthetic thing, everyone goes bare out here.
MIRANDA: Of course they do. L.A. men are too lazy to go searching for anything.
　　　　　—*Sex and the City*, Season 3, Episode 14
(*See also* VAGINA; WAXING)

## Breakfast Club, The

"What we found out is that each one of us is a brain, and an athlete, and a basket case, and a princess, and a criminal. Does that answer your question?"

### breast cancer

Most common cancer among women in the United States; affects one in eight women during their lives. A horrible and tragic epidemic made worse by the countless attempts by companies and organizations ranging from the NFL to Pornhub.com to get consumers to buy their pinkwashed wares.

### breastfeeding

No matter what you're doing, you are probably doing it wrong and hurting your baby.

### breasts

Secondary sex characteristic in females. Big ones are hot, but the women who have them are probably dumb and slutty, and really big ones just make you look fat. Small ones suggest you're cool and possibly athletic, but nowhere near as hot as a woman with big ones (as long as they're not too big). Medium ones can be ruined by nipples that are too big, too small, or too dark, and by moles, zits, hairs, and stretch marks. Naturally large and/or perky ones will eventually be ruined by gravity. Unnaturally perky ones mean you're shallow and appearance-obsessed. Botched unnaturally perky ones mean you're shallow, appearance-obsessed, and ugly. Unnaturally large ones mean you're a porn star. Having them at all means that at some point in your life you will be leered at, catcalled, and/or groped in public. Also, they make food for babies.

### breeder

Pejorative once primarily used by gay people to describe straight ones, but now also used by child-free straight people to describe smug, entitled parents. How far we've come.

### Breeders, The

Indie band founded by two badass lady rock stars: Kim Deal (who was also in the Pixies) and Tanya Donelly (of Throwing Muses and Belly).

### Brewster, Punky

Character in eighties sitcom that, on paper, had a ridiculous setup: a young girl is abandoned by her mother at a shopping mall, and discovered living alone in an empty apartment by the building's curmudgeonly widower landlord, who ends up taking her in and ultimately adopting her. But *Punky Brewster* worked thanks to its star, Soleil Moon Frye, who played the title character with enough spunk and sweetness to make one forget the show's somewhat upsetting premise. The darkness that often ran through the show was offset by Punky's undying optimism and belief in herself, which she expressed through her memorably bright clothing and her constant exclamation of "Punky Power!" She was also a feminist: in the episode "Girls Will Be Boys," she challenges the neighborhood boys, a sexist coach, and even the reservations of her own foster father Henry to gain the right to race her remote control car at a "boys-only" track, eventually winning the race and accepting her giant trophy with this classic quip: "Thanks. This will look great on the shelf, right next to my dolls." (*See also* FRYE, SOLEIL MOON)

### bride

What every single female person over the age of two aspires to be, according to Hollywood. (*See also* MARRIAGE; WEDDING)

### bridesmaids

**1.** Cadre of women chosen to accompany a bride to the altar as part of the "wedding party." Historically, people of rank took such posses with them everywhere they went, and the wealthier and more important you were, the bigger your crew. Today, that practice survives in the wedding party. Bridesmaids are often tasked with the planning of prewedding events like bridal showers and bachelorette parties and are often asked to demonstrate their devotion to the bride by wearing hideous matching dresses and pretending to care about canapés. **2.** 2011 movie cowritten by and starring Kristen Wiig, who plays Annie, a falling-apart thirty-something whose best friend gets engaged and makes her the maid of honor. *Bridesmaids* was supposed to prove, once and for all, that women are not just funny but that a movie stocked with funny women could make box office bank, thus making it easier for other such movies to secure funding. (So, you know, no pressure.) As it happened, *Bridesmaids* grossed about $288 million and scored two Oscar nominations, one for Best Original Screenplay and a Best Supporting Actress nod to the hilarious Melissa McCarthy. And yet, the "Are women funny?" debate goes on. (*See also* McCarthy, Melissa)

### bridesmaids' dresses

Baby blue! Lime green! Fuschia! Ruffles! Butt bows! A total waste of your hard-earned money, even if—or especially if—they're purchased from usually reliable purveyors of good taste like Vera Wang. Their only potential upside is as comic relief.

### Bridges, Ruby (1954–)

American civil rights activist, philanthropist, and something of a living symbol as the first African American child to attend a whites-only school in the South. In 1960, when Bridges was six years old, her parents allowed her to be a part of the NAACP's program to integrate the New Orleans public school system. Bridges described the atmosphere of yelling and shouting as she entered William Frantz Elementary for the first time as being like Mardi Gras. White parents reacted by pulling their kids out of the school, and teachers refused to teach the young pupil. US Marshals were called in, by order of President Eisenhower, to protect her on her way to school. To this day, she continues her work as an advocate against the "grown-up disease" of racism in America. Ruby was immortalized in Norman Rockwell's 1963 painting *The Problem We All Live With*, an image of her walking to school, the canvas fit to her height and cutting the adults around her off at the shoulders, and in 2011, President Obama hung the painting outside the Oval Office to commemorate the fiftieth anniversary of the Supreme Court ruling that made integration possible.

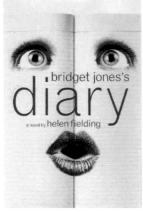

### Bridget Jones's Diary

1996 Helen Fielding novel about a smoking, drinking, BBC-period-drama-watching, slightly chubby single gal in London that became a runaway best-seller—and a pretty good film—for two reasons: it was smart and funny. Unfortunately, writers and publishers eager to replicate its success frequently ignored those two factors, so the rapidly growing genre of "chick lit" soon became known mostly for crappy writing marked by references to unaffordable high heels. Finally, we've reached a point where stories about young female singletons (a word popularized by Bridget Jones) are just called "women's fiction" (as opposed to stories about young male singletons, which are called "literature"), but the "chick lit" era lasted longer than anyone could have imagined, and even managed to cannibalize its original heroine. (*See also* FIELDING, HELEN)

### Bright, Susie (1958–)

Prolific writer, speaker, and sex educator and a pioneer in sex-positive feminism. Academic in her approach to pornography and erotica and instinctual in her approach to intimacy, Bright has been called an X-rated intellectual. Although Bright was often at ideological odds with feminist and anti-pornography activist Andrea Dworkin, she has said that Dworkin was a catalyst for the growing movement around sex positivity. (*See also* DWORKIN, ANDREA; SEX-POSITIVE)

### broad

Term popularized in the 1930s to describe a hard-nosed, well-dressed woman who is allergic to bullshit. Dames are "classy," broads are "ornery." Or in the words of Bette Davis, one of the OBs, "If you want a thing done well, get a couple of old broads to do it."

### Brontë, Anne (1820–1849)

Sort of the forgotten Brontë sister. Wrote *Agnes Grey* and *The Tenant of Wildfell Hall*, which are totally overdue for being made into period movies. Look for them in the next five years.

### Brontë, Charlotte (1816–1855)

Novelist and the best of all possible Brontës. From *Jane Eyre*, published in 1847: "Women are supposed to be very calm generally: but women feel just as men feel; they need exercise for their faculties, and a field for their efforts as much as their brothers do; they suffer from too rigid a restraint, too absolute a stagnation, precisely as men would suffer; and it is narrow-minded in their more privileged fellow-creatures to say that they ought to confine themselves to making puddings and knitting stockings, to playing on the piano and embroidering bags."

### Brontë, Emily (1818–1848)

The middle Brontë sister and author of one novel, *Wuthering Heights*. If your only exposure to the Brontë sisters is *Jane Eyre*, it's time to read this book, the story of a doomed cross-class love affair and its long aftermath. It's brilliant and strange and wild. So was Emily. She was also a near recluse, someone who likely never had a romantic relationship in her life and lived outside her family home for only eighteen months of her thirty years. Writes Anne Carson in *The Glass Essay*, her long poem about Bronte: "Emily made her awkward way / across days and years whose bareness appalls her biographers." But also this:

> in between the neighbour who recalls her
> coming in from a walk on the moors
> with her face 'lit up by a divine light'
> and the sister who tells us
> Emily never made a friend in her life,
> is a space where the little raw soul
> slips through.
> It goes skimming the deep keel like a storm petrel
> out of sight.

To read *Wuthering Heights* is to see this storm-petrel soul in flight.

## Brooks, Gwendolyn (1917-2000)

The most prominent African American woman poet of the twentieth century, winner of the 1950 Pulitzer for poetry, and onetime poet laureate of Illinois and the United States. Brooks began publishing poems in her teens and came out with her first book, *A Street in Bronzeville*, in 1945. At a reading in 1983 at the Guggenheim Museum, she confessed that most people know her as the writer of "We Real Cool," her short, widely anthologized (and occasionally banned) poem about urban boys playing pool on a school day. "I don't mean that I dislike it," she said, "but I would prefer it if the textbook compilers and the anthologists would assume that I've written a few other poems." In fact, she wrote more than twenty books over a half century. Get reading.

## Brooks, Romaine (1874-1970)

American painter known for her life-size nudes and drawings made of continuous curved lines, many of which starred her lovers and members of her social circle, including Natalie Clifford Barney, Gluck, and Renata Borgatti. (*See also* GLUCK)

## Browder, Aurelia (1919-1971)

Civil rights activist arrested for refusing to surrender her Montgomery, Alabama, bus seat to a white passenger, eight months before Rosa Parks did the same.

## THE BROWNS

Why so many notable women named Brown? Perhaps it's due to the "tyranny of the alphabet" (short version: some researchers suggest that, thanks to Western society's penchant for arranging things in alphabetical order—including children in a classroom—the first letter of a person's last name can influence everything from academic achievement and professional ambition to shopping habits). More likely it's simple ubiquity: Brown is one of the most common surnames in a number of English-speaking countries (fourth-most common in the UK; fifth-most common in the US). Supposedly, the name originated as a descriptor of people with brown hair or skin. Which makes sense, we suppose, until one realizes that the large majority of people with the surname, both in this book and elsewhere, reside more on the ivory end of the melanin spectrum.

## Brown, Bobbi (1957-)

American makeup artist and author best known for rebelling against heavy foundation and powders pushed on young girls and women that hid their natural features. In her 2001 guide for teen girls, *Bobbi Brown Teenage Beauty*, she favored "real" girls and has attempted to create makeup that is suitable for women at any life stage and that matches every skin color. And by every skin color, we mean shades in addition to white/Caucasian.

## Brown, Foxy

**1.** 1974 blaxploitation film starring Pam Grier as a vengeful, castrating, hypersexualized but also kind of awesome action heroine of that name. **2.** American hip-hop artist (b. 1978) of the late twentieth and early twenty-first century who gained fame first for her precocious talents and later for her repeated assault charges and eventual jail time.

## Brown, Helen Gurley (1922-2012)

Copywriter turned iconic editor of *Cosmopolitan* magazine; not so much a person as the under-nourished embodiment of a powerful 1960s Madison Avenue realization that single women were, pound for pound, considerably more valuable consumers than their married counterparts

and that their value could be further enhanced by exploiting their insecurities with a steady stream of "must-have" products, possessions, and prognoses. Became the preeminent authority on this glamorous new brand of singledom upon entering into her long and exceptionally codependent marriage to the well-connected magazine editor and film producer David Brown, who masterminded her career-making self-help bestseller *Sex and the Single Girl* and wrote the magazine's famous cover lines. Gurley Brown would be an amazing feminist icon if she hadn't inflicted decades of unrelenting heteronormativity and fearmongering about weight, fashion, and blow job skills on American women. (*See also* COSMOPOLITAN)

### Brown, Julie (1958–)

Not the "Downtown" one. Comedic actress and singer who gave the world *Earth Girls Are Easy* and "The Homecoming Queen's Got a Gun."

### Brown, Margaret Wise (1910–1952)

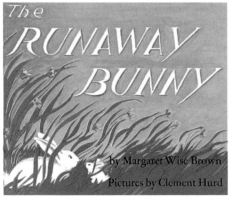

Famed children's author whose most popular works include classics such as *Goodnight Moon* and *The Runaway Bunny*. The bisexual Brown had a ten-year relationship with the actress Michael Strange and was engaged to James Stillman Rockefeller Jr. before her sudden death from an embolism at the early age of forty-two.

### Brown, Molly (1867–1932)

Perhaps the best-known survivor of the RMS *Titanic* disaster. "The Unsinkable Molly Brown" drew notice for her help in evacuating the doomed ship and attempts to save others. A philanthropist and activist for women's suffrage before hitting the iceberg, she later used her fame to promote causes including workers' rights, literacy, and education.

## MURPHY BROWN

Murphy Brown, the investigative television news journalist played by Candice Bergen for ten seasons on the CBS comedy of the same name, has somehow disappeared. The show went off the air in 1998, and as of this writing only the first season is available on DVD. Save for a few cameo clips, the show hasn't even been committed to YouTube. It's not streaming on Hulu or Netflix, and it's not in syndication, making it inaccessible to even the cable-privileged.

Which is why it's so impressive that Murphy Brown, the archetype, is so ubiquitous. The character, created by writer-producer Diane English, is now a convenient shorthand for a particular type of high-achieving woman with a healthy mean streak but plenty of soft spots; the type with a clear career trajectory but a muddy slog through relationships, a combination of professional unflappability and sly self-deprecation that's become the norm for female comedic protagonists. On the wrong side of forty and the right side of rehab, Murphy was no Mary Tyler Moore. She was, in fact, much more like Mary's curmudgeonly boss Lou Grant—unafraid to be unlikable—but with some uniquely feminine hang-ups. In one episode, after dealing with a bout of bad press, Murphy breaks down to her (male) secretary: "Everyone hates me. I've tried not to let it bother me. People have hated me before, but I dealt with it better. I was younger. I was tougher. I was drinking!" The secretary comforts her then promptly quits. (The show's recurring gag of Murphy's string of unsuitable secretaries was a brilliant comedic way of acknowledging ball-busting boss-lady stereotypes without caving to them fully.)

The show is perhaps best remembered for its plot point about Murphy's unplanned pregnancy and her decision to have, and raise, a baby on her own. The political finger-wagging that followed the early 1990s story line was both venomous and appropriate for an era in which which "welfare queen" and "family values" were dominant buzzwords. In May 1992, then Vice President Dan Quayle accused the show of "mocking the importance of fathers by bearing a child alone and calling it 'just another lifestyle choice.'" A Bush White House spokesman jumped into the fray, explaining in a teeth-grindingly patronizing fashion that "the concern now is that the glorification of life as an unwed mother…does not do good service to most unwed mothers who are not highly paid glamorous anchorwomen."

Indeed, Murphy's shoulder-padded struggles weren't exactly the stuff of the common woman. But generations of women—and their fictional counterparts on the big and small screen—have taken Murphy's swagger to heart. As Murphy tells her neurotic, overachieving male producer, "You can't always play by the rules, Miles. Taking risks is how I got here."

## Brown, Tina (1953–)

British-born journalist, author, and, most notably, magazine editor (*Tatler*, *Vanity Fair*, the *New Yorker*, *Talk*, and *Newsweek/Daily Beast*).

### brownies

**1.** A delicious baked treat, sometimes incorporating marijuana. **2.** The second- and third-graders' branch of Girl Scouts of America, perhaps best known for their tiny, adorable beanies. (*See also* GIRL SCOUT)

## Browning, Elizabeth Barrett (1806–1861)

Writer best known for her love poems, *Sonnets from the Portuguese*, written for Robert Browning, a man six years her junior with whom she would eventually elope. Because her family had spent so much time in Jamaica, she believed she had slave ancestors, though there's no way to prove she was right. (She called herself "little and black.") Her guilt over her family's benefit from slavery led her to abolitionism; "if I believed in curses," she wrote to a friend, "I should be afraid." She died just a few years after writing that line, in 1861.

## Brownstein, Carrie (1974–)

Seminal riot grrrl musician turned seminal hipster laceration artist. Brownstein played guitar, sang, and kicked ass in the all-female band Sleater-Kinney from its inception in 1994 until the group went on hiatus in 2006. Now heads the band Wild Flag, which put out its debut album in 2011, and produces, writes, and stars in the sketch show *Portlandia*, where she skewers Portland's culture of tragic hipness, self-congratulatory pseudoactivism, and putting birds on things. (*See also* RIOT GRRRL; SLEATER-KINNEY)

## brunette

Smarter than a blonde. Duller than a redhead.

## Bryn Mawr

Katharine Hepburn swam naked here. (*See also* SEVEN SISTERS)

## Buffy the Vampire Slayer

1992 film written by Joss Whedon and starring Kristy Swanson. A few years after the film's release, Whedon began adapting *Buffy* for the small screen and the show began airing on the fledgling WB network in 1997. Over seven seasons, the show built a powerful portrait of misogyny as a great evil, used magic as a metaphor for the impact of sexual maturity, and introduced groundbreaking lesbian characters like Willow Rosenberg and Tara Maclay. The show also helped build a bench of important female Hollywood writers and producers, like Marti Noxon, who's worked on shows ranging from *Glee* to *Mad Men*, and Jane Espenson, who's continued to work on genre programs like *Battlestar Galactica* and *Once Upon a Time*. (*See also* SUMMERS, BUFFY; WHEDON, JOSS)

## Bull Durham

1988 movie starring Susan Sarandon, Kevin Costner, and Tim Robbins about men who play baseball and the women who love the game and them, mostly in that order. Also, the movie where Sarandon and Robbins met, initiating one of the great romantic and activist partnerships in Hollywood and the origin of the term *Baseball Annie* to describe baseball groupies. Sarandon is Annie Savoy, an intellectual fan of the "Church of Baseball" who mentors and has an affair with a minor-league player on the Durham Bulls (a real Triple-A affiliate of the Tampa Bay Rays) each season. Unusual in its insistence that having sex with athletes neither makes a woman a slut nor precludes her from being a serious fan and student of the game, *Bull Durham* is a depressingly rare combination of a feminist romantic comedy and a plausible sports movie. (*See also* SARANDON, SUSAN)

## burn book

The physical manifestation of girl-on-girl crime. Popularized by the 2004 Tina Fey film *Mean Girls*, a scrapbook used by a clique to insult others by scrawling nasty, hurtful comments underneath a fellow student's name or yearbook picture. Older Jezebels and Judy Blume fans might remember these as "slam books." (Ann M. Martin's novel *Slam Book*, published in 1987, presented a much, much darker portrait of adolescence than the one experienced by The Baby-sitters Club.)

### bush

Slang for pubic hair that is generally very long, very full, and very seventies.

### Bush, Kate (1958–)

English singer-songwriter famous for her haunting soprano and wide range of influences and styles. Although she's hit the UK Top 40 twenty-five times, collaborated with Peter Gabriel, Eric Clapton, and Prince, and reportedly influenced lady songwriters from Tori Amos to Florence Welch, you are probably already singing "Running Up That Hill," and now you will be all day.

### Bush, Laura (1946–)

Wife of the much stupider President George W. Bush and former librarian who spent much of her FLOTUS time promoting education, including working with the Library of Congress to launch the National Book Festival. Extremely likable. For a meaty, albeit fictional, version of her life, check out Curtis Sittenfeld's *American Wife*.

### Bushnell, Candace (1958–)

Writer whose *New York Observer* column "Sex and the City" launched a million clones. (It was later turned into a popular television show, spin-off book series, film franchise, and the bane of New Yorkers deluged with Bradshaw clones unaware of the cold hard reality of freelance writing in one of the world's most expensive cities.) (*See also* Bradshaw, Carrie; Sex and the City)

### bust

Euphemism for breasts. Memorable for its usage in Judy Blume's 1970 YA novel *Are You There God? It's Me, Margaret*. (*See also* Are You There God? It's Me, Margaret; Blume, Judy)

### *BUST* magazine

Jezebel from before the internet. A balls-out sex-positive, tiara-level femme, first-worldy, unapologetically consumerist (though also DIY-ish) women's magazine given to using rhymes in headlines, all of which are strengths or weaknesses depending on your perspective. Co-founder Debbie Stoller told the *New York Times* in 2001 that the secret to attracting young feminists was to pick and choose issues: "I know that celebrating nail polish is not going to save a woman's right to abortion. But I also don't think we have to only point out every single wrong in society." (In that same article, Erica Jong predicted the magazine was totally going to fail, but actually it's been going strong since 1993.) *BUST* is perhaps best known for asking celebrities "Do you consider yourself a feminist?" in interviews, thus directly ruining countless girl-crushes on ladies from whom we expected better answers.

### bustle

A simultaneously practical and ridiculous women's undergarment, designed to hold up the back of a heavy skirt and/or make the wearer's ass look outrageously large. Still sometimes used for wedding gowns with long trains, bustles were last fashionable in the Victorian Era, when fancy ladies had other people to dress them.

### butch

As opposed to "femme," a stereotypically masculine appearance, behavior, and/or presentation.

### Butler, Octavia (1947–2006)

One of the most admired African American science fiction writers of the twentieth century. In 1995, she became the first sci-fi author to win a MacArthur "genius" grant, and she won the Hugo and Nebula Awards twice each. Her *New York Times* obituary described Butler's "evocative, often troubling, novels"—including *Kindred*, the story of a contemporary African American woman who time-travels to the antebellum South—as exploring "far-reaching issues of race, sex, power and, ultimately, what it means to be human."

### Caboodles

Cosmetic organizers. A Caboodles makeup case itself was always more significant than its contents (the too-light raccoon-eye concealer, the dropped-out blushes, the black eye pencil shavings, the hot-pink lipstick rounded from too many blots). Naturally, a beloved organizer often ended up looking quite a bit like a well-worn jewelry box: started with the best of intentions, and eventually crammed with as much shit that one could possibly fit inside while still being able to close the lock.

### Cabot, Meg (1967–)

Author best known for her Princess Diaries series. Has authored more than fifty titles for kids, tweens, teenagers, and adults. Thanks to her conversational tone and ability to write about everything from young royalty to teenage psychics, Cabot has millions of books in print around the world.

---

### cackle of rads

Phrase that onetime vice presidential candidate and reality show star Sarah Palin coined to describe and belittle women who had "hijacked" feminism with their support of abortion rights, same-sex marriage, equal pay, comprehensive sex education, and lack of support of Palin's incessant need to weirdly wink at the camera. Meant to invoke a vision of witches, because it's important for young girls to see positive female role models. (*See also* PALIN, SARAH)

---

### Caesarean section

Surgery to deliver a baby from its mother's uterus, most often performed when a vaginal delivery is impossible and/or dangerous to the health of the mother or child. Sometimes unnecessary and often performed upon request.

### *Cagney & Lacey*

CBS lady-cop show that ran between 1981 and 1988 and starred a youngish, glamorous-ish Sharon Gless (Cagney) opposite Tyne Daly's cute, no-fuss Lacey. (Gless actually replaced actress Meg Foster because the combination of strong-jawed Foster and short-haired Daly came across as too "unfeminine" and/or too "lesbian," depending on whom you ask.) After two seasons of crappy ratings and an actual, if brief, cancellation in 1983, the show was saved by a letter-writing campaign and the support of women up to and including Gloria Steinem and finally settled in for a long, successful run and oodles of Emmys, including two for "outstanding drama series" and multiple best actress awards for both leads. What made this show about a single career gal and a married mother solving crimes on the streets of New York—and holding private confabs in the ladies' room at the station—so special? For starters, it was the first police procedural to feature women partners in the lead roles, and middle-aged women with realistic problems, attitudes, and interests, at that. Most importantly, though, as John J. O'Connor wrote in the *New York Times* in 1984, "The chemistry between Miss Daly and Miss Gless is irresistible, by turns street-smart sassy and intimately moving. The balance there, in terms of admirably professional teamwork, is just about perfect."

### Calle, Sophie (1953–)

French artist who uses the techniques of the detective and voyeur to turn the most painful and banal aspects of private life into objects and experiences for public consumption. She once stalked a stranger from France to Italy, then published surveillance photos of his movements along the way. Calle also had her mother hire a real PI to stalk her around Paris, where she led him on an unwitting tour of her favorite Parisian locales. She asked close to two dozen people to sleep in her bed for eight-hour stretches over the course of a week, photographing them every hour. She uncovered a stranger's address book, dialed the numbers found within, and wrote twenty-eight newspaper articles on its owner. When the writer Gregoire Bouillier broke up with her via e-mail, she asked 107 women (and one parrot) to interpret the letter through the lens of their respective professions—forensics, grammar, psychology, crossword puzzle, dance, origami, marksmanship, and for the parrot, mindless repetition of the letter's parting phrase: "Take care of yourself. Take care of yourself."

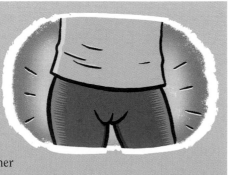

### camel toe

Silhouette resulting from the clinging of fabric around the vulva. Also: Kathleen Turner film *Serial Mom*'s all-lady grunge group, played by L7.

### Camp Fire Girls

Rival youth organization of the Girl Scouts founded in 1910 that went coed in 1975 and is "designed and implemented to reduce sexual, racial and cultural stereotypes." Instead of cookies, members of the organization—now called simply Camp Fire—raise money by selling candy. (Mmm. Almond Roca.)

### Campion, Jane (1954–)

New Zealand filmmaker (*My Brilliant Career, The Piano*) whose interest in human sexuality and the inner lives of women hasn't always made her a critical darling. Almost single-handedly responsible for bringing us all the joy that is the prickly, intelligent performances of Judy Davis. "Listen, the world has always been full of sheep. You want to be a sheep, okay, this is a democracy," Campion once told Jeanette Winterson. "But if you want to find your own way, this is the time to do it. It's not harder to be yourself, it's just more obvious that it's hard—really hard. It's always been hard."

### cankles

Term used to describe an ankle that shows little difference in width from the calf and therefore does not meet societal standards of narrowness. Embodiment of body snarking's final frontier; the *Wall Street Journal* pins the average circumference of a female ankle at eleven inches, a specification that should never have been unleashed upon the world. Notable women who have been reduced to an ill-defined area between foot and calf: Mischa Barton, Hillary Clinton, Miley Cyrus, and the fictional Rachel Green.

### cardigan

Perennial staple of the feminine wardrobe and one beloved by old men, useful thing to have in an air-conditioned office, partial name of one-hit-wonder Swedish band. Also a variety of Corgi.

### Carey, Mariah (1970–)

Classically trained singer with a five-octave vocal range. Also songwriter, actress, pop music standard-bearer. Surpassed Elvis Presley, and second only to the Beatles, for the most number 1 singles in history. Known for bubblegum love songs, cleavage-spilling tube dresses, and a certain film called *Glitter*. Winner of five Grammy awards.

## Carrie

Famous Brian De Palma film based on Stephen King's 1974 novel about a bullied teen who takes revenge on her tormentors with the help of her supernatural powers. Dramatically overstates the importance of menstruation in the lives of teenage girls, culminating in the iconic image of the heroine-villain completely drenched in blood, a bit of symbolism that, when stated baldly on paper, sounds eye-rollingly anvilicious. To make it all even harder to take, the real villain of the movie is—of course—the mother whose sex-phobic rantings sound so silly that even Jerry Falwell would have said, "Hey, wait a second." The icing on the cake is a "gotcha" horror moment at the end that fails to connect to the plot or mean anything at all.

## Carson, Rachel (1907-1964)

American scientist, author, and ecologist responsible for several advances in the environmental movement. Carson launched her career as an aquatic biologist before ultimately focusing on conservation and the dangers of synthetic pesticides, most notably in the publication of the award-winning, bestselling *Silent Spring* in 1962. Carson's fight against chemical companies led to a national pesticide policy and the banning of DDT, and her work spurred a grassroots movement that led to the formation of the US Environmental Protection Agency. In a CBS documentary about *Silent Spring* shortly before her death from breast cancer, Carson remarked, "Man's attitude toward nature is today critically important simply because we have now acquired a fateful power to alter and destroy nature. But man is a part of nature, and his war against nature is inevitably a war against himself. [We are] challenged as mankind has never been challenged before to prove our maturity and our mastery, not of nature, but of ourselves."

## Carter, Angela (1940-1992)

British novelist, essayist, feminist, and feminist-press-founder-ist. Wrote about anorexia, the obnoxiousness of food snobbery, and sexual liberation through S&M before everybody wrote about anorexia, the obnoxiousness of food snobbery, and sexual liberation through S&M. Also wrote many dark fairy tales in which sexual awakening is represented by pools of blood and/or your creepy uncle who runs a puppet shop. Once said that her great aspiration was to create a world in which girls stopped writing weepy novels about the married dudes who broke their hearts and started writing novels about how they, quote, "TORE OFF HIS BALLS." Probably a good thing she didn't live to see *Sex and the City*.

## Carter, Nell (1948-2003)

Performer and the inspiration for Effie in the Broadway production of *Dreamgirls*, a role its original director had hoped she'd play. Was in the chorus of both *Jesus Christ Superstar* and *Hair* before she rose to prominence as a star of *Ain't Misbehavin'*, a musical revue about the Harlem Renaissance, for which she won a Tony in 1978. The sudden fame from her Broadway success threw her into a cocaine addiction that plagued her throughout her Emmy-nominated but criticized-as-mammy-figure role as the sassy housekeeper on *Gimme a Break!* Came from a mythically hardscrabble background in Alabama, bore a child from her rape at gunpoint at fifteen. A beloved brother died of AIDS. Twice married, twice divorced, and mother to two adopted sons who were left to Ann Kaser, her partner from the mid-1990s onward, when she died. Sometimes quoted as saying, "You have to put on more faces to pretend who you are."

### Carter, Rosalynn (1927–)

Former First Lady of the United States. Married future President Jimmy Carter at nineteen. Functioned as the accounting brains of their peanut-farm operation and kept it up in the White House, routinely attending cabinet meetings. Yet still got off to a rocky start as First Lady, thought of as steely and stiff, even as she made mental health her focus. Midway through the Carter administration, Gloria Steinem told the *Washington Post* that she was disappointed that Rosalynn always operated in the president's shadow. After the presidency her image was somewhat rehabilitated; she's now routinely cited alongside Hillary Clinton as one of the more policy-involved presidential wives. But it's hard not to agree with Steinem: her legacy is largely her solid support of her husband.

### Cary, Mary Ann Shadd (1823–1893)

Bear with us, she had a number of distinctions: a black, American Canadian female abolitionist, one of the first female publishers, a writer herself and later a lawyer, nicknamed The Rebel by friends and family. Born free in Delaware, she trained as a teacher, then spent much of her adult life working in Canada, in what is now Ontario, and encouraged African Americans to settle there. Like many trailblazing women, Cary made a lot of men angry by refusing to defer to them in her political activities. We wish they'd made the movie about her instead of Elle Woods.

### Cash, June Carter (1929–2003)

Singer-songwriter who didn't really look anything like Reese Witherspoon. Raised in a family of women (and men!) who sang professionally. Married once before she found true love with her beloved Johnny, giving all of those of us who dated all the wrong people in our twenties some hope. Gave up her career to be "Johnny Cash's wife," a label that may bother us but that made her happy. She likened falling in love with him to falling into a "pit of fire," which led to that song (you know that song). When she died, he was able to carry on by himself for only another four months.

### Cash, Rosanne (1955–)

Singer-songwriter and eldest daughter of Johnny Cash from his first marriage. Something of a proto–Neko Case, a rockabilly before rockabilly was a thing. Never dressed like a country singer, eschewing the big hair and the cutesy gingham outfits; went straight for the soul of the music. Her 1990 album *Interiors* was all about self-exposure—an autobiographical exploration of her divorce—and she managed, somehow, to get her ex to record tracks with her.

### Cassatt, Mary (1844–1926)

American painter and women's suffrage advocate who shed light on the worlds of mothers and children and the private lives of women during the late nineteenth century. Cassatt's struggles as a female artist began in art school in Philadelphia, where she was prohibited to work with live nude models—because God forbid an unmarried woman should see anybody naked—and continued at the Salon in Paris, where, tired of trying to paint what was considered "popular," she eventually fell in with the Impressionists, including mentor Edgar Degas. Cassatt never married because she felt being someone's wife in the nineteenth century would be incompatible with being an accomplished artist. She was forced to give up painting in 1914 after she lost her eyesight to diabetes and cataracts, among other illnesses.

## casting couch

"You think you're going to meet them and you're so excited, like, 'I can't believe this person wants to have a conversation with me,' and you get there and you realize that's not what they want, at all…There are some guys, talking about actors who have been in the business for a while, who are very egocentric and have been able to sleep with a lot of girls for whatever reason, and because they don't know me they think I'm going to be this little cupcake, this Marilyn Monroe-type who's going to bat my eyes and be like a receptacle for them…I just shut them down immediately, right in front of people. It's been so long since someone has told them no, they don't really know how to deal with it. Because of this nonreality they live in, they're fucked up, psychologically."

—MEGAN FOX

**Castleberry, Florence Jean**
Kiss my grits.

## catalogs

Free printed brochures issued and mailed by retailers offering painstakingly photographed, carefully curated, and methodically organized products, often presented in elaborate scenarios intended to sell consumers on a "lifestyle" or aesthetic. Of course, a tailored and ruffled J.Crew blouse will not *actually* make you look like an heiress taking a year off to study architecture in Prague, and a Victoria's Secret bra won't turn your short, soft, flabby torso into that of a lithe Brazilian supermodel. But, as Blondie says, dreaming is free! (Shipping and handling are extra.)

## caterwaul

To cry out shrilly or harshly in protest or displeasure. An expression often ascribed to inconveniently opinionated felines and females. In 2008, a certain professional internet troll once accused Jezebel and its readers of "caterwauling about the patriarchy," to which we responded, "Ha-ha! So what?!" (*See also* PATRIARCHY)

## catfight

Disagreement between women that, for whatever reason, you want to belittle. Originally this referred to a physical alterca-tion, because ladies of course hiss and spit and claw at each other with their delicate nails instead of doing proper dude fighting with fisticuffs. But nowadays it can mean anything from Snooki and JWoww squabbling over tanning oil to Barbara Boxer and Kay Bailey Hutchison disputing a nuanced point of legislation, as long as it's a fight between two women and you therefore wish to portray it as trivial girl business.

### Cather, Willa (1873–1947)

Pulitzer Prize–winning American novelist (*My Ántonia*, *O Pioneers!*, *Death Comes for the Archbishop*, etc.). As a young woman, Cather sometimes dressed in men's clothes and went by "William." She also lived with a woman for nearly forty years, until her death in 1947, although there's debate about whether the relationship was sexual and whether Cather would have identified herself as gay. Cather sometimes disparaged other female writers, but she's notable for the way she challenged the gender norms of her time—and for her beautiful fiction about the Great Plains and the Southwest.

### Catherine II (1729–1796)

Empress of Russia who was born a German princess. Became unhappy during the second half of her arranged marriage to Grand Duke Peter of Holstein, heir to the Russian throne. Maybe she killed him. Maybe not. She definitely assumed his reign, earned the suffix "the Great," and took up with an impressive list of male

"favorites," who reportedly included Gregory Potemkin, Peter Zavadovsky, Ivan Rimsky-Korsakov, Alexander Lanskoy, Alexander Dmitriev-Mamanov, and Plato Zubov. When finished with them, she disposed of her lovers with gifts. Like that of many women who enjoy sex, Catherine's sluttiness has been vastly overstated. Some pin her number at three hundred men and at least one horse; just eleven (human) lovers are substantiated by the historical record.

### Catherine of Aragon (1485–1536)

Spanish princess who was shipped off to England at sixteen to marry Prince Arthur, the heir to the British throne, who died shortly after their wedding. Eight years later she married his little brother, Henry VIII, a tall ginger heartthrob six years her junior. A true love match, they were married for thirty-five years, longer than his five other marriages combined, but their inability to produce the longed-for male heir, combined with his passion for his mistress Anne Boleyn, led Henry to ditch the faithful Catherine. When the pope refused to annul the marriage, Henry had his own archbishop of Canterbury do it, and he banished Catherine to a dismal, remote castle and separated her from her only child. Unbowed, Catherine rejected the divorce and styled herself Queen of England until her death. Despite everything, she could never quit Henry, the great love of her life. On her deathbed, she wrote to him: "Lastly, I make this vow, that mine eyes desire you above all things."

### *Cathy*

Semiautobiographical comic strip by Cathy Guisewite that ran from 1976 through 2010; experts believe this longevity was assisted by its willingness to reuse the same four jokes (shopping is stressful; food is satisfying, yet makes one gain weight; men make disappointing romantic partners; also, your mother is the worst) 234 times a year. Aimed to acknowledge the great feminist progress made in society by sympathetically portraying the daily life and innermost thoughts of a single professional woman. Actually just pictures of a woman screaming in public and stress eating. Pretty accurate. (Ack.)

**cats**
Our collective overlords, if the extensive presence they maintain on the internet is any indication. (*See also* CRAZY CAT LADY; PUSSY)

### Catt, Carrie Chapman (1859–1947)

Leading campaigner for women's suffrage in America, succeeding Susan B. Anthony as the president of the National American Women's Suffrage Association and working toward the eventual passage of the Nineteenth Amendment in 1920. In addition to transforming NAWSA into today's League of Women Voters, Catt ran for president (in 1920, on the Commonwealth Party Ticket) and became an activist for world peace. Her leadership has come under critical review in recent years, however, for her failure to speak out against the imprisonment and mistreatment of Alice Paul and the more

radical suffrage activists, her support for the First World War, her anti-immigrant rhetoric, and, most controversially, remarks she made while pushing Southern states to ratify the Nineteenth Amendment, such as "White supremacy will be strengthened, not weakened, by women's suffrage." African American women did not gain the vote until 1964. (*See also* ANTHONY, SUSAN B.; PAUL, ALICE)

## cattiness
Passive-aggressive form of bitchiness typically employed by mean girls, frenemies, and reality show contestants as a means of attacking another's self-worth while simultaneously preserving/inflating one's own.

> AMBER: Hello? Was I the only one listening? I mean, I thought it reeked.
>
> CHER: I believe that was your Designer Impostors perfume.
>
> —*Clueless*, 1995

## cellulite
Term invented by marketers to describe the dimpling effect of subcutaneous fat on a woman's buttocks and thighs and to sell creams and formulas with false promises to rid women of it. (Convincing women that dimple-free asses and thighs were possible was perhaps the greatest marketing coup of the twentieth century, and it has been argued that Photoshop was invented mainly to perpetuate this deception.) (*See also* PHOTOSHOP)

## Celmins, Vija (1938–)
Latvian artist who uses mixed media, including pencil, oil paint, and printmaking, for her works. Many of her pieces focus on nature's spaces, including the sky and the ocean.

## change of life
Euphemism for menopause that suggests a lifestyle aspect to the eventual exhaustion of a woman's hormone-secreting ovaries.

## Channing, Stockard (1944–)
The coolest of *Grease*'s Pink Ladies and television's first ladies (as Abbey Bartlet on *The West Wing*), the former Susan Stockard is a Radcliffe-educated, Emmy and Tony Award–winning bona fide triple threat. Now let's just get her an Oscar already.

## Chapman, Tracy (1964–)
Singer and songwriter. Notoriously press-shy, perhaps because she's a gay woman of color whose very first album, released when she was twenty-four, sold ten million copies. Once wanted to be a veterinarian but fell into political activism at Tufts. A classmate heard her play, his influential dad introduced her to powerful people in the music industry, and she soon found herself performing in a Free Mandela concert at Wembley Stadium. Really could not care less about what people say about her. Has told reporters she'd rather make music than talk about it; that focus, somehow, kept her from being another success-too-soon story. Briefly dated Alice Walker.

## *Charlie's Angels*
1970s television show that proved threesomes are always the best (even if—or especially if—one of them is a nerdy brunette) and led to the ubiquitousness of Farrah Fawcett *and* flipped and feathered hair. Two feature films from the last decade starred Lucy Liu, Drew Barrymore, and Cameron Diaz

and were most notable for fairly good soundtracks (I) and the sorta-resurgence of Demi Moore's career (II). (*See also* FEATHERED HAIR)

### Charney, Dov (1969–)

Prolific defendant in sexual harassment lawsuits who co-founded the Los Angeles clothing manufacturer-retailer American Apparel in 1989 and presided over its easy credit/cocaine-fueled expansion in the midaughts and the inevitable decline into parodic dysfunction that followed. Famously

masturbated during an in-person interview with *Jane* magazine writer Claudine Ko in 2004; developed hysterical martyr complex when Ko subsequently wrote about it in the magazine. (*See also* AMERICAN APPAREL)

### chastity

Fairly common practice. Doing It Right: choosing to abstain from sexual activity for a set period of time for personal or religious reasons. Doing It Wrong: loudly proclaiming through words, slogans, or jewelry you have given your virginity over to your father or some other male authority figure because you can't be trusted with your own body or decisions.

### chastity belt

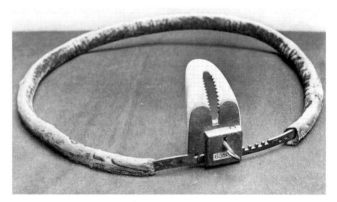

Once the province of the mythical medieval virgin, today's chastity belts are more likely to be worn by the modern submissive, who cedes control of his or her sexual behavior in the service of kinkier sexual pursuits.

### Chase, Angela

Narrator and protagonist of the brilliant, doomed teen drama *My So-Called Life* (1994–1995, RIP). The canonical flailing, self-obsessed, privileged suburban teenager. The one you wanted to be because you knew you weren't cool enough to be Rayanne or Ricky.

## cheerleaders

An organized team, usually consisting of young women, that performs synchronized dance routines and cheers while wearing skimpy costumes, much to everyone's delight. A cross between gymnasts and Vargas girls, cheerleaders provide necessary encouragement for amateur and professional sports teams in the form of rhythmic chanting, human pyramids, and ass-cheek underside viewings. (They also educate spectators, who may never learn to spell S-U-C-C-E-S-S without them.) Their matching uniforms also allow fellow students to easily identify the popular girls in school. Cheerleaders generally insist that cheerleading is a valid athletic pursuit, and they're right—it's extremely physically demanding and takes a lot of training and skill. Their detractors generally insist that cheerleading exploits women, and they're right, too—professional cheerleaders make barely any money and are expected to expend a great deal of cash and effort to look exactly as tan, buff, and flowing-tressed as the male gaze dictates. For not unrelated reasons, TV shows, movies, and other media often use high school cheerleading squads as a convenient shorthand for cliquish, shallowly behaving adolescents.

## cheerleading

Competitive sport that consists of short organized routines in which participants (see above) perform complex stunts and gymnastic maneuvers. The activity is popular among young women in high school and college. Cheerleading can be dangerous, and by one count leads to 65 percent of all female catastrophic injuries in high schools and colleges. Yet many do not consider it a sport worth properly regulating, for reasons outlined above.

---

### Among the indignities visited upon the American cheerleader:

#### In court

US District Judge Stefan Underhill rules that college cheerleading is "too underdeveloped and disorganized" to qualify as a sport.

#### In film

*Bring It On Again; Bring It On: All or Nothing; Bring It On: In It to Win It; Bring It On: Fight to the Finish.*

#### In Texas

A sixteen-year-old cheerleader is removed from her high school squad for refusing to cheer for an athlete who raped her.

#### In fashion

The sparkle brief.

#### In pay

Women are paid $75 to perform on the sidelines at each Washington Redskins football game. They spend up to twenty-five hours a week performing and attending practices (unpaid). They are expected to memorize squad routines on their personal time, using choreography tapes. They perform upward of two dozen charity appearances each year to improve the team's image. They practice throughout the summer with no pay until the season opener. Each year, they receive travel and accommodation to an "exotic" locale, where they pose in bikinis for calendars (the calendars later retail for $15) and online videos for fans. They are instructed to save up vacation days at work to fund the trip. They don't get a cent. Before they make the cut, each potential cheerleader is encouraged to spend $250 on prep classes, $75 on a professional makeup application for audition day, $50 for a pre-audition seminar, up to $100 on a suitable audition outfit, and countless other fees for spray tanning, professional nutritionists, personal trainers, hair extensions, fake eyelashes, and even surgery. At one pre-audition seminar, Lasik eye surgery advocates encouraged women to go under the laser before the auditions, so that "contacts are one less (thing) you have to worry about." Hundreds of women compete for the opportunity every year.

## Cheney, Dick (1941–)

Go fuck *yourself*, mister.

## Cher (1946–)

Grammy Award–winning singer, Academy Award–winning actress, gay icon, and trailblazer, paving the way for celebrities with one name, white women who wear wigs, and superstars who save their faltering careers by hosting late-night infomercials. In 1996, she coproduced, directed, and starred in the made-for-TV movie *If These Walls Could Talk* about women's experiences with abortion and has dedicated herself to raising awareness of injured soldiers at Washington, DC's, former Walter Reed Army Medical Center. Cher has endured a lot in her six decades as a celebrity—her first solo album was released when she was not yet twenty—and her staying power is testament to how tough titties she is—a condition she likely developed from wearing chain-mail shirts with no bra.

## Chicago, Judy (1939–)

Feminist artist best known for her large-scale installation *The Dinner Party*, which includes thirty-nine vagina-inspired place settings dedicated to mythical and historical famous women, which came to represent the ongoing omission of women from the historical record in Western civilization. Chicago doesn't just *make* feminist art, though, she also creates physical spaces where

feminism can flourish. In 1971, she created the first feminist art program at CalArts and a year later she steered it to create the first female-centered art installation, aptly titled *Womanhouse*. She followed this in 1973 with the opening of the Women's Building, which was, of course, governed by a Board of Lady Managers and housed local feminist organizations, businesses, and art galleries, including the Feminist Studio Workshop, the first independent feminist art school.

## chick

Once upon a time, US teen slang for "young woman." Then feminists pointed out that it was a demeaning and infantilizing term, so some people stopped saying it, and others doubled down. Today, it's more or less the female version of "guy," but we prefer the somewhat less politically charged "gal."

## chick lit

School of literature by, for, and about women launched in the 1990s by Brit Helen Fielding's clever *Bridget Jones's Diary* and American author Jennifer Weiner's sly *Good in Bed*. Immediately proliferating high and low, the genre featured the following: an unsatisfied, unmarried girl in a city with a smoking habit/ten extra pounds/love for a tipple; close "urban family" (often less pretty unmarried female and gay best friend); two love interests, one feverishly desired yet slimy and one the surprise white knight; boring cubicle job with difficult boss. Ends in triumphant release from said life. Easily identified by iconic pink cover featuring only a set of legs in high heels. Variant strains: S&F (Shopping and Fucking); Mommy Lit (Bugaboos and Blahniks); Dick Lit (never took off). Although the proliferation of chick lit drew attention to a large, loyal market for women's writing, which is still around today, the phrase is often used as a demeaning, infantilizing, and limiting term. As Pan Macmillan Editorial Director for Fiction Jenny Geras wrote in the *Guardian* in 2012, "[A] whole range of completely different books get lumped together and confused. The only thing that 'these books' really have in common is that they're written primarily by women and about relationships." (*See also* BRIDGET JONES'S DIARY; FIELDING, HELEN)

## Child, Julia (1912–2004)

Former OSS spy. Six feet two inches. The voice of an angel crossed with a Muppet. Learned to cook when she was thirty-seven years old and stationed in Paris. Became obsessed with butter. Went on to publish *Mastering the Art of French Cooking* in 1961, which gave her almost overnight celebrity. Star of the public television program *The French Chef*, which debuted in 1963 and was responsible for the appearance of succulent roast chicken dinners on American tables.

In 2002, blogger Julie Powell began cooking her way through *French Cooking*, leading to her smash-hit 2006 memoir *Julie and Julia* and a subsequent movie starring Meryl Streep as Child (Nora Ephron's final, sumptuous project). Child was known to disapprove of Powell's blog, but we are grateful for anything that led to those scenes of Streep flinging around lobsters and giggling with joy over whipped cream.

## children

Side effect of sex.

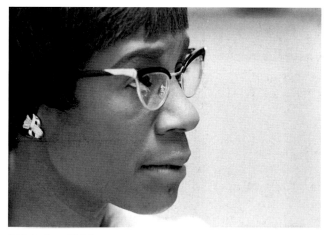

## Chisholm, Shirley (1924–2005)

Brooklyn-born daughter of a Guyanian father and Barbadian mother who was both the first African American woman elected to Congress (1969) and the first female Democrat to run for president (1972), for which she received 152 first-ballot votes. "I ran for the presidency, despite hopeless odds," she wrote in her memoir *The Good Fight*, "to demonstrate the sheer will and refusal to accept the status quo."

## chivalry

Originally, a knightly code of conduct mandating values that were supposed to make knighthood more like *Camelot* and less like *Game of Thrones*—for example, mercy, justice, courage, protection of the needy, and treating women like children or fragile objects in the guise of courtesy and solicitousness. Now, exactly the same thing, minus the mercy, justice, charity, or courage.

## chlamydia

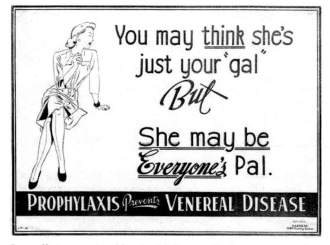

Sexually transmitted bacterial disease that can cause infection and pain in the reproductive organs and eventually lead to blindness. A related form of the disease has hit epidemic proportions among Australian koalas, threatening the species.

## Cho, Margaret (1968–)

Korean American stand-up comedienne and actress who spent the first part of her career taking shit for not being "pretty" enough (read: white and thin enough) by Hollywood standards and has spent the second half telling Hollywood and everyone who shares those standards to go fuck themselves. In 1994, she broke ground as the first Asian American woman to get her own sitcom,

*All-American Girl* (which was also the first one ever about an Asian American family), but criticism of her appearance, her Asian-ness (or lack thereof, depending on the critic), and the show's stereotypical jokes made her miserable. She developed an eating disorder that led to kidney failure and struggled with addiction, but instead of flaming out, she came back stronger in 1999 with a one-woman show, *I'm the One That I Want*, which would become a film and a bestselling book.

### chocolate

**1.** A food derived from cacao beans in a complicated multistage process, the most important part of which is adding a shitload of sugar and then molding it into the shape of a bar or a bunny or one of those little fish in Phish Food ice cream. **2.** When applied on the correct calendar date, the required gesture to prove to a woman that you love her lest you be shamed by all of Western culture. **3.** The linchpin of a massive "feeble jokes on bumper stickers and sweatshirts" industry. **4.** A substance that really genuinely makes you feel better during PMS and you can't prove it doesn't so just go get me some, the 7-Eleven is still open.

### chola

Ethnic slur against Latina females turned reclaimed identity, identified by outsiders by the culture's stereotypical fashions. The chola's signature razor-thin, penciled-in eyebrow has been appropriated by white women like Gwen Stefani, Lady Gaga, and Marlene Dietrich (the last one retroactively).

### Chopin, Kate (ca. 1850–1904)

American novelist best known for *The Awakening*, set in late-nineteenth-century New Orleans, where cheating on your husband could still constitute a feminist act. And under Chopin's hand, Edna Pontellier's petty self-indulgences—reclining in a hammock instead of her husband's bed, swimming too far out to sea without an ounce of training, neglecting her children in favor of a charming resort layabout—resounded instead as radical reversals of a woman's traditional role. In the 107 years it took Elizabeth Gilbert to publish *Eat, Pray, Love*, the activism of adultery lost a bit of its sociological spark. Good for Gilbert: Edna's affair moved her to drown herself in the gulf.

### Christie, Dame Agatha (1890–1976)

Writer whose detective novels her estate claims make her works the third most widely published in the world after William Shakespeare and the Christian Bible. Born to a well-off British family whose matriarch claimed psychic abilities, Christie was homeschooled until age eleven when her father died, and she found it difficult thereafter to adjust to traditional classroom methods. After completing finishing school in Paris, she spent the prewar years writing rejected short stories and husband hunting before settling on novels and Archibald Christie (with whom she had a daughter, Rosalind). Between 1920 and 1926, she published five novels and introduced the world to Hercule Poirot, before her husband announced that he had a mistress and she disappeared for eleven days. (She was discovered in a sanitarium.) Miss Marple, Christie's other most famous character, first appeared in 1930, the year Christie met her second husband, Sir Max Mallowan, a famous archaeologist. During World War I, she worked in a pharmacy, which informed her portrayals of murder-by-poison in later novels. Oft-criticized as too commercial by male writers of her generation, she was nonetheless made Dame Commander of the Order of the British Empire, the female equivalent of a knighting, in 1971. Her fiction, although still widely read, remains controversial for its casual racism against Jews and other nonwhite inhabitants of the now former British Empire and the use of the N-word.

### Christie, Julie (1941–)

British actress who won an Oscar for *Darling*; became a "Swinging London" icon; played Lara in *Doctor Zhivago*; rocked such films as *McCabe and Mrs. Miller, Shampoo*, and *Heaven Can Wait*; slept with Warren Beatty for a while; semi-retired; then hit a certain age and started racking up awards left and right, most recently as an Alzheimer's sufferer in *Away from Her*.

### Chung, Connie (1946–)

American newscaster, journalist, and winner of three Emmys and a Peabody. Began as a correspondent for *CBS News with Walter Cronkite* during the Watergate scandal and moved up through the ranks to finally coanchor her own show, *Satur-*

*day Night with Connie Chung*, in 1989 (the second woman to do so after Barbara Walters). Chung became known for her stand-alone interviews, which were often seen as gentle in comparison to her competitors'. She famously interviewed Magic Johnson after his HIV diagnosis and Gary Condit in the height of the Chandra Levy scandal. Chung caused a scandal of her own when she interviewed Newt Gingrich's mother, Kathleen, in 1995 and asked for her candid opinion on Hillary Clinton, telling her to "whisper it." Chung aired Gingrich's response (that Clinton was a "bitch"), which many saw as a betrayal of confidence. Married to tabloid talk show host Maury Povich, whose show regularly features such highbrow stunts as "Not the Daddy!" paternity tests. We have to admire her for that.

## Ciccone, Madonna Louise

(*See* MADONNA)

## circumcision

Removal of a foreskin from a penis. Point, Nicole Richie: "Some of the guys were uncir-

cumcised, and it was fuckin' disgusting." Counterpoint, Lindsay Bluth: "I think it looks frightening when it's cut off. It's a Doberman, let it have ears." Point, Charlotte York: "There was so much skin. It was like a Shar-Pei." Counterpoint, Samantha Jones: "It's like a Tootsie Pop: hard on the outside, with a delicious surprise inside." Point, Elaine Benes: "No face, no personality, very dull."

## cisgender

Term of uncertain origin—it seems to have cropped up on the internet sometime in the 1990s—meant to indicate people whose gender identity conforms to the one they were assigned at birth. (The prefix *cis* is Latin for "on this side of, and the opposite of 'trans.'") Probably brought into recent wide currency by the trans activist Julia Serano in her excellent 2007 book *Whipping Girl*. The word could have a better ring to it—admittedly, it sounds a little Social Studies 101—but it's one of those definitions that can change things just by existing, just by being used. (*See also* STRAIGHT)

## Cisneros, Sandra (1954–)

Critically acclaimed author and teacher whose award-winning coming-of-age novel *The House on Mango Street* is credited with helping to start the Chicana literature movement. The youngest of seven children and the only daughter, Cisneros describes herself as "nobody's mother and nobody's wife" and says that her childhood, which was marked by repeated, difficult moves between Chicago and Mexico City, influenced her writing and helped develop her voice, an "anti-academic voice—a child's voice, a girl's voice, a poor girl's voice, a spoken voice, the voice of an American-Mexican." Of her work, she has said "my stories are often based on a true framework, just the way a piñata is based on a wire skeleton, but I have to add layers and layers of details to shape and bring them to life. True stories rarely have the symmetry of a beginning, middle, and end."

## Claire's Accessories

Mall staple known as a treasure trove of trendy and disposable jewelry and the site of such rites of passage as ear piercings, tiara selection for prom night, and horrified and excited standing by as one's best friend repeatedly shoplifts various mood rings and velvet choker necklaces.

## *Clan of the Cave Bear, The*

What if, before the Ice Age, Cro-Magnon humans coexisted with Neanderthals, and the Neanderthals occasionally raped those humans? You'd get Jean M. Auel's Earth's Children series, which imagines human–cave man relations some twenty-five thousand years ago. Orphaned by an earthquake in the first volume, *The Clan of the Cave Bear*, Ayla is raised by a clan of grunts, one of whom robs her of her anachronistic conception of virginity. "Broud got impatient, pushed her down, and moved aside his wrap exposing his organ, thick and throbbing," Auel writes. "With a last hard drive that extracted a final agonized scream, he ejected his built-up heat." After Broud's son is delivered (and then confiscated), Ayla sets about establishing the tenets of the modern you-can-have-it-all brand of womanhood, single-handedly discovering birth control, hooking up with sophisticated toolmaker Jondalar, achieving vaginal orgasm, and domesticating wolves.

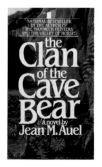

## Clarissa Explains It All

Extremely popular Nickelodeon series featuring the only teenage girl on television with a pet alligator named Elvis. Celebrated for her strong sense of self and individuality, the show's protagonist, Clarissa Darling, had a male best friend, a quirky but loving set of parents, a terribly annoying little brother, and a wardrobe that was somehow both fashion forward and age appropriate (lots of overalls). Her independent streak, sense of humor, intelligence, and creativity often helped her cope with basic teen issues, letting the audience at home know that even though adolescence can be weird and confusing, it doesn't have to be terrifying, especially when you have a role model like Clarissa.

## Claus, Mrs.

Long-suffering wife of a man who takes all the credit. Wasn't even featured in the movies until the 1960s. We picture her at night, kicking away anxious elves, downing a glass of merlot, and listening to Tammy Wynette.

## Cleary, Beverly (1916–)

Children's book author and alleged "slow reader" (she didn't learn how until the third grade) responsible for more than forty immortal children's and young adult books and memoirs. Ramona Quimby, perhaps Cleary's most famous character, was first introduced in Cleary's 1950 book *Henry Huggins* but got her own starring role soon after in a seven-book series that followed her from precocious, imaginative kindergartner years with a penchant for coming to school in her pajamas like a fireman to a somewhat more practical ten-year-old. (*See also* QUIMBY, RAMONA)

## cleavage

Area between the breasts, particularly if they are largish or close set, when visible on an otherwise clothed owner of mammaries. Most frequently referenced either for sartorial/moral judgment ("Does this top show too much cleavage?") or matters of hygiene and gravity ("Crap, I dropped half this cookie into my cleavage AGAIN"). The display of cleavage is generally assumed to indicate sexual availability, and thus to be inappropriate for the office but an excellent cornerstone for multimillion-dollar push-up bra marketing campaigns. Made headlines during the 2008 US presidential campaign, when *Washington Post* columnist Robin Givhan offered extensive coverage and political analysis of a half-inch of Hillary Clinton's décolletage. (*See also* BREASTS)

## Cleaver, June

Mother played by actress Barbara Billingsley on 1950s–1960s sitcom *Leave It to Beaver*, famous for obeying her husband, being charmed by unctuous shithead Eddie Haskell, and doing housework in pearls. Along with Donna Reed, June Cleaver has become shorthand for the ideal 1950s housewife who never really existed.

## Cleopatra (70 BC–30 BC)

Onetime Queen of Egypt and kohl-rimmed muse who has captivated writers, directors, actresses, historians, and drag queens for some two thousand years. (*See also* TAYLOR, ELIZABETH)

## Clifton, Lucille (1936–2010)

American poet and National Book Award winner known for her unsparing lyricism on subjects like abortion, body image, abuse, menstruation, and racism. Served as chancellor of the

Academy of American Poets, was nominated for a Pulitzer twice, served as poet laureate of Maryland, was frequently referenced as the heir to Emily Dickinson, and somehow found the time to write more than sixteen children's books. "I do not think there is an American poet as beloved as Clifton, or one whose influence radiated as widely," said the *New Yorker* on the occasion of her death. When you mention her to college freshmen now, they go "uh, who?" They should read her.

## Clinique

The teenage girl's bridge between Wet n Wild and M.A.C.

## Clinton, Chelsea (1980–)

Only child of Bill and Hillary Rodham Clinton. Former occupant of 1600 Pennsylvania Avenue, current correspondent for NBC News. Clinton became First Daughter when she was twelve years old, an excellent age for any nerdy, gawky girl to experience mind-blowing personal upheaval and unparalleled scrutiny. Despite having to endure public life, vicious jokes about her appearance, and her father's impeachment over a blow job, Chelsea managed to grow into an extremely poised, successful, and levelheaded young woman. We would vote for her for anything, up to and including Queen of the World.

## Clinton, Hillary Rodham (1947–)

Onetime (and possibly future) presidential candidate; US senator; secretary of state; and two-term First Lady. Where to begin? Hillary Rodham went from being the first female chair of the Legal Services Corporation and partner at Little Rock's Rose Law Firm to the First Lady of Arkansas and then the United States, eventually taking husband Bill Clinton's last name to placate complainers. Later, she was the first former First Lady to run for public office (securing a New York Senate seat from 2001 to 2009) and to be appointed to a presidential cabinet (as secretary of state under Barack Obama from 2009 to 2013). In between, she ran her ass off for the Democratic nomination for president in 2008, narrowly losing to Obama and famously putting "eighteen million cracks [i.e., votes] in the highest and hardest glass ceiling." Criticized legitimately for excessive triangulation and race-baiting during the campaign, she was also savaged both for being "cold" and for once fighting back tears while a camera rolled—which of course proved that she was too emotional to lead, and it was probably her time of the month, even though she was in her midsixties. The question from a town hall attendee that immediately preceded that slight welling-up, by the way: "How did you get out the door every day? I mean, as a woman, I know how hard it is to get out of the house and get ready. Who does your hair?"

## clitoridectomy

Acceptable only when cancer has spread to the clitoris.

## Close, Glenn (1947–)

Award-winning actress who will probably end up best remembered as the bunny-boiler in 1987's *Fatal Attraction*. Although she's played everything from the stock girlfriend to the US vice president, most of her best roles are as manipulative whackjobs and/or psychopaths: Besides Alex in *Fatal Attraction*, there's the Marquise Isabelle de Merteuil in *Dangerous Liaisons*, Patty Hewes on *Damages*, Norma Desmond in *Sunset Boulevard* on Broadway, and of course Cruella DeVil. Nobody, but nobody, does "coldly evil" better. (*See also* Fatal Attraction)

## *Clueless*

1995 cult classic written and directed by Amy Heckerling and starring Alicia Silverstone. *Clueless* was a modern-day take on Jane Austen's *Emma*, set in Beverly Hills instead of the rolling English countryside, and Heckerling's heroine, Cher Horowitz, was a snobby teen fashionista with a heart of gold. This film, one of the most quotable in cinematic history, introduced the world to befuddling new vistas of young-people slang: "totally buggin'," "you gave him a toothache,"

and one particular term for a homosexual man, "a disco-dancing, Oscar Wilde-reading, Streisand ticket-holding friend of Dorothy." It also taught a generation of young women the meaning of the word *sporadically*. (*See also* as if; Austen, Jane; Heckerling, Amy)

## Clytemnestra

Greek mythological figure and Helen of Troy's slightly less attractive, anger management issue–having sister. When her husband, Agamemnon, decided to go to war with Troy for Helen, he thought it would be a good idea to sacrifice the couple's youngest daughter to the gods for good luck, and did so. Clytemnestra thought it would be a good idea to wait until Agamemnon came home from the war and then stab him as many times as humanly possible. Clytemnestra was

subsequently killed by her son, Orestes, because he was of the opinion that dads rule and daughters and sisters and moms are like, whatever. These events are covered in *The Oresteia*, which concludes with the goddess Athena's decree that patriarchy should exist so that we won't have to debate whether it's worse to kill a dude or a lady. (HINT: patriarchy literally means "rule of the dads.") Clytemnestra would not be pleased.

## Cody, Diablo (1978–)

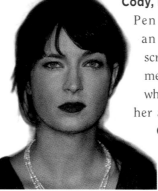

Pen name of Brook Busey, an Academy Award–winning screenwriter, director, producer, memoirist, and former stripper whose first screenplay, *Juno*, won her a Best Original Screenplay Oscar in 2007. Other works include *Jennifer's Body*, *Young Adult*, and the TV series *The United States of Tara*. Following Cody's Oscar win, nude photos of the Illinois-born artist were promptly "leaked" to the press; the fact that Cody had posted these photos to her blog about being a stripper, because she'd written a blog about being a stripper, and also a memoir about being a stripper, because she was basically *extremely open about having been a stripper*, was ignored. (*See also* Collette, Toni; Juno; Page, Ellen)

## Colbert, Stephen (1964–)

**1.** Person: Emmy-winning comedian, actor, and author. Colbert made his mark as the archetypical *Daily Show* correspondent from 1997 to 2005. During that time he also appeared as sexually confused high school teacher and Kansas enthusiast Chuck Noblet on *Strangers with Candy*. In 2005, Colbert began hosting *The Colbert Report*, in which he brilliantly satirizes America's most notorious conservative blowhards. **2.** Persona: Sir Dr. Stephen T. Colbert, D.F.A., is a TV host, pundit, and patriot. Some (primarily Colbert himself) say he *is* America.

> **"Tonight I hereby burn the symbol of male oppression: boxers. Guys, face it—we only wear them because the matriarchy says we need them in case we get hit by a bus."**

### Collette, Toni (1972–)

Australian actress who launched her career with her portrayal of awkward, matrimony-aspiring, Abba-loving Muriel Heslop of Porpoise Spit in *Muriel's Wedding*. (She also turned down the lead role in *Bridget Jones's Diary*, like a boss.) Collette has never been afraid to play the kind of characters who in the hands of lesser actresses would be quirked and pixied and prosthetic-nosed to high heaven. Instead, she manages to turn nutty roles into understated ones—think her warm "Miss Granola Suicide in a yeti costume" in *About a Boy*, and even her titular role as a multiple-personality sufferer in the *United States of Tara*. (*See also* CODY, DIABLO)

### Collins, Eileen (1956–)

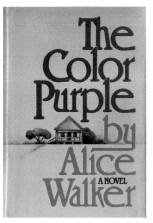

Retired Air Force colonel, the first female pilot and commander of a US space shuttle, logger of more than 872 hours in space during four missions.

### Collins, Gail (1945–)

American feminist, journalist, and author. In 2001, she was named the first female editor of the *New York Times*'s editorial page, where she currently works as a columnist. She is the author of books including *When Everything Changed: The Amazing Journey of American Women from 1960 to the Present*.

### Collins, Joan (1933–)

British actress, author, and gay icon, best known for playing the marvelously vicious Alexis Carrington on the hugely popular prime-time soap *Dynasty* from 1981 to 1989.

### colonic

Where anal sex, celebrity weight loss, and invasive cancer screening meet.

### Color Purple, The

Now classic novel by Alice Walker that earned the 1983 Pulitzer Prize for fiction and has been adapted into an Academy Award–nominated film and Tony-winning Broadway musical. The story centers on Celie, an African American woman in the rural South who endures decades of abuse at the hands of her father and other men. On numerous lists of the best novels of the twentieth century, it's also number 17 on the American Library Association's Top 100 Banned and Challenged Books list for 2000–2009. (*See also* WALKER, ALICE)

### comedienne

(French) Lady comedian. (They need their own word to help people remember they're not the funny kind.)

### commitment-phobes

People, usually men, who date for a while and then back off before it gets too serious, ostensibly because they are terrified of commitment. When they are not merely an invention of women's magazines and sitcoms, commitment-phobes are generally young people who have observed numerous failed long-term relationships and wish to avoid that fate for themselves. (*See also* COMMON SENSE)

### conception

Moment at which a sperm fertilizes an egg, which might, after a few days, create a blastocyst that might embed itself into a female's uterine lining, thereby beginning a pregnancy in which the embryo might survive to the point of viability, after which it might be born, assuming none of the zillion things that could go wrong in that process do, and also that the mother in question (in this case, a human) does not deliberately terminate the pregnancy. If you're a conservative religious type, conception refers to the moment at which a complete human soul miraculously appears in a womb, where it will remain without incident for nine months, provided the support apparatus for that womb (sometimes called a "woman") isn't a dirty, homicidal whore.

## condom

A must-have accessory for protection against two potentially life-threatening conditions: AIDS (among other STIs) and babies. Condoms have been around as early as the fourteenth century, as have complaints about how sex feels better without them.

## Conford, Ellen (1942–)

Children's and young adult author who holds a prime spot in the eighties' Girlhood Pantheon alongside Judy Blume, Paula Danziger, Lois Lowry, and Lois Duncan. For the last twenty-odd years, Conford has been writing the successful *Annabel the Actress* and Jenny Archer series, but we will always love her best for fabulously titled earlier works like *Dear Lovey Heart, I Am Desperate*, *We Interrupt This Semester for an Important Bulletin*, and *If This Is Love, I'll Take Spaghetti*.

## Conley, Lyda (1874–1946)

First woman admitted to the Kansas bar and first Native American female to argue a case before the US Supreme Court. Conley fought the Congress-authorized sale of what is now the Wyandotte National Burying Ground in Kansas City. Descendants themselves of the Wyandotte tribe, Conley and her two sisters worked to protect the sacred land not only through legal challenges and a public relations campaign but by standing guard outside the cemetery with muskets. Though Conley lost the Supreme Court case, thanks to her continued agitation Congress repealed the bill authorizing sale of the land in 1913, and three years later approved a bill designating it a federal park.

## Conner, Darlene

Roseanne Conner's vegetarian-feminist youngest daughter, as played by the adorable yet formidable Sara Gilbert on the 1988–1997 program *Roseanne*. Among Darlene's contributions to high school alterna-girls: "It's a good thing we're in a parking lot full of drunken losers. It shouldn't be hard to spot that white horse"; "my pasties and g-string are in the wash"; upon losing her virginity, "You're not going to,

like, high-five me, are you?"; "The only way I'm going to the prom is if I can sit in the rafters with a bucket of pig's blood." (*See also* ROSEANNE)

## constipation

When you can't poop.

## contraception, contraceptives

(*See* BIRTH CONTROL)

## control top

Foundation garment that, like girdles and Spanx, helps delude women into feeling slightly thinner by squashing their internal organs and creating muffin tops.

## cookies

A sometimes food.

## Cooney, Joan Ganz (1929–)

Producer and cofounder of Children's Television Workshop and *Sesame Street*. Studied to be a teacher and worked as a typist because "it was something that girls of my generation did." Found jobs as a newspaper journalist in Phoenix, a television publicist in New York, and a producer for a public television station before helping to create the groundbreaking television show that revolutionized children's television programming and education. "I've never been qualified for any job I've been hired for," she said later. Like all relevant women of her era, Cooney was investigated as a suspected Communist.

## Cooper, Betty

Perky blonde comic book character who inexplicably keeps waiting around for Archie Andrews to realize she's a better choice than sexy, narcissistic Veronica, even though Archie is average looking at best and kind of a dick. The daughter of druggist and town councilman Hal and Alice, a middle-class Riverdale couple, and the youngest of three children, Cooper is a refutation of the stereotype of the dumb blonde and occasionally the argument that blondes have more fun. She's in many ways traditionally domestic: an excellent cook,

sought-after babysitter and companion for the elderly, and proprietress of a doll hospital. But she's also an athlete as well as a cheerleader, a tambourinist, and later guitarist in the garage band The Archies, handy with a car engine, and for a brief period the recipient of the gift of head-injury-induced extrasensory perception.

## cootie catcher, fortune-teller

Origami-like "toys" that appear similar to one another and are often confused but are in fact distinct. A "fortune-teller" conceals answers like yes, no, and maybe behind folded paper walls. You ask it if you're going to marry your sixth-grade boyfriend, shuffle it a little, and it answers. A "cootie catcher" is folded in the same way but contains no concealed messages— instead it is simply used to pinch "cooties" from the skin and hair of another person. Both likely originated in the 1930s.

## Coppola, Sofia (1971–)

Film director into artfully draped, filmy costume design and hazy, ill-framed film shots in films about pretty rich people who are more or less like herself. Fan of designer Marc Jacobs. Tends also to be a bit hard on women in her films. Exhibit A: The hit on Cameron Diaz by way of Anna Faris's character in *Lost in Translation*.

## *Coraline*

Writer Neil Gaiman's fractured Oedipal tale in which protagonist Coraline Jones risks losing her eyes for not loving her mother enough. There's more to it than that, but you really just have to read it.

## corset

Undergarment that shapes the torso, sort of like Spanx, if Spanx were made with wood or bones instead of spandex.

Corsets enjoyed a solid four-hundred year run in Western women's (and occasionally men's) fashion, before the delightfully named "rational dress movement" of the late Victorian Era started arguing that squashing one's internal organs might be a bad thing—especially if one is pregnant—and created sweeping, feminist sartorial reform. Which paved the way for girdles and Spanx. Yay.

## Cosmopolitan

**1.** A delicious, if overhyped, cocktail made of vodka, triple sec, lime juice, and cranberry juice usually served in a martini glass. **2.** Pioneering but extremely frustrating American women's magazine that began advocating for female sexual freedom in the late 1960s under editor in chief Helen Gurley Brown but then devolved into recycled sex advice, mediocre fashion spreads, and paranoid articles that tell you your man may be cheating if he talks too much, doesn't talk enough, sleeps on his side, coughs a certain way, or breathes. Nearly every issue of *Cosmo*, as the magazine is commonly known, contains long lists of sneak-attack sex tips that would instantly end a relationship if anyone ever actually tried them. These usually include some variation of "rub weird objects on his penis," "bite him," or "stick something up his butt."

The editorial philosophy seems to be that since all men are unfeeling robots who run on sex, manhandling his penis is the solution to all relationship problems. The magazine is proof that the proverbial lowest common denominator can always get lower. (*See also* BROWN, HELEN GURLEY)

### cotillion

Event at which teenagers if they are rich, Southern, and/or from the early twentieth century show off snazzy moves from their ballroom dancing lessons.

### cougar

Sexist and largely nonsensical term for a middle-aged woman who dates younger men.

### Coulter, Ann (1961–)

Conservative political commentator and columnist famous for voicing her controversial opinions and derailing conversations by deploying the three R's to describe her opponents: "racist," "reactionary," and "retard." Hates liberals, loves her little black dress. Subsists on a diet of kittens.

### Couric, Katie (1957–)

Television journalist who still can't quite escape the "perky" and "adorable" labels she got while hosting the *TODAY* show in the 1990s, even though she was widowed with two small children while in her early forties. Couric is famous for, among other things, undergoing a colonoscopy on live TV (to promote awareness of colon cancer, which claimed her husband's life); becoming the first female anchor of a network evening news program (*CBS Evening News*, 2006–2011); interviewing then VP candidate Sarah Palin. In 2011, Couric signed a deal with ABC to host a daytime talk show in the slot vacated by Oprah Winfrey.

### couture

Abbreviation of *haute couture*, the fancy French term for fancy French dressmaking, which legally refers to the work of Paris-based designers who meet strict criteria, but can now also refer to any garment on which a *Project Runway* contestant has hand-sewed a friggin' sequin. (*See also* FASHION)

### coven

Any community of witches—or, in some circles, of women—including actual practicing Wiccans; pointy-hatted, warty-nosed cartoons; and angsty teenaged girls on film. (*See also* CACKLE OF RADS; WITCH)

### CoverGirl

All-American cosmetics brand launched in 1961 that acknowledged in 1992 that "American" was not synonymous with "blonde" by staking its claim as the first mainstream cosmetics company to elevate a black woman to spokesmodel. (The milestone is contested: Revlon hired Veronica Webb the same month CoverGirl signed Lana Ogilvie.)

## cover lies

Magazine editor misrepresentations—often found on the covers of women's service and fashion titles—in order to sensationalize mediocre content, appeal to women's insecurities, and sell lots of copies. (*See also* Allure; Cosmopolitan; Glamour Magazine; Marie Claire; Vogue)

"ORAL SEX" IS STILL TOO NAUGHTY TO PRINT!

Buying Your Man "Lucky" Underwear Strengthens The Relationship

**50 Awkward Things to Do Naked**
(Rather than just having sex)

BE CONFIDENT!
Ignore The Other 236 Pages That Say You're Fat & Use the Wrong Eyeliner)

GIVE UP ON YOUR G-SPOT: We Say, "Fantasize About K-Pats, Stroke Your Clitoris"

THE SEX ARTICLE WE CAN'T DESCRIBE HERE!

Easy, Fun Ways to Fall More in Love With Your Man

**50 Things to Do Butt Naked**

KILLER CONFIDENCE
Make Everyone Wish They Were You!

FIND YOUR G-SPOT: Directions So Close, They're Like GPS

SEX UP YOUR EYES
(With This Awesome Spring Trick)

LADY GAGA
Love Advice Only Gaga Would Give

Speak His Sex Language
We Decode the Secret Clues Men Send in Bed

Weird Reasons You're So Freakin' Tired

MUST-READ
The Rape Danger Zone Most Women Don't Know About

F-ED UP EYE MAKEUP
(Electric Blue Under-Eye Circles Are Sexy For Spring)

LADY GAGA
"Your Career Will Never Wake Up And Tell You That It Doesn't Love You Anymore"

How He Rates You During Sex
Never Forget He's Judging Every Move You Make

Needlessly Complicated, Passive-Aggressive Ways to Express Your Sexual Desires

LIVING IN CONSTANT FEAR
Even When You're Alone in Your Car, You're in Danger of Being Raped

SEX & YEAST INFECTIONS
5 Things Not To Stick in Your Privates

Random Shit We Got For $0!

GUILT TRIP!
MY SLEEP-DEPRIVATION BROKE MY DAUGHTER'S LEG

SEX & YOUR BODY
Your 50 Most Private Questions Answered

Cutest Beauty Stuff Under $10

SO TRUE! WHY THE HAPPIEST WOMEN AREN'T "PERFECT"

**Sexy Jeans!** *Plus* Fun Finds for $49 and Less

Sarah Jessica
On Her Favorite Jeans—and Top Fashion Buys

Best Dos & Donts of the Year
Cool Style, Hot Messes...Oh, and Kim Kardashian Gets a Makeunder

Outsmart the #1 Health Risk of 2010 PAGE 62

Sarah Jessica
On Everything But Matthew Broderick

Best Boobs & Butts of the Year:
See-Through Dresses, Pantsless Wonders... Oh, and a Makeup Ad Disguised as 'Makeunder'

Don't Brush Your Teeth While You're Driving PAGE 62

**Bedazzle Everything!**
*Then* Stick a Fur Hat On Top

**cowgirl**

**1.** The female version of a cowboy. **2.** Euphemism for heterosexual intercourse in which the female is on top. (*See also* O'CONNOR, SANDRA DAY)

**Craft, The**

1996 film that touched on everything from classism to racism to stalking to mean-girl psychology, all to the dark and brooding beat of a supremely nineties soundtrack. (*See also* COVEN)

**crafting, crafts**

The art of creating awesome objects out of anything from beads to yarn to clay. For a long time, crafts such as knitting and decoupaging were dismissed as domestic work and rejected by many modern women for their housewifey–old lady associations. However, since the early 2000s—thanks largely to the enthusiasm of famous crafter-feminists like *Stitch 'n Bitch* author and *BUST* magazine cofounder Debbie Stoller— women have been embracing crafting more fervently. These

days, you can find sewing circles across the globe brimming with awesome women who realize that, no matter its past relationship with the patriarchy, crafting is a heck of a good time.

**Craig, Jenny (1932–)**

Founder of an eponymous international chain of weight loss centers that was sold to Nestlé—the chocolate, ice cream, and Quik folks—for about $600 million in 2006.

**crap e-mail from a dude**

Any e-mailed by-product of common male infelicity with language in the service of communicating feelings, conducting human relationships, or even acknowledging reality as it actually exists, an affliction that often manifests itself most acutely on university campuses and other contexts prone to promoting ambivalence and/or ambiguity in men who may be too emotionally immature to grasp that the two are not the same thing. Common traits include: cartoonish pomposity; tortured syntax; repeated and gratuitous use of the recipient's name; comical use of academic jargon to reference mundane human interactions; Nietzsche. (*See* EXAMPLE BELOW)

---

**"Don't Think I Am Overly Interested in You, But I Love to Hunt. :)"**

So you go out on New Year's Eve. You meet a guy, he seems nice. You share a dance and a good-night kiss and give him your number. He calls the next day; when you don't respond immediately, this arrives.

**"I think you enjoy to be chased. I will call you tomorrow. Don't think I am overly interested in you, but I love to hunt. :)**

**I challenge myself to get you to meet with me although you were not interested in the first place. Lol"**

Okay, so English isn't his first language, but in any language that third line is enough to turn off most women. Well, that and the emoticons. Maybe not dramatically awful—a subspecies of the common inept neg—but definitely jerk territory. Says our friend, "I thought he was weird and an ass, so I didn't text him back. I definitely didn't want to see him at that point." And strangely enough, her mind wasn't changed when the next day she received this:

**"You should know better at the age of 34! Don't be such a cunt! Get back to me. :) You asked me to take your number. Remember? I asked and probed if you really want to and you said yes! Lesson: Do not offer your number if you do not mean it! You gave me a nice hard on with your big ass on the dance floor though:)"**

Well, in *that* case! Needless to say, this did not prompt a response. Well, from her. Because a few hours later:

**"I should have done your friend she had nice big boobs but you pushed in between me and her with your big butt. I could have her in bed by now. Next time make up your mind. I am the german guy whom you met on new years eve."**

Oh. Thanks for clearing that up.

**crazy cat lady**

The stereotype of a woman who prioritizes her career over finding a husband, then finds herself alone and depressed in her thirties, loved only by her increasing collection of felines, who don't mind that she's going bonkers.

### CrazySexyCool

Landmark hip-hop album of the 1990s by all-girl group TLC that defined nineties R&B. Legendary tracks like "Waterfalls" and "Creep" ruled the airwaves and took the album to diamond status.

### Cregg, C. J.

*West Wing* heroine and one of the most satisfyingly smart, funny, and capable female characters ever to appear on television. Most of the credit goes to actress Alison Janney, who took what could have been the dour killjoy second-wave stereotype of a White House press secretary and made C. J. into the kind of woman who usually beats men at their own game and does a highly entertaining dance to The Jackal as she does it.

### Crocker, Betty

1936     1955     1965     1968

Composite advertising icon introduced in 1920s by the Gold Medal Flour Company and a brilliant young home economics major named Marjorie Child Husted as a way to offer consumers a more personalized experience when sending in their questions.

### crotch

Gender-neutral but gross-sounding descriptor for the area where the legs meet the torso.

## THE CROTCH'S DESCENT INTO VULGARITY

- *New York Times*, 1855: "the guys swung out over the river with the boy seated in the crotch, holding on with a hand grasped upon each guy!"
- *New York Times*, 1861: "loose cottondrawers" are requested for Civil War troops, with a "length from waist to crotch on the back, 22 inches."
- *New York Times*, 1921: "Zbyszko throws Stecher...Uses Wristlock and Crotch-Hold to Defeat Nebraskan in Bout at 71st Armory."
- *New York Times*, 1959: "A squirrel perched gracefully in the crotch of an oak tree munching acorns is a familiar sight."
- *New York Times*, 1981: "There was one scene where the girl goes to do her laundry and finds the crotch cut out of her panties and the nipples out of her bras. Any woman would be completely terrified by that."
- *New York Times*, 1999: "Ditka cursed, made an obscene gesture and grabbed his crotch as he left the field at halftime."
- *New York Times*, 2010: "I do think there are men who would see a girl wearing this stuff and think, 'She has so much confidence and she still looks great despite the fact that I don't know where her crotch starts in those pants'...You can still tell when a girl is pretty."

### Crow, Sheryl (1962–)

Backup singer for Michael Jackson, Tina Turner, and Stevie Wonder turned superfamous singer-songwriter, breast cancer survivor, and Kid Rock collaborator.

### Crowley, Candy (1948–)

CNN reporter and award-winning political correspondent who, as a heavy brunette, excelled in a field dominated by men and female eye candy, and racked up a phenomenal record of achievement, including being one of the only women ever to moderate a presidential debate in 2012.

### Crucible, The

1953 Arthur Miller play about the Salem Witch Trials on the surface, but really an allegory about and indictment of McCarthyism. (*See also* WITCH)

## crush

Feeling of ardor for another usually accompanied by a combination of elation and panic. Often obsessive, leading to daydreaming, smiling at and about nothing, reading horoscopes more closely, analyzing song lyrics, and spending time with Magic 8 Balls, Ouija boards, games that revolve around folded pieces of paper, and bubble hearts. Frequently painful. (*See also* ASTROLOGY; COOTIE CATCHER, FORTUNE-TELLER; M.A.S.H.; OUIJA BOARD)

## Cruz, Penelope (1974–)

Spanish actress, muse of director Pedro Almodóvar, homophonic lady friend of Tom Cruise during the early aughts. Currently married to Javier Bardem, a fact that totally does not make us jealous at all. (*See also* ALMODÓVAR, PEDRO)

## crying

Classic Roy Orbison song, and also what women do over every little thing because we are made of emotions instead of logic.

## Crystal Castle

She-Ra's highly vaginal refuge in the peaks of Etheria.

## Cullen, Edward

Vampire character from *Twilight* who sparkles in the sunshine and drives a BMW. Though he has the face (and body) of a teenage boy, he's over one hundred years old, digs high school girls, and doesn't believe in premarital sex. Nope, not creepy at all. (*See also* TWILIGHT)

## cunnilingus

Mandatory.

### cunt

Euphemism for vagina that has been in use since at least the Middle Ages. "I, personally, have a cunt," writes Caitlin Moran in *How to Be a Woman*. "Cunt is a proper, old, historic, strong word. I like that my fire escape also doubles up as the most potent swearword in the English language. Yeah. That's how powerful it is, guys. If I tell you what I've got down there, old ladies and clerics might faint. I like how shocked people are when you say 'cunt.' It's like I have a nuclear bomb in my underpants, or a mad tiger, or a gun." (*See also* MORAN, CAITLIN)

## cupcakes

Began as a charming single-serving cake in nineteenth-century Europe to become a ubiquitous and somewhat nauseating symbol of all things ladylike, demure, and pint-sized. After Carrie and Miranda gingerly ate pink-frosted versions outside New York's Magnolia Bakery on *Sex and the City*, the nationwide craze for the tiny sugar bombs exploded, leading to the expansion of Magnolia and other cupcake empires like Crumbs and Sprinkles, ones that grew so large that they began going to war on the Food Network. These days, the cupcake fad has given way to even more adorably diminutive pastries (ahem, macarons), but they will forever be in our hearts as the most obnoxiously girly food that one can choose to eat. Oh, and they are delicious. (*See also* PIE; SEX AND THE CITY)

## Curie, Marie (1867–1934)

Polish scientist who discovered two elements, won two Nobel prizes (the first woman to win one, and still one of only two scientists to earn two); coined the term *radioactivity* and explained it to the world; survived a tabloid scandal over her affair with a married man; founded a radium institute; gave birth to another female Nobel winner; and made future generations of women wonder what the hell they're doing with their lives.

## Currie, Cherie (1959–)

Lead singer of the legendary all-girl band The Runaways between the ages of fifteen and seventeen. Since then, she's acted in multiple episodes of *Matlock*, recovered from heavy substance abuse, written her memoirs, and become a chainsaw artist who works mostly in wood.

## Curtin, Jane (1947–)

Actress, comedienne, former *Saturday Night Live* cast member, and star of *Kate & Allie* who told Oprah Winfrey that *SNL* "was primarily a misogynistic environment." Female writers, she said, "were working against John [Belushi], who was saying that women are just fundamentally not funny. So you'd go to a table read and if a woman writer had written a piece for John, he would not read it in his full voice. He felt that it was his duty to sabotage pieces written by women." Men still outnumber women three to one in the *SNL* writers' room.

## curves

**1.** Chain of storefront women's fitness centers founded in 1992, known for its "30-minute workout," adorable old lady clientele, and conservative Christian founder, Gary Heavin, who has donated money to antichoice organizations. **2.** The things that make one "curvy" (see below).

## curvy

Popular euphemism for many different iterations of "not skinny," ranging from "voluptuous" to "pudgy" to "fat."

## Cusack, Joan (1962–)

Actress. Her younger brother John might be the more famous sibling, but Joan is the only Cusack to lock down two Oscar nominations—for comedic roles, no less—by the age of thirty-five.

## cute

Pedomorphosis in action. Usually marked by a big head, large round eyes, and, sometimes, fur. Often used—inappropriately—for items of clothing (e.g., "cute shoes").

## cuticle

### dad(dy)

The (usually) male figure who (probably) provided the sperm that helped to make you and (ideally) loved you dearly from day one, unless (hey, it happens) he's an asshole.

### Daily Show, The

Comedic variety show created by Lizz Winstead and Madeleine Smithberg in 1996 and hosted by Craig Kilborn until 1999, when comedian Jon Stewart took it over. Under his watch, the show has become both more successful and more overtly political, with often brilliant work from the women it hires, including Samantha Bee and Kristen Schaal. In 2010, the show issued an open letter by female staffers protesting Jezebel's critical coverage of women's underrepresentation on-screen and as writers. (See also BEE, SAMANTHA; STEWART, JON)

### Daisy Dukes

Revealing denim shorts created by cropping blue jeans, named for the hair-flipping, Jeep-driving character from eighties show *The Dukes of Hazzard* and commemorated in a frenetic Miami bass hip-hop song by 69 Boyz.

### dame

Even better than a broad. (*See also* BROAD)

### damsel

Not even as cool as a princess.

### damsel in distress

Trope to which countless female characters have fallen victim. Usually involves some type of bondage, much shrieking, and occasionally a railroad track. (In more progressive, modern tales, the damsel may sass her captor.)

### Dandridge, Dorothy (1922-1965)

First African American to be nominated for a Best Actress Academy Award for 1954's *Carmen Jones*. (In 1999, Halle Berry played Dandridge in an HBO movie and three years later became the first African American to *win* a Best Actress Oscar. Funny how things turn out.)

### Danziger, Paula (1944–2004)

American author of the Amber Brown series of children's books and a bunch of intelligently written young adult novels about teen angst and various other adolescent maladies, including *The Cat Ate My Gymsuit*, *The Divorce Express*, *There's a Bat in Bunk Five*, *Can You Sue Your Parents for Malpractice?* and *The Pistachio Prescription*.

### Darcy, Mr.

Character described in Jane Austen's *Pride and Prejudice* thusly: "Darcy was clever. He was at the same time haughty, reserved, and fastidious, and his manners, though well-bred, were not inviting…Darcy was continually giving offense." (Weirdly, or perhaps not so weirdly, females still jockeyed for his affections.) Basically, Darcy's a dick. But he secretly has a heart of gold, which is why Elizabeth Bennet eventually falls in love with and (spoiler) marries him, instead of her smooth but untrustworthy first crush, Wickham. The moral: beware of charmers. (Actor Colin Firth played Darcy in a miniseries of *Pride and Prejudice*, which led to his casting as Mark Darcy in *Bridget Jones's Diary* and his ascendance to the pinnacle of square-jawed British hotness.)

### Dare, Virginia (1587–?)

The first child born to English colonists on American soil, specifically a Roanoke Island colony, which—in an incredibly creepy chapter of American history—later mysteriously disappeared.

### "Darling, The"

Short story by Anton Chekhov from 1899 that depicts a woman named Olenka who alters her personality to fit whatever man she happens to take up with. Though not a cautionary tale in the traditional sense, it is a reminder that living through other people isn't always the best idea—and a disturbing portrait of a woman without an identity of her own.

### Daughters of Eve

Lois Duncan's dark and disturbing novel of a high school sorority slowly taken over by a twisted feminist. Through the lens of the girls, the novel explores sexism, sex, abortion, marriage, domestic violence, peer pressure, hazing, and the power of groups, giving a look at women's liberation that is both nuanced and controversial. (*See also* DUNCAN, LOIS)

### David's Bridal

Large, affordable, nationwide chain of bridal stores that has so cornered the market on wedding attire that one in four American brides wears one of its gowns.

### Daria

Hit animated MTV series (1997–2002) that was *The Simpsons* for acerbically smart teenagers of the nineties. It followed the ironic musings of one Daria Morgendorffer, a witty, over-it teenage girl stuck in the snoozy suburb of Lawndale. The *New York Times* called the character "a blend of Dorothy Parker, Fran Lebowitz, and Janeane Garofalo." In contrast to Daria's manic parents; ditzy little sister, Quinn; Goth-artist best friend, Jane Lane; and burnout musician crush, Trent, she came off as the sane voice of reason in an increasingly cynical and shallow world and was known for her biting monotone criticisms of social hypocrisy (which are still highly quotable). A classic exchange:

QUINN: Do you know what existential means? Because today someone told me my writing was existential, so I thought I should coordinate, you know, with wardrobe.

DARIA: Yeah, that's what Camus would have done. For your purposes, existential means "pseudo intellectual poser with accessories from the street fair."

### Davis, Angela (1944–)

Longtime social justice activist and academic. Became famous in the 1960s for her association with the Black Panthers and her leadership of the Communist Party USA, which prompted then California governor Ronald Reagan to pressure the University of California Board of Regents to fire her from her professorship. (She was let go but quickly reinstated by a California judge.) Became the third female to appear on the FBI's Most Wanted Fugitive List due to her involvement in the August 1970 abduction and murder of Judge Harold Haley. (Davis had purchased the firearms used in the attack but was not present when it actually occurred; she was jailed for eighteen months and eventually found not guilty.) From 1991 to 2008, she was a professor in the History of Consciousness and Feminist Studies Departments at the University of California, Santa Cruz.

### Davis, Bette (1908–1989)

Legendary actress known for her voice, her tendency to play unlikable characters, and, of course, her large expressive eyes.

### Davis, Geena (1956–)

Actress and activist known for her work in modern feminist classics such as *Thelma & Louise* and *A League of Their Own*. In 2004, she founded the Geena Davis Institute on Gender in Media, which calls itself "the only research-based organization working within the media and entertainment industry to engage, educate, and influence the need for gender balance, reducing stereotyping and creating a wide variety of female characters for entertainment targeting children 11 and under."

### Davis, Judy (1955–)

Fantastic Australian actress who has played George Sand, Judy Garland, Lillian Hellman, and Nancy Reagan as well as numerous fictional people in movies like *Husbands and Wives*, *Barton Fink*, *Naked Lunch*, and *A Passage to India*. (*See also* CAMPION, JANE)

### D cups

Big breasts. Often associated with sexual harassment, shoulder pain, and porn stars.

### *Death Proof*

Second half of Quentin Tarantino and Robert Rodriguez's 2007 double-feature film *Grindhouse* that showcases both Tarantino's infamous fetish with female feet and his trademark obsession with old movies. *Death Proof* features stuntwoman Zoë Bell (playing herself) and actresses Rosario Dawson and Tracie Thoms (not playing themselves) beating a sadistic misogynist serial killer (played by Kurt Russell) to death in a sequence that upends the typical action movie trope of women in need of rescue.

### Deavere Smith, Anna (1950–)

Actress, playwright, director, and professor. Theatrical dynamo most famous for her heartbreaking one-woman shows in which she plays all of the characters, shifting between races and genders like a chameleon. What is perhaps her best-known play, *Twilight: Los Angeles, 1992*, was constructed from interviews Smith conducted in the aftermath of the violent L.A. riots and earned her a Tony nomination in 1994. Her other theatrical documentary works include *Let Me Down Easy* (a critique of the health care system), *The Arizona*

*Project* (an exploration of women's relationships to the legal system), and the upcoming *The Americans*. She has starred in TV shows and films such as *Nurse Jackie*, *Rachel Getting Married*, and *The West Wing*. Oh, and she was declared a genius in 1996 when she won a MacArthur Fellowship. But we didn't need a grant to tell us that.

### Debbie Does Dallas

Perhaps one of the most recognizable pornographic films ever. Wildly successful upon its release in 1978—during the "Golden Age of Porn"—*DDD*'s biggest contribution to society was the explicit fetishization of cheerleaders. (*See also* CHEER-LEADING)

### Deenie

1973 young adult novel by Judy Blume that, like most of her books, is nothing if not educational on a number of different topics, including: eczema, menstruation, masturbating in bathtubs, the brief window of time a young model has to make it in the business, stage mothers, and most importantly scoliosis, with which the thirteen-year-old aspiring model title character has been diagnosed. (*See also* BLUME, JUDY; MASTURBATION)

### Deee-Lite

Nineties pop-dance group helmed by Lady Miss Kier whose free-spirited, multiethnic members imagined a world in which the eighties never happened and sincerely believed that the groove is in the heart.

### Deep Throat

1972 pornographic film about a woman whose clitoris is located in her throat, making her just about the only woman in the world for whom blow jobs are actually fun and not just a favor. Made for a paltry sum, the movie was a huge hit, grossing about $40 million, but its backstory—namely the biography of star Linda Lovelace—is perhaps what rocketed the film to legendary status.

### Deer, Ada (1935–)

Native American community organizer, social worker, and political leader and the first woman to serve as the head of the US Bureau of Indian Affairs (1993–1997). Born into the Menominee tribe in Keshena, Wisconsin, she went on to get a bachelor's degree from the University of Wisconsin–Madison before becoming the first Native American woman to ever receive a master of social work from Columbia University. Deer unsuccessfully ran for Wisconsin state secretary in 1978 and 1982 and became the first Native American woman to run for one of Wisconsin's congressional seats in 1992.

### deflower

Delicate verb used to describe the "taking" of a woman's virginity, especially if the incident occurs on a wedding night in or before 1952 or the gentleman involved is sporting a handlebar mustache.

### DeGeneres, Ellen (1958–)

Stand-up comedienne, actress, and talk show host who went from well known to world famous when she came out as a lesbian in 1997. In 2003, she began hosting *The Ellen DeGeneres Show*, which has earned thirty-two daytime Emmys—including four each for Outstanding Talk Show and Outstanding Talk

Show Host—and is watched by about three million people a day. Partner of Australian comic actress Portia de Rossi, whom she married in 2008.

### Degrassi Junior High

Painfully earnest, somewhat corny Canadian television program from the 1980s, which had the production values and acting talent you'd expect when two educators-cum-filmmakers (Kit Hood and Linda Schuyler) assemble a crew of mostly nonprofessional adolescent actors to tell stories. Featured regular characters who were fat, zitty, awkward, greasy, and average looking; courageously tackled issues such as teen pregnancy, abortion, and disability and regularly employed story lines about the effects of homophobia, racism, and sexism. (It was also frequently cringe inducing and featured one of the most famous "LSD will make you jump out a window, man!" story lines of the 1980s, not to mention some repressed memory bullshit.) Basically, a show that centered on misfits and demonstrated a sincere commitment to social justice, i.e., what *Glee* thinks it is but never has been.

### dehydration

Horrific epidemic that targets Hollywood stars and has a high comorbidity with exhaustion. (Lindsay Lohan and Charlie Sheen have both fallen victim at one or multiple points.) Dehydration can afflict noncelebrities as well, but the issue is usually solved by ingesting fluids such as water and rarely requires a stay in rehab. (*See also* LOHAN, LINDSAY; SHEEN, CHARLIE)

### Delilah

Ancient and notoriously crafty woman from the Hebrew Bible who got her lover, Samson, to reveal to her the secrets of his power so she could sell him out. Hedy Lamarr, who played her in 1949's *Samson and Delilah*, was pretty crafty herself—she helped patent an idea that later became the basis for modern wireless communications and claimed that she escaped her controlling husband by disguising herself as a maid.

### Democrats

**1.** People who vote for Democratic Party candidates. **2.** Members of the sole electable political party in the US that gives a rat's ass about women's issues, which is depressing on so many levels.

### Dench, Judi (1934–)

BAFTA-, Tony-, Emmy-, and Oscar-winning actress who became Dame Commander of the Order of the British Empire in 1988.

### department store

One-stop shop that offers a wide variety of goods, including clothing, furniture, accessories, makeup, and fragrances. They are often found in malls.

### depression

Mood disorder characterized by periods of sadness, anxiety, hopelessness, and general emo demeanor. Twice as common in women as in men, though it's not totally clear whether the reasons for this are social, cultural, biological, or a combination of all three. The term might apply to both the clinical state and, colloquially, the state of sadness. In times past, depression has been known vaguely as melancholia or ennui. In pharmaceutical company ads of the early 2000s, either anthropomorphized as sad-looking raindrops or expressed by soft-focus people looking dully into the distance while Life goes on around them. (By the end of said commercials, and presumably with the benefit of medications, raindrops and people respectively are able to rejoin Life.) In romantic comedies, conversely, depression is generally not serious and is characterized by unwashed hair and the consumption of ice cream and cured by the intervention of a sassy sidekick. In recent years, great strides have been made toward destigmatizing the illness, and many historical figures, such as Abraham Lincoln, have been posthumously diagnosed by doctors who did not treat them. Not something to be afraid of; definitely something to have checked out, without shame.

### Desdemona

Shakespearean heroine from *Othello* who is important in concept—a white woman married to an older black man, whose interracial marriage the evil Iago destroys for his own somewhat mysterious reasons—but boring in execution. (She's nice; she's gullible; she gets strangled.) For more interesting Shakespearean heroines, check out *Much Ado About Nothing, Twelfth Night,* or *The Taming of the Shrew.*

### Designer Impostors

If you like patchouli and cat piss, you'll love _____.

### dessert

Just order it, already. (Nobody's judging you.)

### Destiny's Child

R&B girl group active from 1997 to 2006 in a number of iterations but perhaps best known as a trio made up of Beyoncé Knowles, Kelly Rowland, and Michelle Williams. (*See also* KNOWLES, BEYONCÉ)

### dewy

An adjective—like "willowy" and "coltish"—reserved exclusively for descriptions of young women in exceptionally bad fiction.

### Diana

Roman goddess of the moon and the hunt, a rough equivalent of the Greek goddess Artemis. Virgin and patron goddess of virgins who now forms the basis of a Wiccan tradition and who inspired the *Wonder Woman* comics (Wonder Woman's real name is Diana of Themyscira). Charles Spencer (Princess Diana's brother) mentioned the goddess in his eulogy for his late sibling, saying, "of all the ironies about Diana, perhaps the greatest was this: a girl given the name of the ancient goddess of hunting was, in the end, the most hunted person of the modern age." (*See also* PRINCESS DIANA)

### Dickinson, Emily (1830–1886)

Nineteenth-century poet and one of most important voices in American literature. Long regarded as a nunnish recluse with little contact with the outside world until Brenda Wineapple's 2008 biography offered an alternate view of the New Englander as a flirtatious, active, engaged letter-writer. Perhaps most famous for her poetry about death—a lifelong obsession—like "Dying":

> *I heard a Fly buzz—when I died—*
> *The stillness in the Room*
> *Was like the Stillness in the Air*
> *Between the Heaves of Storm.*
> *The Eyes around—had wrung them dry,*
> *And Breaths were gathering firm*
> *For that last Onset, when the King*
> *Be witnessed—in the Room—*
> *I willed my Keepsakes—Signed away*
> *What portion of me be*
> *Assignable—and then it was*
> *There interposed a Fly*
> *With Blue—uncertain—stumbling Buzz,*
> *Between the light—and me—*
> *And then the Windows failed—and then*
> *I could not see to see—*

## Didion, Joan (1934–)

Essayist, screenwriter, novelist, and California native celebrated for her formally ambitious, unsparing, astute nonfiction and widely considered to be one of the most important American writers. Best known for her essay collections *The White Album* and *Slouching Towards Bethlehem* and for *The Year of Magical Thinking*, which she wrote after her husband, John Gregory Dunne, died suddenly of a heart attack in 2003.

## DiFranco, Ani (1970–)

Patron saint of budding feminist college girls in the 1990s thanks to a grueling tour schedule and a bunch of catchy, clever pop-folk songs about loving women, loving men, and smashing patriarchy. Although the distinctive sound and devoted following she established as a young musician led to plenty of recording contract offers, she turned them all down and kept putting out albums on her own label, Righteous Babe Records. More than twenty years into a career that started in her late teens, DiFranco is still touring, recording, and wearing her progressive politics on her sleeve. May she never stop.

## dilation and curettage

Common, safe surgical procedure also known as D&C and performed in order to remove tissue from inside the uterus. The "dilation" part refers to the forced widening and opening of the cervix, after which a curette, a spoon-shaped instrument, is inserted into the uterus in order to scrape the lining of the organ or facilitate the suctioning out of material. D&Cs are performed during or after miscarriages, abortions, and childbirth (when remnants of the placenta may still be present). (*See also* ABORTION)

## Dior, Christian (1905–1957)

Pioneering French couturier and ready-to-wear designer who gave his name to a fashion house that continues to be among the world's most successful luxury brands and has been home to such designers as Yves Saint Laurent, Gianfranco Ferré, and John Galliano. (In 2011, Galliano was suspended and then dismissed from his duties as head designer of Dior after he was arrested for going on an abusive anti-Semitic tirade against multiple tourists in Paris.) Born into a wealthy family that lost everything in the Great Depression, Dior worked for couturier Lucien Lelong throughout the occupation of Paris, which meant that he had a hand in dressing the wives of Nazi officers and French collaborators. (Dior's younger sister Catherine, meanwhile, passed messages for a Resistance network that was described by historian Gitta Sereny as "one of the most dynamic intelligence movements in Europe.") In 1946, Dior founded his own couture house. With his first collection, dubbed the New Look by fashion editors, Dior swept away all the restraint and soul-deadening practicality of the fashions produced (under fabric rationing, of course) during the war: Dior's silhouette was voluptuous, wasp-waisted, profligate (some of his dresses consumed twenty yards of fabric)—and extremely beautiful.

## *Dirty Dancing*

Late 1980s movie about, well, many things, including dance, an exceedingly handsome man (Patrick Swayze), "coming-of-age," half-broken class barriers, rapidly evolving Jewishness, and back-alley abortions—the last inserted by screenwriter Eleanor Bergstein to remind the Reagan era of a pre-Roe world. (It also contains the most subtly damning reference to Ayn Rand ever seen in a Hollywood film.) From

the moment we glimpse teenage, sixties-era Baby (Jennifer Grey) reading a book titled *Plight of the Peasant*, *Dirty Dancing* makes clear it is more than your average eighties nostalgia vehicle, a celebration of a romance between two different people transformed by knowing one another without giving up themselves. (*See also* RAND, AYN)

## Disney princesses

Collection of doe-eyed, motherless characters from fairy tales and Disney films—including Snow White, Cinderella, Aurora, Ariel, Pocahontas, Mulan, Tiana, Belle, Jasmine, and Rapunzel—who present a troubling portrait of womanhood and appear on everything from $60 costumes to underwear, curtains, and bicycles but never make eye contact to preserve the integrity of their story lines (and ensure their young fans aren't encouraged to befriend other females). (*See also* JASMINE)

## Ditto, Beth (1981–)

Femme, fat, and lead singer of indie-rock band Gossip. Born dirt-poor in rural Arkansas, now a fashion icon—she has modeled for Jean Paul Gaultier and been the face of Versace. She has also created her own line of makeup, for MAC Cosmetics—while never losing touch with her West Coast riot grrrl roots. Massively famous in Europe and not nearly famous enough in the US. Isn't afraid to speak her mind about other celebrities ("I hate Katy Perry! She's offensive to gay culture"), her weight ("if I lost weight and tried to look the part, that would be the ultimate selling out"), and using her fame and wealth for good ("I also believe in the feminist movement and in helping my sisters and in the queer movement and helping my queer family. I couldn't do that if I didn't capitalize on the things that I've been able to do").

## ditz

Spacey, none-too-bright woman who might be worth keeping around if she's got big tits.

## diva

Originally a celebrated opera singer; then any female singer with serious pipes; then any female singer who made ridiculous demands, with or without the pipes to justify them; today, any woman who gets an occasional manicure or has ever sent a meal back in a restaurant.

## Dixie Chicks

Extremely popular—most of the band's albums have hit number 1 on the country charts—and sometimes controversial pop-country trio. Led by Natalie Maines, who brought the group a monster truckload of grief with the forthright remark she made to cheering fans in London, in 2003: "We do not want this war, this violence, and we're ashamed that the president of the United States is from Texas." Her comment, made in reference to the Iraq War and then president George W. Bush, sparked what would eventually become years of protests against Maines and her bandmates, Martie Maguire and Emily Robison. The women eventually wrote a defiant comeback song in 2006—"I'm not ready to make nice / I'm not ready to back down." The group has been on hiatus since about 2007, the same year that their record responding to the controversy, *Taking the Long Way*, won a Grammy for Album of the Year. (*See also* KOPPLE, BARBARA)

## dolls

Miniature anthropomorphic figures often classified as emblematic of traditional femininity, fraught with maternal expectation, and eschewed by certain progressive parents. Independent of any sociopolitical significance, dolls are a source of horror and anxiety to many people due to their general creepiness, a fear exploited by such motion pictures as *Child's Play* and *Child's Play 2*. Also a source of enduring pleasure and fascination for many people. Prominent dolls include Barbie, Raggedy Ann, Madame Alexander, and Betsy Wetsy, a doll capable of urinating.

## dolphins

Marine mammal that, for some reason, little girls are drawn to. (*See also* UNICORNS)

## domestic

One who's paid to do work in the home—child care, cleaning, cooking, and so on. The term is usually associated with women, since much of that work is so often thought of as "women's work."

## domestic violence

Broad term for what happens in abusive relationships, from physical and sexual violence to emotional and financial manipulation. According to the National Coalition Against Domestic Violence, 85 percent of victims of domestic violence are women, 1.3 million American women experience abuse by an intimate partner each year, and nearly one-third of the victims who report such violence to the police are eventually murdered by their intimate partner.

## douche

Product used to rinse and flush out the vaginal canal with liquid (often water or a combination of water, vinegar, antiseptics, and fragrances) and transported via a tube connected to a bottle or bag, which has somehow become synonymous with male *Jersey Shore* cast members. (*See* DOUCHE BAG) Once used to treat vaginal infections, prevent pregnancy, and combat that infamous "not so fresh feeling" but later proven to be medically unnecessary and possibly dangerous. Bad for vaginas, period.

## douche bag

**1.** Pouch that holds the liquid component of a douche.
**2.** Synonym for "asshole" first popularized in the 1970s and then mostly forgotten until it came back strong in the aughts,

thanks to the internet, which never did settle whether the term was misogynistic ("It's mean and lady-adjacent!") or secretly feminist.

## douching

Act of using a douche.

## Douglas, Gabrielle (1995–)

American gymnast who, at the 2012 London Olympics, became the first woman of color—and first African American gymnast—to win the individual all-around competition and the first female American gymnast to earn gold in both the individual and team all-around in the same Olympics.

## Douglas, Helen Gahagan (1900–1980)

Democratic congresswoman from California who, like Ronald Reagan, started off acting. (Her costuming and performance in the 1935 movie *She* inspired the look and affect of the Evil Queen in Disney's animated feature *Snow White*.) Unlike Reagan, however, Douglas was intelligent and quick-witted, though she was eventually unseated by a campaign that went so far as to mention the supposed color of her underwear.

## dowager

Wealthy widow. With opinions.

### Dowd, Maureen (1952–)

Pulitzer Prize–winning reporter and *New York Times* columnist who, during the 2008 presidential primaries, was designated the World's Most Obnoxious Feminist Concern Troll by the feminist blog Shakesville.com. Which about sums it up.

### drawers

Excellent word for underwear.

### Dr. Drew

Physician and addiction expert who is in the process of sullying his reputation by becoming involved in increasingly questionable reality TV ventures. Got his start in 1984 on the radio show *Loveline* and, after years of advising legions of young and/or profoundly stupid callers on everything from safe sex to anal fissures, rose to national fame in 2008 with the VH1 show *Celebrity Rehab with Dr. Drew*, which rapidly devolved into an exploitative romp.

### Driggs, Elsie (1898–1992)

American painter who depicted the modern landscape and infrastructure of twentieth-century America with a Precisionist take on bridges, factories, and skyscrapers.

### drinking

Really fun, until it's not. Often leads to sex with people you're not that attracted to, unexplained bruises, karaoke, and headaches.

### droop

What happens to everything on your body after you turn thirty.

### drunk dialing

Practice of calling someone on the telephone when you should really be going to bed and sleeping it off. Common perpetrators include alcoholics, the recently broken-up-with, and Virginia Thomas.

### Drew, Nancy

Cultural icon, influencer of Supreme Court justices, girl detective. Nancy Drew first appeared in the 1930s, the star of her own book series created by Edward Stratemeyer, who wanted to capitalize on the fact that girls liked the Hardy Boys series and might like a girl detective even more. The books were initially written by Mildred Wirt Benson, using the pen name Carolyn Keene. Sometimes assisted in her sleuthing by her two best friends or her boyfriend, Ned Nickerson, Nancy was smart, observant, and determined. And a little bit racist. In the 1950s, the books were revised to solve that last problem, though critics remarked that the revisions also served to make her more stereotypically feminine. But she is something of a supergirl, with a staggering if somewhat unrealistic range of skills including painting, sewing, and horseback riding. Over time, the character has evolved and endured, appearing in television shows and movies and dozens of foreign translations of the books. After eighty years, more than 80 million Nancy Drew books have been sold worldwide, and women like Hillary Rodham Clinton and Sonia Sotomayor cite her as an inspiration. (*See also* CLINTON, HILLARY RODHAM; KEENE, CAROLYN; SOTOMAYOR, SONIA)

## dude

Slang term for a person. Often associated with Californian surfers, stoners, and fraternity brothers, *dude* has yet to achieve the gender-blind status achieved in recent years by *guys* and is usually applied only to boys and men. Its proudest moment as a noun came in 2009, when MSNBC host Rachel Maddow, a Californian, got frustrated in an interview with an antigay researcher who denied having ever made one particular homophobic claim. Maddow said, with audible exasperation, "I'm reading it from your book, dude." Its least proud moment came in the form of the 2000 movie *Dude, Where's My Car?* (*See also* MADDOW, RACHEL)

## due date

Approximate time at which a pregnant person can be expected to give birth, calculated from the first day of the last menstrual period. Also the name of a 2010 movie starring Robert Downey Jr. and Zach Galifianakis that looked fucking dreadful.

## du Maurier, Daphne (1907-1989)

English playwright and author, most famously, of the Gothic novel *Rebecca*, which was later made into a classic film by Alfred Hitchcock. *Rebecca* is the story of an unnamed young woman who marries the wealthy widower Maxim de Winter and suffers psychological torture at the hands of her husband's longtime housekeeper Mrs. Danvers, learning that nothing about the de Winter estate is as it seems.

## Duncan, Lois (1934-)

Young adult novelist best known for her dark, suspenseful works combining the supernatural with the struggles of adolescence. In *A Gift of Magic*, heroine Nancy copes with her parents' divorce while coming to understand her powers as a psychic; in *Stranger with My Face*, Duncan couples adoption with astral projection; in *Down a Dark Hall*, we find the students at a boarding school possessed by ghosts. Duncan's own daughter Kaitlyn was murdered, an event she depicted in 1992's nonfiction work *Who Killed My Daughter?* (*See also* DAUGHTERS OF EVE)

## Dunham, Lena (1986-)

Writer, actress, director, and cultural lightning rod. Came to national attention with her 2010 breakout film *Tiny Furniture* and her much-explicated HBO series *Girls*, which makes a certain kind of guy blusteringly angry and Dunham therefore a heroine.

## dutch

How you should pay on a first date, even if it's with someone who really, really wants to show off.

## Dutch oven

Pulling the bedcovers over someone else's head after you fart. Always a winner.

## Dworkin, Andrea (1946-2005)

Writer and cultural critic who did *not* say that all sex—heterosexual or otherwise—was rape (though she was quoted as such). Frequently mocked for having a less-than-pleasing-to-the-American-straight-male appearance, Dworkin was wrong about quite a few things—the essence of porn for one—but it's hard to imagine a world without her 1987 book *Intercourse*, which gave us ideas and aphorisms like: "While gossip among women is universally ridiculed as low and trivial, gossip among men, especially if it is about women, is called theory, or idea, or fact." Dworkin had a blunt manner, but her loud, unhinged poundings on the door have a way of waking you up. To paraphrase Susie Bright, Dworkin's great talent was aiming pies right at the crotch of Mr. Big Stuff, even when her aim was wildly off.

### E., Sheila (1957–)

Mind-bogglingly talented percussionist, singer, and frequent Prince collaborator best known for her 1984 hit "The Glamorous Life."

### Earhart, Amelia (1897–1937)

Aviator and the first woman to fly across the Atlantic solo. Actually worked for a while as an editor at *Cosmopolitan* and as a fashion designer, but her careers in magazines and clothing did not keep her from being an ardent feminist. Was, as

she told her husband, George P. Putnam, very reluctant to marry, refused to change her last name, and didn't hold Putnam to fidelity, according to a neat prenup letter she wrote. When her plane disappeared near the South Pacific's Howland Island as she tried to circumnavigate the globe, she was just thirty-nine years old. May have died a castaway. (*See also* Cosmopolitan)

### earrings

Objects better removed before a fight.

### earworm

See Kylie (na na na, na na na na na); Suzanne Vega (doot do dooo do, doot do doo do, doot do do do, doot do doo do).

### *Eat, Pray, Love*

(*See* Gilbert, Elizabeth)

### Eckford, Elizabeth (1941–)

One of the Little Rock Nine, the group of African American students who first integrated the public school system in Little Rock, Arkansas. In 1957, when she was only fifteen years old, Eckford and eight others showed up for class at Little Rock Central High School amid a storm of abuse, threats, and publicity. Due to a logistical mix-up, Eckford was the only one to arrive at the front entrance, which was blocked by an angry mob and by the National Guard. When the Nine were finally able to enter the school successfully several weeks later, a crowd of a thousand segregationists showed up to intimidate them. Eventually, President Eisenhower called in the US Army to ensure that the Nine could enter each day, though once inside the school Eckford endured violence at the hands of her white classmates. In 1999, she was awarded the Congressional Gold Medal by President Clinton. The image of Eckford walking to school with a crowd of jeering white segregationists at her back remains one of the most powerful visual symbols of the civil rights movement.

### Edwards, Elizabeth (1949–2010)

Lawyer, health care advocate, bestselling author, and unofficial manager and partner in husband John Edwards's campaigns for the Senate, vice presidency, and presidency. A smart, driven woman ahead of her time, Edwards perhaps should have had a political career of her own. She did not. But she battled cancer, inequality, maternal grief, and other indignities with grace and gusto. She once told the *New York Times* that she hoped to give her children wings so that they might be able to "stand by themselves in a stiff wind."

### egalitarianism

Philosophy that holds all human beings are born equal and deserve equal respect.

### Egan, Jennifer (1962–)

Very Serious Novelist, and a common modern-day answer to the debate about whether women can produce canonworthy literary fiction. Her best-known novel, *A Visit from the Goon Squad*, a series of linked stories about a record executive and his constellation of family and acquaintances, won the Pulitzer Prize for fiction in 2011. In the book, she plays with linear time and format, including one chapter in the form of a PowerPoint presentation. Her writing is smart and crisp and vivid and sad. An example: "If I had a view like this to look down on every day, I would have the energy and inspiration to conquer the world. The trouble is, when you most need such a view, no one gives it to you."

### egg freezing

Practice of preserving one's eggs—at great expense—in the hopes of getting pregnant with them when one would otherwise be too old or unhealthy. Which you wouldn't have to do if you'd quit being so obsessed with your career, *gawd*.

### ego

Per Freud, the part of the human mind that thinks rationally about how to strike a balance between the devil and angel on each of your shoulders. (Id: "I WANT SEX NOW." Superego: "Not on the first date!" Ego: "Look, just use protection.")

### Ehrenreich, Barbara (1941–)

Social commentator, feminist, and investigative journalist who began her career as a scientist (she received her PhD in biology from Rockefeller University in 1968). Best known for her 2001 book *Nickel and Dimed: On (Not) Getting By in America*, which documented her experience working for three months at minimum wage and shed light on the myriad of obstacles put in the way of poor people in the US.

### eligible

Any single man anywhere near your age, according to your mother.

### Eliot, George (1819–1880)

Pen name of Victorian author and Englishwoman Mary Ann Evans, who gave us politically rich novels like *Middlemarch* and *The Mill on the Floss*, wrote under a male name to get the professional respect she deserved, and drove the point home by writing the memorably titled essay "Silly Novels by Lady Novelists." Lived in sin for many years with married philosopher George Henry Lewes and then legally married a man twenty years her junior seven months before she died. Boss.

### Elliott, "Mama" Cass (1941–1974)

Founding member of The Mamas and the Papas, known for her big voice and body. Died of a heart attack in her sleep at age thirty-two, but you've probably heard that she choked on a ham sandwich from some asshole who thinks fat jokes about gifted people who died tragically young are hilarious.

### emasculate

To treat a man the way you'd treat a woman, which men tend to think is horrifying. Wonder why.

**embryo**

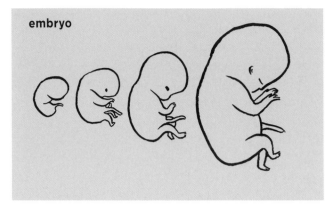

The medical term for a developing pregnancy during the first eight weeks of development. Prior to being an embryo, the developing human is a zygote. After the embryonic stage, the proper term is fetus. And the official GOP term for an embryo that results from a woman being raped is a *blessing*.

**emery board**

A file, usually made of cardboard covered in a sandpaperlike material made of ground emery and used to shape and smooth fingernails and toenails.

**Emin, Tracey (1963–)**

British artist who rose to fame with confrontational, often sexually charged works including *Everyone I Have Ever Slept With 1963–1995* (a little blue tent emblazoned with appliquéd names) and *My Bed* (Emin's actual dirty bed strewn with bloody period-panties and condoms). Nominated for a Turner Prize in 1999, represented Britain at the Venice Biennale in 2007, and opened the Turner Contemporary gallery with Jools Holland in 2011. Professor of drawing at London's Royal Academy of Arts (founded 1768)—one of only two female professors in its history. (*See also* PANTIES; PERIOD)

**emotional**

**1.** Experiencing a full range of human feeling.
**2.** Totally irrational, according to a dude losing an argument.

**emotions**

What women employ instead of logic.

**empathy**

What emotion (as opposed to logic) allows you to feel.

**Ensler, Eve (1953–)**

Activist and playwright who wrote *The Vagina Monologues* in 1996, waking several generations of women to the fact that *their vaginas are angry*, and helped millions of women realize that it's not only *okay* to love their bodies—it's a social and political imperative. Now, almost twenty years after its debut, it's pretty easy to make fun of *The Vagina Monologues*—some of its woo-woo goddessy undertones are pretty dated—but there's no shaking the truth that it's a massively powerful, important, groundbreaking piece of work.

***Entourage***

Hit HBO series and unintentional satire of male culture that ran from 2004 to 2011 and centered on fictional film actor Vinnie Chase (Adrien Grenier), his fictional friends, and how they all reacted to Chase's fictional silver screen success. (The secondary "hero" of the show was Ari Gold, an agent with a serious, undiagnosed case of borderline personality disorder.) Executive-produced by and loosely based on the life of actor Mark Wahlberg, the show was absolutely unself-conscious in its anxiety about the homosexual undertones around its depiction of a group of men who spend all their time together. (Except, of course, for the rotating cast of women they regard, at best, as ornamental.) Sort of like *The Hills*, except it's not clear who actually watched it.

### Ephron, Nora (1941–2012)

Beloved and decorated writer and director. Got her start as a journalist in the 1960s (after an internship in the Kennedy White House), covering politics, fashion, and everything in between for the *New York Post, Cosmopolitan*, and *Esquire*. Married journalist Carl Bernstein in 1976 (her first screenwriting gig was helping to rewrite the script of *All the President's Men*, the movie about how Bob Woodward and Bernstein uncovered the Watergate Scandal). Divorced Bernstein while pregnant with the couple's second son after discovering he was having an affair with a family friend; her devastation and recovery was chronicled in her bestselling 1983 roman à clef, *Heartburn*. Ephron's illustrious career was a testament to the power of storytelling, whether on-screen (*When Harry Met Sally, Sleepless in Seattle, You've Got Mail, Julie and Julia*), onstage (*Love, Loss, and What I Wore*), or on the printed page (*Crazy Salad, Heartburn, I Feel Bad about My Neck, I Remember Nothing*). In *I Remember Nothing*, Ephron wrote a list of things she would and would not miss about life, when it ended. On the "won't miss" list: "Polls that show that 32 percent of the American people believe in creationism," "mammograms," and "Panels on Women in Film." On the "will miss" list: "My kids," "waffles" and "the concept of waffles," and "*Pride and Prejudice*."

### epidural

Pain-relieving procedure involving the insertion of a catheter through which a narcotic or other anesthesia is delivered in order to block sensation and pain in a specific region of the body. Often used during labor and delivery, and pooh-poohed by proponents of "natural" childbirth. (*See also* NATURAL CHILDBIRTH)

### episiotomy

Incision made in the perineum, the area between the anus and the vagina, to enlarge the vaginal opening and assist with birth. There are a number of types, including the median, or midline (a straight up-and-down cut); mediolateral (a diagonal cut); and J shaped, which begins as a midline cut then becomes diagonal. Episiotomies were introduced in the eighteenth century to prevent vaginal tears during birth, because of a mistaken belief that a surgical incision would heal faster than a natural tear, though the big push for them came in the 1920s from Dr. J. B. DeLee, who described women's bodies as "badly designed for birth." (Research suggests that spontaneous tears heal just as fast, if not faster, and that episiotomies may cause more harm than good, including more pain and blood loss and increased likelihood of tears that extend all the way down to the rectum.)

### Equal

### equal opportunity

Depending on whom you ask, (a) an explicit constitutional obligation; (b) a concession to the deities of political correctness; or (c) what's keeping the White Man down. In fact it is none of those things. Equal opportunity is not mentioned in the Fourteenth Amendment—the phrase there is "equal protection"—but the "equal" word does impose a certain obligation of fairness that takes white men out of charge of, well, everything.

### Equal Rights Amendment

Suggested constitutional amendment first proposed in 1923 to create a precedent against sex-based discrimination. Reintroduced in every Congress since then, the ERA has been ratified by thirty-five out of the necessary thirty-eight states. Supporters say that ratifying the ERA will provide stronger legal standing in areas such as the wage gap, debates over contraception and abortion, and employment discrimination. Opponents claim the ERA will upend traditional gender roles, destabilizing the nuclear family and creating a world in which women are obligated to support themselves. But as Alice Paul once explained, "We shall not be safe until the principle of equal rights is written into the framework of our government." (*See also* PAUL, ALICE; SCHLAFLY, PHYLLIS)

### espadrille

### Esprit

Quintessential clothing label of the 1980s, when apparel manufacturers moved their factories to Asia and suddenly purple leg warmers, hysterically oversize sweaters, polka-dot stirrups, shoulder-padded hounds-  tooth blazers (essentially, any wild statement that didn't involve tailoring or any other feature that might require an intuitive grasp of the contours of its target customer's body) ruled fashion. The ur-American Apparel, Esprit is currently headquartered in Hong Kong, where a longtime supplier acquired the brand in the wake of the messy divorce of San Franciscan cofounders Doug and Susie Tompkins.

### Eve

Everything, ever, is that bitch's fault.

### exercise

Physical activity in which the body is moved back and forth and up and down until (if you're doing it right) you start to sweat profusely and kind of feel like you are going to die but also, eventually, be strong and capable and awesome.

### expecting, expectant

Something a pregnant person and her partner can be together, as opposed to *pregnant*, which is a solo adjective.

## F

### fab, fabulous

An art and state of being that no one can agree on how to achieve. As a quality, fabulousness is easily overdone, leading to campiness or (heaven forbid) tackiness. This is separate and distinct from fabulosity, which is either the default state of Kimora Lee Simmons or an alternative universe swathed in cheetah print.

### face

Surface that covers the front of the head on all vertebrates. On humans, consists of the eyes, which are used to see things, the nose, which is used to smell things, the mouth, which is used to taste things and pleasure your sexual partner, and the skin, which holds it all together. Ladies are told that the way their faces look are very important. Ladies, your faces are very important.

### Facebook

Social networking service. Do you even remember a world without Facebook? When you couldn't keep tabs on your exes and frenemies from the comfort of your home, and being tagged meant you were it, not that potentially embarrassing photos of you were all over the internet? What started as a social network open only to Harvard students quickly morphed into a behemoth that welcomes anyone over the age of thirteen who has an e-mail address; as of 2013, there are more than one billion users worldwide. It's unlikely that founder Mark Zuckerberg ever imagined that his life would play out on the big screen (2010's *The Social Network*) and in print (2009's *The Accidental Billionaires*, on which the film is loosely based), but he did seem to understand the magnitude of his creation when he said, "By giving people the power to share, we are starting to see people make their voices heard on a different scale from what has historically been possible." (*See also* SORKIN, AARON)

### face-lift

Cosmetic surgical procedure. In the ongoing war against Mother Nature, the face-lift is the nuclear option. In this simple-yet-horrifying procedure, incisions are made around the perimeter of the patient's face, after which a surgeon lifts the skin from the facial muscles and yanks it back so as to create a tightened "lift" to the patient's face. Remarkably, people pay (a lot) to have this done.

### facial

**1.** Incredibly painful process in which the pores on the face are squeezed, exfoliated, and generally roughed up. **2.** Term for when a man ejaculates all over the face of his sexual partner. (The latter is commonly considered to have been popularized by porn; the former has yet to be.)

### fact

**1.** A true thing that really happened or exists. **2.** Anything that bolsters your argument.

### Facts of Life, The

*Diff'rent Strokes* spinoff sitcom that ran for an unaccountably long time (1979–1988), set at a girls' boarding school in upstate New York. In addition to the tsk-tsking but warm housemother (Mrs. Garrett), the show's parade of stereotypes included the nasty blonde rich one (Blair), the butch

one with a chip on her shoulder (Jo), the jolly fat one (Natalie), the disabled one who teaches us all a valuable lesson (Blair's cousin Geri), and the sassy black one (Tootie) whose only method of travel is roller skates (we don't know, it was the eighties). Season 1 is worth a possible rewatch for a very young Molly Ringwald and season 7 for a very young George Clooney.

### fad

The widespread adoption of a certain look, behavior, or obsession that is too frivolous and fleeting to be considered a bona fide trend. Fads are generally stupid and silly and, thankfully, short-lived. (Memes before there were memes.) Examples include Furbies, slap bracelets, and dog yoga.

### fag, faggot

Pejorative term for a gay man, or a man perceived to be gay, or any male who has a run-in with a homophobic jackass who thinks that "gay" is the worst thing you can call someone.

### fag hag

Pejorative term for women who hang out with gay men, presumably because they can't get straight ones to pay attention to them.

### fairy

Supernatural/mythical/magical creature, often female, usually winged, rooted in old English and Irish folklore, but now up there with "princess" as a feminine being that many little girls in Western cultures admire. Also, term used by homophobic Neanderthals to question a person's masculinity or heterosexuality.

### fairy tales

Folkloric short stories featuring a large number of lopped-off heels, legs, and arms that have nowadays vanished in favor of the Disney–Industrial Complex princess conveyor belt. Perhaps we always got a sexist gloss on the story. The Grimms were devout nineteenth-century Christians, Andersen a celibate serial unrequited lover. Their appreciation of gender dynamics was not ideal and sometimes veered right into misogyny—too many villains who were witches and stepmothers. But without the half-baked sexism they propagated, we would never have had either Ariel or the films of Catherine Breillat. Some trade-offs are worth it. (*See also* DISNEY PRINCESSES)

### faith

You gotta have.

### fake

Term that's a modern replacement for the underused "two-faced," normally leveled at women (and gay men) and often accompanied by the word *bitch*. *Fake* has multiple uses. Sometimes it refers to the status of one's aesthetic choices (e.g., "Everything about that bitch is fake: hair, lashes, titties!"). But most often it means someone who is insincere in his or her interactions with other people (e.g., "That fake bitch—wait till I see her on the reunion show!"). Anti-Anthem: TLC's "Case of the Fake People."

### fake bake

How to get a Bright Bronzed Look without the harmful damaging effects of the Sun's Rays!

### Falco, Edie (1963–)

American actress and four-time Emmy Award winner best known for her role as Carmela Soprano on *The Sopranos* and as Nurse Jackie on the titular series. Projects the aura of a woman who just could not give a fuck:

**"Like, forgive me, I don't know if you're friends with her—but who the hell is Kim Kardashian? Like, who are these people and why are they famous and why are they advertising things and being asked their opinions about things? I just don't understand what these people did to be in a position of having everyone ask their opinions about stuff."**

—to an interviewer in 2011

### fallopian tubes

Thin tubes that connect the ovaries to the uterus. Named after a man, of course: Gabriele Falloppio, a sixteenth-century Italian priest-cum-anatomist. Falloppio is also credited with inventing a chemical-soaked linen penis sheath—i.e., an early but probably uncomfortable condom—to prevent syphilis, and arguing with another contemporary anatomist over which of them really "discovered" the clitoris, though both were reportedly shouted down by a more famous scientist who swore to God it didn't exist.

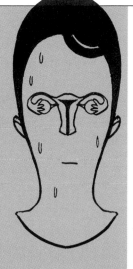

### falsies

Breast enhancers. (Think "merkin for your boobs.") Available in a variety of different types and sizes, from silicone "chicken cutlets" that can be slipped into any bra, to in-bra inflatables, to gel inserts, to those little teardrop-shaped polyester-batting things that are often sold with bras and swimwear. The history of falsies is as long as our culture's habit of choosing, every ten years or so, one of the many available sizes and shapes of the human female breast to anoint as "fashionable." In the nineteenth century, falsies were known as "breast pads," and clothing and corsets commonly included pockets into which such pads—often made of rubber—could be inserted. In the 1920s, a flat-chested figure was considered the height of chic, so breast binding came into vogue. Falsies differ from prosthetic breasts, such as those worn by some breast cancer survivors, in that prostheses (which are often custom-made), are intended to appear like actual breasts, while falsies are all about boosting cleavage and making your existing boobs look bigger. They are often hot, heavy, and somewhat restricting to wear.

### Faludi, Susan (1959–)

Journalist, Pulitzer Prize–winner, and author of nineties feminist classics *Backlash: The Undeclared War Against American Women* and *Stiffed: The Betrayal of the American Man*. Brought the

term *backlash* into the feminist lexicon. Kind of lost it weith her post-911 tome *The Terror Dream*, but she's forgiven on account of her general asesomeness. "Sisterhood, to me, is not about 'us girls against the guys,'" she wrote in *Slate* in 1997. "It's about public solidarity with women who don't have the choices you have, who are not yet free to blow off a job they don't like, who can't raise their children the way they yearn to, who have all this potential creativity and talent that is unexpressed and withering on the vine."

### fanny

**1.** Buttocks (United States). **2.** Vagina (United Kingdom). **3.** May have led to some international wrong-hole misunderstandings in the bedroom.

### Farrell, Suzanne (1945–)

American ballerina, one of the greatest ballet dancers of the twentieth century. Farrell, known for her lyricism, joined George Balanchine's New York City Ballet in 1961, became one of his muses, and danced for decades with some of City Ballet's best-loved leading men, including Jacques d'Amboise, Arthur Mitchell, and Peter Martins.

### Farrow, Mia (1945–)

Actress, activist, reigning queen of the pixie haircut (long after she grew it out), and model of a Woman Scorned. Mother to Ronan Farrow, a child genius who agrees his father, director Woody Allen, is a putz. Most famous for *Rosemary's Baby*, but her best line was in Allen's *The Purple Rose of Cairo*, one cherished by any woman who has fallen in love with Gilbert Blythe, Mr. Darcy, or Rhett Butler: "He's fictional, but you can't have everything." (*See also* ANNE OF GREEN GABLES; DARCY, MR.)

### farts

Natural by-product of digestion in the form of foul-smelling gaseous compounds that are expelled through the anus. Fortunately, female readers of this book need not worry, because scientists confirm that females are indeed incapable of farting. (Our gaseous waste is converted to things like "maternal instinct," "female intuition," and "caring about shoes.") Isn't science wonderful?

### fashion

Industry revolving around the production of clothes; the art of designing garments. Depending on whom you ask—a fashion designer, a fashion photographer, a fashion editor, or a fashion blogger—you may get a different definition of this term. But in any case, fashion is never synonymous with style.

### fashion forward

That which is new, or so on trend, fashion-wise, that it is almost ahead of its time. (*See also* FASHION MODEL; SUPERMODEL)

### fashionista

Stylish person. (Not to be confused with fashion victim; someone who's obsessed with fashion, or with wearing all of *Vogue* magazine's Ten Top Fall Trends! at once.) Instead, someone who gets dressed with a sense of purpose—perhaps with a hint of eccentricty, or what your mother would call "pizzazz." In this matter, heiresses have something to teach us. Daphne Guinness = fashionista; Tinsley Mortimer = fashion victim.

### fashion model

Tall and thin female who poses for photographs in order to sell clothes or accessories. (That fourteen-year-old Polish hyperthyroid case staring back at you glumly from the pages of *Purple* magazine is a fashion model and was probably not paid for the eighteen hours it took for the photographer to shoot her wearing twelve different outfits.) (*See also* SUPERMODEL)

### fashion show

Presentation of clothing, usually on live human models walking a central runway in front of an audience of editors, celebrities, and hangers-on. (*See also* FASHION WEEK)

### fashion victim

(*See* FASHIONISTA)

### Fashion Week

Semiannual trade show for the garment industry that currently takes place over four successive weeks in New York City, London, Milan, and Paris, and throughout the year in other cities. Fashion Week is probably more exciting than spending a week at the DMV (although the lines are about as long and the people behind the desks just as skeptical), but only because there's often free champagne (and very expensive drugs). Basically exists so that designers can display their new seasonal collections to an invite-only crowd: critics and reporters, runway photographers, buyers from major retailers, event sponsors, and their closest celebrity friends. Whom they pay to show up. Seating is based on a guest's position in the industry's archaic yet constantly shifting pecking order. Dozens of shows take place each day—New York Fashion Week, for example, plays host to over three hundred shows—and every night there are parties at which the same editors and buyers gossip about each other, and the same celebrities step and repeat and drink cocktails with the sponsor's logo facing outward, like good soldiers, and issue the same sound bites to the same reporters.

### *Fast Food Nation*

2001 book by Eric Schlosser, whose searing exposé made us all quit eating at McDonald's for six weeks.

### fat

State of having a larger than average amount of adipose tissue on one's body.

### fat acceptance

Forty-odd-year-old movement that wishes people would define *fat* as above, instead of polluting the definition with moralizing and subjective aesthetic crap.

### *Fatal Attraction*

1987 male fantasia about how cheating gets you nothing but a psychotic sex-crazed harlot rising from the dead in your bathtub. They might as well have titled it *Bitch Crazy*. Glenn Close deserved better. (*See also* CLOSE, GLENN)

### fat shaming

Umbrella term for remarks and actions meant to make a fat person (or person perceived as anywhere above an "ideal" weight) feel lame, stupid, and shitty because of his or her size—ideally too small, stupid, and shitty to protest, or even to think for a moment that he or she doesn't deserve it. Comes in a nearly infinite variety of manifestations and contexts.

### feathered hair

This IS Farrah Fawcett, basically. Just look up Farrah Fawcett in the dictionary. See that? That's feathered hair. (Or, for the dude version, think Don Johnson circa 1982.) It's where the hair is really fluffy and kind of points out horizontally and falls in overlapping layers like a furry layer cake or a bird's butt. You do it with a hairbrush and a blow dryer, probably. For more information, ask 1976. (*See also* CHARLIE'S ANGELS)

### Feinstein, Dianne (1933–)

Senior senator from California and liver of a life full of first-woman-tos. (San Francisco Board of Supervisors' president, early 1970s; mayor, 1978; chair of the Senate Select Committee on Intelligence, 2009 to present; chair of the Joint Congressional Committee on Inaugural Ceremonies, 2009.) It didn't come easily to Feinstein; she was raised by an abusive mother, whom she once saw try to drown her younger sibling. After graduating from Stanford with a degree in history, Feinstein set her sights on politics, and she counts among her greatest achievements the now-expired 1994 assault weapons ban; in 1993, she said, "Banning guns addresses a fundamental right of all Americans to feel safe." A few weeks after the Newtown, Connecticut, massacre of twenty children and seven adults—including his mother—by a suicidal twenty-year-old in December 2012, Feinstein introduced an assault weapons ban bill in Congress.

### feisty

Adjective that portrays legitimate female anger or steadfastness as cute and nonthreatening. Former Speaker of the House and current House Minority Leader Nancy Pelosi has been a common recipient of the term. (*See also* PELOSI, NANCY)

### *Felicity*

Television series created by J. J. Abrams that ran from 1998 to 2002 and was built on a sort of frightening premise: that following the hot guy from high school to the wrong college would turn out totally great. Made a generation think that Dean & DeLuca was the hottest coffee shop in New York and that all dorm rooms had beautiful scrollwork and huge bay windows, but  offered a reality check in demonstrating that a short haircut—as modeled by series star Keri Russell—is not always a good idea for everyone.

### fellatio

Term for a sexual act that comes from *fellatus*, which is Latin for "to suck," and therefore a much more accurate description for orally stimulating a penis than the colloquial (and thus ironic) term *blow job*.

### female

**1.** Adjective describing the egg-producing members of a species. **2.** A noun used interchangeably with "woman," mostly by people who, secretly or not-so-secretly, despise the egg-producing members of their species.

# EUPHEMISMS FOR THE WORD "FEMALE"

## Lady

Extremely versatile: potentially in waiting, royalty, a tramp, or the special canine friend of a tramp. Used by salespeople ("This lady is looking for a bra in a 34B"). When irritating, preceded by the word *listen.* Appropriate for ages twenty and above.

## Woman

Generic female. Used by less polite salespeople when discussing a female in front of said female ("This woman is looking for this bra in a 34B"). Appropriate for ages thirty and above.

## Girl

Young, carefree, possibly innocent. Often preceded by a "hey" and followed by a high five. Appropriate for ages zero and up.

## Gal

Youthful but slightly knowing and experienced. Used in earnest in the 1940s and now employed in a cutesy, retro way. Often preceded by a "what a" or "that's my."

## Chick

Historically, a long-haired (frizzy, center-part) patchouli-schpritzed Woodstock attendee or long-haired (ironed, center part) fan or subject of beat poetry; during the 1990s, a pixie- or medium layered-haired fan of Sarah McLachlan and Ani DiFranco, or a reader of *Bridget Jones's Diary* and viewer of Sandra Bullock films.

## Bird

Young, usually attractive female (no relation to "chick"). Often modified by "fit" and used by the British.

## Lass/Lassie

Unmarried; dons woolen sweaters and scarves and has a fondness for plaids. Inhabits colder, foggy climates, which is good because she sunburns easily. Generally well-behaved, visibly moved by bagpipes.

## Skirt

Young, attractive female under the age of, say, fifty, and commonly found working in an office in front of a manual typewriter. Frequent target of harassment by men smoking cigars, wearing fedoras and trench coats.

## Wench

Vulgar, brash, employed by a bar, inn, or pub. Can be found serving mead, eating a chicken leg with her hands, or texting.

Often slapped on the rear by drunk men. May be drunk herself.

## The fairer sex

Sits with her ankles crossed, never burps, farts, goes to the bathroom, sweats, or curses.

## Babe

Cute, hot, sexy, bodacious, somewhat innocent. Often preceded by "she's a total."

## Fox

Hot-to-trot, less innocent than babe. Often preceded by "check out that."

## Vixen

Sexually voracious; less innocent than fox. Fond of playing tricks.

## Vamp

Like a vixen but slightly dangerous. May travel with a knife in her knee-high boot.

## Missus

Usually married and possibly a mother. Often zaftig, voluptuous, and laden with grocery bags.

## Bitch

Mean or verbally self-respecting girl, lady, or woman. (When used by misogynists, a girl, lady, or woman.)

## Doll

Nice, sweet, and/or pretty, without necessarily being sexy.

## Biddy

Older female or attractive younger female.

## Sheila

Australian.

## fembot

Robot given feminine characteristics. Sometimes for good (Rosie the maid on *The Jetsons*), sometimes for evil (the Austin Powers androids or the silver creatures with breasts in SVEDKA Vodka ads). (*See also* BIONIC WOMAN, THE; STEPFORD WIVES, THE)

## feminazi

Term of endearment initially coined by Rush Limbaugh's close friend Thomas Hazlett, a former chief economist of the FCC and law professor who has written scholarly papers blaming apartheid on socialism and currently spends most of his time fighting net neutrality regulations. Like a feminist, but also a Nazi! Geddit? Hur.

## feminine, femininity

"Girly, Girliness," basically. Feminine people behave in a way associated with females: they wear makeup, or swing their hips when they walk, or cross their legs when they sit. People who appear to be female are expected to be feminine and are assumed to be lesbians if they aren't, and people who appear to BE male are not expected to be feminine and are assumed to be gay if they are. Femininity and its converse, masculinity, look different in every culture, but all cultures have one thing in common, which is that they all start teaching people how to be feminine or masculine from day one. In the West, a baby girl is wrapped in a pink hospital blanket and a baby boy in a blue blanket, because pink is feminine and blue is masculine, and studies show that parents are more likely to reprimand a little boy for crying than they are to reprimand a little girl. Because crying is feminine. Learning how to properly "perform" your femininity—or how to avoid performing it, if you're a boy—starts very early. (*See also* PINK)

## feminine itch

Natural consequence of that not-so-fresh feeling.

## Feminine Mystique, The

1963 blockbuster feminist classic by Betty Friedan in which the writer and activist railed against the pervasive domestic ennui afflicting American women and declared, "We can no longer ignore that voice within women that says: 'I want something more than my husband and my children and my home.'" In Friedan's 2006 *New York Times* obituary, Margalit Fox wrote that *The Feminine Mystique* "ignited the contemporary women's movement in 1963 and as a result permanently transformed the social fabric of the United States and countries around the world." Back in the sixties, though, the *Times* was not impressed. Reviewer Lucy Freeman thought women like Friedan should probably just quit whining and pull themselves up by their bra straps: "It is superficial to blame the 'culture' and its handmaidens, the women's magazines, as she does. What is to stop a woman who is interested in national and international affairs from reading magazines that deal with those subjects? To paraphrase a famous line, 'The fault, dear Mrs. Friedan, is not in our culture, but in ourselves.'"

## feminism

According to Merriam-Webster, "1: the theory of the political, economic, and social equality of the sexes; 2: organized activity on behalf of women's rights and interests." Period.

That *should* be it. In reality, the word *feminism* and the movement it represents have a bunch of problematic connotations, some of which they deserve. The 1970s stereotype of the hairy-legged, man-hating bra burner persists today, even though it was always bullshit (well, not always the hairy legs, but seriously, *that's* what we're going to get hung up on?), yet legitimate criticism of second-wave feminism and its legacy—chiefly that it centers on white, straight, middle-class cisgender women, at the expense of everyone else—still goes ignored all too often.

## feminist

Person who believes in the political, economic, and social equality of the sexes. Period. Though in the light of the recent tendency of people like Sarah Palin to call themselves "feminists," we should probably add "and who doesn't actively work to undermine women's interests."

## femme fatale

Beautiful. Glamorous. Occasionally dangerous. Often found in film noir and uses her looks, seduction, and charm to get ahead in a man's world. Sexily star-crossed, she is normally the center of epic tales of murder, betrayal, and intrigue. See Lana Turner, Linda Fiorentino. Men, take heed; women, take notes. (*See also* GRIER, PAM; WONG, ANNA MAY)

## Ferraro, Geraldine (1935–2011)

First woman to run for vice president on a major party ticket. Worked as a teacher and then an attorney before becoming head of the Queens County Special Victims Bureau (you're welcome, Dick Wolf). First ran for Congress in 1978. In 1984, Democratic frontrunner Walter Mondale picked her to be his running mate, and even though they lost spectacularly, they made history. Ferraro went on to run unsuccessfully for Senate on two occasions but remained active and respected in Democratic Party politics. In 2008, she served as a consultant on Hillary Rodham Clinton's groundbreaking primary campaign, which ultimately also failed. During

Barack Obama's successful campaign for president, Ferraro's legacy was tarnished after she came under fire for comments about Obama receiving preferential treatment because he was a black man.

"If Obama was a white man, he would not be in this position," she said. "And if he was a woman of any color, he would not be in this position. He happens to be very lucky to be who he is."

## fetus

Something that could be a baby someday.

## Fey, Tina (1970–)

Writer, comedienne, and actress who has a list of accomplishments as long as your actual arm, including, in no particular order: first female head writer on *SNL*, best "Weekend Update" cohost we can remember, *Mean Girls* screenwriter, *30 Rock* creator, Liz Lemon portrayer, Sarah Palin imitator, *Bossypants* author, *Baby Mama* and *Date Night* actress, which, well, we don't really want to talk about *Baby Mama* and *Date Night*. All this and a vocal feminist, so, yeah. Fey is amazing. And yet, like your obnoxious Facebook status, It Is Complicated: Fey's oddly rich-white-lady-centric focus and frequent attitude of judginess toward other ladies (okay, we do want to talk about *Baby Mama*) has been a frequent subject of discussion on feminist blogs.

Oh, hey, here's another accomplishment of Tina Fey's: she's the only person to devote an entire episode of her TV show to making fun of feminist blogs without being a douche (*See* JOAN OF SNARK). Our love: It is so conflicted! Yet, oh, so real! (*See also* BABY MAMA; LEMON, LIZ; MEAN GIRLS)

## fibroid

As a wise philosopher once said, "It's not a tumor!" Except it totally is, albeit a noncancerous one that's particular to lady parts. Fibroids can form in the uterus, outside the uterus, underneath the uterus, and in the cervix. As is the case with much of what goes on Down There, the exact cause of fibroids is unknown but is thought to have something to do with hormone levels. While fibroids are rarely life threatening, they can be quite painful and are generally a giant pain in the ass. (Er, lower torso.)

## fiction

Stories invented by the author, as in novels, television programs, movies, comic books, and several popular "memoirs" of the 2000s.

### Field, Patricia (1941–)

Flame-haired openly gay designer and stylist known for her flamboyant, maximalist, street-inspired ensembles. In the 1990s, Field's NYC store was frequented by club kids and drag queens; toward the turn of the century she became the costume designer for a little premium cable show called *Sex and the City*, which won her an Emmy. Later received an Oscar nomination for her work designing costumes for the film *The Devil Wears Prada*. (*See also* SEX AND THE CITY)

### Fielding, Helen (1958–)

English novelist who created the character of Bridget Jones for a newspaper column in 1995, then expanded her diary entries into a bestselling novel and media empire. (*See also* BRIDGET JONES'S DIARY)

### *Fifty Shades of Grey*

Self-published trilogy by the author E. L. James originally conceived as *Twilight* fan fiction. The story of a gorgeous twenty-seven-year-old billionaire with *Phantom of the Opera* tendencies and an S&M playroom (generally described as inaccurate by practitioners of the BDSM lifestyle) and the unimpressive virgin who loves him. The first book and its sequels have become an international sensation and launched the trend known dismissively by people who have loudly not read them as "mommy porn."

### figure

Term for a person's—usually a woman's—body shape or phenotype. You know, like, "Oh, I can't have that donut, I'm *watching my figure*." Women are expected to always watch their figures, mostly because men are watching women's figures, too. If our figure is "wrong" (too fat, too lumpy, too saggy, too old) we are deemed a shitty woman. If our figure is "right," it's often the only thing people care about. A fundamental goal of feminism (and, more specifically, body-positive activism) is to decouple a woman's societal value from the "rightness" of her figure. Because, really, it's just a body. It's a tool, it's an amazing machine, and it's YOURS. You can do whatever you want with it. Go figure.

### fingering

To high school boys, the holy grail of third base. To more mature adults, a minefield. Done alone or with a skillful partner, it can be a pleasurable penetrating sensation that stimulates the G-spot. Done with a jabby klutz, it can be a disaster.

### First Lady

Role that morphs with time and circumstance. Generally the wife of the president, but sometimes a female relative or relative-in-law who is skilled in public relations. (President Woodrow Wilson's daughter, Margaret, served as First Lady after her mother's death in 1914; her tenure lasted until her father remarried a year later.) Unofficial duties include adopting a cause, being the White House hostess, interpreting fashion by the whims and moods of the country, providing a sympathetic ear to the oft-termed Leader of the Free World, and political feats of alchemy. (*See also* BUSH, LAURA; CLINTON, HILLARY RODHAM; FORD, BETTY; JOHNSON, LADY BIRD; OBAMA, MICHELLE; ROOSEVELT, ELEANOR)

### Firth, Colin (1960–)

"I'm fully aware...that if I were to change professions tomorrow, become an astronaut and be the first man to land on Mars, the headlines in the newspapers would read: MR. DARCY LANDS ON MARS."
—to *NOW* magazine, 2001.
(*See also* DARCY, MR.)

### Fisher, Carrie (1956–)

Actress, writer, every fanboy's original fantasy girl from the pre-Manic Pixie Dream Girl age, and all the more admirable for not being completely okay with that. The daughter of Debbie Reynolds and Eddie Fisher, she is also a recovering alcoholic and drug addict who once woke up next to her best friend's dead body—he'd overdosed on OxyContin and cocaine and died in the night—and had the father of her daughter turn out to be gay. Was once married to Paul Simon, which means that she's the one-half-wandering Jew in "Hearts and Bones." Has a refreshingly biting, sarcastic perspective on everything from being "complained about in song" to the "vague smell" legacy of playing Princess Leia in the *Star Wars* franchise. (*See also* MANIC PIXIE DREAM GIRL)

### fistula (obstetric)

Hole between the vagina and the rectum or bladder that develops as a result of trauma to the area, such as rape, botched surgery, pregnancy at an early age, or difficult labor. Fistulas can usually be fixed by a relatively simple surgery, but in many parts of world where people don't have access to decent medical care, the money to pay for it, or even the information that such a treatment exists, women with fistula live with the incontinence, related infections, nerve damage, and social ostracism it elicits.

### fitness

The state of being in good cardiovascular condition, with strong muscles and healthy joints. Not to be confused with "thinness." (*See also* EXERCISE)

### Fitzgerald, Ella (1917–1996)

Legendary jazz singer who dominated the 1930s, 1940s, 1950s, and 1960s, thanks to the flawless, fluid quality of her voice. Fitzgerald was the first black singer to perform at the Mocambo in Hollywood—a nightclub where Frank Sinatra had performed. Music critics called her voice "beautiful," "sonically perfect," and "radiant." In addition to her amazing range and scatting skills, Fitzgerald knew how to breathe new life into old standards, making them sound fresh again.

### Fitzhugh, Louise (1928–1974)

American author and illustrator of children's books. In *Harriet the Spy*, Fitzhugh created one of the best-loved children's heroines of the twentieth century, the plucky and rebellious little girl who keeps scrupulous notes on everyone and everything in her life, with disastrous consequences. Fitzhugh lived most of her life in New York City after escaping a lonely and difficult childhood in her native Memphis. (Fitzhugh barely saw her mother after her father won full custody rights following their divorce.) Attended Barnard College and briefly married her high school sweetheart before coming out as a lesbian. (*See also* BARNARD COLLEGE; HARRIET THE SPY; NORDSTROM, URSULA)

### flab, flabby

Favorite term of tabloids and women's magazines to describe fat and/or nonmuscular areas that you should be ashamed of, you pig.

### Flanagan, Caitlin (1961–)

*Atlantic* contributor, author of *To Hell with All That: Loving and Loathing Our Inner Housewife* and feminist concern troll gravely concerned about, among other things, the long-term effects of mothers working outside the home on their poor, neglected, probably unloved children. (Who cares about families in which the long-term effects of mothers not working include "homelessness" and "starvation"?)

### flappers

Young women in the 1920s who bobbed their hair, listened to jazz, preferred fringed dresses and pearls, and had laid-back attitudes about sex and alcohol. Zelda Fitzgerald, F. Scott's wife and the muse of the Jazz Age, is widely considered the first flapper.

### Fleiss, Heidi (1965–)

Beverly Hills–born rich kid who rose to infamy after being outed as "the Hollywood Madam" who provided escorts to high-profile clients. Fleiss was arrested on state prostitution charges in 1993 and was convicted in 1994, but the conviction was overturned in 1996. (She was also tried on federal tax evasion charges and subsequently convicted, serving twenty months in prison.) After maximizing her fame with books and television appearances in the nineties and aughts, she tried creating a "Stud Ranch" for women seeking male company in Nevada. After that venture failed, she spent her days caring for exotic birds and appearing on reality shows like *Celebrity Big Brother* and *Celebrity Rehab with Dr. Drew*. Survived an abusive relationship with actor Tom Sizemore.

### Flick, Tracy

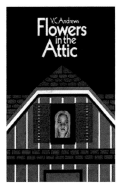

Character from Tom Perrotta's novel *Election* (and Alexander Payne's 1999 film of the same name). The kind of ambitious, ruthless young woman that young men imagine to be a sociopath and the rest of us aren't quite sure what to do with. (Who doesn't want to grow up to be Hillary Clinton? Why is ruthless ambition wrong in a girl and not in a man? Isn't this movie about how gross that teacher is, anyway?) As played by Reese Witherspoon, Tracy in all her ambiguity came through beautifully. So the next time someone tries to insult you with the name, wear it with pride.

**floozy**

One of the more delightful derogatory terms for a woman who has sex outside of marriage. It's "slut" mixed with a bit of "ditz" and it calls to mind a Brooklyn-accented platinum blonde from a black-and-white movie.

**flounce**

COMMENT 1: I am so offended, I am never coming back to this website!

COMMENT 2: Did you hear that? I said I'm leaving! No more page views for you!

COMMENT 3: Seriously, I am done. DONE. Look how very done I am!

COMMENT 4: Hey, I'm back!

### Flowers in the Attic

Harrowing yet titillating story of V. C. Andrews's Dollanganger clan. Four beautiful children are imprisoned for years in an attic so that their mother can receive the hefty inheritance promised to her on the condition that she remain childless. Close quarters lead to an incestuous relationship between the eldest girl, Cathy, and her brother Christopher, and the two become quasi-parents to their younger twin siblings. Brutal scenes include grandmother tarring Cathy's hair for misbehavior; Cathy's brother welcoming her to sex with a brutal rape; the twins growing up with unnaturally large heads due to lack of light; and the discovery that their mother is responsible both for their imprisonment and their slow poisoning (on powdered donuts, if you're interested), not their horrid grandmother. (*See also* ANDREWS, V. C.)

### Fluke, Sandra (1981–)

Georgetown Law School student denied the ability to testify about birth control and the Affordable Care Act before the House Oversight and Government Reform Committee, chaired by California Republican Darrell Issa, on the grounds that the panel was a discussion on the implications mandatory copay-free contraception would have on religious people's feelings, rather than what copay-free birth control would mean for the women who needed it. Fluke later testified before House Democrats and whipped conservatives into a fury (most notably, radio host Rush Limbaugh, who called Fluke a slut and demonstrated that he doesn't understand how birth control works by implying that women who have lots of sex somehow need to take it more often than women who have less sex or use birth control for nonsexual reasons, comments that caused dozens of advertisers to flee his show). Fluke, who graduated from Georgetown Law in 2012, continues to be a vocal proponent of women's public health issues and was invited to speak at the 2012 Democratic National Convention. Rush Limbaugh still can't stand her.

### Flynt, Larry (1942–)

Pornographer. Flynt was born into poverty in rural Kentucky, dropped out of high school, enlisted in the army as a teen with a fake birth certificate, was discharged, worked at a GM plant, got into moonshine, enlisted in the navy and found himself part of the team on the USS *Enterprise* that recovered John Glenn's space capsule, and eventually earned his GED. Whether that makes it more or less strange that he then became one of the world's most successful pornographers and infamous free speech advocates, history has yet to decide. But in 1965, Flynt opened his first Hustler Club with nude dancers and eventually parlayed it into a national strip club chain, the pornographic *Hustler* magazine, and—under the moniker LFP, Inc.—a number of other pornographic and nonpornographic magazines, a pornographic video production and distribution company, and a casino. Flynt's life became the subject of the 1996 film *The People vs. Larry Flynt*, which documented the growth of his business, his marriage to and the bathtub drowning death of his wife, Althea, and an attempted assassination in 1978—which resulted in permanent paralysis—during one of his many obscenity trials. Flynt's legal battles over obscenity standards, libel, and free speech have landed him at the Supreme Court three times, redefined the law, and garnered him a six-month federal prison sentence for desecrating the flag by wearing it as a diaper to court. Flynt's pornographic magazine efforts, a deliberate effort to produce more "raw" and down-market pornography than the ubiquitous *Playboy*, has drawn feminists' ire for being even more graphic (he was one of the first to showcase models' labia), more misogynistic (a 2012 issue of the magazine featured a rendering of conservative pundit S. E. Cupp performing fellatio as a commentary on her politics), and more dehumanizing (a 1978 cover following Flynt's short-lived Christian conversion ironically featured a lifelike rendering of a woman being put through a meat grinder, with only her legs and bare ass sticking out of the top, with the promise from Flynt: "We will no longer hang up women like pieces of meat.") than its competitors.

### Fonda, Jane (1937–)

(Sorry, *Lady* Jane Fonda.) Academy Award–winning actress, fitness guru (she started the 1980s aerobic exercise craze; we wouldn't be able to work out from our living room carpets if she hadn't popularized the at-home fitness program), former model, political activist. (In 1972, Fonda, an outspoken Vietnam War detractor, visited Hanoi and was famously photographed while sitting on an antiaircraft gun. She later claimed she was manipulated into taking the photo, but the "Hanoi Jane" moniker stuck.) Vocal supporter of feminist causes, from the Jane Fonda Center for Adolescent Reproductive Health at Emory University that she founded in Atlanta, Georgia, in 2000 to (little-known fun fact!) her role as a mentor to the first ever all-transgender cast of *The Vagina Monologues*. Fonda, who has been married three times, said she felt she had also divorced the world of patriarchy when she split from media mogul and CNN founder Ted Turner in 2001. Burn.

### Ford, Betty (1818–2011)

Onetime model and dancer. Wife of President Gerald Ford. First Lady of the United States (1974–1977) who made her mark by speaking out about everything from breast cancer awareness to substance abuse and addiction. Ahead of her time and not in step with much of the Republican Party, she was a supporter of the Equal Rights Amendment and abortion rights and a passionate advocate for the arts. After her family's intervention in 1978, Ford sought treatment for alcoholism and an addiction to pills, which she'd originally been pre-scribed in the 1960s for a pinched nerve; in 1982, she estab-lished the Betty Ford Center in Rancho Mirage, California.

### Ford, Eileen (1922–)

Barnard alum and cofounder of Ford Models, one of the pre-eminent modeling agencies in the world. Ford was one of the first to make celebrities into models and models into celebri-ties and was known for cultivating a fetish for "fresh-faced," "American" beauty in the fashion industry. Ford and her agency have represented "American"—read "Caucasian"—models such as Martha Stewart, Ali MacGraw, Candice Ber-gen, Jerry Hall, Carol Alt, Kim Basinger, Christie Brinkley, Lauren Hutton, and Janice Dickinson, among countless others. (*See also* BARNARD COLLEGE; FASHION; MODEL; SUPERMODEL)

### Ford, Tom (1961–)

Cocky, handsome American fashion designer who became the creative director of Gucci in 1994. Ford's designs for the label were slick, sexy, and glamorous—so much so that Madonna wore head-to-toe Gucci at the 1995 MTV Music Awards. Ford designed for the company until 2004, after which he launched his own eponymous label. In 2009, Ford directed a feature-length film, *A Single Man*, which was nominated for several Golden Globes.

### foreplay

Women like it. Men are bored by it. Usually involves "heavy petting" or anything that you don't consider actual sex.

### foreskin

Fold of skin that covers the glans penis and that is removed during circumcision. Across the United States the rates of men who have been circumcised vary. In Nevada, only 12 percent of boys were circumcised in 2009, whereas in West Virginia, 87 percent were—and these rates, which peaked in the late 1990s, are dropping again. And in Europe, it's not the norm; only about 10 percent opt for it. No wonder so many are confused about whether to snip or not to snip.

### Forever 21

Nearly $3 billion Los Angeles–based retailer of men's, women's, and children's apparel and accessories founded in 1984 that specializes in contracting with sweatshops to produce super-cheap copies of designers' work. Has been sued more than fifty times for alleged intellectual property violations but has never lost a case in court, mostly because it prefers to settle confi-dentially with plaintiffs rather than risk an adverse verdict.

### Foster, Jodie (1962–)

Actress and director. Friend to Mel Gibson. Came to us as a kid star, gum-cracking and streetwise, went to Yale, then went underground after she got tangled up in the Reagan assassina-tion attempt, famously designed to impress her. Her performance in *The Accused* as a sexual assault victim who wasn't the "right kind" of woman but deserved justice all the same cemented her in all of our hearts. Reminds us of a Judy Blume heroine, a bit, in the way she's led her life. We suspect she's still a gum-snapper at fifty. (*See also* ACCUSED, THE)

### *Four Weddings and a Funeral*

1994 romantic comedy that made us all wish Hugh Grant would be our charmingly spluttery boyfriend and that Andie MacDowell would take some goddamn acting lessons.

### Frank, Anne (1929–1945)

Author and German Jewish teen who died, at age fifteen, in the Bergen-Belsen concentration camp as a result of the Jewish Ho-locaust during World War II. Her diary, which she kept while hiding from the Nazis in a small annex (hidden by a bookcase) in Amsterdam and which was later recovered and pub-lished by her father, Otto, is perhaps the most-known personal memoir in the world. The best thing about Frank's diary, besides all of the important historical de-tails, is how much of an emotional teenager she seemed—she worked out her crush on Peter van Pels, she sassed her mother, she wondered what she would look like when she grew up, and she was so, so hopeful. Even in her darkest moments, she wrote, in a quote re-produced thousands of times, that, "in spite of every-thing I still believe that people are really good at heart."

### Frank, Lisa (1955–)

Artist and designer. Not even a seventh grader on acid could dream up the electric-hued designs and animals that Lisa Frank put on folders, stickers, pencil boxes, stationery, and more in the 1980s and early 1990s. During that heyday, young girls snapped up Frank products, which featured neon pandas, tigers, polar bears, dolphins, and other whimsical creatures doing whatever it is whimsical creatures do. Although Frank's popularity waned by the turn of this century, nineties nostalgia has apparently created a market for "vintage, limited edition" items, with Urban Outfitters selling erasers for $10, desk sets for $20, and poster books for $28. (*See also* UNICORNS)

### Frankenthaler, Helen (1928–2011)

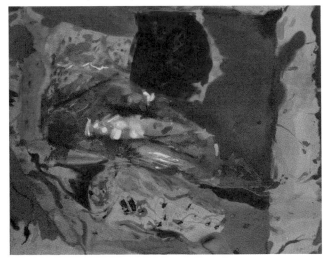

American abstract expressionist painter whose *Mountains and Sea* piece tricked the senses; although painted in oil, it looks like watercolor. Her "soak stain" technique involved heavily diluting the oil paint with turpentine and allowing it to go right into the canvas. Frankenthaler did not consider herself special for being a woman in the art world; according to John Gruen's book *The Party's Over Now*, she said, "For me, being a 'lady painter' was never an issue. I don't resent being a female painter. I don't exploit it. I paint."

### Franklin, Aretha (1942–)

Singer. Two years before her birth, her celebrity preacher dad impregnated a twelve-year-old; when she was six, her mother moved halfway across the country (she died four years later); by thirteen she'd been knocked up by a local Detroit youth. (If you've ever found yourself moved to tears at the super-

market by the sound of "Until You Come Back to Me" or "Ain't No Way," remember that very poor romantic choices are the foundation of so much great art.) And yet it was her eminently prudent, considered career decision to sign with Columbia Records over the (then fledgling) Motown that muzzled Franklin's true artistic greatness. But after six years, nine albums, and more than twenty singles spent catering to their every whim and musical genre, Franklin decided to leave—and was immediately swept off her feet (and into the Top 10, nine times in the first eighteen months) by a musical soul mate named Jerry. (That would be Jerry Wexler, an Atlantic Records producer with such sterling R&B credentials he is literally credited with coining the term *rhythm & blues* as a *Billboard* reporter.) By the time she was twenty-six, everyone acknowledged Aretha Franklin to be the undisputed queen of a kind of music that hadn't actually been formally established before. There were oceans of struggle and heartbreak (and the inevitable bad disco album and series of horrific outfits) still to come, but never again would we look upon Aretha Franklin or the innumerable octave-hopping, genre-indifferent, unapologetically and naturally woman artists she inspired without the proverbial r-e-s-p-e-c-t.

### frat house, fraternity

**1.** College-based social community for men, often based around communal living, service, and long traditions of proud man formation. **2.** A point of reference used in implicating other organizations for being particularly immature, bacchanalian, predatory, privileged, homophobic, and destructive; e.g., "Working at Bear Stearns was basically like waking up, dressing in heels, and going to a frat house every weekday." **3.** Home of the backward baseball cap, the phrase Eiffel Towering, and butt chugging.

### Frau

German's aurally unpleasant answer to *Mrs.*, i.e., a married woman. Coincidentally rhymes with *cow.*

### Freaky Friday

A franchise of sorts comprised of a book (1972), two movies you know about (1976 and 2003), and one movie you don't know about (1995), all based on the same bone-chilling premise: a girl and her mother switch bodies for twenty-four hours. (Though marketed as a comedy, it's basically a horror story.) Jodie Foster starred in the first movie (as the daughter), Shelley Long was in the second (as the mother), and Lindsay Lohan and Jamie Lee Curtis were in the third (as the daughter and mother, respectively.) (*See also* FOSTER, JODIE; LOHAN, LINDSAY)

### Free to Be…You and Me

Beloved multimedia social justice extravaganza (book, album, television show) created by, among others, actress Marlo Thomas and the Ms. Foundation for Women in 1972. "When we started mapping out the album," writes Thomas on the Free to Be Foundation's website, "I thought we'd collect some already published stories that were truly humanist in feeling

as well as well-written, amusing, or touching, and totally free of stereotypes of sex, class, and race. After a lot of research, it became clear that if I wanted such stories, I'd have to write or commission them myself." The "we" included Letty Cottin Pogrebin and original *Sesame Street* writer Carole Hart. Cottin Pogrebin described the project's themes as "independence and self-fulfillment; the human need for love, sharing and mutual assistance; the joys of creative, cooperative relationships with one's parents, siblings, and friends," and although the project seems a bit quaint and earnest forty years later—hot tracks on the album included "Parents Are People," "Helping," and "It's All Right to Cry"—it was enough of a BFD at the time to attract heavy-hitting talent like Alan Alda, Harry Belafonte, Judy Blume, Mel Brooks, Rita Coolidge, Roberta Flack, Rosey Grier, Dustin Hoffman, Michael Jackson, Kris Kristofferson, Carl Reiner, Diana Ross, Shel Silverstein, Cicely Tyson, and Dionne Warwick. In 2012, cultural historians Lori Rotskoff and Laura Lovett released an anthology called *When We Were Free to Be: Looking Back at a Children's Classic and the Difference It Made.*

### French, Dawn (1957–)

English actress and comedienne. Reasons to love her: **1.** She is balls-out hilarious. **2.** She's that rare celebrity who seems legitimately beloved by everyone who ever talks about her in public. **3.** See # 2, factor in that she's fat, and it's even more amazing. **4.** She and Jennifer Saunders hated each other at first, then went on to become basically the best female comic duo ever. **5.** She cofounded the plus-size clothing label Sixteen47. **6.** According to Wikipedia, "On television, French has kissed (in some cases, for charity) Brad Pitt, Johnny Depp, George Clooney, Richard Armitage, Gordon Ramsay, Michael Bublé and Paul O'Grady." (*See also* SAUNDERS, JENNIFER)

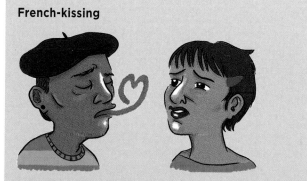

### French-kissing

Tongue-jousting for the purposes of assisting in sexual arousal. If badly done, described as "tonsil hockey." Like coffee and hard liquor, takes a little getting used to as a thing that's hot.

### frenemy

That person whom you can't stand but keep real close because she could ruin your life because we're all in high school still.

### Friday, Nancy (1933–)

Pioneering writer who specializes in "feminist erotica"—seeking to explore women's vibrant inner fantasy lives and dismantle the intense shame surrounding female sexuality. The author of 1973's *My Secret Garden*, a collection of women's fantasies about sex, Friday argued that the traditional ideal of "womanhood" is restrictive, outdated, and stifling, and that women need to abandon "niceness" and give in to "selfishness."

### Friedan, Betty (1921–2006)

Writer and activist whose 1963 book *The Feminine Mystique* opened a long-overdue cultural conversation about marriage, motherhood, and fulfillment or lack thereof. Three years after publishing her book, the former Betty Goldstein cofounded the National Organization for Women, and she was a leader in the 1970 Women's Strike for Equality, the National Women's Political Caucus, and what would become NARAL Pro-Choice America. "She played a very pivotal, very critical role in launching the second wave of the modern women's movement," then NOW president Kim Gandy told the *Wash-*

*ington Post* upon Friedan's death, although Friedan had left the group in the 1970s, unhappy with the way younger feminists were handling things. (Like how they gave a damn about lesbians and didn't pay enough attention to her, according to some reports.) Always controversial, sometimes prickly, sometimes closed-minded, Friedan left a complicated yet critical legacy. (*See also* FEMININE MYSTIQUE, THE)

### friending

Social media action that has almost nothing to do with actual friendship.

### friends with benefits

Perhaps the trickiest of sexual relationships, one that requires a delicate balance between being "friends" with a sexual partner while keeping the relationship "casual" and typically not "exclusive." One of those phrases older people used to seize upon as evidence of the moral degradation of youth, but now a Justin Timberlake/Mila Kunis movie. (*Plus ça change...* )

## ODE TO FEMALE FRIENDSHIP

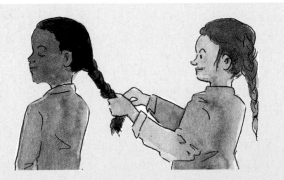

You lock eyes across the party. You love her style. That belt! Where did she get it? She seems so confident. You have to talk to this woman. And you're not surprised to find out she's funny. And she lives in your neighborhood! You've already got brunch plans. Movie plans. You're practically planning a vacation to Colombia together. Even for the single, straight woman, meeting a man at a party holds the possibility of weeks of fulfillment. Maybe months. Maaaaaybe years. But truly connecting with another woman? A lifetime of friendship and support and laughter.

It's shocking that no one is celebrating this. Let's run through the style-section trends, shall we? People are marrying later and later. Women are settling. Or refusing to settle. Either way, our relationships are probably doomed: the divorce rate continues to climb. In any case, it's clear that the notion of lifelong romantic partnership, like the lifelong career, has become passé. But what if the authors of all those hand-wringing pieces about single womanhood were to look around them and realize that it's friendship—particularly friendship between women—that's the lasting, reliable, lifelong relationship we should all be investing in.

This is not to say we should begin planning *Golden Girls*-style retirement scenarios prematurely. It just means it's time to acknowledge that friendship, really good friendship, transcends life phases. And rather than wring our hands about the crumbling pillars of family and society, we should acknowledge how friendship has stayed solid. More than solid—if anything, delayed marriage and increased divorce have conspired to make platonic love a more powerful force than ever. Maybe it's not so ridiculous to talk about buying adjacent apartments. Maybe we shouldn't just joke about adopting a baby together. At the very least, we should stop worrying about dying alone. We mean, *Beaches*.

A liberating concept, nonetheless. The phrase's origins are unclear but many believe Alanis Morissette coined it in her song "Head Over Feet," which has a verse that goes: "You're the best listener that I've ever met / You're my best friend / Best friend with benefits."

### frigid

Insult (around since the 1650s) aimed at women deemed insufficiently interested in sex or unable to reach orgasm from vaginal penetration. Usually used by a man when a particular woman doesn't show interest in sex at any given moment with said man. Another way to police women's sexuality when that sexuality is deemed inconvenient, and attempt to bully a recalcitrant woman into something she doesn't want in order to prove she's not "abnormal."

### frou-frou

Ornate, in the most stereotypically feminine way possible.

### Frye, Soleil Moon (1976–)

Actress famous as a child for her starring role on *Punky Brewster*. Famous as an adult for developing giant breasts, which she then had reduced. (*See also* Brewster, Punky; D cups)

### fuck

Adjective, verb, noun, and general multitasker; Manic Pixie Dream Girl of words. Considered vulgar yet titillating in most contexts. Some would venture that the term is not appropriate language for a lady; tell those people to go fuck themselves. (*See also* Manic Pixie Dream Girl)

### fucksaw

Motorized sex toy, described by the A. V. Club Chicago as "a dildo attached to a reciprocating saw which, when cranked up to full blast, can drive a person to orgasm." In 2011, Northwestern University Human Sexuality professor John Michael Bailey staged an extracurricular demonstration of a fucksaw in action on a female volunteer, and then acted surprised when people went a little nuts about it.

### fug

**1.** Euphemism for "fuckin' ugly" and usually employed to describe a person or her outfit. (Modern usage.) **2.** Euphemism

for "fuck" as seen in early- to midtwentieth-century novels like *Cannery Row* and *The Naked and the Dead*.

### Fuller, Margaret (1810–1850)

Fuller might not be a household name, but her *Woman in the Nineteenth Century* was the nineteenth century's *Feminine Mystique*. Known as a big reader at a time when that wasn't a good thing, Fuller parlayed her skills into a job as the first female book reviewer, like, *ever* for the *New York Tribune*.

### FUPA

Acronym for "fat upper pubic area," aka one's pelvic area and abdomen. We can only assume this makes one's legs the "lower pubic area," and face the "far north pubic area."

### Furstenberg, Diane von (1946–)

Belgian-born Jewish daughter of a Holocaust survivor whose dynastic first marriage (to Prince Egon von Fürstenberg) joined her to a mother-in-law who attended the 1936 Olympics as Hitler's guest. Married mother of two by age twenty-four

turned fashion designer who says she designed her most famous garment, the wrap dress, to facilitate one-night stands. (No zippers, no buttons, no fumbling.) Feminist who says gender-essentialist things like "Feel like a woman. Wear a dress." One of the biggest designers at New York Fashion Week. Optimist.

# G

### gab

What you do with your gal pals while you split a slice of chocolate cake because none of you could bear to be seen eating a whole dessert.

### Gaga, Lady (1986–)

Singer, pianist, songwriter, and performer who combines art, music, and fashion to comment on culture and society. Fan of elaborate couture ensembles often featuring wigs, sky-high platform shoes, and face-obscuring hats, veils, and sunglasses. Gay rights advocate ("Born This Way" song and foundation). Recovering anorexic and bulimic who launched the "Body Revolution" movement to help those struggling with loving their bodies and maintaining a healthy self-image.

Marketing expert with an uncanny ability to make a statement without saying a word. (That meat dress, for instance: can you name another pop star who would have dared comment on the true nature of the music industry's attitude toward women?)

### Gaia

Ancient earth goddess (often referred to as Gaea) who slept with her son, Uranus, and brought forth a bunch of gods and Cyclopes and whatnot, one of whom took a flint sickle she made and used it to castrate his dad. (And then Aphrodite was born of Uranus's testicles. Obviously.) Often invoked by hippies as a synonym for Earth.

### gal

Variant of girl. According to *Merriam-Webster*, its first known use was in 1795, but at the time of this writing, it's virtually impossible to say without picturing a 1950s secretary (*see* GAL FRIDAY) or your grandma. Still, it's quite possibly due for a semi-ironic comeback, à la "lady."

### Galatea

Name for the ivory statue Pygmalion created with his own two hands and then fell in love with *before* the goddess Aphrodite brought her to life, which we're supposed to believe is totally romantic and not at all creepy as fuck.

### gal Friday

Early-twentieth-century jill-of-all-trades, willing to cheerfully perform any task asked of her by male superiors. Well, maybe not *any* task.

### gal pal

Cutesy name for female friends; term of choice for tabloid editors afraid to use the word *lesbian*.

**gamine**

Woman who looks like a Margaret Keane painting, but in a really chic way.

**Gandhi, Indira (1917–1984)**

Politician and the third person—and first woman—to serve as prime minister of India. Born into a long line of politicians: Gandhi was the only child of Jawaharlal Nehru, the leader of the Indian Independence Movement and the first prime minister of independent India; she married Feroze Gandhi in 1942 and served as unofficial personal assistant to her father during his tenure as prime minister. In 1966, Gandhi became prime minister herself and served three consecutive terms in office, remaining in power until 1977. As one of the first female world leaders, Gandhi didn't shy away from displays of traditional strength: she went to war with Pakistan, developed India's nuclear program, and, in Operation Blue Star, authorized the army to enter a Sikh temple and forcibly remove dissidents. "My father was a statesman, I am a political woman," she said. "My father was a saint. I am not." Gandhi won another term in office in 1980, but her life was cut short in October 1984 when she was assassinated by two of her bodyguards in retaliation for Operation Blue Star.

**gangbang**

"A series of acts of often forcible sexual intercourse engaged in by several persons successively with one passive partner," says Dictionary.com. Popular in porn. (Related: the world is horrible.)

**Gap, The**

Clothing conglomerate that once sold basic clothes for the young professional who couldn't afford the higher price point and more tailored, fashion-forward stylings of J.Crew. The first Gap store was opened in 1969, but its heyday as a brand came in the late 1980s, thanks in part to a series of advertisements featuring living and dead celebrities. Gap, Inc., acquired Banana Republic (further up the yuppie scale and more expensive) in 1983 and launched Old Navy (less yuppie, cheaper) in 1994; it added two more brands, Piperlime and Athleta, in the 2000s.

**Garbo, Greta (1905–1990)**

Swedish actress known for retiring in her midthirties and then telling everyone who wanted a piece of her to take a hike. Was pretty terrific playing a series of ill-fated heroines, including Anna Christie, Anna Karenina, Camille, Mata Hari, and Queen Christina.

**Garden of Eden**
Where Adam and Eve lived until a serpent talked the latter into eating from the Tree of Knowledge of Good and Evil, after which she was blamed for everything men ever did wrong. (*See also* EVE)

**Gardasil**

Vaccine that protects against two types of HPV that cause about 75 percent of cervical cancers and two more that cause about 90 percent of genital warts cases in girls and young women ages nine to twenty-six. Medical professionals consider the vaccine safe and advise that girls receive it at some point during their adolescence; conservatives balk at the vaccine's use, claiming that it promotes sexual activity, or, in the words of Minnesota Congresswoman Michele Bachmann, "mental retardation." Studies have not borne this theory out.

**garter(s)**
Article of clothing made to hold up your stockings or, more commonly, to be worn by virginal blushing brides on their wedding days so that the groom may, in full view of the world, reach up under his bride's wedding dress, pull it off (often with his teeth), and then toss it to the awaiting mob of single male guests (just in case anyone is still unclear that her hymen belongs to him). (*See also* BRIDE; WEDDING)

**Gaultier, Jean Paul (1952–)**
French fashion designer responsible for Madonna's cone bra era, among other things.

**gaze, male**
Film theory, proposed by Laura Mulvey's 1975 book *Visual Pleasure and Narrative Cinema*, that posits that a movie camera lens, usually overseen and operated by males, is an inherent mechanism through which men watch women and women watch other women being watched by men. In Mulvey's formulation, men therefore identify as subjects and view women as objects, and women identify as both male heroes *and* their sexual conquests.

**geisha**
Female Japanese performers stigmatized in Western culture as subservient feminine ornaments and in Japanese culture as immodestly enterprising businesswomen who have shirked domestic lives as wives and mothers to study theater, dance, and song.

**gel**
Styling product. The worst modern use of gel has got to be the spiky look, which, combined with frosted tips, basically defined the aesthetic of middle school boys for what felt like the better part of the nineties. For women, it's been a way to battle frizz and actually "tame" curls for much longer. And who can forget the classic scene in *There's Something About Mary*…when there's clearly something about Mary's hair that's not gel…Oh, and *The Jersey Shore*'s Pauly D, who said, "There's no way I'm going to Jersey without my hair gel. Can't leave without my gel."

**gender**
Before 1955: a designation as to whether or not a person was biologically male or female. After 1955: a distinction proposed by sexologist John Money to differentiate between biological sex and social gender, sparking the idea that genitals don't determine clothing style, color affiliations, pronoun identification, sex partners, or chromosomal makeup— freeing men to "get in touch with their femininity," trans people to transition from female to male or vice versa, gender queer people to fuck the binary, and gender traditionalists to try to stop them by denying gender-nonconforming people legislative rights, beating them to death, or submitting them to chromosomal testing before allowing them to compete in sporting competitions.

**genitals**

Sex organs. (*See* JUNK)

**gentleman**

Once, a man of leisure who lacked aristocratic rank but derived influence from his considerable wealth and property. Now, a man who believes that by conforming to a certain code of behavior—opening doors, pulling out chairs, laying down coats over muddied areas, fighting other men on a woman's behalf—he may cultivate a benevolent superiority over women and a competitive advantage over other men. (*See also* NICE GUYS)

**Gerber baby**

Ubiquitous advertising logo of the Gerber Product Company created in 1928 by Dorothy Hope Smith. For over eighty years, the international model of Gerber's self-described "happy, healthy" infancy has been white, blond, and American, which speaks to the enduring power of the original picture and reminds us that

the beauty norms that shape our perceptions start at birth. (The identity of the child in Ms. Smith's sketch—a celebrity? a politician?—remained a mystery until 1978, when it was revealed that Smith's model was her onetime neighbor, Ann Turner Cook, a former English teacher and mystery novelist, who had posed for Smith as a baby.)

**Gevinson, Tavi (1996–)**

Founder, owner, and editor of *Rookie*, an online magazine for teenage girls that showcases writing on topics including body image, fashion, self-expression, education, feminism, and politics. Gevinson became known at the age of eleven when she founded the blog Style Rookie, where she published thoughts mostly related to

fashion. The quality of her writing and her taste, combined with her youth, caught the eye of designers including Miuccia Prada, Rei Kawakubo (Comme des Garçons), and Laura and Kate Mulleavy (Rodarte). She then founded *Rookie* at age fifteen (Ira Glass of *This American Life* helped Gevinson negotiate the deal with her backers) and has published writing by Emma Straub, Sady Doyle, and Sarah Sophie Flicker.

**Gibson girl**

White, narrow-waisted, large-breasted, wide-hipped, long-haired, fashionable, wealthy, fun-loving-but-not-feminist imaginary woman who served as the model of ideal female beauty in early-twentieth-century America—think old-timey Barbie, but with her hourglass figure created by a restrictive lace-up corset instead of expertly molded plastic. A generation of women's anxieties were created by Massachusetts-bred, member of US political royalty, and *Life* magazine illustrator Charles Dana Gibson, whose own wife, Irene, served as a model for the model.

**giggle**

Tee-hee.

**Gilbert, Elizabeth (1969–)**

Writer. Bestselling eater, prayer, lover, and author of several books. Portrayed on-screen by Julia Roberts in the film version of her hugely popular 2006 memoir *Eat, Pray, Love.* Alternately hailed as an inspiring writer and the worst kind of first-world whiner, Gilbert has inspired numerous pilgrimages, with varying results. (It's hard for any single woman to travel abroad nowadays without a disclaimer that her journey has nothing to do with spiritual self-discovery or the pursuit of a book deal.)

**Gillard, Julia (1961–)**

First woman to serve as the prime minister of Australia. In 2010, Gillard was deputy prime minister (the first woman to be that, too) under PM Kevin Rudd. But she wrested the spot from him,

and with that one swift political move, misogyny in Australia ended forever. Just kidding: Gillard was the target of vicious sexism, especially because she wasn't married to her partner and chose to remain in a de facto relationship with him after moving into the official residence. (He was a hairdresser who reportedly blew out Gillard's hair every day.) Gillard won affection and fist pumps from feminists around the world when a fifteen-minute video of her lambasting the opposition leader for his misogyny and hypocrisy about sexism directly to his smug face went viral in 2012.

### Gilman, Charlotte Perkins (1860–1935)

Writer and onetime paradigmatic lonely, imaginative child who transformed from a tomboy into radical feminist. Longed to be different from her mother, a disenchanted musician who had been forced when Charlotte was two to sell her piano, and who could never afford another. As a grown woman, Gilman surrendered her child to the second wife of her ex-husband and harbored guilt about it. Later in life, she married her third cousin in a love match and became a tireless advocate of women's suffrage and socialist causes. A hundred years before Andrea Dworkin articulated it, observed that a prostitute (in the parlance of the age) and a wife held economically similar positions. (*See also* "YELLOW WALLPAPER, THE")

### *Gilmore Girls*

Amy Sherman-Palladino-created drama about a young single mother and her teenage daughter that was a surprise breakout hit for the then nascent WB Network in the early aughts. Lauren Graham, playing mom Lorelai, and Alexis Bledel, playing daughter Rory Gilmore, struck the perfect

balance between the show's two signature characteristics: witty, rapid-fire dialogue and cozy, huggable warmth. It didn't hurt that pros Melissa McCarthy and Kelly Bishop played Lorelai's best friend and her snooty but practical mother, respectively. How could you not want to live in Stars Hollow, where there was a fire in every fireplace and a hilarious pop culture reference on every tongue? Unfortunately, after a 2006 contract dispute, Sherman-Palladino and her writer-husband Daniel left the show, which killed it within a year. (*See also* McCARTHY, MELISSA)

### gin

For purists, the only acceptable basis for a martini. For everyone else, alcohol to be combined with tonic and ice. And consumed with pizza.

### Ginsburg, Ruth Bader (1933–)

Second female justice ever to sit on the US Supreme Court, after being appointed by President Bill Clinton in 1993. Much earlier in her career, Ginsburg was the first woman on both the *Harvard* and *Columbia Law Reviews*, and the first tenured female professor at Columbia Law School. She cofounded the journal *Women's Rights Law Reporter* and the ACLU Women's Rights Project, for which she was chief litigator in the 1970s. She also raised two kids, stayed married to the same man for fifty-six years (until his death in 2010), and survived two bouts of cancer. NO BIG WHOOP.

## girdle

Restraining device worn underneath clothing to support the buttocks, hips, waist, and/or breasts and to give a streamlined appearance to an outfit. (*See also* CONTROL TOP; CORSET; SPANX)

### girl

A term for a child or adolescent woman, often adopted by adult women to avoid taking on the negative cultural connotations that pile up as they age and are sucked of all fun, robbed of their sexualities, and relegated to the mother role.

## girlfriend

A close female friend or sex partner. Fittingly, the title of Justin Bieber's debut single for his over-eighteen, pseudo-Timberlakey career incarnation.

## girlie, girly

Stuff girls are supposed to like—soft, pink, ruffled, glittery, laced, squealing, shining, and otherwise set apart from the normalized accoutrements of the world of adult men. (*Don't see also* BOYIE, *because it doesn't exist*)

## girlie mags

Men's magazines featuring scantily clad women, a publishing tradition that's stretched from the French cheesecake of the early 1900s through the painted pinups of World War II and into the stunt stripping of the modern era, where struggling mags like *Playboy* and *Hustler* offer million-dollar prizes to damaged starlets for baring all at their lowest points—the literary equivalent of crying during sex.

## *Girls*

Cringe-, praise-, and fury-inducing Emmy Award–winning television show created by and starring the Emmy-nominated actress, writer, and director Lena Dunham. *Girls* premiered on HBO in 2012 and was widely hailed as "the new *Sex and the City*" because it was about four female friends, one of whom was kind of a writer, living in New York City. As it turned out, *Girls* was far darker and more complicated than *Sex and the City*, a troubling hand-drawn graphic novel to its predecessor's bright, sparkly cartoon. (As its name suggests, is also a whole lot younger than its predecessor: twentysomethings Hannah, Marnie, Jessa, and Shoshanna are or are about to be post-college.) Dunham, her semiautobiographical Hannah, and her friends elicit fury in cultural commentators because they are privileged and live in a nearly melanin-free version of New York City. They elicit cringes because despite all that, plenty of viewers see themselves in Hannah and her friends. And Hannah and her friends screw up, a lot, and often with mortifying consequences. (*See also* DUNHAM, LENA)

### Girl Scout

Member of an association of young girls who don green skirts, sashes, and berets and are socialized to be model citizens through training in first aid, sport, art, craft, and survival, for which they accumulate various insignia. Better than the Boy Scouts because they accept gays, trans people, and atheists, but not without their traditional gender hangups—one academic study of Scouts badges found that Boy Scouts' awards are more focused on science, and Girl Scouts', art; Boy Scouts', solitary badges, Girl Scouts', communal ones; Boy Scouts', stoicism, Girl Scouts', playfulness; Girl Scouts', literary pursuits, Boy Scouts', practical ones; Boy Scouts', careers, Girl Scouts', hobbies.

### Girls Gone Wild

Franchise created by Joe Francis in 1997 that is best described by Ariel Levy in the first chapter of her book *Female Chauvinist Pigs: Women and the Rise of Raunch Culture*: "If you ever watch television when you have insomnia, then you are already familiar with *Girls Gone Wild*: late at night, infomercials show bleeped-out snippets of the brand's wildly popular, utterly plotless videos, composed entirely from footage of young women flashing their breasts, their buttocks, or occasionally their genitals at the camera, and usually shrieking 'Whoo!' while they do it." (*See also* LEVY, ARIEL)

### Givenchy, Hubert de

Audrey Hepburn's designer. Swoon.

### glamorous

Beautiful in a rich way.

### Glamour magazine

Condé Nast–owned women's magazine founded in 1939 that covers issues like fashion, body image, sex, relationships, and celebrity. Less offensive than *Cosmopolitan*, more mass market than *Vogue*. (*See also* COSMOPOLITAN; COVER LIES; MARIE CLAIRE; VOGUE)

## glass slipper

Romantic conceit—first proposed by European folklore and Disneyfied in 1950—that proposes an escape route for poor, abused women. Here's how it works. The woman is (a) exceptionally beautiful, (b) in the path of a rich and powerful man at the right time, (c) in possession of a bizarrely specific shoe size, and (d) secretly actually an aristocrat. Apologies, all other destitute ladies!

## *Glee*

Hour-long television program about a ragtag show choir that seemed groundbreaking and adorable in its first season and became steadily more boring and obnoxious after.

## glitter

Sparkles of foil and plastic painted to reflect the light in order to project a superficial and temporary illusion of glamour. Can be painted on with an eye shadow brush and removed with a little bit of rubbing alcohol. Also the name of a roundly panned movie starring Mariah Carey. (*See also* CAREY, MARIAH)

## Gluck (Hannah Gluckstein) (1895–1978)

British painter Hannah Gluckstein—known as Gluck—gained notoriety in the 1920s when she began to wear tradi-tional men's attire. She painted everything from floral arrangements to portraits and designed and patented the Gluck Frame, which was three-tiered and created to blend in with a gallery's aesthetic. (*See also* BROOKS, ROMAINE)

*Golden Girls*
Thank you for being a friend.

### Goldin, Nan (1953–)

Photographer whose "snapshot aesthetic" anticipated Instagram. Enjoyed, among other things, taking pictures of herself in bed. One of Goldin's most famous photographs is of her bruised face after a boyfriend beat her up; she called her series of photographs about that relationship and her friendships of the era *The Ballad of Sexual Dependency*. Has been less than thrilled by the way her aesthetic has been reappropriated as "heroin chic" by perfume and fashion ads: "I find that really reprehensible and evil," she told the *Guardian* in 2002.

### Goncharova, Natalia (1881–1962)

Russian avant-garde artist whose 1909 painting *Picking Apples* sold for the highest price recorded for a female artist in 2007, at which point American newspapers wrung their hands because they'd not heard of her. Was arrested as a pornographer in pre-Revolutionary Russia. Rather liked making people angry. She and her lover cross-dressed and painted each other and paraded out in public this way. Even went topless in Moscow, which we hope happened in summer.

### Goodall, Jane (1934–)

Female primatologist who lives out our collective YouTubed fantasy of living among wild animals. Within the scientific community, best known for showing that chimpanzees are carnivores who can make tools. Her affectionate attachment  to the chimpanzees, however, makes research scientists treat her as a dilettante. Chicks, man: always letting their emotions get in the way of science. Was once a baroness.

### Gordon, Kim (1953–)

Singer and musician. As two thirds of the alt-rock group Sonic Youth, Gordon and bandmate boyfriend Thurston Moore were the bizarro version of Kurt and Courtney: the legendary rock couple that aged gracefully instead of spiraling into tragedy. Gordon and Moore formed Sonic Youth in 1981, married in 1984, had a daughter, named her Coco, established themselves as indie rock tastemakers, then worked studiously for decades, dabbling in art, fashion, and *Gossip Girl* cameos, and quietly separated after twenty-seven years of marriage in 2011.

### Gordon, Ruth (1896–1985)

Beloved American actress best known for her role as the life-loving Maude in the 1971 classic *Harold and Maude*. Gordon's professional career began in earnest in 1915 when she began acting on Broadway at the tender age of nineteen. During the thirties, she was signed to MGM but didn't make a film until 1941, when she starred alongside Greta Garbo in *Two-Faced Woman*. In addition to taking supporting roles in movies, Gordon began writing screenplays and received Oscar nods for the scripts of the Spencer Tracy–Katharine Hepburn vehicles *Adam's Rib* and *Pat and Mike*. Won a Best Supporting Actress Oscar in 1969 for her role as the Satanist neighbor in *Rosemary's Baby*.

### Gosling, Ryan (1980–)

Actor. An early turn as sappy romantic lead in Nicholas Sparks's joint *The Notebook* + an extended off-screen ro-

Hey girl.

Sharpen your pencil—I just got the go-ahead to teach only the works of Octavia Butler from now until I retire.

mance with costar Rachel McAdams + tabloid reports of spontaneous acts of Good Samaritanism, including single-handedly saving a journalist from walking into oncoming traffic + handsome + abs = the popular legend of actor Ryan Gosling, which has conflated his on-screen and off-screen personas into the ultimate sensitive hunk, represented in internet memes that superimpose romantic platitudes over Gosling's face, each beginning with the salutation "Hey, girl." Over the years, Gosling's legend has gained intellectual depth, spawning the memes "Feminist Ryan Gosling" ("Hey, girl. Yes means yes") and "Biostatistics Ryan Gosling" ("Hey, girl: let's forget about casual interference because I can't imagine a pseudo-population without you").

### Gossip Girl

Young adult soap opera on the WB about a group of attractive, wealthy, privately schooled Upper East Side teenagers whose lives are ruled by an anonymous mass texting system for sharing gossip as they fuck, drug, date rape, beat, rob, impregnate, impersonate, marry, defame, and wage clumsy class war with each other and their families. Based on series of young adult novels by Cecily von Ziegesar.

### Grable, Betty (1916–1973)
Actress remembered for her spectacular legs.

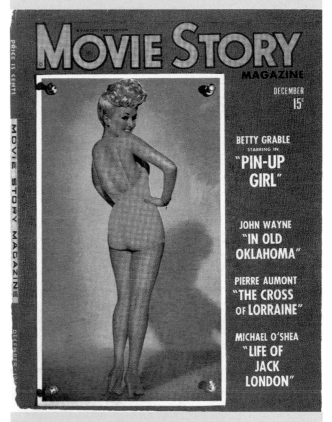

### Graham, Martha (1894–1991)
Influential dancer and choreographer. Of dancing, Graham said, "It's permitting life to use you in a very intense way. Sometimes it is not pleasant. Sometimes it is fearful. But nevertheless it is inevitable." In 1926 she founded the Martha Graham Dance Company, which is the oldest continually performing dance company on the entire earth. And those *cheekbones*.

## Grandin, Temple (1947–)

Activist, professor, and doctor of animal science who revolutionized both animal welfare activism and autism treatment

and visibility. Invented what's known as the "squeeze machine" or "hug box," which is used to calm hypersensitive individuals by applying deep, steady pressure to the body. Her understanding of anxiety and neurology also informed her development of humane livestock corrals, designed to reduce stress on animals being led to slaughter. Grandin's essay "Animals Are Not Things" is still a fundamental text in the philosophy of animal rights. Also, Claire Danes played her in a movie.

## Granger, Hermione

Harry Potter's muggle-born, know-it-all bestie. In a piece for Global Comment, in which she posited that the entire Potter series should really be known as the Hermione Granger series, Sady Doyle wrote:

> "Hermione is not Chosen. That's the best thing about her. Hermione is a hero because she decides to be a hero; she's brave, she's principled, she works hard, and she never apologizes for the fact that her goal is to be very, extremely good at this whole "wizard" deal. Just as Hermione's origins are nothing special, we're left with the impression that her much-vaunted intelligence might not be anything special, on its own. But Hermione is never comfortable with relying on her "gifts" to get by. There's no prophecy assuring her importance; the only way for Hermione to

have the life she wants is to work for it. So Hermione Granger, generation-defining role model, works her adorable British ass off for seven straight books in a row. Although she deals with the slings and arrows of any coming-of-age tale—being told that she's "bossy," stuck-up, boring, "annoying," etc.—she's too strong to let that stop her."

(*See also* ROWLING, J. K.)

## Greer, Germaine (1939–)

Australian firebrand feminist and author of *The Female Eunuch* (1970) whose sheer nerve would be much easier to love

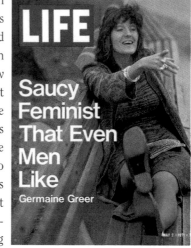

if she didn't hold such reprehensible views about trans people. Tried to keep a trans woman from being elected a fellow of Newnham College at Cambridge in the late 1980s on the grounds that people who were "born" men ought not to hold tenure at women's colleges. Unrepentant about this. Took the opportunity in 2009, during the Caster Semenya affair, to swipe at the "ghastly parody" of trans women. Appeared on the United Kingdom's version of *Celebrity Big Brother* and then appeared to be surprised that the show was cruel and psychologically taxing. In other words, unfortunately now something of a punch line.

## Grey, Sasha (1988–)

Retired adult film star. Over the course of her porn career, which began when she was just eighteen, Grey asked Rocco Siffredi to punch her in the stomach, and she joined an impromptu twelve-person orgy, among other things. She quit porn at twenty-one, having achieved "crossover appeal" in the mainstream entertainment world by aligning herself with porn's most extreme expectations (and talking all about it on *Tyra*). Her screen presence in the face of adversity led to an okay Steven Soderbergh movie, the arty coffee table book industry, and an industrial music career.

### Grey's Anatomy

Initially appealing television show about how to survive in a workplace where you accidentally (no, really!) screwed your boss before you started the job. Later became evidence of the necessity of an ancient law: network dramedies should not, absent exceptional circumstances, be allowed to exceed three seasons. Launched a thousand terrible Katherine Heigl vehicles but gave us Dr. Bailey, so we'll call it even.

### Grier, Pam (1949–)

Actress and undisputed Queen of Blaxploitation films. Grier's bold, violent, take-no-prisoners roles in low-budget seventies movies like *Sheba, Baby*, *Foxy Brown*, and *Coffy*—in which she would wield a firearm while dressed to the nines and spitting lines like "This is the end of your rotten life, you motherfuckin' dope pusher!"—made her a legend in her own time. Quentin Tarantino, who cast her in his 1997 film *Jackie Brown*, considers her the first female action star.

### Griffin, Kathy (1960–)

Actress and comedienne. Longtime supporter of LGBT issues. Left her big Irish American family in Illinois for Los Angeles when she was eighteen, where she worked with the improv troupe The Groundlings. Guest spots on *Seinfeld* and *ER* led to comedy specials and a starring role on *Suddenly Susan*, but her star rose thanks to her *Kathy Griffin: My Life on the D-List* reality show, which documented her attempts to climb her way to the top of Hollywood. No stranger to controversy, Griffin is known to provoke conservatives, Catholics, and thin-skinned actors and actresses.

### G-spot

Highly sensitive area either inside the vagina, inside some vaginas, or inside no vaginas, depending on whom you ask. Named after German gynecologist Ernst Gräfenberg. Everyone started talking about it in 1982, when Alice Kahn Ladas, Beverly Whipple, and John D. Perry published *The G Spot: And Other Recent Discoveries about Human Sexuality*. Thirty years later, we're still arguing over whether it exists.

### G-string

Absolute tiniest piece of clothing a person can wear in public without getting arrested.

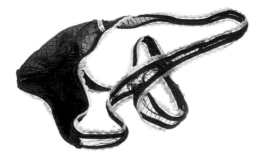

THE ADVANTAGES OF BEING A WOMAN ARTIST:

Working without the pressure of success
Not having to be in shows with men
Having an escape from the art world in your 4 free-lance jobs
Knowing your career might pick up after you're eighty
Being reassured that whatever kind of art you make it will be labeled feminine
Not being stuck in a tenured teaching position
Seeing your ideas live on in the work of others
Having the opportunity to choose between career and motherhood
Not having to choke on those big cigars or paint in Italian suits
Having more time to work when your mate dumps you for someone younger
Being included in revised versions of art history
Not having to undergo the embarrassment of being called a genius
Getting your picture in the art magazines wearing a gorilla suit

A PUBLIC SERVICE MESSAGE FROM **GUERRILLA GIRLS** CONSCIENCE OF THE ART WORLD

### Guerrilla Girls

Anonymous feminist gate-crashers who began, in 1985, as a collective fed up with representations of women in the art world. The final straw was a splashy exhibition at MoMA called "An International Survey of Recent Painting and Sculpture," which, despite casting a wide net, found only seventeen women worthy of inclusion in a show featuring 169 artists. Adding insult to injury was the bold statement that anyone not included "should rethink his career." The group uses "facts, humor and outrageous visuals to expose sexism, racism and corruption in politics, art, film and pop culture" and adopts pseudonyms of dead famous female artists. "We've discovered that ridicule and humiliation, backed up by irrefutable information, can disarm the powers that be, put them on the spot, and force them to examine themselves," they once said.

### Guess jeans

American clothing brand that gave birth to the world's hunger for so-called designer jeans. Claudia Schiffer and a whole slew of other supermodels (RIP, Anna Nicole) have all posed in ads for the brand, and Marty McFly rocked the denim line throughout *Back to the Future*.

### GURL.com

Old-school online mag and message board support system for teen girls to hash out relevant issues, from vaccine schedules to the Booty Pop. Created by Esther Drill, Heather McDonald, and Rebecca Odes, it reached peak relevance as a midnineties zine-y teen reference guide and pioneered the culture of highly formatted, multicolored, animated-GIFed message board signatures. It carries on today under new management, lost in the crush of girl sites that came after it.

### Guthrie, Janet (1938–)

Aerospace engineer turned race-car driver who became the first woman to compete in the Indy and Daytona 500s, disproving the haters who said that a female body didn't fit behind the wheel. "A driver is primarily a person, not a man or a woman, and a great deal of driving is mental," Guthrie said. Though her racing career suffered from a lack of endorsements, forty years later lady drivers are still dealing with an overemphasis on the physical and are often expected to rep companies by slipping out of their jumpsuits, not into them.

### Gypsy

Classic stage mom epic of stage and screen inspired by the life and memoir of innovative burlesque artist Gypsy Rose Lee. Lee always found herself overshadowed by her stage-star younger sister (when she was born, her mother named her Ellen June, then later changed her name to Rose Louise in order to give "Ellen June" to her more talented sis), until she bottomed out on the theater circuit, stumbled into a bordello, found that she could use her powers of wit, charm, and clothing removal to win over crowds, and chose her own name.

### Hadid, Zaha (1950–)

Architect. Although she's secured the highest honors in her field, Hadid is often scrutinized not just for her impressive structures (like her masterpiece, Rome's MAXXI art museum) but for her imposing physical presence. Critic Blake Gopnik called her a "diva" in *Newsweek*, then went on to describe her clothing ("shiny black leggings and a Miyake top"), her eyes ("hidden behind big Prada glasses, Liz Taylor style"), and her voice ("talks with a Lauren Bacall growl") before addressing her work. "If I was a guy they would think I'm just opinionated," Hadid has said in response to the diva charge. "But as a woman, I'm 'difficult.' I mean, I can't change sex." Born and raised in Iraq. Despite the fact that she's won numerous awards, including the prestigious Pritzker Prize, Hadid's gender and provenance have been used against her. As she told the *Guardian* in 2012, "You cannot believe the enormous resistance I've faced

just for being an Arab, and a woman on top of that. It is like a double-edged sword. The moment my woman-ness is accepted, the Arab-ness seems to become a problem."

### hair

Biomaterial that grows on the heads and bodies of mammals; when on female humans, highly politicized, with a short hairstyle signifying feminist abandon, lesbianism, maternity, or advanced age; a long hairstyle signifying femininity; the presence of hair on the legs and armpits signifying man-hating or lack of personal care; and its absence on the genitals signifying the pornification of America. (If you're African American, in addition to all of the above, you may need to spend a great deal of time and money trying to approximate the texture and/or color of white hair, lest you be deemed "too political" to be employed and too unattractive to be loved. But no pressure!)

### Hairspray

**1.** Delightful 1988 John Waters film about civil rights and flying your freak flag. **2.** Broadway musical based on #1. **3.** Dreadful 2007 film based on that, and starring John Travolta in a role originated by Divine, which is basically all you need to know. (*See also* AQUA NET)

### Hamer, Fannie Lou (1917–1977)

Civil rights and antipoverty activist. The youngest of twenty children, Hamer worked as a sharecropper alongside her husband and was forcibly sterilized without her knowledge in 1961 as part of a statewide effort to reduce the state's population of black people. After the activist group SNCC (Student Nonviolent Coordinating Committee) visited her church to promote voting rights in the year 1962, Hamer registered to vote and was consequently terrorized, along with sympathetic family members and friends, by white members of her Mississippi community. In 1963, a year after joining SNCC, Hamer was arrested for voter registration activism, and while in jail she was subjected to a vicious beating orchestrated by the police, which left her with lifelong kidney problems and partial blindness. The following year, in her role as vice chairman of the Mississippi Freedom Democratic Party (a group organized to wrest control of the state's Democratic Party from prosegregation forces), she helped crash the 1964 Democratic National Convention with the demand that the party unseat the all-white Mississippi delegation. "If the Freedom Democratic Party is not seated now, I question America," she announced in a speech to the convention's credentials committee that was taped and broadcast on all the major networks. "Is this America, the land of the free and the home of the brave where we have to sleep with our telephones off the hooks because our lives [are being] threatened daily because we want to live as decent human beings—in America?"

### Hamm, Mia (1972–)

Retired American soccer player who scored 158 international goals during her years as a forward for the US women's soccer team—more than any other player, male or female, in the history of soccer. Many consider her one of the most important athletes of the last fifteen years. Married to former Red Sox shortstop Nomar Garciaparra.

### handbags

What women have to carry because putting pockets in their clothes would mess up the lines. Available in an endless array of colors and designs, and one of the easiest ways to liven up a boring outfit. Also: heavy, a source of consumer stress, and responsible for the death of millions of cows.

### Handler, Chelsea (1975–)

Entertainer, producer, and stand-up comedienne with her own late-night comedy show on E! Entertainment Television, *Chelsea Lately*. Author of four books that have appeared on the *New York Times* bestsellers list. Handler's humor is divisive: some love her bawdy party-girl routine, while others think there's a limit to how many puns you can make about having a dirty mouth and a fondness for martinis.

### Handler, Ruth (1916–2002)

Cofounder of Mattel who invented Barbie and helped develop prosthetic breasts after she had a mastectomy and couldn't find anything she liked. As you do. (*See also* BARBIE)

### Handmaid's Tale, The

1985 novel that even in twenty-first-century America feels more prophetic than fantastic. Imagines a United States reorganized as a theocracy where women are classed by their reproductive capabilities, some as Wives and others as barefoot-and-pregnant Handmaids. Saves the kicker for the Wife character of Serena Joy, theoretically a villain but also a tragic figure, in that she once advocated for family values as a popular evangelist and later finds that she doesn't like having to live by them. Made into impossibly campy movie in which Faye Dunaway continues to channel her nutbar-Joan-Crawford alter ego in royal blue polyester. (*See also* ATWOOD, MARGARET)

### Hanna, Kathleen (1969–)

Feminist and founding member of the bands Bikini Kill and Le Tigre who basically invented zines, the riot grrrl movement, and DIY punk. Seminal figure in the early nineties Olympia, Washington, music scene (along with Bratmobile, Calvin Johnson, and a billion other influential people). (*See also* BIKINI KILL; LOVE, COURTNEY)

### Hansberry, Lorraine (1930–1965)

Best known as the playwright behind *A Raisin in the Sun*, the first play by a black woman ever staged on Broadway, for which she won the Drama Critics Circle award when she was just twenty-eight. Close friends with Nina Simone. Member of the Daughters of Bilitis, the first lesbian civil and political rights

organization in the United States. (According to *Root* reporter Kai Wright, "It's unclear whether Hansberry would have called herself a "lesbian," primarily because she and others were still in the process of developing the concept of such a clearly defined sexual identity.") Married to American songwriter and theatrical producer Robert Nemiroff, who was instrumental in bringing her works to Broadway, Hansberry divorced him shortly before she died of cancer at thirty-four. (*See also* SIMONE, NINA)

*Happiness*

Two kinds of ice cream. Knowing a secret. Climbing a tree. That song had it right, man.

### Harajuku girls

Japanese youth street fashion subculture marked by the frills of gothic Lolita and the sci-fi accoutrements of cosplay ("costumed play"), co-opted by Gwen Stefani in service of her music, live performances, and fashion line. In the early aughts, Stefani recruited four Harajuku Girls, named them after vague concepts—Maya Chino ("Love"), Jennifer Kita ("Angel"), Rino Nakasone Razalan ("Music"), and Mayuko Kitayama ("Baby")—and directed them to dance and pose behind their blonde, white leader at public events, sometimes tittering with hands over their mouths. (*See also* STEFANI, GWEN)

### Hardison, Bethann ("older than Iman")

Fashion industry heavyweight and modeling agency owner. As a model, she was part of the pioneering Palace of Versailles fashion show of 1973 that announced American designers as serious members of the French-dominated fashion industry through its show, using exclusively African American models. As a modeling agent, she has made a point of representing women of color in the modeling and fashion industries and calling attention to the industries' (disturbing) historic disregard for the inclusion of minorities. Also, discovered Tyson Beckford, Veronica Webb, and cofounded, with African supermodel Iman, the Black Girls Coalition. (*See also* FASHION; FASHION MODEL; SUPERMODEL)

## Hardy, Ed (1945–)

Tattoo artist who became famous for his incorporation of American folk imagery into his work, which was then licensed by French jeans designer Christian Audigier for a clothing line that has been seen on the bodies of everyone from Madonna to Britney Spears to Jon Gosselin. Hardy (real name: Don Ed Hardy) and his wife, Francesca, make an estimated $10 million annually from the deal, and in 2009 the fashion conglomerate Iconix Brand Group bought 50 percent of the brand for a reported $17 million.

## harpy

Half-bird, half-woman creatures in Greek mythology who snatched food from King Phineus. Homer, according to one scholar, thought they were "personified storm winds." Hesiod, the Greek poet, thought they were pretty; in our contemporary imagination, they're rather witchlike. Harpy was a favorite insult of Shakespeare's, but the one time an actual harpy appears in one of his plays, it's a man (Ariel in *The Tempest*). Make abundant fun of any man who uses this as an insult.

## harlot

Word of unknown origin, though probably dating back to the thirteenth century or thereabout, that originally referred to a homeless man. Became a political term in the early eighteenth century as London started to clean up the streets. A popular 1732 engraved serial of "moral work" by the painter William Hogarth was called *A Harlot's Progress* and depicted the transition of a girl named Moll Hackabout from an innocent girl into a mistress, followed by her early death from syphilis. Women of the period had scenes from *Harlot's Progress* printed on their fans. Now just a fun word to say.

## *Harriet the Spy*

Beloved 1964 children's chapter book by Louise Fitzhugh about a curious eleven-year-old tomboy and wannabe spy named Harriet who spends her free time canvassing her Upper East Side neighborhood and writing down her observations in a black-and-white composition book. Enjoys brutal honesty, tomato sandwiches, her nanny, Ole Golly, and her best friends, Sport and Janie. Will be damned if she goes to dancing school. Undergoes a crisis of confidence after her notebook is found and mocked by a group of her private school friends, resulting in her brief ostracization. The book, Fitzhugh's first solo effort, was banned from numerous schools and libraries because it was said to encourage children to lie to, swear at, spy on, and sass adults. (*See also* FITZHUGH, LOUISE; NORDSTROM, URSULA)

## Harris, Emmylou (1947–)

Folk-country's great duet partner, best known for backing, interpreting, and elevating the works of dudes like Gram Parsons, Mark Knopfler, Neil Young, and Ryan Adams.

### Harris-Perry, Melissa (1973–)

Professor of political science at Tulane University, author of the 2011 book *Sister Citizen*, and host of an eponymous weekend political talk show on MSNBC. Brought unapologetically intersectional analysis to mainstream television and refers to her show, the place to which she takes her viewers every weekend, as "Nerdland." Harris-Perry's show has had its share of breathtaking television moments; on one broadcast, she lost her cool with a business and finance expert, exclaiming that she had no patience for the Republican talking point that it is "risky" for the wealthy to make large investments. "What is riskier than living poor in America?" Harris-Perry demanded. "Seriously, what in the world is riskier than being a poor person in America?" On other occasions, has spoken frankly and compellingly about being a survivor of sexual assault.

### Harron, Mary (1953–)

Film director and writer. Living proof that you needn't give up your dream of radical feminist filmmaking before your early forties, which is how old she was when 1996's *I Shot Andy Warhol* came out. (Granted, she'd been a respected music and theater critic first.) Turned *American Psycho* into a great movie, despite its basis in Bret Easton Ellis's boring ode to male-shockerdom and a bunch of male fans who complained she hadn't indulged their dreams of seeing women ripped apart in gory detail. Took fourteen years to make *The Notorious Bettie Page*, while never actually meeting her subject after being forbidden to speak to her after a legal conflict. Dated Tony Blair when both were undergraduates.

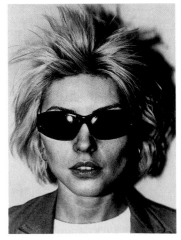

### Harry, Debbie (1945–)

*Playboy* bunny turned punk princess turned (original) *Hairspray* villain so associated with the color of her hair that her iconic rock band—Harry plus four dudes—was forced to launch a marketing campaign clarifying that "Blondie is a group." She hated it. "I was always Blondie," Harry said later. "People always called me Blondie, ever since I was a little kid." On the band's reunion tour in 1999, Harry proposed a new nickname: "I couldn't be Blondie anymore, so I became Dirty Harry." (*See also* HAIRSPRAY)

### Hart, Melissa Joan (1976–)

(*See* CLARISSA EXPLAINS IT ALL)

### Hartley, Nina (1959–)

Sex-positive feminist, author, sex educator, director, and pornographic actress who has starred in more than six hundred adult films. Rising to fame in the 1980s, she was the first adult film actress to advocate and articulate her belief in the legitimacy of the adult film industry.

**haters**
Gonna hate.

### haute couture

Expensive, exclusive, tailored-to-fit, entirely unsustainable fancy French clothing that even designers themselves cannot afford to make. A French thing. (*See also* COUTURE; FASHION)

### Hawn, Goldie (1945–)

Actress and enduring dumb blonde of film who stretched the archetype from the hippie pixie of *Rowan & Martin's Laugh-In* to self-mocking washed-up B-actress of *The First Wives Club*. Mother of nineties It Girl Kate Hudson.

### Hayek, Salma (1966–)

Actress who parlayed a gig in the Mexican soap opera *Teresa* into a star turn in one of the most acclaimed Mexican films of all time, *El Callejón de los Milagros*. Then decamped to Hollywood to toil in a series of disposable Sexy Latina roles (sexy HBO maid!) and more formidable Sexy Latina roles (sexy free-spirited Mexican American photographer who becomes sexily, unexpectedly pregnant with Matthew

Perry's baby!), formed her own production company, painted on Frida Kahlo's unibrow, snagged an Oscar nom, and turned the Sexy Latina stereotype on its head with tongue-in-cheek guest spots in *Ugly Betty* and *30 Rock*.

## health of the mother

Phrase spoken by Arizona Senator John McCain with accompanying air quotes during a discussion of abortion in one of his 2008 presidential debates with Barack Obama. Playing to

a base more conservative than his politically moderate track record would suggest, McCain's sharp veer to the right led to this widely mocked moment when the senator sneeringly explained that abortion exceptions like "health of the mother" were extreme. *Daily Show* host Jon Stewart coined the term *dick fingers* to describe McCain's gesture.

## *Heathers*

1988 cult hit about a group of horrible high school girls, starring Christian Slater and Winona Ryder, who go on a mission to take them out. Will fuck you gently with a chain saw and make your eating disorder passé. Filmed in a time when women actually wore scrunchies outside the house. Depressing to watch now because (a) what happened to Christian Slater and (b) what happened to films this adventurous and salty about teenage girls?

## Heche, Anne (1969–)

Actress and onetime rising star. In 1998, Heche was Harrison Ford's love interest in *Six Days Seven Nights*, one of *People*'s 50 Most Beautiful people, and the other half of the highest-profile lesbian coupling in history. By 2000, she was best known as a crazy bisexual person after being found disoriented on the doorstep of a Fresno farmhouse, claiming to be God and offering to take everyone to heaven with her in a spaceship. Heche later owned

the "crazy" thing, wrote a memoir called *Call Me Crazy*, and said, "I'm not crazy, but it's a crazy life." (*See also* DeGeneres, Ellen)

## Heckerling, Amy (1954–)

Film director. Even by today's standards, celebrated female auteurs are few and far between, so it was unheard of when, at just twenty-eight years old, Amy Heckerling broke into the strictly dickly boys' club of mainstream filmmaking with her major studio directorial debut *Fast Times at Ridgemont High* (1982). The film not only went on to achieve iconic status but redefined a new genre in cinema: the realistic teen movie. Heckerling went on to direct films that made tens of millions of dollars—like *European Vacation*, *Look Who's Talking*, and *Clueless*—and is one of the few female directors in history to enjoy that kind of box-office success. She's also acutely aware of the gender inequality in her chosen profession and how it affects the stories that are told about women. "It's a disgusting industry," she's said. "Especially now. I can't stomach most of the movies about women. [It's like] again with the fucking wedding and the only time women say anything is about men." (*See also* Clueless)

## Hefner, Hugh (1926–)

Hey, Hef, here's some more rope: "The notion that *Playboy* turns women into sex objects is ridiculous. Women are sex objects."—the *Playboy* founder to the *New York Daily News*, 2010 (*See also* Playboy)

## Hellman, Lillian (1905–1984)

Writer mostly remembered as the playwright of *The Children's Hour* and *The Little Foxes* (deservedly so), but in her own time known as a hell-raiser and man-eater, often in the best possible way. Could and did swear blue streaks when women didn't do that and stood up to Joseph McCarthy's House Committee on Un-American Activities. Had a long involvement with Dashiell Hammett, whose literary executor she became; along the way, she also somehow became executor of Dorothy Parker's estate. Famously pronounced a liar by Mary McCarthy on the *Dick Cavett Show*. (Hellman proved herself humorless about the insult by suing.) (*See also* Davis, Judy; McCarthy, Mary; Parker, Dorothy)

### Hello Kitty

Japanese cartoon feline known for her sweet face and ubiquitous bow. Nowadays, her image graces everything from electric guitars to toasters, but the iconic white cat came from humble beginnings: her first appearance was in 1974 on a vinyl coin purse. The fact that she appeals to all ages (yep, you can even find her likeness on vibrators) has helped keep Hello Kitty a moneymaker for decades; in 2009, Sanrio reported $5 billion in sales worldwide. Not too shabby for a cat without a mouth.

### Henderson, Florence (1934-)

Best known as matriarch of *The Brady Bunch* and the Wesson Oil lady from the eighties, she was briefly in the public eye again when Barry "Greg Brady" Williams released a memoir saying they'd gone on a date while working together. But then it turned out to be more like one "Aww, aren't you cute?" meal together. (*See also* BRADY, JAN)

### Henry, Marguerite (1902-1997)

Beloved author of the horse-loving girl's classic *Misty of Chincoteague*.

### Hepburn, Audrey (1929-1993)

British dancer and actress who starred in *Roman Holiday*, *My Fair Lady*, and *Breakfast at Tiffany's* and is still regarded as one of the most elegant women who ever lived. Her frequent collaboration with designer Hubert de Givenchy made her the woman we still want to dress like. She also spoke five

## HEROINES OF YOUNG ADULT LITERATURE

### Meg Murry

Brash, blunt puncher of bullies and bold saver of worlds, Madeleine L'Engle's Meg Murry was introduced to the reader with the author's groundbreaking **A Wrinkle in Time**, wherein she rescues her father and brother from The Black Thing, the source of all evil, by confronting it with the glories of science, math, logic, and literature. Meg also appears in two follow-ups from L'Engle, along with another series of novels featuring her husband, Calvin, and their daughter Polyhymnia.

### Karana

Based on a real person, this **Island of the Blue Dolphins** (Scott O'Dell) heroine survives alone on an island with her dog, Rontu, for nearly twenty years after her tribe leaves for the mainland. As she slowly fortifies herself against elements both mental and psychological, Karana's struggle to survive is about coping with isolation through ingenuity, both physical and mental.

### Ludell

The plucky heroine of the eponymous novel by Brenda Wilkinson and its sequels **Ludell and Willie** and **Ludell's New York Time**, teenage Ludell, raised by her grandmother in the rural South of the 1950s, takes the reader on a both humorous and pointed examination of everything from discrimination, poverty, and hard work to young love, literature, religion, and freedom.

### Louise

Twin to beautiful and talented Caroline in Katherine Paterson's classic **Jacob Have I Loved**, volatile Louise, raised on a small crabbing island in Maryland during WWII, offers a complex and searing portrait of jealousy and a path to adulthood.

### Deenie

The heroine of Judy Blume's eponymous novel is a wannabe teenage model who is resolutely typical and mostly indifferent to her looks. Nonetheless, when she's diagnosed with scoliosis and forced to wear a brace, she must cope with the ramifications on her relationship with her mother, her burgeoning sexuality, her place in her school's hierarchy, and her own view of herself.

### Laura Ingalls

Heroine of the Little House on the Prairie series, Laura is the fractious, funny, complex lens through which the reader learns the equally complex story of frontier America, from killing bears to wagon trains to building the railroads to Indian lands to epic blizzards to prairie schoolhouses. In the series, we meet Laura's two most important partners: beautiful sister Mary, her childhood antagonist and adult

languages and earned a Presidential Medal of Freedom for her humanitarian work with UNICEF, no big deal. (*See also* GIVENCHY, HUBERT DE)

### Hepburn, Katharine (1907–2003)

No relation to Audrey, but also a gorgeous actress who achieved eternal stardom before most of us were born.

Played *Little Women*'s Jo March, *The Philadelphia Story*'s Tracy Lord, and *The African Queen*'s Rose Sayer, among many others.

### heroines

Like heroes, but ladies.

friend, and future husband Manzo (a nickname for Almanzo), who is in both **Farmer Boy**, his own volume, and with Laura and their young family in **The First Four Years**.

### Claudia Kincaid

Who cannot be impressed by and envious of the fearless Claudia Kincaid, an eleven-year-old who escapes her stifling parents to hide in grand style in the Metropolitan Museum of Art with her brother Jamie, eating at the Automat by day and cadging coins from the museum's fountain at night? Her adventure, in E. L. Konigsburg's **From the Mixed-Up Files of Mrs. Basil E. Frankweiler**, becomes a search for the unknown sculptor of a beautiful angel in the museum's collection, leading the two to the mansion of the lady of the title, who contains the closest proof of its provenance.

### Turtle

Of all the motley crew of Ellen Raskin's **The Westing Game**, the underestimated and perennially curious Turtle is the youngest of the inhabitants of Sunset Towers who are mysteriously challenged to solve the mysterious murder of Samuel Westing. Her braids flying behind her as she bikes around the building in search of the answer to the puzzle, Turtle is a reminder that charm and cuteness run a distant second to ambition, intelligence, and generally annoying everyone in pursuit of a worthy goal.

### Harriet M. Welsch

Honestly, some of us prefer Sport and Mouse. But one cannot gainsay the sway of the scribbling investigator of **Harriet the Spy** who, in her search for the answers to life's persistent questions, finds that spying on her neighbors and

friends—to say nothing of keeping a precise notebook of her findings while she eats tomato sandwiches and absorbs the wisdom of her nanny, Ole Golly—is not always the most productive way to find Truth.

### Cathy Dollenganger

No, incest is not best. But apparently when you are locked in a room with your brother and two younger twin siblings for years, left to piece together a motley family in a one-room jail with a staircase to an attic playroom, it's necessary. As the heroine of a purple novel like V. C. Andrews's **Flowers in the Attic** has to be, Cathy is both wholly vulnerable and triumphant as she creeps through the effed-up narrative, setting the stage for three more novels in the trilogy and then endless spin-offs involving self-destructive clans who are equal parts glamour, telenovela, and soft-core porn.

### Marcy Lewis

This bespectacled self-described "blimp," the antihero of Paula Danziger's **The Cat Ate My Gymsuit**, is moved from cynical self-consciousness to rabble-rousing when a beloved teacher gets fired for being a seventies mildly radical intellectual. Marcy's path to freedom, which involves much grousing, also includes getting herself out from under the thumb of her unsupportive (to say the least) father and linking forces with a future love interest, Joel, who is less interested in her extra pounds than in her mind.

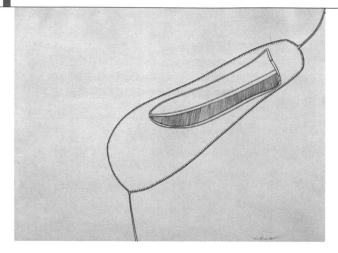

## Hesse, Eva (1936–1970)

Artist. Escaped Nazi Germany, moved to New York, watched her parents' marriage fail, grappled with the aftermath of her mother's suicide, then pioneered postminimalist art with her abstract expressionist sculpture. She did all of this before the age of thirty-four, when she died of a brain tumor. Posthumously, she did even more: inspired the feminist art movement, which was just coming into consciousness at the time of her death in 1970.

## heterosexuality

**1.** Being sexually attracted to people of the opposite gender, assuming there are only two. **2**. What everyone in this culture is assumed to be unless they have a nonstereotypical gender presentation and/or constantly remind people that not everyone is heterosexual. **3.** A sexual orientation. No more, no less.

## Hewitt, Jennifer Love (1979–)

Actress who's so genuinely bubbly (and, it must be said, busty) that she's managed to become famous despite never having been in anything good, ever. Seriously. Look it up. In 2007 Hewitt bitched out the media for calling her "fat"—but lest you think she's actually got subversive opinions about body positivity, let it be known that she is also a vocal fan of vajazzling. (*See also* VAJAZZLING)

## HGTV

Home and garden television network that manages to dramatize the most banal reality television programming possible—everyday people considering purchasing property for *House Hunters*, a show a former participant later revealed as a sham.

## Hill, Anita (1956–)

Brandeis University professor and author who entered the history books in 1991 when she testified that then Supreme Court nominee Clarence Thomas had sexually harassed her when he was her supervisor at the Department of Education and Equal Employment Opportunity Commission. During Thomas's confirmation hearings, the Senate Judiciary Committee savaged Hill, "impugning everything from her competence to her sanity to her sexuality," according to a 2011 *Newsweek* article. Although Hill passed a polygraph test and Thomas declined to take one, he was confirmed. Thomas became a creepy, right-wing Supreme Court justice, and Hill became a feminist icon who mostly chose to keep a low profile over the next two decades, although she wrote and spoke frequently about racism and gender discrimination. Hill was thrust into the spotlight again, in 2010, when Thomas's wife, Virginia, left her a bizarre voice-mail message asking that she "consider an apology sometime and some full explanation of why you did what you did with my husband." Hill's response to ABC News: "I don't apologize. I have no intention of apologizing, and I stand by my testimony in 1991." A year later, she told *Newsweek*, "I think we let go of anger bit by bit. To me, the best way to do that is to think about what my contribution can be, to make sure this doesn't happen to other people. The larger goal is both gender equality and racial equality, because both racism and sexism contributed to my being victimized."

## Hilton, Paris (1981–)

Sorta-model, maybe-billionaire heiress, reality television scourge, unwitting sex-tape participant, and
nightclub regular whose dubious
cultural products—signature phrase
"that's hot," signature pose of limp
hand on jutted hip, signature sex
move of taking a phone call, plus
some shoes and perfumes—have
made her millions of her own.

## Hinton, S. E. (1950–)

Writer born Susan Eloise Hinton who by the age of seventeen
had penned the definitive YA coming-of-age-novel on 1960s
greaser tweens, despite unacceptably being a female. Her
publisher truncated her first and middle names to achieve a
more macho abbreviation that could convince tween boys
and adult book buyers to accept her story, which she titled
*The Outsiders*. (So far, 8 million or so of them have done so.)
"I don't mind having two identities," her publisher, Random
House, quotes her as saying. "And since my alter ego is clearly
a fifteen-year-old boy, having an authorial self that doesn't
suggest a gender is just fine with me."

## hipster

Identifier claimed by no one but freely subjected on any
person more Navajo-printed, leather-jacketed, asymmetrically
hairstyled, unshowered, ironically racist, Pitchfork-reading,
warehouse-dwelling, amateur-mandolin-playing, or neon
than you.

## ho

Perjorative term for a woman. According to Ludacris's "You's
a Ho," a ho engages in "ho activities, with ho tendencies" and
"ho energy to do watcha do, blew watcha blew, screw watcha
screw." Really, a ho refers to any woman the speaker wishes
to denigrate as promiscuous.

## Hobbes, Miranda

*Sex and the City*'s resident manhating short-haired cynical
feminist attorney who—this close to a Very Special Abortion
Episode—turned into maternal long-haired softie Brook-
lynite when she canceled her appointment at the last minute
and decided to raise the results of her one-night stand with
one-balled ex-boyfriend Steve. Doomed a generation of
women who are dedicated to and successful in their jobs to
being "such a Miranda." (*See also* BUSHNELL, CANDACE; SEX
AND THE CITY)

## Hoch, Hannah (1889–1978)

Artist. As the token woman in the German Dada movement,
Hoch incorporated dystopian images of the feminine into her
absurdist collages.

## Hoffs, Judy

Lone female lead character on the best "baby-faced cops go
undercover in high schools, because of course they do" show
of the late eighties and early nineties, *21 Jump Street*. Played
by Holly Robinson Peete (then minus the Peete), Judy was
also one of three leads of color for most of the series; that the
show's "hot chick" was also smart and African American was
never presented as an issue, although there were rumors that
Fox nixed a first-season romance between Hoffs and Johnny
Depp's Tom Hanson as too controversial. Twenty-odd years

later, when the genuinely groundbreaking, if painfully earnest, *21 Jump Street* was remade as a crappy feature film comedy, Robinson Peete made a cameo as Hoffs, but this time the female lead was a young, blonde, white girl. Yay, progress. (*See also* PEETE, HOLLY ROBINSON)

### Hoffs, Susanna (1959–)

(*See* BANGLES, THE)

### Hole

Lipstick-smeared, torn-hemmed, girl-fronted nineties girl rock band that tore through American girlhood after Courtney Love, burned out on flitting from Portland to L.A. to San Francisco to the UK, working as an actress, a stripper, and a Faith No More singer, put an ad in a fanzine reading "I want to start a band. My influences are Big Black, Sonic Youth, and Fleetwood Mac." The band rocketed Love to superstardom—1994's most mainstream riot grrrl manifesto, *Live Through This*, was hailed as one of the best albums of the year—but her coupling with grunge king Kurt Cobain overshadowed her own work, and when Cobain shot himself that year, rumors spread that Cobain had in fact written Love's album himself. Hole disbanded in 2002, reconnected briefly in 2010 for *Nobody's Daughter*, then called it quits again. In 2012, Love took to social media to declare that "Hole is dead." (*See also* LOVE, COURTNEY)

### Holiday, Billie (1915–1959)

Possibly the most influential female jazz vocalist of all time. Released twelve studio albums and scads of singles and compilations, became famous for her jazz-trumpet-inspired vocal style, and cowrote several heartbreakingly personal songs that became standards. Her past was difficult, and her present was usually difficult, too; she endured childhood rape, poverty, prostitution, drug abuse, domestic abuse, and alcoholism that eventually killed her. But she had a towering impact on the future of music. Six of Holiday's recordings ("Crazy He Calls Me," "Embraceable You," "Strange Fruit,"

"God Bless the Child," "Lover Man (Oh Where Can You Be?)," and the album *Lady in Satin*) have been posthumously inducted into the Grammy Hall of Fame, and four compilations of her music have received the Grammy for Best Historical Album. Frank Sinatra told *EBONY* magazine in 1958 that "every major pop singer in the US during her generation has been touched in some way by her genius," and though he couldn't know at the time, that didn't end with her generation.

### Hollaback!

International crowd-sourced anti–street harassment movement founded in 2005 that allows women to share, via social media, stories about receiving unwanted catcalls and worse. The goal? "For most folks, it's not about catching the turd—it's about having a badass response," the founders say on their website, adding that they believe opening up about street harassment is a safe but also empowering and actionable way to combat creeps who think they have the right to yell "Nice tits, wanna fuck?" at you on your way to the grocery store. (*See also* STREET HARASSMENT)

### Holloway, Joan

"Peggy, this isn't China," the *Mad Men* spitfire once told her coworker. "There's no money in virginity." It turns out there might be in a red hairpiece, some really great office dresses,

and übercompetence, though. Joan started out as the woman who was gonna have it all—the good job, the great husband, the family in the suburbs—and ended up somewhere else entirely. Though she's fictional, she represents a kind of woman that was a mother and/or grandmother to most of us: someone whose smarts and talents deserved better than what the world had to offer. And who knew it. (*See also* MAD MEN; OLSON, PEGGY)

### Holzer, Jenny (1950–)

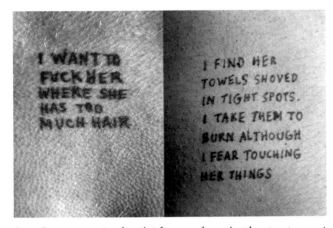

American conceptual artist famous for using language as art in pieces called *Truisms*, printed anonymously on white paper and pasted to buildings and telephone booths all over lower Manhattan. Also inspired one of the best parody Twitter accounts ever, Jenny Holzer's Mom. Sample tweet: **"AN INTENSE LONGING AND THAT ALONE IS NOT A MEANS TO A NEW CARDIGAN BUT YOU GETTING A JOB MIGHT HELP."**

### homemaker

Old-fashioned term for stay-at-home mom. These days, it's outdated and is often considered an insult. You know, because raising kids isn't, like, important or anything.

### homosexuality

Gayness.

### homosexuals

What right-wing religious fundamentalists say through gritted teeth when referring to gay people, because these days you never know who might frown disapprovingly at you if you say "faggot" or "dyke."

### hooks, bell (1952–)

Writer, feminist. You know every really smart thing that every social-justice-minded friend of yours has ever said? Everything that blew your mind open and made you realize that you're either being oppressed or dripping in stinky privilege or (most

likely) both? Yeah, that pretty much all came from bell hooks. hooks (deliberately uncapitalized, because DON'T TELL BELL HOOKS WHAT TO DO, PATRIARCHY) writes about the crippling and often invisible systems of domination and oppression that perpetuate inequalities in gender, race, and socioeconomic status. Fuck yeah bell hooks.

### Hooters

All-American *Playboy* Club for the common man, and, oddly, sometimes his wife, and, awfully, their children. A breast-themed family restaurant—"breastaurant"— founded in 1983 and plagued by celery-heavy wings platters and high-profile legal issues, including the accusation that the chain has disqualified male employees outright, disqualified female employees on the basis of their dimensions, and forced even its suitably pushed-up women to fork over their own funding for the obligatory panty hose that keep its orange hot pants demure. (The panty-hose policy reads in part: "The approved color is Suntan. A darker shade may be worn if the employees [*sic*] skin is darker than the Suntan hose. Lighter shades may not be worn. Tights or other forms of leggings may not be worn. If the panty hose run or snag, they must be replaced with a new pair. Males may not wear panty hose.")

### hormones

Glandular chemicals that tell the human body when to sleep (melatonin), smile (serotonin), fight (adrenaline), flee (noradrenaline), orgasm (oxytocin), secrete milk (prolactin), grow breasts (estradiol), and serve as perennial excuses for freaking out, humping, gaining weight, breaking out, crying, or coming at bros.

### Horne, Lena (1917–2010)

Multiracial singer and actress. White enough to make it as a Hollywood star, black enough to be cast off to the nightclub circuit when she spoke up about how absolutely terribly she was treated. Horne—African American, Native American, and European American—used her musical and acting talents to fight segregation in the USO, lynching in the South, and the Communist scare that ultimately blacklisted her from Hollywood films. "I don't have to be an imitation of a white woman that Hollywood sort of hoped I'd become," Horne said later. "I'm me, and I'm like nobody else."

### hot flashes

One of the special treats that ladies get when they go through the change of life. Basically, it happens in a flash, and your whole body gets HOT. It totally sucks. If you're asleep, it's called a "night sweat." If you are premenopausal and experiencing hot flashes, you should go to the doctor because your pituitary gland might be messed up. Pro tip. (*See also* CHANGE OF LIFE)

### Houston, Whitney (1963–2012)

Actress and singer. Revolutionary in the 1980s—a black woman with a voice deemed fit for pop radio and a face featured on the cover of *Seventeen* and videos in heavy rotation on MTV—Houston leveraged her appeal among white audiences to quietly change the cultural tide on race. As a model, she boycotted South Africa's apartheid government and as an actress formed one-half of *The Bodyguard*'s blockbuster interracial romance and starred in *Waiting to Exhale*'s real-talk about the lives of suburban black women. Then, Houston's

image took a turn—she fell into a violent relationship with Bobby Brown, said "I make too much money to ever smoke crack" on television, and was abandoned by the popular culture she helped build until she died young and alone in a bathroom in 2012, and her former supporters lit up jukeboxes across America with "I Will Always Love You."

### Huffington, Arianna (1950–)

Writer and entrepreneur; accused plagiarist. Pioneered an aggregatorial model of web newsmaking with the *Huffington Post*. With her image, became the human aggregator, slinking into whichever shell happened to be trending at the time—shipping heiress, Republican political wife, California gubernatorial candidate, Rajneesh devotee, Pulitzer Prize–winning new media publisher, forever career opportunist.

### Huffman, Felicity (1962–)

Longtime small-screen actress of *Sports Night* and *Desperate Housewives* and power-couple other-half to William H. Macy who—like a handful of cisgender actresses—courted Serious Critical Acclaim by playing a trans person.

### Hughes, John (1950–2009)

Undisputed king of American teen movies. The coming-of-age films he wrote and directed between 1984 and 1987—notably *The Breakfast Club, Sixteen Candles, Some Kind of Wonderful*, and *Ferris Bueller's Day Off*—rewired the brains of an entire generation of yuppies-to-be and basically made the careers of the precocious, offbeat-pretty young actors known as the Brat Pack. Basically, if you watch those films, *Say Anything*, and maybe *Better Off Dead*, you will at a minimum double your ability to understand the psyche of any lower- to upper-middle-class white person born between 1970 and 1985: guarded, yearning, hyperverbal, self-obsessed, and mildly racist.

### Hunger Games, The

Phenomenon of young adult books and movies—more gritty than *Harry Potter*, less gaslighty than *Twilight*, with an ass-kicking and uncompromising female hero who has so little time for teen girl bullshit that it takes her three books to understand that she's in the center of a love triangle. The basic premise: In a post-apocalyptic America, the citizens are kept subdued by an annual gladiator competition/reality show/Shirley Jackson lottery in which randomly chosen teenagers battle to the death until only one survives. Katniss Everdeen, the protagonist, volunteers for the Games as a substitute for her little sister. She wins them, natch, using a combination of luck, cunning, diplomacy, and videogenic skin, and goes on to start a revolution. Before and after the Games she is also outfitted in a number of pretty dresses, because it's still a series for teenage girls. The first Hunger Games book was published in 2008, and the first movie, starring Jennifer Lawrence, came out in 2012 and broke box office records—$155 million in North America alone—its first weekend of release.

### Hunter-Gault, Charlayne (1942–)

American journalist and civil rights figure. Hunter-Gault was one of the first two African American students to attend the University of Georgia in the wake of *Brown v. Board of Education of Topeka, Kansas*. A Peabody and two-time Emmy winner, she has reported for NPR, the *New York Times*, and *PBS NewsHour*, and she was CNN's Johannesburg bureau chief for half a decade. After a childhood spent experiencing the brutality of segregation and the controversy of desegregation in America, she dedicated much of her adult life to reporting on the effects of apartheid in South Africa.

### Hurston, Zora Neale (1891–1960)

Novelist. Famously lied about her age when she got to Baltimore and wanted to attend high school, saying she was ten years younger than she was. Hilarious, referring to her white

patrons as "Negrotarians." Became an ethnographer of the Caribbean and the South. The latter gave her the idiosyncratic speech patterns that inflected her most important novel, *Their Eyes Were Watching God*. She was forgotten for many years, until Alice Walker revived her reputation in 1975. Really knew how to wear a hat.

## Huxtable, Clair

The most awesome TV mom ever (portrayed with aplomb by Phylicia Rashad) and a funny, smart, and successful lawyer  married to a funny, smart, and successful doctor, living with their five loving and quirky children in a huge Brooklyn brownstone. The stuff dreams are made of—accomplished, fashionable, sophisticated, loved, respected—Huxtable was introduced to America by way of *The Cosby Show* and remains one of very few portrayals of an attractive, successful black woman in pop culture—since the dominant images of black women on TV stick to stereotypical scripts.

## Hyde Amendment

"I certainly would like to prevent, if I could legally, anybody having an abortion, a rich woman, a middle-class woman, or a poor woman," said Representative Henry Hyde in 1976. "Unfortunately, the only vehicle available is the…Medicaid bill." Thanks to the success of a legislative rider prohibiting federal funding of practically all abortions that persists to this day, Henry Hyde managed to make sure he'd be remembered for more than just being a onetime adulterer who led attempts to impeach Bill Clinton for lying about an affair. Exceptions to the Hyde Amendment have fluctuated over the years, but since 1993 they've included rape, incest, and life endangerment, requirements that in fiscal year 2010 only 331 women met. Unless a low-income woman on Medicaid lives in one of the minority of states that use their own funds to cover abortion, she's either on her own or can try the limited coffers of her local abortion fund. As Senator Edward Brooke put it back in the early days of Hyde, "A right without access is no right at all." (*See also* ABORTION; PRO-LIFE)

## hysteria

Word whose Greek roots mean something like "illness that comes from the uterus." (The idea that we're all being driven mad by our sacred wombs can at least be thanked for inspiring the invention of the vibrator.) Still a gendered insult; try calling a man hysterical sometime and gauge the precise degree of scarlet his ears will turn.

### IBS

Irritable bowel syndrome. Every woman we know over thirty is trying to figure out if our generation has an unusually high occurrence of it, or if we're just way more comfortable talking about poop than our mothers were.

### ibuprofen

Over-the-counter painkiller useful for hangovers and cramps.

### ice cream

We all scream.

### iced coffee

For when it's hot out and you need a jolt of caffeine but basically want to drink sweetened milk.

### *I Dream of Jeannie*

Midsixties television series that you loved as a kid, then thought about later and said, "Wow, that was *fucked up*." Barbara Eden is a two-thousand-year-old genie who falls in love with a thirty-something astronaut (Larry Hagman) after he lets her out of a bottle. She then breaks up his engagement so she can stay with him forever as his wife-type thing, even though she always calls him Master and they don't sleep together. This is ostensibly a fantasy, but we're really not sure whose.

### *I Love Lucy*

Classic American sitcom vehicle for the amazing Lucille Ball. (*See also* BALL, LUCILLE)

### image

For women, a highly constructed visual presence based on an impossible set of cultural expectations. As Tina Fey put it in her book *Bossypants*:

> "Now every girl is expected to have Caucasian blue eyes, full Spanish lips, a classic button nose, hairless Asian skin with a California tan, a Jamaican dance hall ass, long Swedish legs, small Japanese feet, the abs of a lesbian gym owner, the hips of a nine-year-old boy, the arms of Michelle Obama, and doll tits. The person closest to actually achieving this look is Kim Kardashian, who, as we know, was made by Russian scientists to sabotage our athletes."

### Iman (1955–)

Regally beautiful supermodel, born in Somalia, photographed for *Vogue* in 1976, founder of her own cosmetics line in 1994 and a Global Chic fashion line for HSN in 2007. Besides being stunning, smart, and charitable, she's been married to David Bowie since 1992. Jealous?

### Immaculate Conception

NOT Jesus's conception, but the conception of the Virgin Mary—which confuses people because the conception mechanism involved intercourse, whereas Jesus's conception made use of the virginity-preserving Sperm of God. The general idea is that Mary was without sin from the moment of fertilization so it was immaculate in that sense. Which might raise interesting questions about abortion and choice and fetal development and the definition of "personhood," except we're talking about Catholicism here, so duh. (*See also* VIRGIN MARY)

### inappropriate

Euphemism for "Knock it off before I kill you." Traditional: "Jim, grabbing my ass as I walk past your desk is highly *inappropriate*." Modern: "Eleanor, get off the table! *Inappropriate!*"

### income

If you're a white woman, about 77 percent of that of a man doing the same job. If you're a woman of color, even less.

### Indigo Girls

Folk-rock duo operating continuously from 1984 through the present, but mostly famous in the 1990s for sweet harmonies, lesbianism, and being the rumored objects of Ani DiFranco's indie-purist scorn. (*See also* DIFRANCO, ANI)

### indulge

According to American marketers, what women do when they eat anything with flavor, especially chocolate.

### infinity dresses

Circle skirts with nine-foot straps that can supposedly be wrapped into countless chic configurations. No one wears them.

### ingrown hair

Something you're happily relieved to find out you actually have after a week of agonizing about herpes.

## inhibitions

Things that usually keep us from dancing on bars, punching people we have to share public transportation with, telling our bosses what we really think of them, and wearing pajama bottoms to cocktail parties. Things that sometimes keep us from approaching attractive people, asking for raises we deserve, and otherwise taking risks that might pay off big in the long run.

## injustice

Holes in the civil and criminal law enforcement system that allow innocent men to be sentenced to death, rapists to rape again, and the NYPD to perform more frisks on young black men in New York City than there are young black men in New York City.

## innocence, innocent

Lacking in worldliness, street smarts, experience, and sex partners—one of the most fucked-up traditional feminine ideals.

## instant gratification

Netflix streaming and a TV dinner.

## instinct

What makes women care for babies instead of leaving them to die. Supposedly.

## insatiable

Capable of consuming limitless amounts of food, drink, or, most often, sex—and a common term for women who like just a moderate amount of those things.

**internet**

The most mind-blowingly fast and effective communications system in history. Don't read the comments section, though.

**Intervention**

Exploitative reality television program that masquerades as a legitimate documentary television program (shaky hand-held camera style) in order to trick people addicted to alcohol, meth, eating, dieting, shopping, plastic surgery, pills, gambling, cutting, or playing video games into exhibiting their addictions for camera crews before ambushing them and demanding they stop engaging in the self-destructive behavior that feeds the ratings for *Intervention*. Few succeed.

**intimate**

**1.** Euphemism for genital. **2.** Euphemism for fucking.

**intolerance**

Euphemism for bigotry, except when preceded by *lactose*.

**In Touch Weekly**

Lowest of lowbrow glossy tabloids that advertises itself as the cheapest celebrity rag on the stand. Just $2.99 keeps readers in touch with developing scoops like "Cellulite at 22" and the final photos of Anna Nicole Smith's son before his death by accidental overdose of prescription drugs.

**invitations**

Websites like Evite have made sending cute ones easy, green, and free, but etiquette mavens, mothers, and paper goods manufacturers stubbornly insist that a proper, mailed version is better.

**Iron Chef**

Competitive reality cooking show that gave us the phrase "Kitchen Stadium."

**ironing**

A method for removing wrinkles from clothing invented in 1882, dooming decades of women to hunch over a scalding piece of metal to make their husbands' work shirts look presentable.

**irritable**

What women are described as when we refuse to suffer fools.

**Islam, Runa (1970–)**

London-based Bangladeshi film artist who's said she favors the medium because "it can re-articulate time. Films from other epochs allow you to go back in time. But so much of contemporary life is also envisioned through film and TV. We remember people we've never met because we've seen them on a screen."

**Israel, Margaret Ponce (1929–1987)**

Cuban-born painter, ceramist, collagist, bamboo artist, and professor who set up a studio in a converted horse stable, lived with a rooster, hens, doves, rabbit, dogs, and cat, and depicted them in her work before being struck and killed by a tractor trailer on Twenty-Third Street at the age of fifty-seven.

**It Girl**

"To have 'It,'" wrote Elinor Glyn in 1927, "the fortunate possessor must have that strange magnetism which attracts both sexes. He or she must be entirely unself-conscious and full of self-confidence, indifferent to the effect he or she is producing, and uninfluenced by others. There must be physical attraction, but beauty is unnecessary." In other words: the It Girl, first personified on screen by actress Clara Bow (in a film called—yep—*It*), is the woman that every man wants and that every woman wants to be. She embodies the spirit of her era with effortless style, grace, sexuality, and confidence and is generally the life of any party (and any party she doesn't attend simply isn't a party worth attending). The It Girl is easily replaceable and has a relatively short shelf life—she burns bright and either flames out, fades away, or reinvents herself as an artist who doesn't need to be the center of attention to draw the world to her work. (*See also* FAD)

## Iturbide, Graciela (1942-)

Mexican feminist photographer who has documented her country's women-run villages, indigenous rituals, sexual subcultures, and contentious northern border. Creator of a famous photograph—titled *Lady of the Iguanas*—that featured a woman who wore on top of her head lizards that she planned to sell as food.

## IUD

Intrauterine device, a highly effective, long-term, reversible form of contraception that unfortunately got a terrible rap in the 1970s, when one make of IUD—the Dalkon Shield—was linked to pelvic inflammatory disease, infertility, and fatal infections. Combine that with the basic squick factor of "Well, what we do is, we stick a metal thing into your uterus and leave it there for years," and American women understandably freaked out. Today's models are quite safe, though, and a hell of a lot more convenient than the pill, lasting up to twelve years.

## Ivins, Molly (1944-2007)

Wickedly funny Texan writer who gave George W. Bush the nickname Shrub and was known for her no-bullshit, genuinely populist, faux-folksy political wisdom. Although barbs like "If his IQ went any lower, we'd have to water him twice a day" made her famous outside Texas, her intelligence and sincere patriotism shone through even her most vitriolic columns. After the 2004 presidential election, Ivins addressed readers who whine, "There's nothing *I* can do about it" in her *Colombus Free Press* column: "If the last election didn't teach you that every vote counts, you may want to consider assisted living. Of course, you don't have as much say in this country as the people who give big money to the politicians—but that can be fixed. As an American living today, your one vote means you have more political power than 99 percent of all the people who ever lived on this planet. Think about it: Who ever had this much power? A peasant in ancient Egypt? A Roman slave? A medieval shoemaker? A French farmer? Your grandfather? Why throw power away? Use it. Leverage it."

# J

### Jackson, Janet (1966–)

Youngest sister of legendary pop singer Michael Jackson, and a legendary pop culture fixture in her own right. Privacy is her middle name. Her last name is Control. No, her first name ain't "baby." It's Janet. Ms. Jackson, if ya nasty.

### Jackson, Shirley (1916–1965)

Writer. You know her as the lady who wrote "The Lottery," that story you read in middle school about a ritual public stoning in a small town. You *should* know her as the author of the equally creepy novels *We Have Always Lived in the Castle* and *The Haunting of Hill House*. Before her unexpected death at forty-eight, Jackson had also published four other novels, two memoirs, four children's works, and dozens of stories in the *New Yorker*, *Ladies' Home Journal*, *Playboy*, *Harper's Magazine*, and *Good Housekeeping*, among others.

### Jacobs, Jane (1916–2006)

Celebrated urban theorist. Though she's best known for planting herself in the way of Robert Moses's plan for New York City, she lived in Toronto from 1968 until her death, in protest of the Vietnam War and its accompanying draft. Was more than willing to belittle men other than Moses.

> "Some men tend to cling to old intellectual excitements, just as some belles, when they are old ladies, still cling to the fashions and coiffures of their exciting youth."
>
> —*The Death and Life of Great American Cities* (1961)

### jailbait

Teenage girl you would like to bang, if only it weren't for those pesky statutory rape laws! Ha-ha-ha! Get it? (*See also* AGE OF CONSENT)

### Jamison, Judith (1943–)

An icon of contemporary dance, Jamison toured the world with the Alvin Ailey American Dance Theater before taking over as its artistic director, securing her role as the most prominent black woman in modern dance.

### *Jane* magazine

Lady mag launched in 1997 by Jane Pratt. Framed as the older sister to Pratt's late, great *Sassy*, *Jane* never quite managed to elicit the same kind of devotional love from its readership, and it folded in July 2007.

## Jasmine

Disney's only Middle Eastern cartoon princess to date, Jasmine is the love interest in *Aladdin* (1992), in which she sang to us about a whole new woooorld where Middle Eastern cartoon princesses are still voiced by blonde white ladies. (*See also* DISNEY PRINCESSES)

## jealousy

The plague of womankind, if you ask romantic comedies, sitcoms, or douche bags. Women are so naturally jealous of each other, we can't be trusted to make true female friends, meet each other's boyfriends, or behave professionally on a consistent basis. In a stunning coincidence, this assumed innate weakness is extremely convenient for folks who would like to control women. (*See also* DOUCHE BAG)

## Jemison, Mae (1956–)

Physician. Dancer. Astronaut. Enrolled in Stanford University when she was just sixteen years old, where she received degrees in Afro-American studies and chemical engineering. Her courses in the latter presented a challenge. "Some professors would just pretend I wasn't there," she told the *New York Times* in 2000. "I would ask a question and a professor would act as if it was just so dumb, the dumbest question he had ever heard. Then, when a white guy would ask the same ques-

tion, the professor would say, 'That's a very astute observation.'" In September 1992, Jemison became the first African American woman in space when she traveled aboard the space shuttle *Endeavour* as a science mission specialist. (The mission, STS-47, was devoted to experiments in the life and material sciences, including studies of weightlessness and motion sickness.) "I always assumed I'd go into space," the Arkansas-born Jemison told an audience at Denison University in 2004. Applying to be an astronaut, she once said, was preferable to "waiting around in a cornfield, waiting for ET to pick me up or something."

### Jennifer

Singer-songwriter Mike Doughty, born in 1970, wrote a song with the lyric "I went to school with twenty-seven Jennifers." If you were born in the 1980s, replace with "Jessica." (If you were born in the 1990s, stop reminding us how old we are.)

### Jersey

Very comfortable fabric; Bruce Springsteen's home state.

### *Jersey Shore*

Much-bemoaned popular MTV reality series. Within weeks of its 2009 premiere, the show wasn't just the punch line of late-night hosts' monologues—its cast members were guests on the couches. Seemingly overnight, they became pop culture icons, and their nicknames (Snooki, the Situation, JWOWW, etc.) and slang (smash, GTL, guidette, etc.) became part of the American lexicon. And, because everybody watched it (the show earned network-like ratings), everybody had something to say about it, from New Jersey governor Chris Christie (he was not a fan, insisting that it perpetuated misconceptions about the state) to Barbara Walters, who featured the cast on her Most Fascinating People list in 2010. Controversy around the show was not hard to come by: some took offense at the cast's liberal—and favorable—use of the word *guido*, which UNICO denounced as an ethnic slur. Later, it was the show's depiction of misogyny and its dual subversion of and conformation to stereotypical gender roles. (The men wax their eyebrows and cook dinner, while the women drink heavily and fistfight.) As for sexual behavior, critics all seemed to be in agreement that it was normal for guys to sleep around but disgusting for women to do the same.

### Jett, Joan (1958–)

Singer-songwriter. Walking advertisement for the restorative powers of eyeliner. Also a testament to levelheadedness in the face of ridiculous, literal-rock-star fame. Sang the iconic version of "I Love Rock 'n' Roll" and has thus forever given rock a female voice it has to contend with. Looks like she survives on champagne and cigarettes but actually doesn't drink and is a proselytizing vegetarian. Had the good sense to turn down Steven Tyler when he, by his own admission, sat outside her hotel door naked and begging.

### jewelry

Accessory, often expensive—especially if there are diamonds involved. Most often, but not exclusively, worn by human females.

### Jezebel

Baal-worshiping Phoenician princess who married Ahab, the king of Israel, convinced him to convert, and had a bunch of Jewish prophets killed before she was tossed out a window and left to be eaten by dogs. Apparently, she prettied up her face with cosmetics before the defenestration, which led to the cultural association of her name with women who wear makeup, i.e., prostitutes. Yeah, we don't completely get it, either—but by 2007, it was snappy shorthand for a woman of ill repute, which made it the perfect name for Gawker Media's new ladyblog.

*Bette*
**DAVIS**

**JEZEBEL**

*with*
HENRY FONDA  GEORGE BRENT
MARGARET LINDSAY  DONALD CRISP  FAY BAINTER

### Joan of Arc

*Question, in six parts:* Is Joan of Arc, fifteenth-century martyr/saint and French heroine, more like Sarah Palin: a boundary-crossing, alarmingly militaristic up-front-and-in-charge lady from humble beginnings who seeks divine guidance for the good of her country and the thwarting of its enemies? Or is Joan of Arc more like Sarah Palin: an obvious tool used by the real power brokers to drum up peasant support for an agenda that was killing lots of peasants? Did Joan of Arc receive direct, personal guidance from God? Or did she claim to have done so because that's what you had to do in the 1400s if you were a woman and you wanted to be listened to and taken seriously? Does this make it all the more galling that today all such women are lumped together under the heading Women Mystics? Have the various literary, musical, and artistic works devoted to her served as a Rorschach test for prevailing notions about gender and war at the time said works were created?

*Answer:* Quite possibly.

### Joan of Arcadia

Two-season CBS drama about Amber Tamblyn talking to God. Bafflingly, it was kind of good.

### Joan of Snark

Fictional parody website. On February 25, 2011, the Tina Fey–created NBC sitcom *30 Rock* aired an episode about feminism that was inspired by Jezebel's critical examination of the role of women (or lack thereof) at *The Daily Show*. In it, Jezebel was fictionalized as a website called "Joan of Snark," described by Liz Lemon as a place "where women talk about how far we've come and which celebrities have the worst beach bodies." OMG SHE KNOWS US. (*See also* DAILY SHOW, THE; FEY, TINA; LEMON, LIZ; MUNN, OLIVIA)

### Johnson, Lady Bird (1912–2007)

Wife of Lyndon Baines Johnson, thirty-sixth president of the United States. She is best known for her beautification efforts in DC and around the country.

### jojoba

Desert shrub whose oil was the magic beauty elixir of the seventies and eighties.

### Jolie, Angelina (1975–)

Actress and activist. Alleged archenemy of Jennifer Aniston, temptress of Brad Pitt, and talented home wrecker; collector of adopted children from poverty-stricken nations; object of tabloid speculation about her "thin" frame; red carpet stunner; former wife of Billy Bob Thornton and Jonny Lee Miller; biological mother of three of Brad Pitt's children (one of whom is thought, according to controversy-desperate tabloids, to be a tough little lesbian); onetime wearer of vials of blood; UN ambassador for something peace-related that makes it technically impossible to hate her; and possessor of enviably full lips that are more natural than not. In 2013 Jolie announced that she had undergone a double masectomy in order to lower her chances of contracting breast cancer, which took the life of her mother, Marcheline Bertrand, in 2007.

## Jones, Grace (1948–)

Jamaican-born singer of new-wave club hits and bond hench-woman opposite Roger Moore. Jones's real talent is her severe, elaborate, and androgynous look, which she honed in the 1980s with the aid of artist and stylist Jean-Paul Goude, sporting elements like an early flattop, nun hats, crustacean eyewear, and yin-yang headpieces, which helped to dictate trends for decades of drag queens, derivative pop starlets, and even straight guys. Ignore or imitate her at your own peril. Jones once clawed at an interviewer's face for not looking at her enough, and said of Lady Gaga: "I've seen some things she's worn that I've worn, and that does kind of piss me off."

## Jones, Sarah (1973–)

Performer and poet whose one-woman show *Bridge & Tunnel* was produced off Broadway by none other than Meryl Streep. Refreshingly covered a wider array of New York City experiences than just the upper-middle-class white one. When MTV came to her to offer her riches and fame she turned them down. "I want to hear everything," she told *Vanity Fair* in 2004, "but I'm tired of hearing just one thing."

## Jong, Erica (1942–)

Bestselling author of the feminist classic *Fear of Flying* (1973). Jong's debut novel, still the book for which she is best known, is about a woman whose marital malaise drives her to explore her sexual fantasies outside her marriage. *Fear of Flying* introduced into the lexicon the phrase "zipless fuck,"

sex between two people who don't know each other and between whom "there is no power game. The man is not 'taking' and the woman is not 'giving'...The zipless fuck is the purest thing there is," Jong wrote, "and it is rarer than the unicorn." No reason to stop looking for it, though, right?

## Jordan, Barbara (1936–1996)

First black Texas state senator post-Reconstruction (her most recent predecessor was elected in 1883). First black woman in the twentieth century to be voted into the House of Representatives from the Deep South. First black woman to give the Democratic National Convention's keynote address. (At the time of her death, the first black woman buried in the Texas State Cemetery.) But tellingly, Jordan was often the almost-first, her political career stunted by the time in which she lived (and in which we still do). She was *almost* chosen as Jimmy Carter's running mate; *almost* appointed to the Supreme Court by President Clinton; and *almost* an openly lesbian black politician in 1960s Texas, until campaign handlers advised her to keep her long-term partner private on the trail.

### journalist, lady

**1.** Thin, pretty, thirty-something woman, usually white, who is sometimes allowed to handle the less-hard-hitting television news. **2.** A writer capable of covering fashion, celebrity gossip, and the mommy wars, but who's better off leaving long-form investigative reporting to more qualified colleagues. **3.** Just like a regular journalist, only without all the awards. **4.** A smart, tough woman who loves news enough to fight through all that bullshit and do it anyway.

### Joyner, Florence Griffith (1959–1998)

Track and field athlete often called "the fastest woman of all time." Although she won five Olympic medals and set records in the one hundred and two hundred meters, FloJo is also remembered for her flamboyant style: brightly colored extralong (often six inches!) fingernails; long, full mane of hair; one-legged fluorescent spandex running tights.

### Juicy Couture

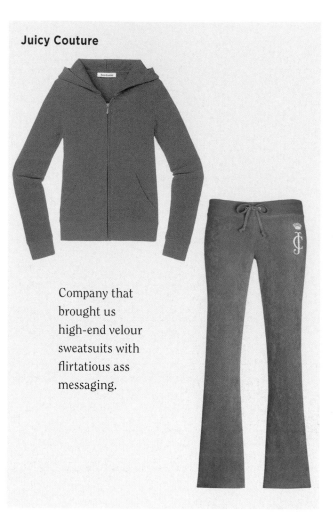

Company that brought us high-end velour sweatsuits with flirtatious ass messaging.

### Juliet

**1.** Teenage girl who, over the course of a few days, makes out with a hot guy at a party; finds out he's among her family's sworn enemies; secretly marries him; finds out he killed her cousin and has been banished from town for it; processes that for five minutes before she bangs him anyway; concocts a plan to fake her own death and get entombed for a little while, until hubby and his bestie can spring her; wakes to find he's poisoned himself because he thought she was actually dead, and therefore plunges a dagger into her own chest. **2.** Still shorthand for "best girlfriend ever" in Western culture, four hundred years or so after Shakespeare created her, in case you were wondering whether we really need feminism.

### junk

You know, parts. (*See also* GENITALS)

*Juno*

2007 film about a pregnant teen that everybody loved until they
got sort of sick of Diablo Cody. (*See also* Cody, Diablo; Page, Ellen)

# K

### Kabbalah

Strain of Jewish mysticism popularized by Madonna in the midaughts and briefly adopted by a whole bunch of lesser celebs—Britney Spears and Jerry Hall via the L.A.–based Kabbalah Centre.

### Kael, Pauline (1919-2001)

Our Lady of the Sharp Pen and endless appetite for trashy movies. Locked horns with Joan Didion. Came into her career as a film critic in her thirties, proving that not everything belongs to the young. A breath of unpretentious fresh air in a formerly patrician profession. Worshipped by Quentin Tarantino and Wes Anderson, along with an army of mostly male acolytes known as the Paulettes. Known to be brash and abrasive in person. A proto-Jezebel if ever there was one.

### Kagan, Elena (1960-)

The fourth female justice appointed to the US Supreme Court. Previously first female US solicitor general, first female dean of Harvard Law School, White House domestic policy adviser (during the Clinton administration), and, at age thirty-one, a University of Chicago law professor.

### Kahlo, Frida (1907-1954)

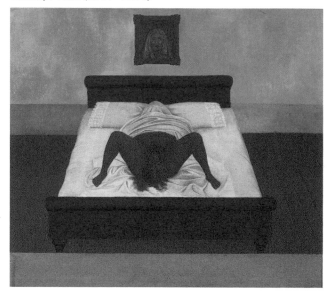

So much more than her unibrow. Self-taught Mexican painter who used herself as her primary subject, crafting haunting, surreal images of her own internal struggles. After a childhood battle with polio left her right leg disabled and a bus accident in 1925 left her in a full body cast (and reproductively sterile), Kahlo began painting brightly colored portraits from her sickbed as a way to grapple with the pain of illness, depression, and infertility. She married (and then divorced, and then remarried) the tempestuous muralist Diego Rivera but proceeded to engage in affairs with both men and women, including the Communist revolutionary Leon Trotsky. Shortly before she died after a year of severe illness, she wrote in her diary: "I hope the exit is joyful—and I hope never to return." But she did return—after a period of obscurity, she became famous again in the 1980s as a beacon of feminist painting, and now her work appears in nearly every major museum, a Julie Taymor film, and, of course, Google doodles.

## Kaling, Mindy (1979–)

Indian American writer, actor, and comedienne.

## Kardashians

There's a reality show, and there are three pretty sisters whose names all begin with *K*, and Bruce Jenner is married to their mom, and a whole lot of people seem to care a whole lot about what those three sisters do, say, wear, endorse, and give birth to, for reasons that are totally inscrutable to the rest of us.

## Karr, Mary (1955–)

Poet and memoirist. Blunt. Texan. Her first memoir, *The Liars' Club* (1995), detailed her troubled and yet quip-filled family history. Known as a bit of a ballbuster, particularly where it came to her relationship with David Foster Wallace. Karr told Wallace she "hated" his first novel because she didn't like pyrotechnics and tried to get him to write from the heart. For all that hubris she still has a wonderful way of criticizing herself: "I'd spent way more years worrying about how to look like a poet—buying black clothes, smearing on scarlet lipstick, languidly draping myself over thrift-store furniture—than I had learning how to assemble words in some discernible order," she wrote in *Lit* (2009), her most recent memoir.

## Kate & Allie

Eighties sitcom featuring two divorced best friends living in a NYC brownstone and raising their families together. Strong, independent women, Kate and Allie—played by Susan Saint James and Jane Curtin—seemed open to remarriage but were perfectly happy without husbands or boyfriends, depending on each other, their kids, and their own inner strength to make things work.

## Keds

Brand of shoewear. If you call sneakers sneakers, you have Keds to thank; they popularized the term in 1916, thanks to the shoes' quiet rubber soles. They haven't always been cool; once seen as the cheaper alternative to Converse, they've made a comeback among the young and hip. Onetime Hollywood It Girl Mischa Barton got her own line of them in 2006. Now the shoes are so trendy that Taylor Swift has jumped on the bandwagon. (Of course, Jennifer Grey in *Dirty Dancing* and half the casts of *Saved by the Bell* and *Full House* were way ahead of the curve.) (*See also* It Girl)

## Keene, Carolyn

A pseudonym used by the myriad of writers who authored the Nancy Drew books. The first of these was Mildred Wirt Benson, who moved on from ghostwriting to become an amateur archaeologist and pilot planes. Some women really get to live the dream. (*See also* Drew, Nancy)

### Kennedy, Flo (1916–2000)

Feminist icon who rocked cowboy hats and pink sunglasses while holding a middle finger to the system. Started out by threatening to sue Columbia Law School if they denied her entrance based on her gender, then took on women's equality and civil rights cases. Kennedy's advocacy was both colorful and controversial—she once protested Harvard's lack of women's bathrooms by hosting a "pee-in" on the historic Cambridge, Massachusetts, campus. Kennedy flowed between social movements, agitating for change both within the activist community and in society at large. Her enduring advice: "Don't agonize. Organize."

### Kewpie

Doll based on Rose O'Neill's turn-of-the-century comic illustrations for *Ladies' Home Journal* and known for their

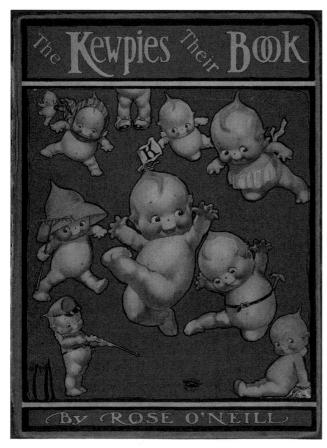

nudity and evil smile side-eyes. Have been haunting children's dreams since 1913.

### Kick-Ass

2010 movie based on a comic by Mark Millar and John Romita Jr. most notable for giving us the foulmouthed, ruthless, and completely fucking awesome eleven-year-old assassin, Hit Girl.

### kickass summer, have a

Universal yearbook wish for people you don't really care about.

### killjoy

Someone with no sense of humor who hates fun and ruins everything and needs to lighten up and/or get laid—e.g., a feminist who thinks mutual consent should be a prerequisite for sex *every time*.

### kindred spirit

The less giggleworthy alternative to "bosom friend" in *Anne of Green Gables*.

### King, Billie Jean (1943–)

Champion tennis player. Beat a guy whose name everyone has now forgotten in a famous "Battle of the Sexes" match in 1973. Huge advocate of Title IX legislation, not least because when she won the 1972 US Open, the prize was $15,000 less than that of the male champion. One of the first profssional athletes to be identified as gay. (Didn't get to choose her own coming-out; in 1981, a former partner filed for palimony and the press found out.)

> "It's funny how when a woman does something they always think we only affect half of the population, and people will come up to me and say thanks for what you did for women's tennis all the time, and I know they'd never say that to a guy. If they walked up to a male, they would just say thanks for what you did for tennis."
> —to NPR, 2008

## kiss

(*See also* FRENCH-KISSING]

## kiss off

Ten is for EVERYTHING, EVERYTHING, EVERYTHING, EVERYTHING.

## kitchen

Are you a lady? Then why aren't you in there right now?

## kittens

Gateway drugs of Crazy Cat Ladies the world over. (*See also* CRAZY CAT LADY; CUTE)

## Klein, Naomi (1970–)

Activist, writer, and Canadian who never finished her university degree—she was too busy writing books and magazine articles. Most famous for *No Logo*, her jeremiad against consumer culture and its co-optation of political action. Worried that real liberation was being overlooked in favor of superficial gender- and race-representative advertising or, in other words, that feminism was being co-opted to market crap. Which, judging by all those United Colors of Benetton and

Nike "let me play sports" ads that saturated the 1980s and '90s, wasn't half-wrong.

## knickers

If you were an American girl in the early 1980s: billowy, usually corduroy pants that ended in a tight hem just below your knee. If you're from an English-speaking country other than the US or Canada: undies. Either way: what you get in a twist when you start feeling like you might need to kill some joy. (*See also* KILLJOY)

## knitting

Hobby practiced strictly by grandmothers until the whole third-wave, DIY, crafty thing happened in the nineties. (*See also* CRAFTING, CRAFTS)

## knocked up

**1.** Preggers. **2.** To be awakened by someone rapping on a door, if you're a British person trying to entertain American visitors with a good story about wacky linguistic differences. **3.** Judd Apatow comedy about a one-night stand resulting in #1 (as well as the memorable line, "Was your *vagina* drunk?") criticized by shrill humorless feminists for its insufficient discussion of abortion, dramatic attractiveness asymmetry of lead actors Katherine Heigl and Seth Rogen, and overall portrayal of female characters as shrill humorless feminists. (*See also* APATOW, JUDD)

## knockers

A little less classy than hooters; a little classier than jugs.

## knockoff

Cheap copy of some desirable high-end item that becomes middlebrow and undesirable anyway as soon as the cheap copies arrive.

## know-it-all

(*See* GRANGER, HERMIONE)

### Knowles, Beyoncé (1981–)

Singer, actress, designer, entrepreneur. Buoyed by an amazingly strong voice and persistent, costume-designing stage mother, Beyoncé Knowles led R&B girl group Destiny's Child to a reported 50 million record sales worldwide. She then moved on to an insanely successful solo career, a pretty damn successful acting career on the side, a collaboration with Lady Gaga, and marriage to Jay-Z, with whom she produced a darling baby girl named Blue Ivy. If she has not actually achieved human perfection yet, she's working on it. In the meantime, she's certainly the closest thing we have.

### Knox, Shelby (1986–)

Feminist activist. Subject of *The Education of Shelby Knox*, a 2005 documentary about her efforts to get a sex ed program started in her Texas high school. Onetime roommate of mentor Gloria Steinem.

### Komen, Susan G.

Breast cancer charity clearinghouse responsible for raising billions of dollars to "fight breast cancer" since 1982. Target of critics who argue that the organization takes advantage of donors' good intentions and promotes a culture of frilly corporate feel-goodery rather than actual investigations into the causes and prevention of breast cancer. In 2012, the organization's reputation took a hit when it ceased funding Planned Parenthood's breast health program on the grounds that the women's health provider was under congressional investigation. Later, it was revealed that high-ranking Komen officials, one of whom had run for governor of Georgia on a strongly antiabortion platform, had pushed the foundation to pull its support from Planned Parenthood. Funding was returned to PP, but the damage to Komen's reputation had been done.

### Kopple, Barbara (1946–)

American documentary filmmaker and two-time Oscar winner. Kopple, who worked with the documentarians Albert and David Maysles (*Grey Gardens*) before striking out on her own, won her first Academy Award for her 1976 film *Harlan County, USA*, which documented a violent and protracted Kentucky coal miners' strike. Her other films have continued to focus on social justice and freedom, including 2006's *Shut Up and Sing*, which documented the fallout faced by the Dixie Chicks after their lead singer criticized then president George W. Bush. "With documentaries you have no idea what's going to happen, you don't know what's around each turn," she told the *Atlantic* in 2011. "You don't think, 'Is this an issue about free speech?' You just know that it's a story about people."

### Krasner, Lee (1908–1984)

Abstract American painter whose critical eye is said to have strongly influenced the work of her husband, the better-known Jackson Pollock. Despite her limited collection (Krasner liked to cut up her paintings after she was done with them), she remains one of the few women to have had a retrospective exhibition at New York's Museum of Modern Art.

## Kruger, Barbara (1945–)

Conceptual artist who works largely in bold blocks of text questioning materialism, desire, and popular culture through a feminist lens. Kruger has said, "I work with pictures and words because they have the ability to determine who we are and who we aren't." In one notable work questioning the pledge of allegiance titled *Untitled (Questions)*, Kruger asked:

> "Who is free to choose? Who is beyond the law? Who is healed? Who is housed? Who speaks? Who is silenced? Who salutes longest? Who prays loudest? Who dies first? Who laughs last?"

## Krupnik, Anastasia

Bespectacled, spunky, and imaginative protagonist of a delightful series of children's books by author Lois Lowry. Red Sox fan. Daughter of a poet (her dad) and artist (her mom). Maker of Likes and Dislikes lists, a literary conceit that seems inspired by the scribblings of her predecessor in highly opinionated girl heroines, Harriet M. Welsch of *Harriet the Spy*. Older sister to brother Sam. Owner of a bust of Sigmund Freud and a number of science-project gerbils. Lover of warts. (*See also* HARRIET THE SPY; LOWRY, LOIS)

## Kyi, Aung San Suu (1945–)

Burmese freedom fighter, Nobel Peace Prize winner, and the closest we have ever come to a female Gandhi (or Martin Luther King Jr.). Started out as a dissenting politician, working for democratization. From 1989, has been held under house arrest, on and off, and separated from her children and from her British husband, whom she was not permitted to see before he died of cancer. Asked by an interviewer if she had been mentally or emotionally captured by the SLORC, the military junta that held her under arrest, she whipped out an example from George Eliot's *Middlemarch*:

> "There was a character called Dr. Lydgate, whose marriage turned out to be a disappointment. I remember a remark about him, something to the effect that what he was afraid of was that he might no longer be able to love his wife who had been a disappointment to him. When I first read this remark I found it rather puzzling. It shows that I was very immature at that time. My attitude was—shouldn't he have been more afraid that she might have stopped loving him? But now I understand why he felt like that. If he had stopped loving his wife, he would have been entirely defeated. His whole life would have been a disappointment. But what she did and how she felt was something quite different. I've always felt that if I had really started hating my captors, hating the SLORC, and the army, I would have defeated myself."

## Kylie

Na na na, na na na na na na, na na na, na na na na na. (*See also* EARWORM)

### label

Something that lets everyone else know roughly or exactly what you spent on a desirable, exclusive item. Like sweatpants that say *Juicy* on the ass. (*See also* JUICY COUTURE)

### labia

Anatomical structures, in the form of folds of skin and tissue, that help make up the external female reproductive organs (namely the vulva) and protect the urethra, clitoris, and vagina. Every set—there are two, labia majora and labia minora—is unique in character. Just like a snowflake!

### labor

**1.** Work. **2.** The act of giving birth. You connect the dots.

### lactation

(*See* BREASTFEEDING)

### lad

British term for either *male child* or *fratty shitbag*.

### ladies

Your grandmother preferred being called a "lady" because it implied refinement. Your mother preferred to be called a "woman," because she felt the distinction between "lady" and "woman" was dumb, old-fashioned bullshit. You started ironically referring to yourself and your female friends as "ladies" somewhere in the late nineties or early aughts, at first because you felt weird referring to yourself as a "woman," and then later out of habit. By the time your daughters are grown, it will seem like a dumb, old-fashioned bullshit term again.

### ladylike

A type of behavior some people think women should aspire to even though the refinement thing went out during your great-grandma's time.

### landing strip

Bit of pubic hair left on the body after a bikini wax. (*See also* BIKINI WAX; BRAZILIAN WAX)

### lang, k.d. (1961–)

Singer. Still the only Canadian butch lesbian pop-country singer on the scene, as far as we know. Has kept that haircut in the face of a decade's worth of jokes and criticism, which suggests an admirable degree of stubbornness. Has been out

of the closet for most of her career, even at a time when that was a dicey prospect for an entertainer

> "Women send me their 8-by-10s and their measurements, but the last thing I want to do is sleep with a fan. Because k.d. lang the performer is so much cooler than me. Not that there's really a difference, but as a lover I'm not as self-assured and cocky and invincible as she is."
>
> —to *Rolling Stone*, 1993

**laptop**
Lucky for ladies, they come in pink.

**Lassie**
Beloved midcentury fictional collie, always played by male dogs in the movies and on TV, because even canine actresses can't catch a break.

**latchkey kid**
What a ton of us were in the 1980s, after our parents got divorced and/or our moms went back to work. The media fretted for us on a regular basis, but coming home to cartoons, snacks, and no supervision was less traumatic for children than the experts imagined.

**Latina, wise**
(*See also* SOTOMAYOR, SONIA)

**laughter**
According to heterosexual dating wisdom, the best women engage in this freely, but never inspire it.

**laundry**

**Lauper, Cyndi (1953–)**
Grammy-winning singer, songwriter, actress. Outspoken feminist, gay icon, and LGBT rights activist. Lauper started writing her own music at age twelve and spent the seventies performing in New York–based cover bands before damaging her vocal cords and taking a year off. She and her band Blue Angel (named in homage to a Marlene Dietrich film) released a critically acclaimed but commercially unsuccessful album in 1980. Her first solo album, *She's So Unusual*, featured her iconic hit "Girls Just Want to Have Fun," written by Robert Hazard but altered to be "less misogynist" by Lauper. Her wild success with the album—including the popular ode to female masturbation "She Bop"—led to her featured vocals in the aid song "We Are the World," a turn as the musical director of the *Goonies* soundtrack (and the two-part video for her own song "The Goonies 'R' Good Enough"). Married the actor David Thornton in 1991, gave birth to their son in 1997. Won an Emmy for her guest work on the sitcom *Mad About You*, appeared in a handful of movies and television shows (including a turn as a psychic in *Bones* in 2009). (*See also* "SHE BOP")

**lazy**
What you clearly are if your house isn't spotless, your meals aren't homemade and delicious, your kids aren't superstars, your boss ever depends on other employees, or your husband isn't getting his knob polished on a regular basis.

**leading lady**
Actress with the biggest role in a film or play; too often means "simpering girlfriend of the complex character you're actually supposed to care about."

***League of Their Own, A***
1992 movie directed by Penny Marshall, starring Geena Davis, Tom Hanks, Lori Petty, and Madonna, and based on the true story of the All-American Girls Professional Baseball League (AAGPBL), which was founded during World War II to fill the void left when all of America's professional ballplayers shipped off to war. The movie centers on two sisters, Dottie (Davis) and Kit (Petty), who are recruited from their Oregon farm to play for the Rockford Peaches. Their ragtag team of players from all over the country, sort of led by their washed-up alcoholic former pro Jimmy Dugan (Hanks), make it all the way to the first women's (oh, fine, *girls'*) World Series. Along the way, there are awesome training montages, sisterly heart-to-hearts, funny jabs at old-timey sexism, swing dancing, 1940s fashion and makeup, and serious sexual tension between Geena Davis and Tom Hanks. It is, in short, the perfect movie.

**Lebowski, Maude**

As played by Julianne Moore, the avant-garde feminist artist daughter of the *other* Jeffrey "The Big" Lebowski in the 1998 Coen Brothers movie *The Big Lebowski*, Maude first hires men to assault Jeff "The Dude" Lebowski and take his rug, and then sleeps with him in an effort to conceive a child. "My art," she tells The Dude when she meets him, "has been commended as being strongly vaginal, which bothers some men."

**lech**
Charmingly out-of-date term for "disgusting, usually old, pervert," perhaps due for a comeback.

**Lee, Harper (1926–)**
Author. Lee's first and only published work, *To Kill a Mockingbird*, has sold more than 30 million copies since its release in 1960 and remains a staple of high school curricula. The semiautobiographical story of a motherless girl, Scout, her brother, Jem, and her father, Atticus, it is one of the decisive works of fiction on racism in America, along with *Invisible Man* and *Black Boy*. Known familiarly as Nell, Lee, who avoids the media but is a very public member of her community in her hometown of Monroeville, Alabama, placed childhood friend Truman Capote in the novel as her neighbor Dill.

**Lee, Nikki S. (1970–)**

Korean American artist who works principally in photography and film. Her photographs usually involve an elaborate getup that toys with external signs of identity—in her first series, *Projects*, she dressed up as an Ohioan, a drag queen, and a hip-hop fan, among others. Doesn't usually take the pictures herself, more often serving as the subject of them. Made a film about how she really had two personalities, one academic and withdrawn, the other a girl-about-art-town, praised as a star and party lover.

**legislature**
The branch of government that decides what women can do with their bodies.

### legitimate rape

Phrase coined by Republican Missouri Senate candidate Todd Akin in 2012 after a reporter asked him why he didn't support an exception in the case of rape in his proposed abortion ban. ("If it's a legitimate rape, the female body has ways to try to shut that whole thing down," he explained.) The startling combination of an earnest belief that real rape victims excrete a mystical form of contraception and that pregnant rape victims are just lying sluts who make the whole thing up went on to define Akin's campaign. His popularity plummeted and he went on to lose to incumbent Claire McCaskill, who won with 55 percent of the vote. (*See also* "RAPE-RAPE")

### leg warmers

### Leibovitz, Annie (1949–)

Portrait photographer whose work was a staple of publications like *Rolling Stone* and *Vanity Fair* in the 1970s and '80s (and the woman behind the lens for those infamous "Hollywood" editions of the latter). Leibovitz was also partners with Susan Sontag for many years before Sontag's death. In recent years, it has been discovered that Leibovitz is unfortunately less talented at managing her vast wealth than at taking photographs, and she almost lost the rights to all of her work.

### Lemon, Liz

Semiautiobiographical character created and portrayed by Tina Fey in Fey's award-winning comedy *30 Rock*. Known to her coworker Tracy Jordan as LL and in poorly translated Chinese as Lesbian Yellow Sour Fruit, Liz is head writer for a terrible sketch comedy show, *TGS with Tracy Jordan*, on a failing network, NBC. She's romantically and sexually dysfunctional, eats her feelings, and once had a prescription drug–induced haze in which she mistook an adolescent girl for Oprah Winfrey. Lemon became something of a symbol of well-intentioned white lady feminism, an issue that the show explored on many occasions, as well as an emblem of the frustrating Hollywood tendency to pretend that good-looking women— Tina Fey is hot, you guys—are not good-looking. Lemon, a high-powered woman who has worked long and hard to carve out a career for herself, often struggles with work-life balance, a conflict best illustrated when she is given the choice between stopping the man she loves from leaving town and eating the world's most delicious sandwich, and she refuses to choose. Stuffing her face and frantically swallowing, she cries, "I cab hab ib ALL!" (*See also* FEY, TINA; JOAN OF SNARK)

### Lennox, Annie (1954–)

Singer. First rose to fame as one-half of the British pop duo The Eurythmics (her onetime boyfriend, Dave Stewart, comprised the other half), but over the last thirty years, Annie Lennox has become one of those people who's just consistently fucking awesome, no matter what she's doing. Breakout solo album (1992's *Diva*)? Check. Album of covers, in which she sings a bunch of famous men's songs better than they did (1995's *Medusa*)? Check. Triumphant professional reunion with Stewart? Academy Award for Best Song, plus four Grammys, eight Brit Awards, and too many other honors to count? Human rights and AIDS activism? Sexification of androgynous fashion? LGBT icon status? Star of a video in which a young Hugh Laurie and John Malkovich do her bidding? Victoria and Albert Museum exhibit of cool stuff she's collected over the years? Voice like a motherfucking angel? Check times a billion.

> **lesbian**
> Female who is sexually attracted to and loves other females. Or, in popular culture, a woman who playfully makes out with other women for the benefit of horny dudes.

### lesbian shitasses

What Scott Baio's wife, Renee, called the writers and readers of Jezebel in an impassioned Facebook post following her husband's great Twitter meltdown of 2009. When called out on the blatant homophobia of that statement, Renee Baio did not say, "Some of my best friends are lesbians." She did, however, say, "True fact: I have lesbian friends that couldn't be nicer." (*See also* BAIO, SCOTT)

### letters

Writing platform in which women, long boxed out of literature, were allowed to cultivate the art of prose, as long as they kept it between themselves and their direct recipients. Even when the forms collided into the epistolary novel, notable books of letters between "women" were still largely written by men: see Claude Barbin's 1669 book *The Love Letters of a Portuguese Nun* and Honoré de Balzac's *Letters of Two Brides*.

> **lettuce**
> Along with celery, a dieter's best friend. That vaguely mean, passive-aggressive friend who's never blatantly offensive but always makes you feel kind of bad about yourself.

### Levitt, Helen (1913–2009)

Self-taught American documentary photographer and filmmaker whose photographs of kids laughing, fighting, exploring, and destroying are some of the finest images of urban children's street culture ever taken. During the 1930s and '40s, the New York–born Levitt, who also worked as a film editor, keenly but unsentimentally documented the public performances and private dramas of kids as they played on the streets and sidewalks of the city's poorer neighborhoods. "She recognized real, formative moments in a child's life," museum curator Arthur Ollman told the *Los Angeles Times* in 2004. "She saw the dignity of children, they were not strange 'other' beings to her." Levitt herself was not so sanguine. "People think I love children, but I don't," she told the *New Yorker* in 2001. "Not more than the next person. It was just that children were out in the street."

### Levy, Ariel (1974–)

Staff writer for the *New Yorker*. Best known as the author of *Female Chauvinist Pigs: Women and the Rise of Raunch Culture*, the book that reignited the Sex Wars in the mid-2000s. Not a big fan of mainstream porn or the *Girls Gone Wild* phenomenon, Levy worried that young women don't really enjoy their newfound empowered sexuality. Any protestations they might make to the contrary are the result of a false consciousness. Jury's still out on that one. (*See also* GIRLS GONE WILD)

**E. LEWIS. SCULPTOR.**

### Lewis, Edmonia (ca. 1840-1907)
Sculptor. As a black orphan during the Civil War, Lewis with her family wove and sold traditional baskets in New York to survive. Studied art at Oberlin, one of the few colleges in the country that accepted black women. Technically. As a student, was accused of poisoning two fellow students (they recovered) and was dragged and beaten by a mob in retaliation before she was acquitted and allowed to pursue her career as a sculptor. She eventually took off for Italy, where she applied the neoclassical style to busts of figures from the Civil War, abolitionism, and classic literature.

### liberal
Person with dangerous left-wing political opinions, such as "women are human."

### libido
You're a lady; you don't need to worry about that.

### librarian
Highly educated person who oversees a library collection and facility. Or, in popular culture, a quiet brunette with glasses, hiding a slammin' body and a libido set to eleven under that cardigan and tweed skirt.

### lightweight
Derogatory term for a person who gets drunk quickly, often deployed by skeevy guys trying to convince tipsy women to have another.

### Lin, Maya (1959-)
American architectural designer and artist whose Vietnam Veterans Memorial was initially controversial because its design was seen as "unconventional" (a less sexist way of saying it was the world's first war memorial to be shaped more like a vagina than a dick).

## Lincoln, Mary Todd (1818–1882)

Wife of the sixteenth president of the United States. Well-educated daughter of a wealthy Kentucky family. Though she was first courted by Stephen Douglas—whose senatorial debates with Abraham Lincoln in 1858 set the stage for Lincoln's eventual presidency—she instead fell in love with Lincoln and married him over the objections of her family. She gave birth to four sons, but only two survived childhood, and only one outlived her. Suffered from migraines and depression much of her adult life, and historians speculate—based on reports of her temper and outbursts—that she may have suffered from bipolar disorder. After her husband was elected president, she became one of the most reviled figures in wartime Washington, due to her supposedly coarse "Western" manners, her slave-state heritage, her unwillingness to "act like a lady" and defer to men in conversation, and her spending on the White House and its social events. After the death of her son William in 1862, she became so depressed that even her husband worried for her mental health and she curtailed entertaining and dabbled in spiritualism, which garnered her even more opprobrium from official Washington—though Lincoln continued to proclaim his love for her. When Lincoln was shot in 1865 while attending a play with her, she accompanied him to a rooming house across the street only to be barred from his deathbed by War Secretary Edwin Stanton. Her depression deepened even further after her son Thomas died in 1871, and her surviving son, Robert, had her committed to an asylum in 1875 after she displayed erratic behavior, including spending sprees and an attempt to escape a nonexistent fire through a window. Two months into her incarceration, she managed to smuggle letters to her lawyer and the resulting publicity ended with her release to her sister's care, estrangement from her only living son, and her taking off for Europe lest he try to commit her again. (*See also* FIRST LADY)

### lingerie

### liposuction

Surgical removal of fat from the body. Ew.

### lipstick

Cosmetic used to pigment lips, scrawl messages to other women on bathroom stalls, or falsely assert the wider economic importance of the beauty-industrial complex—Estee Lauder chairman emeritus Leonard Lauder claimed the "lipstick index" to be an inverse indicator of the strength of the economy, meaning that women buy more lipstick when times are tough (the claim has since been disproven). Similar claims have been made about women's hemlines and nail polish. (*See also* MAKEUP; SEPHORA)

### liquid courage

### literature

Read by women, who support 80 percent of the fiction market. Controlled by men, who write 80 percent of books reviewed by the *New York Review of Books* and 80 percent of the reviews of those books.

### Little House on the Prairie

Series of autobiographical novels by Laura Ingalls Wilder about her childhood living in, and moving around, the wilds of the midwestern US in the late nineteenth century. The books, which have been in print continuously since they began being published in the 1930s, were the basis for a popular television show of the same name, which ran from 1974 to 1983. (*See also* LITTLE HOUSE BOOKS)

# LITTLE HOUSE BOOKS

Perhaps the most famous children's series of all time, the autobiographical *Little House* books, by Laura Ingalls Wilder, follow Laura Ingalls, a girl growing up in the late 1800s, and her family: Pa, a fiddle-playing, bootless dreamer; the far more conservative and lovely Ma; sisters Mary and Carrie, brother Charles, and Grace, the youngest, as they make their way across the exploding America of the late 1800s, the most exciting character of all.

As traveler Pa takes the Ingalls family from the Big Woods of Wisconsin across young America, the series engraves indelible images in its readers' brains: a young Laura and Mary tossing around the bladder balloon of a pig in *Little House in the Big Woods*; the girls learning to housekeep in a house carved out of a stream's banks in *On the Banks of Plum Creek*; Pa's working on the railroads in *By the Shores of Silver Lake*; the family's foray into Indian territory— and its consequences on the people—in *Little House on the Prairie*. (Let us not leave out, of course, the appearance of Laura's rival, the blonde and be-curled Nellie Oleson.)

But the series serves a dual purpose. First of all, it presents one of the first heroines who is both lovable and flawed. Laura is spirited and sulky; brave yet heedless; brown-haired while Mary is blonde and well-behaved. She's the first foil to a far more perfect character, revealing Mary to be more a boring character than one to aspire to. (As the girls grow, Mary's character deepens as well as Laura's, and the sisters grow into a close friendship, particularly after a fever leaves Mary blind.)

More mature readers will notice that the series also tells a more complex story: the story of the formation of America. The Ingalls family goes from log-cabin settlers to the first inhabitants to kick Indians off their lands, build the railroads, settle in a town supported by the trains they've built, farm and trade, and create a country driven by commerce instead of self-sufficiency. By the same token, Laura is one of the first women to grow outside the home: as a schoolteacher, she is part of the creation of the skilled middle class of the rapidly growing center of America, as well as a world in which women work outside the home.

But that history is also rocky—the Ingalls have their crops wiped out by locusts; survive near continuous blizzards for seven months; and are part of the ruthless process that strips the lands from Native Americans in the oft-violent name of progress.

Most important, the seemingly genial Little House series is a reader's exposure to the grand complexities of life, both emotional—the relationship between two divergent sisters; economical—Pa's efforts to balance his adventurous spirit with his family's prosperity; communal—the family's move from an isolated cabin to what becomes a thriving metropolis in which they play a key part; and elemental—the family's exposure to the exigencies of the weather, the land, and all of its inhabitants. There's no mistake that these are the joys, challenges, and problems of America still, and that is why readers return to the series: to learn about our past, but also to learn about ourselves.

**locket**

**Logan, Lara (1971–)**

South African foreign correspondent for CBS and *60 Minutes* who has covered embassy bombings in Nairobi, wars in Kosovo, and crimes against humanity, including her own: While covering the Egyptian Revolution in February 2011,

she was sexually assaulted in Tahrir Square by a crowd of men who ripped off her clothes, dragged her through the square, and raped her "with their hands" for half an hour. When a group of women and Egyptian soldiers crowded around her to fend off the mob, Logan was rescued, then airlifted back to the United States where she recovered in a hospital and eventually reported on her own story, breaking the culture of silence around assaults on female reporters who report on conflicts around the world.

## logical

Opposite of emotional, according to a man who's losing an argument to a woman.

## Lohan, Lindsay (1986–)

(*See also* CHILD STARS; PUBLIC TRAIN WRECKS, CULTURE OF; WALKING PUNCH LINES; WASTED POTENTIAL)

## *Lolita*

1955 Vladimir Nabokov novel widely misunderstood to glorify pedophilia when in fact one is supposed to marvel at what a creep this Humbert Humbert guy is. The beauty of the book's language belies an ugliness of subject.

## loofah

Excellent in a bubble bath. Not as good in a pita pocket, no matter how much hummus and tahini you put on it. Take note, Bill O'Reilly.

## loose woman

Opposite of a lady, according to your grandma.

## Lopez, Jennifer (1969–)

Actress, singer, and dancer most famous for, in no particular order: playing the late singer Selena; her butt; her engagement to Ben Affleck; her marriage to and divorce from Marc Anthony; dating P. Diddy when he was just Puffy; *American Idol*; making jumpsuits her thing. (Oh, and that Versace dress from the 2000 Grammy Awards.) Lopez is actually a pretty good actress, especially in *Out of Sight* with George Clooney. (*See also* ASS)

## Lorde, Audre (1934–1992)

Self-described "black lesbian feminist mother lover poet" who famously wrote "The Master's Tools Will Never Dismantle the Master's House," as well as numerous other influential feminist essays. From the 1960s forward, she was a strong voice calling leaders of the women's movement, such as Betty Friedan, to task for focusing almost exclusively on problems affecting white, middle-class, heterosexual women and thus marginalizing the concerns of women of color and queer women. (She was equally hard on African American men in the civil rights movement who ignored their own male privilege and women's voices.) "The oppression of women knows no ethnic nor racial boundaries, true, but that does not mean it is identical within those differences," she wrote in an open letter to Mary Daly in 1979. "Nor do the reservoirs of our ancient power know these boundaries. To deal with one without even alluding to the other is to distort our commonality as well as our difference."

## loser

Cultural dropout who has failed so spectacularly at the widely accepted metrics of life success that she begins to identify positively with her failure.

## loudmouth

Woman with opinions.

## love

Nice if you can get it, though as practiced at the dawn of the twenty-first century, just as often a concept held out to women as a means of suggesting that life really is just like *Dirty Dancing* and if you don't have a Nicholas Sparks moment you ARE GOING TO DIE. (Tip: you're going to die anyway.) *See also* "A secondhand emotion." "A many-splendored thing." "Means never having to say you're sorry." "Soft as an easy chair." "Grand." "The alpha and the omega."

## Love, Courtney (1964–)

Equal parts 1990s grunge icon, lightning rod for controversy, and off-and-on hot substance-abusing mess. Made famous for her brash, in-your-face lyrics as the frontwoman of Hole (and infamous for her onstage antics and tumultuous marriage to Kurt Cobain), she spent much of the last twenty years in the limelight, as a musician, artist, fashion designer, muse, television personality, and disgruntled fan whipping girl in turns. While Love's attitude and lyrics emerged around the same time as the riot grrrl movement, she was famously apathetic about the whole thing, trashing the genre in print and taking out some of her animus by punching riot pioneer Kathleen Hanna in 1995. (*See also* HOLE; RIOT GRRRL)

## love handles

Fat deposits in the waist area, about which grown human beings with jobs and friends and dreams are expected to spend time being embarrassed and working to eliminate.

## Lowry, Lois (1937–)

Writer. Author of *The Giver*, the start of a groundbreaking series set in a dystopia focused on creation, family, and his-

tory. Lowry also wrote the very different—and humorously modern—Anastasia series, which chronicles the trials and travails of a snappy young heroine and her wry, intellectual, Boston parentals. (*See also* KRUPNIK, ANASTASIA)

## lump

According to women's magazines, a woman's natural enemy, for reasons both frivolous (the unflattering fit of a pencil skirt) and serious (breast cancer).

## LUSH

British brand of handmade cosmetics that make everything within a thirty-foot radius smell like the whole Strawberry Shortcake gang farted in unison.

## lust

(*See* INSATIABLE; LIBIDO)
According to women's magazines: chocolate, a glass of wine,

and/or a hot bath. According to men's magazines: expensive cars, suits, and real estate.

## Lynch, Jane (1960–)

Actress who looks goddamn amazing in a tracksuit and has made great use of her flat Illinois vowels. Lynch's big breakthrough came when she was forty, as a disciplinarian dog trainer in Christopher Guest's *Best in Show*. A recovering alcoholic who didn't come out to her parents until she was in her thirties. Went through a self-described Indigo Girls phase. Hilariously threw shade at *Entourage* at the 2011 Emmys by joking that it made her gay, provoking whining from cast members of said show.

## ma'am

Ostensibly a respectful term for an older woman (or ranking member of the military), *ma'am* is in fact routinely used with mocking disrespect. (See *Married with Children*'s misogynist clubhouse, "NO MA'AM", aka the National Organization of Men Against Amazonian Masterhood.) Sometimes a woman rejects the term, as when Barbara Boxer asked to be called *senator* instead of *ma'am* on the Senate floor in 2009.

## Machiavelli (1469–1527)

Italian political scientist whose book *The Prince* (first disseminated in 1513) presented a method for laying down the ultimate power play, a technique that is often invoked by modern smiters hoping to make a claim to intellectual relevance. "It changed my life," Lindsay Lohan said in 2007. "I was going out with someone and they said I should read Machiavelli and I was like, 'Nah,' and then I was, 'Oh, I'll read it,' and now it is always with me." (*See also* LOHAN, LINDSAY)

## machismo

Term coined by feminist scholars to describe the traditional structure of masculinity/patriarchy in Latin American cultures. The basic tenets of machismo include male dominance, hyper-masculinity, female submission, and ultratraditional gender roles. Defenders of machismo liken it more to nurturance, hard work, and responsibility, which is a nice idea, but...FYI, you don't get to make a new definition for a thing until you've dismantled the old one. Especially when the old definition is still oppressing people.

## macho

Often used as a synonym for "ultramasculine." A macho man is physically strong and emotionally stoic and eschews girly stuff like flowers, classical music, and naked men. Or he may be a member of the super-gay band the Village People, known for their 1978 hit "Macho Man." (*See also* MACHISMO)

## Macintosh

Model of Apple computer, arguably preferable to a PC because of its superior oh my God shut up no one cares.

## MacKinnon, Catharine (1946–)

Lawyer and activist best known for her efforts to mount legal oppositions to pornography, which she and Andrea Dworkin defined (in preparing an antiporn ordinance for the city government of Minneapolis) not as images of humans fucking but "graphic sexually explicit subordination of women through pictures or words" where women are dehumanized, objectified, and made to seem to enjoy pain, submission, and humiliation. Antipornography ordinances based on MacKinnon's framework have been declared unconstitutional, and MacKinnon and Dworkin have been dismissed forever as prudish feminists who hate sex. MacKinnon was more successful with another crusade: establishing the legal framework for prosecuting harassment as sex discrimination in the workplace, which she pioneered in her 1979 paper "Sexual Harassment of Working Women." The Equal Employment Opportunity Commission adopted her guidelines in 1980.

## MacLaine, Shirley (1934–)

Oscar-winning star of *The Apartment* and *Terms of Endearment*; filmmaker; sister to Warren Beatty; the woman who gave us both Ouiser Boudreaux and a perfect foil for the Dowager Countess but will probably only be remembered for all that past-life bullshit.

### macrobiotic

"Holistic" diet targeted at combatting cancer that eschews animal products, promotes digestion thorough chewing, and varies depending on the season, the climate, and a person's age and gender. Regular fixture of Gwyneth Paltrow's for-normal-everyday-gorgeous-wealthy-women newsletter, goop.

### Mad Men

American television series created by Matthew Weiner that premiered in 2007. Set during the advertising boom of the 1960s, the show chronicles the lives of the employees of Sterling Cooper, a fictional Madison Avenue advertising agency with Don Draper, the agency's partner and creative director, at its center. In addition, the series portrays the rapid social changes of the sixties, especially female advancement in the workplace and the unapologetic, condoned institutional sexism and racism endured by women and minorities at the hands of the hard-drinking, overentitled white male ruling class. Peggy Olson, the firm's first female secretary to make the jump to copywriter, is celebrated as a feminist hero, thanks to her professional ambition and personal rejection of traditional gender norms and expectations. (She has premarital sex, uses birth control, and lives with her boyfriend.) *Mad Men* is also widely praised for its impeccable styling, both in wardrobe and in set decoration. (*See also* HOLLOWAY, JOAN; OLSON, PEGGY)

### madam

Female owner of a brothel or bawdy, drag queen-esque puppet "Madame" created and voiced by Wayland Flowers.

### Maddow, Rachel (1973–)

Rhodes scholar, author, and the first openly gay anchor of a major news program in the United States. Suck it, Anderson Cooper.

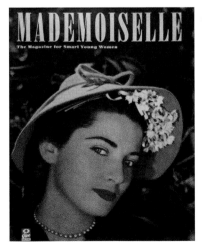

### *Mademoiselle*

For sixty-six years, a Condé Nast publication that catered to "the smart young woman," aiming for a readership of college-educated females. The magazine published noted authors like Flannery O' Connor, Joyce Carol Oates, and Sylvia Plath, who based her novel *The Bell Jar* on her time as guest editor at the magazine. In 1961, *Mademoiselle* was the first mainstream fashion magazine to feature an African American model in its pages. While it continued to be a "top-shelf" magazine in subsequent decades, the publication shuttered in 2001 after the September 11 attacks devastated the economy.

the transferring-of-the-pop-star-power to Britney Spears via tongue-kissing phase; the besties with Gwyneth phase; the disco roller-skating Malawi adoption phase; the sinewy-armed geriatric dance-off at the SuperBowl halftime show phase.

### maenad

Wild woman of Greek mythology. The maenads were followers of Dionysus, the god of awesome parties, and their religious fervor would whip them into frenzies of lustful, violent, drunken ecstasy. If you ran into a band of maenads, you'd be likely to think it was really cool at first, since they are basically a fifty-legged walking drunken sex party that can conjure milk and honey right out of the earth. But they're also prone to ripping nearby animals and/or humans to pieces. Just a word to the wise.

### maiden

An unmarried virginal woman, or else a ship's first voyage, or else a horse that has never won a race, indicating that a woman is lacking in experience, status, and worth until she has successfully snagged a man for life. Also a onetime Scottish beheading device.

### maiden name

Woman's actual surname, given to her at birth under the presumption that it will be changed to her husband's when she marries. Modern excuses for a woman continuing the tradition of surrendering her personal identity to signal the transferring of male ownership from father to husband include: "I never really liked my name anyway" (as if women are the only ones burdened with inelegant last names), "it was just my father's name anyway" (as if women are the only ones burdened with the names of their fathers), and "I want our kids to have the same name" (as if women should be the only ones burdened with simplifying the bureaucratic process of childbearing).

### maid of honor

Sort of superbridesmaid as seen in the strange social hierarchy of the wedding and tasked with handling everything from bachelorette party to toast to bride emotional management and rewarded with the cultural cachet of being recognized as the bride's ultimate bestie. (*See also* BRIDESMAIDS)

**Madonna (1958–)**
Pop star against which all others are measured—herself included. Career transformations include: the bleached-out synth, crucifixy, rolling around on the floor in a wedding dress phase; the dating and marrying Sean Penn, dabbling in acting phase; the divorcing Sean Penn, sponsored by Pepsi, burning crosses on MTV phase; the *League of Their Own* phase; the naked coffee table book phase; the Eva Perón extended dance remix phase; the Jewish mysticism phase;

### makeup

Any paint or pigment a person puts on your face to make yourself look different. At one end of the range you have makeup that's supposed to make you look as if you don't have makeup on, such as mascara that's basically the color of your eyelashes—in other words, the stuff *Cosmo* will tell you is culturally required to bring yourself to a baseline level of attractiveness. From there, the spectrum runs through Amy Winehouse cat eyes, goths, State Fair face paint, RuPaul, and finally clowns and those aliens from *Avatar*. All stops on that train are potentially awesome; ladymags don't recommend them all for date looks, but who cares. Women who are confused by makeup often believe they're experiencing a catastrophic failure of femininity, but for the most part, skill or lack thereof with makeup actually comes down to artistic training and ability, since you are essentially brush and finger painting on your own face.

### Malcolm, Janet (1934–)

Apostle of the storied American tradition of Women Journalists Who Send Men into Apoplexies. (*See also* Didion, Joan; McCarthy, Mary) Started out as a shopping columnist for the *New Yorker*; now one of the biggest names in the business. Wrote the best book on Sylvia Plath, *The Silent Woman*

(1995). Fun game: quote the first line of *The Journalist and the Murderer* (1990), "Every journalist who is not too stupid or too full of himself to notice what is going on knows that what he does is morally indefensible" to other journalists and watch them freak out.

## male

Adjective that describes men and other nonlady animals. Or a noun, if you must.

## male chauvinist pig

1960s and '70s sitcom term for sexist.

### Mama

**1.** Affectionate nickname given to one's mother, often shortly after one's birth. Term of endearment also bestowed on matriarchs of families, musical groups, and other gangs. **2.** Nickname for Thelma Harper, a fictional character played by Vicki Lawrence on *The Carol Burnett Show* and *Mama's Family*.

"GIVE MAMA A HUG!"

## mammary gland

Organ that produces mother's milk. In human beings, located in the female breast, which some overly squeamish people find terribly confusing and wrong.

## mammogram

X-ray in which a woman's breasts are squashed flatter than she ever thought possible.

## man

**1.** A general term referring to the entirety of the human race. **2.** A singular human possessing an X and a Y chromosome, male sex organs, a desire to identify as a "man," or any combination thereof. **3.** When capitalized and preceded by "the," a term used to refer to the power structure that has historically made the rich richer and the poor poorer. The Man is a self-replicating, self-preserving system in place for only its own benefit, at the expense of all others. Catastrophes commonly blamed on The Man: all financial crises, the subjugation of women, racism, classism, the failure of the War on Drugs, cancer, honeybee extinction, and the fact that Chris Brown still has a record deal and millions of devoted fans. **4.** (archaic) An individual who displays leadership, strength, stoicism, courage, and decisiveness. Can also be used as a verb. (Example: "man up.")

### Manic Pixie Dream Girl

Term coined by *Onion A.V. Club* scribe Nathan Rabin to describe a deeply annoying female trope in film: "that bubbly, shallow cinematic creature that exists solely in the fevered imaginations of sensitivewriter-directors to teach broodingly soulful young men to embrace life and its infinite mysteries and adventures." Most irksome example: Natalie Portman's character in *Garden State*, who ruined The Shins for everyone.

## manicure

Chiefly cosmetic hand and nail treatment that was once the province of rich grandmas and models but is now just as common as highlights, waxing, and other costly, time-consuming beauty endeavors.

## manipulative

A short list of things that are manipulative: romantic comedies, political rhetoric, passive-aggressive yoga instructors, pickup artists, chiropractors (in a literal sense), and that asshole ex of yours.

### Mankiller, Wilma (1945–2010)

First female deputy chief of the Cherokee Nation (1985 to 1995). When she was just eleven, her father moved her family to San Francisco from their native Oklahoma with a grant from the government. There she lived in a mostly African American neighborhood and learned that "poor people have a much, much greater capacity for solving their own problems than most people give them credit for." As chief, she was preoccupied with the building of infrastructure, specifically schools and health centers, for the Cherokee Nation. She once said that she'd encountered more discrimination as a woman than as an Indian, and she received the blowback you might expect. But she was never one to let gender get in her way. "I think that what women need to do is that they need to stop looking elsewhere for leadership and look to themselves for leadership," she told an Oklahoma oral history project in 2009.

### manly

**1.** Masculine. **2.** Really, really masculine. **3.** Laura's nickname for Almanzo in *Little House on the Prairie*. (*See also* LITTLE HOUSE ON THE PRAIRIE)

### Mann, Sally (1951–)

Photographer best known for her portraits of her own children, and fairly often naked, in defiant, adult-looking poses. Sometimes they were depicted as injured, as in one famous photograph in which her daughter looks beaten up but is actually recovering from gnat bites. Mann's collection of such images, published in her book *Immediate Family* (1992), created an uproar, with publications like *Artforum* refusing to print the photographs and angry op-eds asking, "But what about the kids?" The kids, as it turned out, had wanted the pictures to be published, and their mother had paid them twenty-five cents a shot. The book was a huge hit and made their mother rich.

### mannequin

**1.** A humanlike form on which clothes are displayed. **2.** A 1987 film in which Kim Cattrall plays a department store window dummy who comes to life and rides off on the back of Andrew McCarthy's motorcycle, but not before she's embarrassed him all over town by making it look like he's "dating" a regular old inanimate mannequin. Awkward! And creepy as fuck! Also notable for dumping Starship's "Nothing's Gonna Stop Us Now" on the world.

### manners

Detailed knowledge of etiquette and/or commonsense decent behavior, depending on whom you ask.

### Mansfield, Katherine (1888–1923)

Short story writer. Despite a limited literary output and a brief life, the subject of multiple biographies because her thirty-four years were just that fascinating. She was bisexual, and her first relationship was with a young Maori woman, whose own journals would resurface in at least one of Mansfield's stories. Got pregnant in her early twenties. (She either miscarried or had a stillbirth, depending on which biographer you ask.) Had love affairs with just about everyone. Would end up marrying her editor, John Middleton Murry, who was somewhat indifferent to her in life but obsessed in death. After she died, from complications related to tuberculosis, he was the keeper of her literary legacy for years, editing all of her pluck and anger out of her journals in the interest of maintaining her sweet and romantic image.

### mansplain

Patronizing explanation of a topic to an already informed audience. Often, this misplaced intellectual authority is the product of the assumed male command of all relevant topics, but the same effect can be achieved through the indulgence of any privileged perspective over others. (*See also* WHITE SPLAINING)

### marabou

African stork whose feathers trim the kitten-heeled slippers that match some women's long red negligees.

## marathons

26.2-mile road races that used to be badges of honor for serious athletes but are now excuses for everyone you know to exercise obsessively for several months and hit you up for money.

## March, Jo

Second eldest of the four sisters whose lives are chronicled in Louisa May Alcott's classic 1868 novel *Little Women*. Strong-willed, tomboyish, and creative and perhaps the most beloved of the sisters, aspiring writer Jo is outspoken against injustice and refuses to bend to the norms of the time, even rejecting the marriage proposal of the family's handsome and wealthy neighbor Laurie in favor of the poor but kind professor Friedrich Bhaer. The character of Jo is generally accepted to be a reflection of Alcott herself or, at the very least, a reflection of the woman Alcott yearned to be, and a representation of the evolving standard of girlhood in the late 1800s. (*See also* ALCOTT, LOUISA MAY)

## Mardi Gras

Festival of debauchery preceding a period of austerity in which intoxicated bros gather in packs to invite women to reveal their tits in exchange for cheap plastic beads. Christian.

## Margolyes, Miriam (1941–)

English actress and voice artist, Professor Sprout in *Harry Potter*, Fly the dog in *Babe*, openly gay and happily partnered for a very long time, witty and delightful in interviews.

## Margulies, Julianna (1966–)

Actress. We liked her on *ER*. We love her on *The Good Wife*.

## *Marie Claire*

Women's fashion and service magazine, first published in France in 1937 and in the United States in 1994. Better than *Cosmopolitan*. Worse than *Elle*. (*See also* COSMOPOLITAN)

## marijuana

Dried flowers and leaves of the *female* cannabis plant used as a recreational drug and a medicinal substance to treat, among other things, gynecological disorders, menstrual cramps, anxiety, depression, and boredom.

## marriage

Between a man and a woman. Or any other combination of two consenting adults who wish to enter into such a contract, for fuck's sake, why is this even an issue?

## Mars

Where men are from, which explains why they—no wait, sorry, it explains nothing. And is also not a real thing. Well, Mars is a real thing, and we recently sent a car called Curiosity up there on a rocket ship, which is seriously badass, but no, men are not from there.

## Mars, Veronica

Cutesy noir heroine from a TV series of the same name. Sometimes veers a little far into the perk zone but is nonetheless appealingly angry and jaded. Also generally full of good advice for others, viz.: "When entering a frat house full of accused rapists, the pantsuit is a solid wardrobe choice. It's fashion's way of saying: 'Move along. Nothing to see here!'"

## Marshall, Penny (1943–)

Director of some pretty terrific films, like *Big* and *A League of Their Own*, but doomed to be known forever as (a) Garry's sister and (b) Laverne DeFazio.

### Mary Kay Cosmetics

Direct sales cosmetics company. Once a year tens of thousands of women carrying hundreds of thousands of garment bags fly from more than thirty-five countries to Dallas, Texas, and hole up at convention center hotels for a virtually women-only weekend of makeovers, motivational speeches, multiple costume changes, ritual photo ops taken sitting fully clothed in pink bathtubs before life-size full-body portraits of the late Mary Kay Ash clad in a flowing white fairy godmother gown, and, of course, the annual presentation of keys to the newest crop of proud pink Cadillac owners. Ash was a forty-five-year-old executive board member at the World Gift Company with twenty-seven years of direct sales experience when she finally broke out on her own in 1963 to start Mary Kay Cosmetics, knowing exactly what would go over: makeup parties for women, with flowers and chocolate and booze. Duh! Today, a $3 billion business. Though a nice selection of models and colors are available to star reps, most still choose the classic pink Cadillac, due more to the camp factor than anything else.

### Mary Magdalene

Most noteworthy female disciple of Jesus Christ. Happened to be a sex worker.

### masculine

Traits associated, biologically and/or stereotypically, with men.

### masochism

Receiving pleasure from humiliation, sexually, professionally, or socially.

### massage

Manipulation of human skin and muscle and bone to achieve relaxation or medical healing. Sometimes a euphemism for a hand job.

### mass media

Film, television, radio, newspaper, magazine, and online content designed to reach huge numbers of people at once, effectively creating an international cultural community—one still controlled by a small group made up primarily of white guys.

### mastitis

Painful mammary gland infection common in breastfeeding women.

### M.A.S.H.

An acronym for Mansion Apartment Shack House and a fortune-telling game played by children throughout the United States and beyond. To participate, the player must list the names of four suitors, four brands of cars, four types of residences, and four numbers of broods of children (though categories may vary depending on who's playing). After the list is complete, a fellow player will begin either making ticks in a box or drawing circles inside one another until the key player says to stop. After that, the number of ticks or rings are counted and that number determines the rotations per round. By the end of the game, it is foretold whom the player will marry, where they will live, what car they will drive, and how many children they will have. Results can range from ideal to awful and are always infallible. (*See also* COOTIE CATCHER, FORTUNE-TELLER; OUIJA BOARD)

## masturbation

Literally, feeling yourself up. Figuratively, talking yourself up.

## Mata Hari (1876–1917)

The original honey trap (maybe). Dutch exotic dancer born Margaretha Zelle and executed on suspicion of spying for Germany in World War I. Following the end of an abusive marriage and the death of her eldest child, she threw herself into studying dance and Indonesian traditions, eventually choosing her stage name and rising to stardom as a performer. Hari's frequent travel during WWI caught the attention of world leaders, and, although documents show Mata Hari was engaged in espionage, her legend has outstripped her actual deeds. Was she really a double agent? She was known to fib about her background—she represented herself as a Javanese princess trained in Indian dance—but that kind of exotic, orientalized backstory was kind of standard for someone in her profession at the time (and anyway, she really *did* study dance in Indonesia). Executed by firing squad in 1917. The French dossier on her supposed spying activities is slated for public release in 2017, and rumor has it that the information it contains will prove she was mainly guilty of being a sexy lady who enjoyed well-paid dalliances with high-ranking officials in an unfriendly time.

## maternal

Characteristic of a mother; motherly and nurturing; in other words, a proper woman.

## maternity

State of being a mother, and the belly-friendly clothes you wear during and after pregnancy.

## math

Subject that former Harvard University president and onetime treasury secretary Larry Summers thinks women might just be bad at. (Other, more reasonable people believe women are poorly represented in math and science because they're deterred from those disciplines at a young age.) *The Wonder Years* actress-turned-mathematician Danica McKellar is one advocate who's labored to recruit more girls to math, by dishing out math tips (and workout advice!) to young girls using sexy book titles like *Girls Get Curves: Geometry Takes Shape*.

## Matlin, Marlee (1965–)

Actress who rose to prominence when she became the youngest actress and the only deaf one to win the Best Actress Academy Award, for 1986's *Children of a Lesser God*. *West Wing* cast member, reality show contestant (*Dancing with the Stars*; *Celebrity Apprentice*), and activist.

## matriarchy

In theory, a society ruled by women. *Only* in theory because, with few exceptions, women with power choose not to rule over men but rather form egalitarian communities in which men and women hold equal standing, a concept that is also known as "feminism."

## matronly

Term that, like "maternal," comes from the Latin for "mother," a descriptor with a negative connotation because it basically means fat, old, and dumpy. The opposite of MILF.

### Maude
CBS television series that ran from 1972 to 1978 and starred Bea Arthur as Maude Findlay, twice-divorced liberal feminist cousin to *All in the Family*'s Edith Bunker. If you've ever laughed at Liz Lemon trying so hard to demonstrate her lack of racism that she does just the opposite, you can thank Maude, who pioneered that gag forty years ago. You can also thank the show, its writers, and its stars for bringing all of the following into prime time: divorce, single parenthood, alcoholism, domestic violence, and—the first thing anyone will bring up when you mention *Maude*—abortion. Pre-Roe. On a sitcom. Sometimes the 1970s don't sound so bad. (*See also* ARTHUR, BEA)

### Max, Tucker (1975–)
**1.** Nickname of the violent crimes section of a state prison in Arkansas. **2.** Diabolically self-promoting author of short stories about drinking multiple gallons of liquor, despoiling fast-food restaurants, puking, and intercourse. (Incidentally, a Penn State student who submitted herself to one of Max's "jackhammering" sessions reported that he farted loudly and repeatedly throughout the act.) Franchise player in the spate of male mating gurus who attained fame during the midaughts by advising affection-starved men to follow strict regimens of high-speed insult-bombing to achieve their means; foreswore such methods following his reunion with an old girlfriend who introduced him to a psychotherapist and "mother figure" who caused him to realize that all his assumptions about women had been informed by the "self-selecting" sample of drunk sluts who "come to me based on their own dysfunction." Max did not, however, forswear obnoxious self-promotion; shortly after a 2012 interview in which he mused, "Who gives a shit if you're rich—if you're a dick to your wife or you're not in touch with your feelings, what does that matter? It doesn't mean shit. What matters is the quality of your relationship," Max made a public show of attempting to donate $500,000 to Planned Parenthood in exchange for securing naming rights to one of its clinics. Tellingly, Max is also a junior member of the endless list of evildoing media whores indoctrinated by the University of Chicago economics department.

### maxi pads
What you use when you're so young you think tampons will steal your virginity, or so old your flow makes you want to call in Sunshine Cleaning every time you take a leak.

### May, Elaine (1932–)
Writer and director. *Ishtar* actually received mixed reviews. But it went down in film history as one of the industry's most storied flops, and so writer-director May's impressive film career—her celebrated screenplays for *Heaven Can Wait* and *The Birdcage*, and her uncredited treatments for *Tootsie*, *Reds*, and *Labyrinth*—will always end with a punch line.

### Mayer, Marissa (1975–)
Technology and business executive who served as Google's first female engineer and proved instrumental to the tech company's profitable rise and public image. (No small feat in Silicon Valley, where the public faces of most tech companies are decidedly not female.) In 2012, the then pregnant Mayer left Google for competitor Yahoo, where she achieved the distinction of being the youngest CEO of a Fortune 500 company and stirred up controversy when she vowed to take

a short maternity leave so that she could focus on her job. Unlike Sheryl Sandberg, Mayer has shied away from publicly commenting on her role as a high-ranking female in a male-dominated industry. Maybe she thought no one would notice? (*See also* SANDBERG, SHERYL)

### McAdams, Rachel (1978–)
Canadian ingenue of romantic film who models the dance every successful woman must perform—outplaying every throwaway role awarded to her. Brought dignity to Nicholas Sparks's joint *The Notebook*, intelligence to Vince Vaughn buddy comedy *Wedding Crashers*, and grace to a too-harried-by-her-career-to-be-loved rom-com *Morning Glory*.

### McCarthy, Jenny (1972–)

Cousin to Melissa, which is about the only point in her favor. Onetime annoyingly wacky MTV dating show host who then decided that vaccines caused her son's autism and that "a gluten-free, casein-free diet," supplemented by vitamins, detox of metals, and antifungals for yeast overgrowth cured it. Now, one of the world's foremost proponents of New Age bullshit, one we can't help but think of every time we hear about new cases of whooping cough and measles.

### McCarthy, Mary (1912–1989)

Writer best friends with Hannah Arendt and mortal enemies with Lillian Hellman. Besides being an amazing intellect, she was open about her enjoyment of sex before that was a Thing. In her memoir written late in life she compared dicks, recalling one in particular that was "about the size and shape of a lead pencil." Speaking of penis size, she wrote a novel so popular and widely enjoyed (*The Group*) that naturally Norman Mailer sputtered all over the *New York Review of Books* about it and claimed it was a "shabby little boutique" of a lady writer's book and all the rest of it. Even before that he had some kind of issue with her intelligence, idiotically challenging her to a boxing match. Men can get so catty sometimes, you know? (*See also* HELLMAN, LILLIAN)

### McCarthy, Melissa (1970–)

Breakout *Bridesmaids* star who stole the show as a limp-ponytailed, bowling-shirted, sexually aggressive woman who comes on to air marshals on planes and has telepathic deep-sea conversations with dolphins. McCarthy's star turn sparked debate over the role of fat women in comedy, with some arguing that her casting as Megan stigmatized fat women, and others that it represented a positive reversal from the rail-thin women who nab most mainstream comedy roles.

### McCartney, Stella (1971–)

Fashion designer who became creative director of Chloë in 1997 and launched her own fashion house in 2001. In addition to her eponymous clothing line, her empire now includes a fragrance, skin-care products, handbags, and a kids' collection. Daughter of Paul and Linda McCartney.

### McCloskey, Deirdre (1942–)

As far as we know, the first out trans woman who's also a famous economist.

### McDaniel, Hattie (1895–1952)

Controversial trailblazer and actress. The daughter of slaves, McDaniel spent her life playing the sassy, wisecracking sidekick-maid to a series of prominent white characters. Best known for her Academy Award–winning role as Mammy in *Gone with the Wind*. When she raised ire for taking roles that reinforced the idea of black subservience to whites, McDaniel's oft-quoted response was "I'd rather play a maid and make $700 a week than be one for $7." While she often stood against the NAACP and accepted the segregated realities of Hollywood, McDaniel also fought for civil rights on other fronts (like home ownership) and threw herself into public service through her donations and work with the Red Cross. The circumstances following her death paralleled the bigotry she endured in life: her request to be buried at the Hollywood Cemetery was denied as the cemetery did not accept African Americans. In 1999, the new owner of the cemetery wanted to right the wrong, and there is now a memorial to McDaniel on the grounds.

# A HISTORY OF FEMALE DICTATORS

Megalomania and mass murder have never been strictly the purview of men: history conveniently forgets that when given the opportunity, women are capable of equal depravity in the service of personal power. And though some people assert that more women in power will make for a gentler, kinder world, a short sampling of history's greatest dictatresses puts the lie to that theory (especially for those unlucky enough to be related to them).

## Cleopatra (Egypt, 69 BC–30 BC)

She raised an army to wrest power from her brother and used Caesar's lust for her to gain military advantage over and permanently defeat her brother. She bore Caesar a son he wouldn't officially acknowledge, then got involved with Marc Antony in order to promote her son to the Roman throne and retake the eastern part of the Egyptian Empire. They failed and eventually both committed suicide.

## Wu Zetian (China, 624–705)

Though she began as the teenage concubine of the emperor, Taizong, she used his death to beat a path to his son, Gaozong, and bear him two male heirs. (Gaozong was married at the time, and there are historical debates about Zetian's involvement in the death of his childless wife.) By the time Goazong died, Zetian had poisoned or exiled most of her male rivals and so assumed the throne herself. She installed a system of secret police and informants, and had her secret police falsely accuse, torture, and execute rivals and those who spoke against her and anyone she just deemed incompetent.

## Hind al-Hunnud (Kindah, now Saudi Arabia, seventh century)

Led forces into battle against Muhammad and his followers and was known to toast her own battle prowess from atop a pile of corpses. Rumored to have eaten the liver of the man who killed her father (and made jewelry out of his skin and nails) and led a guerrilla war against Muhammad before eventually converting.

## Isabel I of Castile (Spain, 1451–1504)

When she succeeded her brother as the monarch of Castile, she instituted a series of legal reforms that had the effect of jailing more people than ever. She also expelled both Jews and Muslims from the country, institutionalized the Inquisition, and sent Christopher Columbus to "India," which as you may know had roundly negative consequences for the native peoples of the Western hemisphere.

## Catherine the Great (Russia, 1729–1796)

Arrested her husband and probably had him killed so that she could rule Russia, then had hewr only other rival for the throne killed as well. Though she did give serfs the right of legal petition to the courts, she did so only to prevent having to deal with them herself, and their lot in life didn't improve, for the most part. She also fought several wars, annexed Crimea, partitioned Poland, and executed plenty of people. Oh, and she purportedly had lots of sex, but that's not a crime.

## Tzu-Hsi or Cixi (China, 1835–1908)

As teenage concubine to the emperor Xianfeng, she was the only one to bear him a son, which elevated her. When Xianfeng died, she managed to oust several of the regents appointed to rule in her son Tongzhi's stead and executed three of them. She ruled directly until Tongzhi's seventeenth birthday, when he was married and presented with a group of concubines. Tongzhi later took to utilizing the services of prostitutes outside the castle walls when his mother interfered in his sex life, which may have resulted in his death from a sexually transmitted infection. After his death, Tzu-Hsi retook the throne and violently held off all social reforms until after the Boxer Rebellion, when she instituted some of the very changes she'd killed people to prevent.

## Indira Gandhi (India, 1917–1984)

Though she was initially democratically elected as prime minister, her reelection campaign in 1971 was marred by allegations of malpractice and thrown out by the courts. In reaction, Gandhi jailed many of her political rivals and instituted two states of emergency and an emergency decree extending her rule before finally agreeing to hold elections in 1977. She was arrested by political rivals and thrown out of Parliament almost immediately after ending the second state of emergency, but after three years of intergovernmental strife, Gandhi ran for office again and was reelected in 1979. After she ordered the Indian army to attack a Sikh temple to prevent what she called a potential uprising in 1984, and they killed and injured hundreds of civilians, she blocked media and foreigners from access to the entire province. In October 1984, she was assassinated by two of her Sikh bodyguards in an apparent act of revenge.

## McGraw, Dr. Phil (1950–)

Psychologist who met Oprah Winfrey in the late 1990s and became a relationship and life guru who regularly appeared on her show. Went on to author several books and launched a syndicated talk show, *Dr. Phil*. Target of numerous critics and lover of media stunts. In 2008 he attempted to stage an intervention with a hospitalized Britney Spears, then talked about it to anyone who would listen. (*See also* OPRAH; WINFREY, OPRAH)

### Mean Girls

Tina Fey–penned comedy dissecting the social machinations of high school girls, who employ gossip, negs, and fake stupidity to engineer each others' downfall and land the hot boy for themselves. Launched Fey's acting and solo writing career, cemented Rachel McAdams's rise, and still inspires commentators to lament that fallen star Lindsay Lohan had "so much talent." (*See also* FEY, TINA; LOHAN, LINDSAY)

## Medea

Woman from Greek mythology who married Jason and killed a bunch of people, most notably her own children, which makes her name enduring shorthand for women who don't act sufficiently maternal.

### Mehretu, Julie (1970–)

Ethiopian-born artist whose large-scale works of acrylic, pencil, and pen draw on her own nomadic experience, layering the emblems of architecture and infrastructure—columns, charts, trains, maps—to create enormous hives of urban activity that stretch across space, time, and perspective.

## meltdown

What toddlers and grown women have when beset by too many feelings all at once. (Men just get steamed.)

### Menchú, Rigoberta (1959–)

Guatemalan activist and prominent member of the country's indigenous K'iche' ethnic group. In 1981, Menchú was forced to flee Guatemala for Mexico shortly after the murder of her guerrilla father by the Guatemalan army. The next year, she collaborated on an autobiography with Venezuelan anthropologist Elisabeth Burgos entitled *My Name Is Rigoberta Menchú and This Is How My Consciousness Was Raised* (commonly known as *I, Rigoberta Menchú*). The book, published in several languages, made her an international icon for the struggles of Guatemalans though much of its content was later questioned, with Menchú accused of changing her life story to better fit into the guerrilla rhetoric. Received a Nobel Peace Prize in 1992 and now runs Salud para Todos, a pharmaceutical company whose goal is making medicine more available to those of varying income levels. Cofounder of the Nobel Women's Initiative.

## menstruation

That thing where blood pours out of your vagina once a month. Maybe you've heard of it? To deal, you have to cork up your hole with this thing that's like a severed toe made out of cotton, and if you don't swap it out often enough your legs fall off and you die. Or you can wear a diaper. Or, if you have a super-chunky flow, you do both so you don't get stigmata

on your pants. (Hippies have other methods. Talk to them.) Also your uterus fucking hurts and you poop a bunch and you're hormonal and you get acne. For some reason girls in the seventies couldn't wait to get their periods and incessantly wrote books about it. "Oh, I hope I get it today!" Uh, get better priorities, Margaret. (*See also* ARE YOU THERE GOD? IT'S ME, MARGARET; TAMPONS)

**meow**

Terribly clever thing to say when one woman says something to another that can plausibly be interpreted as mean. (*See also* CATFIGHT)

### Merkel, Angela (1954–)

First female chancellor of Germany and the most powerful woman in the world, according to *Forbes*. Famously given a shoulder massage by President George W. Bush, because he apparently forgot where he was or who he was or who she was or not to be a disgusting asshole.

### Meyer, Stephenie (1973–)

Bestselling writer of the Twilight series. When Meyer birthed her first son, she decided to forgo her law school dreams—she "just wanted to be his mom." Then came the vampire dreams, which she began translating into YA romance as a hobby, sold for $750,000, and used to share her BYU-bred ideas about love, sex, and the glittery occult with young girls and their mothers. Her protagonist, Bella Swan, mirrors Meyer's pre-Twilight life—full of intellectual and emotional potential, fully obsessed with boys and babies. Bella never ends up diverting her energy to any cause outside the family. But now, Meyer rakes in $50 million a year off the franchise while her husband, Christian, stays home with the kids.

### M.I.A. (1975–)

English singer and rapper of Tamil descent, born Mathangi "Maya" Arulpragasam. M.I.A. started making music in the early years of the twenty-first century but shot to international fame with her 2008 single "Paper Planes." The song, whose lyrics are both funny and politically charged, is emblematic of M.I.A.'s brash, rebellious, and overtly political music. People who

always forget its title refer to it as "that one with all the gunshots in it." The video for her 2010 song "Born Free" caused a controversy—it was banned from YouTube in the US and UK—for its depiction of the genocide of redhaired people.

### Midler, Bette (1945–)

Actress. Broad. Started out as a singer in a bathhouse, which, come to think of it, explains a lot. Described by a friend as "one of the last real entertainers." Married a man in 1984 after knowing him for just six weeks; as of this writing, they're still together.

**midwife**

Person (usually a woman) specially trained to assist during pregnancy, labor, childbirth, and postpartum. There's a bit of a perception that midwives encourage women to give birth squatting in a kiddie pool while listening to Gregorian chants under the moon. But they also perform births at hospitals—often with an obstetrician present or on call—and act as a buffer between the pregnant woman and a medical profession that can seem brusque, impersonal, and weirdly episiotomy-happy.

**MILF** Acronym for "Mom I'd Like to Fuck" referring to a mother, generally the parent of a friend, with whom you would like to have sex. First popularized by the 1999 teen film *American Pie*. DILF (Dad I'd Like to Fuck) and GILF (Grandparent I'd Like to Fuck) are spin-offs of the phrase, though neither variation has permeated the culture the way MILF has.

## Millay, Edna St. Vincent (1892–1950)

American poet and feminist who wrote the lines "My candle burns at both ends / it will not last the night / But ah, my foes, and oh, my friends— / It gives a lovely light!"

## Millett, Kate (1934–)

Second-wave feminist best known for the book *Sexual Politics*.

## Mills, Hayley (1946–)

English actress who paved the way for the Lindsay Lohans and Miley Cyruses of the world as a 1960s Disney starlet with leading roles in *Pollyanna*, *The Parent Trap*, and *That Darn*

*Cat!* Parlayed her fame into more movie, stage, and television roles from the 1960s to today, including starring as the title character of 1987's *Good Morning, Miss Bliss*, which was reformatted to become *Saved by the Bell*.

## miniskirt

(*See also* SKIRT)

## Mirren, Helen (1945–)

Comely young English actress who achieved major Hollywood fame later in life—in *Teaching Mrs. Tingle* at fiftyfour, *Gosford Park* at fifty-six, *The Queen* at sixty-one, host of *SNL* at sixty-five. Oscar winner. Noted for her sharp wit and preternaturally hot retirement-age body.

## misandry

Systemic hatred of men. Misogyny's corollary, but not its equivalent, because men are a structurally privileged group and women are not. (For this reason, you will rarely hear anyone but a butthurt Men's Rights Activist use the word.)

## misogyny

Fear and hatred of women, which is actually a real thing that fucks up a whole class of people.

## A ROGUE'S GALLERY OF WRETCHED MISOGYNISTS

With its long history, long reach, and impressive staying power, misogyny is truly universal. Yet some individuals cry out for a particular public shaming for their cringe-inducing contributions to the world of women hatred.

### Aristotle

Carried the sexist torch of Socrates, ultimately surpassing his own mentor in the Greek Philosophers' Misogyny Olympics. Some of Aristotle's most quotable statements reportedly include "Woman may be said to be an inferior man"; "The female is, as it were, a mutilated male"; and "Females are weaker and colder in nature, and we must look upon the female character as being a sort of natural deficiency."

### God

His books overflow with misogynist messages. In Genesis, the first woman is created from a man's rib, has a weakness for snakes and fruit, and is responsible for destroying the blissful Garden of Eden. In the New Testament, the Immaculate Conception creates the impossible and unbearable Madonna/whore dichotomy our society still suffers under today.

### Friedrich Nietzsche

Wrote that women are not yet capable of friendship, since they "are still cats, and birds. Or at best cows." The German philosopher also said that women are "typically sick, changeable, inconstant...she needs a religion of weakness that glorifies being weak...she makes the strong weak." Somewhat tragically, Nietzsche suffered a nervous breakdown at the age of forty-four, cutting short his career as a professional sexist pig.

### Ayn Rand

Said she wouldn't vote for a female presidential candidate. The Russian-born mother of heartless American libertarianism, you see, didn't believe that "any good woman would want that position" anyway and that a female president would be "unspeakable."

### Norman Mailer

Once said that "a little bit of rape is good for a man's soul." The hard-charging American man of letters also stabbed his second wife (out of six), puncturing her in the area around her heart and requiring emergency surgery.

### Phyllis Schlafly

Doesn't believe in marital rape: "By getting married, the woman has consented to sex, and I don't think you can call it

## Miss

Like Mrs., only less important, because she's not married.

### Miss America

Title bestowed upon the winner of the Miss America Pageant. Before it turned into a glitz and glamour extravaganza, the competition was a two-day beauty contest held in Atlantic City. Winners were crowned starting in 1921, and a talent portion was added in 1935. (Women of color were not allowed to compete in those days—the official pageant rulebook stated that "contestants must be of good health and of the white race"—although, by the late 1940s, that barrier was eventually broken by Native American, Asian American, and Puerto Rican women. It wasn't until 1970—two years after the Miss Black America pageant was held—that Iowa's Cheryl Brown became the first black contestant.) The pageant, first televised in 1954, peaked ratings-wise in the 1960s and has been on the decline ever since.

### Miss Congeniality

**1.** An actual award given out in some pageants to the woman judged to have the best personality. **2.** Canonical euphemism for "not the prettiest." **3.** When italicized, a 2000 movie starring Sandra Bullock.

rape." The Equal Rights Amendment opponent and well-educated career woman also urges women to stay home, making her part of the proud tradition of right-wing moralistic fundamentalist hypocrites. Do as she says, not as she does.

### Jerry Lewis

Once said, "A woman doing comedy doesn't offend me but sets me back a bit. I, as a viewer, have trouble with it. I think of her as a producing machine that brings babies in [*sic*] the world."

### Mel Gibson

Once threatened the mother of his child, Oksana Grigorieva, by yelling into the phone: "You look like a f***ing pig in heat, and if you get raped by a pack of n***ers, it will be your fault." Also told her: "I am going to come and burn the f***king house down...but you will blow me first." Grigorieva accused Gibson of punching her in the face, giving her a concussion, and knocking out her teeth.

### Rush Limbaugh

Publicly called then Georgetown Law School student Sandra Fluke a slut after she testified about the importance of insurance coverage for birth control. Rush, on his fourth wife but still apparently flummoxed by the biology of the female body, complained that Fluke is "having so much sex she can't afford the contraception."

### The Republican Party

Regularly issues cringe-inducing statements on sexual assault; opposes the Violence against Women Act, equal pay, reproductive rights, and a whole host of other things.

### Donald Trump

Routinely criticizes women who disagree with him by mocking their appearance. Sent *New York Times* columnist Gail Collins an annotated version of one of her op-eds in which he likened her looks to those of a dog. Called comedienne and talk show host Rosie O'Donnell a "fat pig" who is "disgusting—both inside and out." (He used the same language to insult media maven and author Arianna Huffington.) He has offered to show high-profile attorney Gloria Allred his penis after a transgender contestant was disqualified from the Miss Universe pageant and claims not to care about bad press because "it really doesn't matter what [the media] write as long as you've got a young and beautiful piece of ass."

### Allen West

Voted to defund Planned Parenthood, which he accused of "neutering American men." Called Representative Debbie Wasserman Schultz (D-FL) the "most vile, unprofessional, and despicable member of the US House of Representatives," adding that the DNC chairwoman is "not a lady." While serving in the Iraq War, wrote his wife to ask, "Are you committed to being my porn star?" and informed her that certain sex acts would be "the standard and it is non-negotiable."

### missionary position

Dude on top of lady. No sudden movements.

### Miss Piggy

Porcine Muppet who may suffer from some kind of mood disorder, vacillating between extremes of sometimes violent anger and smothering affection.

### mistress

The French find her totally normal; in America, she's still a bit of a bogeywoman. Even in the eyes of men who have mistresses, it's still rather a fantasy of someone who only takes what she is given and asks for no more. There may be someone somewhere who is happy living like this, and godspeed to her. For everyone else, it'd be nice if we could dispel the idea that this was anything other than a second marriage. Mistresses should, we think, be able to get health insurance at least.

### Mitchell, Joan (1925–1992)

Painter of airy, colorful brushstroke canvases, colleague of Willem de Kooning and Jackson Pollock but never the household names they were. Always had trouble selling her work; as a dealer once told her, "Gee, Joan, if only you were French and male and dead." One of the few women the Abstract Expressionist boys' club accepted, and wonderfully acerbic about their "yak-yak-yakking about blah-blah-nothing." Fan of the pageboy haircut. Romanced another painter, Jean-Paul Riopelle, and told the *New York Times Magazine* she did not recommend dating another artist: "Someone gets squished."

### model

(*See* FASHION MODEL; SUPERMODEL)

### mommy wars

Largely media-propagated phenomenon in which women are encouraged to bitch about each other's child-rearing choices. Team Housewives, who changed their name to the more ego-friendly Team Stay-at-Home Mothers, sneers at women who have paid employment outside of the home, viewing them as haughty narcissists who are too busy climbing the corporate ladder to love their children. Team Career Women laughs at housewives, imagining them to be softheaded relics afraid to have their intellectual inadequacies challenged or exposed in the workforce. Magazines such as *Newsweek* and the *Atlantic* have published an innumerable number of articles promoting the mommy wars over the years, invariably containing the phrase "have it all." This "all" that women can't have is rarely described, except to say that women cannot actually achieve it. Our best guess is that "having it all" actually means "having what men have," i.e., an ability to have both a family and a career, but it is considered impolite to state this directly. The world painted in mommy wars articles is one where all mothers are married to men who make enough to support the entire family, leaving them free to choose home or office. Single mothers, divorced mothers, or mothers whose households need

### Mitchell, Joni (1943–)

Probably the best female folksinger of the 1970s. Some of Mitchell's most famous songs pay tribute to California, Paris, and New York City, but she actually grew up mainly in Saskatoon, where she was known as Roberta Joan Anderson. A childhood bout of polio forced her to give up athletics in favor of singing and songwriting. By the time she put out her first, self-titled album in 1968, songs she had written had been recorded by George Hamilton, Buffy Sainte-Marie, and Judy Collins. Many of her tunes became folk staples, including "Both Sides Now," "The Circle Game," "A Case of You," "Chelsea Morning," "Free Man in Paris," and "River." Mitchell's later work veered into jazz and synth-pop, which was not as successful, but whatever, by that time she was Joni fucking Mitchell and could do what she pleased. The recipient of nine Grammys and member of the Rock and Roll Hall of Fame and the Canadian Music Hall of Fame.

the second income may be mentioned in passing, but their struggles are considered uninteresting compared to those of upper-middle-class wives of lawyers trying to decide whether or not to use their Princeton degrees for a career in pushing a stroller around gentrified Brooklyn.

## Monistat
Over-the-counter yeast infection treatment that, we hear, also doubles as a nice antichafing gel.

## Monroe, Marilyn (1926–1962)

"I've never fooled anyone. I've let men sometimes fool themselves. Men sometimes didn't bother to find out who and what I was. Instead they would invent a character for me. I wouldn't argue with them. They were obviously loving somebody I wasn't."

—from her posthumous, ghostwritten "autobiography," *My Story*, released in 1974

## Montgomery, Lucy Maud (1874–1942)
Canadian author who worked as a teacher before publishing *Anne of Green Gables* in 1908. An immediate bestseller, Montgomery's book spawned several sequels, with young readers falling hard for the imaginative and adventurous title character and kindred spirit. (*See also* ANNE OF GREEN GABLES)

## Moore, Mary Tyler (1936–)
Actress and star of the 1970s eponymous sitcom that featured the first-ever unmarried career woman—thirty-something single Minneapolis TV producer Mary Richards—on television, paving the way for future classics in the ladies-with-jobs genre: *Murphy Brown, Parks and Recreation*, and *30 Rock*. (*See also* RHODA)

## Moral Majority
Jerry Falwell–founded organization that marshaled right-wing Christian political power beginning in the late 1970s. Subject of one of the sickest one-line burns ever (though no one recalls who said it first): "The Moral Majority is neither."

## Moran, Caitlin (1975–)
English writer and broadcaster who was a working journalist and published novelist by age seventeen and rose to international prominence in 2012 with her bestselling pop-feminist memoir *How to Be a Woman*. In an interview with The Hairpin, Moran gave a lovely answer to a question about some Twitter-based criticism of her use of the word *tranny* in the book: "Initially I was kind of equally tetchy, like, 'There's no greater friend of the gays! How dare you?' But after the misunderstanding that happened on Twitter, I researched lots and came across the word 'cis' which I'd never come across before, and again it comes back to the idea of normality, so that educated me and that's fantastic, that's why it's brilliant that Twitter's there. It educated me about 'cis' and 'tranny' and 'trans' in a way that I have educated people about feminism, so it was all very useful." Not long after that, though, she got into another Twitter jam with social justice proponents after defending Lena Dunham's show *Girls* for depicting a New York City that's unrealistically low on people of color—and not really giving a shit when people got upset with her for that. At this writing, there's been no reflection and apology on that front, but it's hard not to love her anyway, because she is motherfucking hilarious.

## Moraga, Cherrie (1952–)
Chicana. Coeditor, with Gloria Anzaldúa, of *This Bridge Called My Back: Writings by Radical Women of Color*. Playwright and poet who, inexplicably, has never quite become the feminist household name she should be.

"Fundamentally, I started writing to save my life. Yes, my own life first. I see the same impulse in my students—the dark, the queer, the mixed-blood, the violated—turning to the written page with a relentless passion, a drive to avenge their own silence, invisibility, and erasure as living, innately expressive human beings."

—from "Art in América con Acento," in *The Last Generation* (1993)

### Moreno, Rita (1931–)

Fantastic, tulle-wrapped living legend, singer/actress/performer who won the Best Supporting Actress Oscar for her role in the screen adaptation of *West Side Story*, becoming the first Hispanic woman and second Puerto Rican ever to win an Academy Award. Also the recipient of a Tony, an Emmy, and a Grammy, which earns her a place in the EGOT pantheon. Once dated Marlon Brando. Recipient of the Presidential Medal of Freedom.

### Morgan, Robin (1941–)

Key figure of feminism's second wave; edited an anthology called *Sisterhood Is Powerful* (1970). Sometimes a poet or novelist; mostly an essayist. Originally wanted to be a book editor and was fired for unionizing the office; was arrested in the same office after she staged a sit-in to get Malcolm X's widow, Betty Shabazz, her proper share of his royalties. Somehow manages to identify as both atheist and Wiccan, which makes her sound like an awesome, grown-up version of Willow Rosenberg. Like many second-wavers, has a difficult record on trans rights and kicked a trans woman out of a lesbian rights conference in 1973 with the deeply unfortunate accusation that said trans woman had "the mentality of a rapist," a statement which she does not seem to have ever retracted.

### Morgendorffer, Daria

(*See* DARIA)

### Morissette, Alanis (1974–)

Quintessential nineties lady alt-rocker who lifted the legacy of the righteously angry riot grrrl and spun it into the commercially viable, quasifeminist crusade for "girl power!" Her pièce de résistance: asking ex-boyfriend Dave Coulier whether his new lady friend performed blow jobs on him at the movies, in song.

### morning-after pill

Pill that launched a thousand pharmacist side-eyes. A highly stigmatized medication that—taken within seventy-two hours of unprotected sex—prevents the meeting of egg and sperm. Initially offered just to victims of sexual assault but now available over the counter to women eighteen and over, all of whom have been painted as sluts and abortionists by social conservatives.

### morning sickness

Hollywood's idea of how most women find out they're pregnant.

### Morrison, Toni (1931–)

Gentlewoman, scholar, and writer of beautiful epic magical-realism-tinged novels, many of which center on black women and family history. Morrison (née Chloe Wofford) was born in Ohio, and after a bookish working-class childhood went on to study English at Howard and Cornell. After finishing her master's, she worked as a teacher and editor before turning to publish fiction. Her best-known work is probably 1977's *Song of Solomon*, a complex, controversial, classic novel that Barack Obama has called his favorite book. Recipient of the National Book Critics' Circle Award (1977, for *Song of Solomon*), the Pulitzer Prize (1988, for *Beloved*), and the Nobel Prize in literature in 1993, so, you know, NO BIG DEAL. Morrison has also taught at Howard, Yale, Bard College, SUNY, and Princeton and published essays on race, literature, and education. And she has enough degrees, honorary and regular-style, to wallpaper a small office. (*See also* BELOVED)

### Moss, Kate (1974–)

Fashion model discovered at the age of fourteen while walking through an airport. Made a name for herself in the 1990s as the face of Calvin Klein. Over the course of her career, she's modeled for everyone from Dior to Rimmel and been featured on the cover of *W* and *Harper's BAZAAR*. Her private life has never really been private—pictures of her allegedly doing lines of cocaine were featured on the front of the *Daily Mirror*, and her high-profile relationships with Johnny Depp and Pete Doherty were all tabloid fodder—but the gossip has quieted a bit since her 2011 wedding to The Kills' Jamie Hince.

### mother

Female parent expected to bear the majority of child-rearing duties, from birth to emotional support to professional sacrifice to cooking to cleaning until the identification of "mom" subsumes a woman's entire personal identity, all pants she wears become "mom jeans," her sexual attractiveness is rated on a MILF scale, and her life is converted into a punch line of "your mom" jokes.

### Motley, Constance Baker (1921–2005)

Lawyer, civil rights activist, author of the original complaint in *Brown v. Board of Education* in 1951, and the first black woman to argue in front of the Supreme Court in 1962. Later went on to win nine of the ten cases she argued before the high court. She was also the first black woman elected to the New York State Senate, and she served as Manhattan's borough president.

### mouthy

Opinionated, loud, or talkative. Usually female.

### Moyet, Alison (1961–)

Formed the band Yazoo with Depeche Mode's Vince Clarke. Circled just around pop stardom for decades.

### MRAs

Acronym for Men's Rights Activists and a group of terrible garbage people who consider a certain movement known as feminism extremely threatening. Started relatively inoffensively, with various gentle man-hippies who witnessed the women's rights movement and decided that they needed all-male spaces to work their stuff out. Over time, it transformed into one of the most virulent plagues the internet has ever known. Modern-day MRAs promote, among other things, false domestic violence statistics and the elimination of child support laws and are responsible for such Top 10 hits as "But Women Lie About Rape (Why Reporting Rape Should Be Illegal)," "Women Rule the Divorce Courts (That Bitch Got the Car)," and "Feminism Is Just Female Supremacy (I Have No Idea What the Word 'Feminism' Means, I Can't Read, Send Help)." Conveniently, their acronym also stands for More Raging Assholes, which is how you will start referring to them after you've heard all their "arguments" a few hundred times.

### Mr. Big

Once a heartless lover of steak, wine, and hot tubs, he became Mr. Carrie Bradshaw (née John) in the first *Sex and the City* movie. This change of heart convinced single women worldwide that they, too, could convert an emotionally unavailable, selfish man into a doting partner for life. (*See also* BRADSHAW, CARRIE; BUSHNELL, CANDACE; SEX AND THE CITY)

## MRS Degree

Title appointed to women who attend university with the hopes of getting married rather than educated.

## Ms.

Feminine form of Mister, i.e., a term of address that doesn't rely on the addressee's marital status, because who cares? (Everyone did, until the 1970s.)

### Ms. Magazine

American feminist magazine founded in 1971 by Gloria Steinem, Letty Cottin Pogrebin, Patricia Carbine, Joanne Edgar, Nina Finkelstein, and Mary Peacock. In 1972, a year before *Roe v. Wade*, published a list of women who admitted having illegal abortions and was the first national magazine to cover domestic violence. Now a quarterly magazine that feels kind of earnest and serious. (*See sidebar*)

## muff

Hand warmer. Euphemism for vagina. (*See also* BUSH)

## muffin top

Name given to flesh that puffs up or spills over the waistband of low-rise pants. Also Jenna Maroney's hit single.

## multiple personality disorder

Psychological disorder now known as dissociative identity disorder and made famous by Shirley Mason, who was immortalized as Sybil Dorsett in Flora Rheta Schreiber's *Sybil* and who later admitted that she made everything up. A lot of evidence suggests the whole disorder is made up, in fact, but we wouldn't want to say that anywhere near a comments section on the internet.

# *MS.*-UNDERSTOOD

It's strange to imagine that *Ms. Magazine* was once the "it" magazine of the moment. Launched as a special insert in Clay Felker's *New York Magazine* in 1971, it was an instant hit. And not in the niche, urban way of *New York Magazine* and its coastal ilk. From the first issue, *Ms.* was shipped around the country and flew off newsstands so quickly that Gloria Steinem initially thought there had been a shipping error and the magazines had not arrived at all. Readers, so intrigued by the editorial collective's promise to tell real women's stories, hid the magazine from their husbands and surreptitiously shared it with their daughters. The letters section was particularly active, as the magazine received hundreds of responses to each issue and published pages' worth of them.

The very fact that it's now strange to think of *Ms.* as such a central part of the cultural zeitgeist is also a cautionary tale. As the years went by, torn apart by internal ideological battles and the same financial pressures that weigh on most print magazines, it slid from cultural relevance to stodgy oblivion. For those of us who love both feminist politics and popular media, the lesson of *Ms.* is that it's impossible to serve both a readership and a movement. They intersect, of course, but the overlap is never clean. Eventually, the editors have to decide which one to prioritize. And the staff of *Ms.* chose the movement.

"Those of us who wanted better cover images and better cover lines got resistance from people for whom ideology ruled everything. They didn't seem to understand what the medium was," cofounding editor Mary Peacock told *New York Magazine* in an oral history of *Ms.* that *New York Magazine* published in 2011. "The idea was to entice people to read the magazine." The idea *was*. Not anymore. The transition was complete in 2001, when the Feminist Majority Foundation assumed ownership of the magazine and dropped its publishing schedule to four issues a year. Not that most American women missed it. Which is a shame. While many mainstream women's magazines professed to have taken up *Ms.*'s original editorial mandate of speaking to real women's experiences, few have succeeded. The sad part is, as the mouthpiece for a movement, neither did *Ms.*, which is said to have a circulation of 110,000.

## multitasking

Overrated.

## Munn, Olivia (1980–)

Actress, comedienne, memoirist, and *Maxim* cover girl who climbed the comedy ranks with her "one of the boys, except a hot girl!" image on gamer-bro network G4, where she was once dressed in a sexy maid outfit and was instructed to jump into a gigantic pie. In 2010 *The Daily Show* awarded her a rare female correspondent slot, which turned into a full-on Michael Bay–style firestorm after Jezebel criticized the show's ultramale writing and performing staffs and Munn's style of man-pandering humor. Munn is actually more interesting than her sexy shtick, and her success at transcending those look-at-me-put-these-sausages-near-my-mouth comedy roles should be celebrated. Unfortunately, Munn also has a history of accusing female critics of being fat, sandwich-eating ladies who are just jealous. (*See also* DAILY SHOW, THE; "YOU'RE JUST JEALOUS")

## Munro, Alice (1931–)

Canadian goddess of the short story.

## Murdoch, Iris (1919–1999)

Brilliant Dublin-born philosopher and novelist who became a symbol for the tragedy of degenerative mental disorders when she was diagnosed with Alzheimer's in the midnineties, wrote it off as writer's block, and mentally declined until her death in 1999.

## musical theater

Form of mainstream absurd performance where emotion builds into outbursts of song. Traditional refuge for self-expression of women and gays.

## muumuu

Item of comfortable, shapeless apparel also known as a schmatta. (The opposite of Spanx.) It doesn't really matter that muumuus' lack of definition around the waist and comically loud prints are severely unflattering, because the loose-fitting dresses are typically worn around the home, which is why they lend themselves so well to bralessness.

## My Little Pony

Colorful plastic toy created in 1981 by illustrator and designer Bonnie Zackerle and marketed on backpacks, lunch boxes, and anything else that could be emblazoned with their images. Subject of a syndicated cartoon and even a movie, 1986's *My Little Pony: The Movie*, featuring the voices of Danny DeVito and Madeline Kahn. In 2010, the latest animated incarnation, *My Little Pony: Friendship Is Magic*, debuted, which was a surprise hit with teen and adult males (known as "bronies").

# N

### nachos

Yes, please.

### naive

Ignorant of the ways of the world. Innocent. Maybe a little dumb.

### naked

Flip side of the pornographic nude; a purer term for the un-clothed and one applied to small children splashing in a bath, Adam and Eve pre-Original Sin, and "all natural" foods.

### nanny

Usually a woman—the career is so female-oriented that male practitioners are derisively nicknamed "mannies"—hired by a family of means to outsource the raising of their children.

### Napolitano, Janet (1957–)

First female attorney general of Arizona, first woman to be reelected as governor of that state, and first female secretary of homeland security, who self-identifies as a "straight, single workaholic."

### National Organization for Women

Organization launched in 1966 by the *Feminine Mystique*'s Betty Friedan, the Episcopal Church's first black woman priest, Reverend Pauli Murray, and the first woman to seek the Democratic presidential nomination, Shirley Chisholm. Formed to "take action to bring women into full participation in the mainstream of American society now, exercising all privileges and responsibilities thereof in truly equal partner-ship with men." It later got more specific, honing its focus on reproductive rights, domestic violence, equal rights in the Constitution, antiracism, LGBT rights, and economic equality. (*See also* CHISHOLM, SHIRLEY)

**National Woman's Party**
Political group formed by Alice Paul in 1913 to advocate for women's suffrage. (*See also* PAUL, ALICE; SUFFRAGETTE)

### natural childbirth

Labor and delivery of a baby without (often, though not always, necessary) medical interventions such as epidurals, C-sections, and episiotomies. Occasionally nature-fetishist, hippy-dippy crap that makes women feel guilty for requesting any of the above.

### neckline

Do you have breasts? Are you wearing a turtleneck? If the answers are yes and no, respectively, yours is too low. Cover that up.

### negotiation

In the workplace, an excuse lobbed at women who do not receive equal pay to men—"Women don't ask for more money!" (In fact, it's been proven that women perceived as pushy have been denied raises.) In the bedroom, an excuse lobbed at women whose sexual boundaries are violated—"She says no, but she means yes" (when in fact it is incumbent upon the assailant not to assault a partner in the first place).

### nephew, niece

Child of a sibling, a partner's sibling, or a dear friend. They work well both as practice kids and as reminders to use birth control.

### nervous breakdown

A thing that 1950s housewives used to have when they ran out of antianxiety meds. Treatment: a slap across the face and a hearty "Get ahold of yourself, woman!" It's a vague, unscientific term that refers to an acute anxious or depressive episode—a sort of mental illness lite for delicate, frazzled ladies. That vagueness cuts both ways—it contributes to the sensationalism around women's mental health (as in, once a month our brains liquefy and bleed out our vaginas and that's why we can never be president!), while simultaneously trivializing women's actual concerns (as in, sometimes *shit really is fucked*, but no big, it's "just" a nervous breakdown and we'll be fine). Similar to "hysteria"—you know, just spray us with the hose and we'll snap out of it. (*See also* MELTDOWN)

### nesting

During pregnancy, obsessively redecorating and organizing the house before a baby's arrival. At all other times, watching Netflix in your pj's instead of meeting your friends out at a bar.

### networking

Ostensibly a dead-eyed, big-smile, arm-grab handshaking, business card–slipping, party-circulation activity through which professional connections are lubed.

### neurosis

Once an old-timey diagnosis for emotional disorders that defied psychological explanation but now scientifically pinpointed as the experience of a particular anxiety—OCD, phobias, separation anxiety—as well as a broad-stroke term for afflicted personalities of Woody Allen–type boys and Courtney Love-esque girls.

### neuter

Nicer, more accessible word than *castrate*.

### Nevelson, Louise (1899–1988)

Russian-born artist who emigrated to the United States as a toddler and became one of the most prominent American sculptors of the early twentieth century. Historians have placed Nevelson's totemlike monumental structures at the dawn of the feminist art movement, crediting her work with flipping the expectation that female artists only work in the most feminine disciplines. (Nevelson said she was "not a feminist," just "an artist who happens to be a woman." Both feminists and misogynists disagreed.) Her contemporaries still knocked her works for not being masculine enough. "We learned the artist is a woman, in time to check our enthusiasm," a critic of her work wrote in 1941. "Had it been otherwise, we might have hailed these sculptural expressions as by surely a great figure among moderns."

### Newkirk, Ingrid (1949–)

President of People for the Ethical Treatment of Animals (PETA) and divisive figure known to support fairly radical guerrilla tactics when it comes to animal rights, including some actions of the Animal Liberation Front. "I *do* support getting animals out in the same way I would have supported getting human slaves out," Newkirk said of ALF, "child labor, sex slaves, the whole lot." Loves puppies.

### nice guys

Everyone in the feminist blogosphere has written a definition of this term—not that it stops entitled, manipulative single dudes from insisting that no, really, they can't get laid because they're just *too nice*. Writer Amanda Marcotte puts it this way: "Nice guys are angry at women—at least the ones they will admit are women." "If a guy refers to himself as a 'Nice Guy,' chances are he isn't," adds Feministe's "Zuzu," stating the if-only-it-were-obvious. "Guys who consider themselves 'Nice Guys' tend to see women as an undifferentiated mass rather than as individuals. They also tend to see possession of a woman as a prize or a right." The website Heartless Bitches International describes typical NG behavior: "Whether it is targeting women who are troubled to begin with, setting themselves up to be taken advantage of, or acting in a manipulative, patronizing or obsequious fashion, these guys sabotage themselves and often blame 'all women' for their misfortunes." And card-carrying dude Jeff Fecke encapsulates it: "Pity the Nice Guy®. No, please, pity him. He desperately wants you to. And while you're pitying him, would it kill you to give him a mercy fuck?" (*See* SIDEBAR)

# A TAXONOMY OF NICE GUYS

The good news: feminism happened, so men don't get to just run around slapping our asses with impunity anymore. The bad news: now that overtly piggish behavior is heavily, heavily socially discouraged, there's a subset of men who resort to more subtle means when they want to act like jerks. Chief among them is the Nice Guy. A "Nice Guy" with a capital NG doesn't refer to a man who happens to be a genuinely kind person. Hooray for kind, caring, conscientious people! We mean the sort of Guy who has declared himself to be Nice, and thus deserving of positive (usually sexual) attention from the female of his choice, upon whom he has often projected an elaborate fantasy of perfection and willingness that rarely has anything to do with the subject's actual feelings or desires. When a Nice Guy is romantically rejected by a woman he wants, he lashes out at her, wondering why that dumb cunt won't go out with him. After all, he has been Nice!

## The Predatory Bestie

He offers to listen to you cry and cry about your ex. So you let him. He offers to help you move a heavy dresser to your fourth-floor walk-up. So you let him. He admits that he cried during *The Notebook.* So did you. He tries to touch your boobs one night. You don't let him. You bitch.

**Likes:** All the same things you like, even *Grey's Anatomy.*

**Dislikes:** All those assholes you keep dating who are definitely just doing _____ to get in your pants, unlike Predatory Bestie, who is most definitely not just hanging around waiting for you to be single and vulnerable so he can make a move and then guilt you into having sex with him.

**Pop culture muse:** Duckie from *Pretty in Pink.*

## The Chivalrous Stranger

He gets all up in your face as you're walking down the sidewalk. "SMILE!" he says, "I bet you'd be so pretty when you SMILE!" You don't smile. You bitch.

**Likes:** YOU! Smiling!

**Dislikes:** Frowny sourpuss ladies who aren't decorative enough.

**Pop culture muse:** Pete Campbell.

## The Aspirational Fuck Buddy

It's just a sex thing and you're not ready for a relationship. You've told him this. But he won't listen. He doesn't understand rule number 1 of taking your pants off is that you can't fuck your way into a relationship.

**Likes:** Making you soup when you're sick.

**Dislikes:** The fact that you are not his girlfriend and have told him that you should stop sleeping together.

**Pop culture muse:** The dude from *500 Days of Summer.*

## The Fake Reformed Ex

When you were together, he was a butthole factory. A factory that makes only buttholes. But you broke up with him, and he didn't take it well. Now he's changed, he swears. He's so different. He's learned. He's changed so much in the last three weeks. Except when you tell him that it's really, for real over, he punches a wall and fractures his hand.

**Likes:** Things with flames on them. Calling you "turkey legs" because your thighs touch at the top, unlike those of his last girlfriend.

**Dislikes:** Being told no, anything you like.

**Pop culture muse:** Chris Brown.

## The Liberated Pig

He's an old guy at a cocktail party who name-drops feminist authors because he figures you're in the age-group that would appreciate that sort of thing. He's with it. He's down with the feminisms. But then he asks for your phone number. You tell him you have a boyfriend. You dumb bitch.

**Likes:** Bourbon. Saying "Simone de Beauvoir" with a high school level French accent.

**Dislikes:** Being corrected.

**Pop culture muse:** Henry Higgins (the super-mansplainy guy from *My Fair Lady*).

## The Incredible Hulk

One minute, he's just a guy making an ill-fated move. But the act of rejection turns him into an explosive tyrant. Also his team missing a field goal makes him into an explosive tyrant, but that's a whole other thing altogether.

**Likes:** You. WAIT, WHAT? FUCK YOU!

**Dislikes:** THIS FUCKING BEER! ROAAAR!

**Pop culture muse:** Biff from *Back to the Future.*

## The Dejected Unknown Piner

You have no idea who he is, but he's made up this whole story in his head about how he's just a sad, shy Nice Guy who you can't even see because you're SO BLIND to anyone who isn't a football player, etc., etc., etc. By the way, you're adults, so there are no football players involved here.

**Likes:** Reddit. MEAN BUT TRUE.

**Dislikes:** Football players, talking to girls.

**Pop culture muse:** Taylor Swift. *Did I just blow your mind?* Women can be Nice Guys, too.

### Nichols, Nichelle (1932–)

Actress and singer who toured with Duke Ellington and Lionel Hampton's bands and starred as Lieutenant Uhura on *Star Trek*. Got to enjoy one-half of television's first interracial kiss. (With William Shatner!) When she considered leaving the show, Martin Luther King Jr. reportedly told her she was too important as a role model. (Mae Jemison, the first African American woman in space, cites her as an inspiration.) (*See also* JEMISON, MAE)

### Nicks, Stevie (1948–)

Flower-childlike singer of songs about Welsh witches. Unabashed fan of flowing muslin skirts and shawls. Made her name headlining a little band called Fleetwood Mac, then went on to a multiplatinum solo career. Known for being openly and nakedly ambitious. Never settled down; dated a number of fellow rock stars but married only briefly, once, and halfheartedly. She told a British interviewer in

2007 that "even though I'm pushing sixty I don't feel that I'm that old yet." Idolized Janis Joplin, whom she once opened for. Managed to survive extensive, public battles with Klonopin and cocaine; still didn't want Lindsay Lohan to play her in a movie. "Over my dead body," Nicks said. "She needs to stop doing drugs and get a grip. Then maybe we'll talk."

### Nightingale, Florence (1820–1910)

Crimean War badass who rejected her wealthy parents' wishes that she get married and instead essentially invented the profession of nursing. Patients dubbed her The Lady with the Lamp for her penchant for wandering around checking in on them in the middle of the night.

### nightmare

Bad dream based off the "mare," a witchy female creature of Germanic lore who would "ride" men, horses, and even trees in the night, sucking up and perverting their energy and forms.

### Nin, Anaïs (1903–1977)

Writer whose diaries of bohemian life in Paris in the 1930s were a favorite of sex-starved housewives living vicariously. Onetime lover of Henry Miller.

## nip slip

Annoyingly cutesy term for a wardrobe malfunction that occurs when woman flashes one or more nipples to the public or paparazzi, unknowingly or otherwise. For famous moments in nip slip history, see Janet Jackson's 2004 Super Bowl performance (also known as Nipplegate), Madonna's 2012 MDNA tour, and Lindsay Lohan on most Friday nights.

## nip & tuck

**1.** Slang for body-altering plastic surgery designed to make the recipient appear more youthful and fecund. Often found on the coasts, especially among celebrities who have taken time off to spend "with family" and now claim to have discovered the miraculous, suspiciously surgical-looking benefits of "yoga." **2.** Way that scandalized elders from coast to coast referred to *Nip/Tuck*, a TV drama that aired from 2003 to 2010 on FX and appealed to television viewers who found the final season of *Twin Peaks* too realistic.

## Nixon, Cynthia (1966-)

Lesbian *Sex and the City* alum (portrayed Miranda Hobbes) who rocked the gay activism world by stating, after having serious relationships with both men and women, that she "chose" to be gay with partner Christine Marinoni. "For me, it is a choice," Nixon told the *New York Times*. "You don't get to define my gayness for me." (*See also* SEX AND THE CITY)

## Nixon, Pat (1912-1993)

FLOTUS from 1969 to 1974 and a champion of charitable causes throughout her life. Always much better liked than her husband, Richard.

> **"no means no"**
> Not really a difficult concept.

## Nordstrom, Ursula (1910-1988)

Grandmother of modern children's literature. A veteran editor and publisher for Harper & Row (and that company's first female vice president), Nordstrom helped to revolutionize children's literature with a focus on books for kids that eschewed high-handed or folksy moralizing in favor of narratives with nuance and, in some cases, negativity. Over the course of her decades-long career, Nordstrom edited and oversaw such authors and books as E. B. White (*Charlotte's Web*), Margaret Wise Brown (*Goodnight Moon*) Louise Fitzhugh (*Harriet the Spy*), Maurice Sendak (*Where the Wild Things Are*), and Shel Silverstein (*Where the Sidewalk Ends*). According to the *New York Times*, the Nordstrom-published book *William's Doll*, written by Charlotte Zolotow and published in 1972, "appalled many men in publishing and enthralled feminists"; it also made its way, in musical form, into Marlo Thomas's midseventies feminist multimedia explosion *Free to Be…You and Me*. According to a 1998 collection of Nordstrom's correspondence, when she was asked by a New York Public Library superintendent—unimpressed that Nordstrom lacked teaching credentials or experience as a parent, Nordstrom replied, "Well, I am a former child, and I haven't forgotten a thing." (*See also* BROWN, MARGARET WISE; FITZHUGH, LOUISE; FREE TO BE…YOU AND ME; THOMAS, MARLO)

## Nyro, Laura (1947-1997)

Hall of Fame R&B artist who piloted an accelerated career—sold a song to Peter, Paul and Mary by seventeen, established a publishing company with David Geffen by eighteen, released her first album by twenty-one, retired from the music business by twenty-four, returned at thirty, retired again to have her first child at thirty-one, returned to the touring circuit at forty, and died of ovarian cancer at forty-nine.

### Oakley, Annie (1860–1926)

Ambidextrous Ohioan who proved WOMEN could be sharpshooters, too. Hardly butch, she curtsied on her way onto the national stage and blew kisses on her way off and was not a suffragette or even an advocate of what were then called bloomers. Fought with younger costars of *Buffalo Bill's Wild West*. Sued the pants off William Randolph Hearst when he claimed she stole a man's pants to buy cocaine, and won. Lindsay Lohan, at one time, should have taken note.

### Oates, Joyce Carol (1938–)

American author of more than forty novels and hundreds more novellas, short stories, plays, essays, memoirs, poems, and young adult books. "So many books! So many! Obviously JCO has a full career behind her, if one chooses to look at it that way," Oates  has responded to critics. "Many more titles and she might as well…what?…give up all hopes for a 'reputation'?"

### ob-gyn

One of the few medical fields in which female practitioners outnumber male ones (because, vaginas). Initial medical experiments with women's bodies were undertaken by tinkering male doctors, from the first Caesarian section in 1500 to the first use of ether in childbirth in 1846 to the first artificial insemination in 1866 to the first in vitro fertilization in 1978.

## Obama, Barack (1961–)

Husband of Michelle. Forty-fourth president of the United States, and that country's first African American commander in chief.

## Obama, Michelle (1964–)

America's first African American First Lady. Obama, née Robinson, first met the future POTUS at the Chicago law firm Sidley Austin, where she was his mentor. And she's just a boss, generally. She graduated from Princeton, then went to Harvard Law School, and worked as the VP for community and external affairs at the University of Chicago Medical Center until 2007. She and Barack, whom she married in 1992, have two daughters, Malia and Sasha.

America, it seemed, wasn't ready for the Michelle they were given in the early days of Barack's presidential campaign, and his team made a conscious effort to soften her image away from that of the Angry Black Woman that many voters seemed to project onto her. Since moving into the White House, Obama has stuck to more or less apolitical issues: organic gardening, military families, and childhood obesity. She has also become something of an American style icon. Her speech at the 2012 Democratic National Convention demonstrated just how much speech-giving practice she had had in her four years as First Lady, and made a lot of people wish they could vote for her after—or even instead of—her husband. (*See also* FIRST LADY)

## Occam's razor

Let us put it this way: when the female portion of the population makes 77 cents on the male portion's dollar, Occam's razor would suggest that sexism is involved.

## Occupy movement

International protest movement, inspired in part by the Arab Spring and outrage at the global financial crisis, that first gained attention when hundreds of protesters descended upon New York City's Zuccotti Park in September 2011 to demand economic equality, bank reform, and the removal of corporate influence from politics. The movement also popularized the slogan "We Are the 99 Percent," in reference to the extreme concentration of wealth held by just 1 percent of earners.

## O'Connor, Flannery (1925–1964)

Short story writer who was made housebound by lupus by age twenty-five and died before her fortieth birthday but left behind some of the most influential American writing of the twentieth century, particularly the collection *A Good Man Is Hard to Find* (1955). (Thankfully, not a dating manual.)

Though she's sometimes thought to have been a lesbian, she rebuffed the overtures of her longtime penpal Betty Hester and did have a male partner early on. A model of drawling, morose, sarcastic wit we'd all be proud to emulate. A proto-Jezebel in her early diagnosis of Ayn Rand's nuttery: "She makes Mickey Spillane look like Dostoyevsky." (*See also* RAND, AYN)

### O'Connor, Sandra Day (1930–)

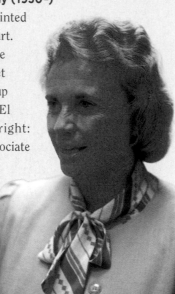

The first woman appointed to the US Supreme Court. And it only took the court 192 years to get there! O'Connor grew up on a cattle ranch in El Paso, Texas. That's right: America's first lady associate justice was a cowgirl before she was a judge. She was appointed to the SCOTUS in 1981 by President Ronald Reagan after serving as attorney general of Arizona, as a state senator, and as a Court of Appeals judge. In 1992, O'Connor sided with the majority in preserving the right to abortion in *Planned Parenthood v. Casey. Casey* was a chance to overturn *Roe v. Wade*, and because she had been appointed by a Republican president who knew that she found abortion "personally repugnant," O'Connor was expected to vote to do that. Instead, she joined the majority in preserving the fundamentals of *Roe*. Still, the *Casey* ruling maintained the rights of individual states to restrict access to abortion, provided that the restrictions did not place an "undue burden" on women. You know, like medically unnecessary but mandatory transvaginal ultrasounds. Nothing too undue or burdensome. O'Connor retired from the court in 2006 and her seat was filled by Justice Samuel Alito, the human incarnation of an undue burden. (*See also* COWGIRL; PLANNED PARENTHOOD; ROE V. WADE)

### O'Connor, Sinead (1966–)

Radical pacifist shaved-head ordained priest made famous for singing Prince's words ("Nothing Compares 2U"), and spitting her own, most notably during a 1992 appearance on *Saturday Night Live* in which she tore up a photograph of Pope John Paul II as she declared, "Fight the real enemy."

### Odetta (1930–2008)

Singer who was crowned "The Voice of the Civil Rights Movement" by people who knew what they were talking about. (Rosa Parks was a fan, and Martin Luther King Jr. called her the queen of American folk music.) Inspired basically every singer who mattered in the 1950s and '60s, including Bob Dylan and Janis Joplin, and kept touring until she was seventy-seven, a year before she died.

## O'Donnell, Rosie (1962–)

*so there's this woman*
*she's from long island*
*lost her mother way too young,*
*funny as hell, though*
*real gift for stand-up*
*next seinfeld maybe*
*she's fat, which distracts*
*people from talking about her sexuality,*
*at least. and mental illness*
*and all the things no one*
*talks about yet*
*it's the '80s*
*stand-up up up*
*into the '90s*
*league of their own. beautiful girls*
*(the shaved beaver speech omg)*
*and it's the Rosie O'Donnell Show*
*queen of nice. and koosh balls.*
*and a big fake crush on tom cruise*
*top of the world*
*then a memoir*
*"I'm a dyke!"*
*no more talk show.*
*new girl on the view*
*outs star's weight loss surgery*
*mouths off, feuds with trump,*
*hates war*
*one more new talk show*
*new oprah?*
*nope-rah.*
*but still*
*there's always the blog*
*the strange, sweet poetry*
*of rosie dot com*

### offensive

**1.** What misogynists believe feminists find everything.
**2.** Misogynists.

### ogle

Catcall without words. What creeps do to breasts, butts, or any lady part unfortunate enough to cross their lecherous paths.

### Oh, Sandra (1971–)

Korean-Canadian actress best known for playing Cristina Yang on *Grey's Anatomy*.

### O'Keeffe, Georgia (1887–1986)

American painter who rose to prominence in 1915 when she made a series of abstract charcoal paintings as a way of expressing her personal ideas and feelings. In the mid-1920s O'Keeffe began the series of large-scale, yonic close-ups of flowers for which she is best known. (Vaginas!) O'Keeffe denied any Freudian symbolism in her flower paintings, saying anything anyone saw in them was "talking about their own self, not me." Lived a ferociously independent life in a time that did not reward women for self-reliance. Or expect it.

GEORGIA O'KEEFFE IN NEW MEXICO
**Stark visions of a pioneer painter**

MARCH 1 · 1968 · 35¢

### old

Any woman who no longer buys Clearasil on the regular, according to Hollywood. (*See also* ACNE)

### Olsen twins (1986–)

Sad-eyed prisoners of sappy child fame. Not actually identical twins; in adulthood Mary-Kate and Ashley look quite different from each other. Resurfaced in 2005 from long, dark exile to Walmart as NYU students with vague artistic aspirations. Dropped out. Popularized a style of dress that might best be termed "ersatz homeless." Doesn't really matter what they do now because they have more money than God.

## Olson, Peggy

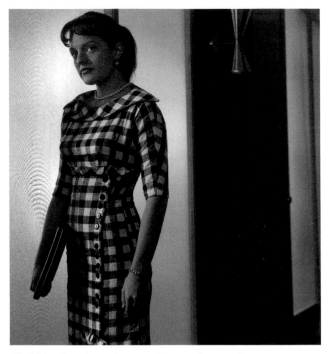

*Mad Men* heroine whose trajectory from naive secretary at Sterling Cooper to advertising executive Don Draper's work wife and only true friend to executive at a rival firm offers an essential portrait of the uneven progress toward equality for professional women in the sixties. Where her colleague and queen of the secretarial pool Joan Holloway trades on her sexuality all the way to a limited partnership in what becomes Sterling Cooper Draper Pryce, Peggy—after an initial liaison with executive Pete Campbell results in a pregnancy she denies and a child she ultimately gives up for adoption— competes with her male colleagues rather than working on a parallel track to them. While Draper initially facilitates her rise as a copywriter, his inability to appreciate or credit Peggy's work highlights their clash of working styles and the slow evolution of male-dominated professional spaces like Madison Avenue, just as Peggy's acceptance of an invitation to move in with her boyfriend when she expected a proposal illustrates the promise of sexual liberation and the emotional ambiguities of that new landscape. As underscored in a memorable scene from *Mad Men*'s fifth season, Peggy's journey reminds us that sometimes a room of one's own may just be a motel with dogs rutting outside the window, but that doesn't mean it's any less important to seize that independence. (*See also* HOLLOWAY, JOAN; MAD MEN)

## OMG

Ancient English shorthand for *Oh, My God* and dating back at least to World War I, when the then seventy-six-year-old British naval strategist John Arbuthnot Fisher invoked the abbreviation in a letter to his known frenemy Winston Churchill.

## Ono, Yoko (1933–)

Accomplished artist, musician, filmmaker, and activist; wife of the late John Lennon, who described her as "the world's most famous unknown artist. Everybody knows her name, but nobody knows what she does." As a child, suffered through the March 1945 bombing of Tokyo; her daughter from her second marriage was kidnapped by her husband and raised in a cult. Her propensity for elliptical statements still makes her unpopular with the press. Exhibit A:

> "I think that all women are witches, in the sense that a witch is a magical being. And a wizard, which is a male version of a witch, is kind of revered, and people respect wizards. But a witch, my god, we have to burn them. It's the male chauvinistic society that we're living in for the longest time, three thousand years or whatever. And so I just wanted to point out the fact that men and women are magical beings. We are very blessed that way, so I'm just bringing that out. Don't be scared of witches, because we are good witches, and you should appreciate our magical power."

—to Pitchfork in 2007.

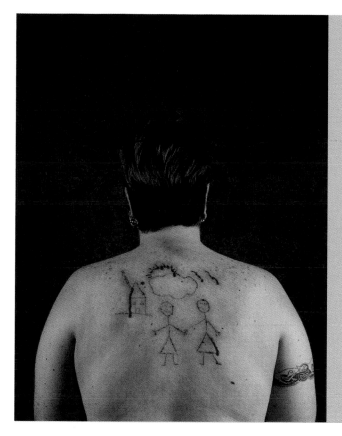

### Opie, Catherine (1961–)

Documentary photographer best known for her work depicting different American demographics. In her portraits of insular groups—she's focused her lens on lesbians, surfers, and high school football players—Opie reveals how the human body is shaped by the pressures and peculiarities of community, whether the body belongs to a vaunted small-town stadium star or a topless butch badass crouching outdoors in her combat boots. "I am an American photographer. I have represented this country and this culture. And I'm glad that there is a queer, out, dyke artist that's being called an American photographer."

### opinionated

(*See* LOUDMOUTH; MOUTHY)

### *Oprah*

Onetime crown jewel in the queen of daytime talk's media empire that was, for a quarter century, one of the most influential television programs in the world. Winfrey's confessional style and mix of sentiment and attention to social issues lured hard-to-get guests like Michael Jackson to her couch, the site of indelible television moments like Ellen DeGeneres's 1997 coming-out and Tom Cruise's profession of love for Katie Holmes. The platform she built let Winfrey make products with segments like Oprah's Book Club and her holiday giveaway special, Oprah's Favorite Things, and personalities like psychologist Dr. Phil, physician Dr. Mehmet Oz, and financial adviser Suze Orman. (*See also* McGRAW, PHIL; ORMAN, SUZE; WINFREY, OPRAH)

Winfrey's willingness to speak about her experiences of childhood sexual abuse, drug use, and her struggles with weight loss made *Oprah* a building block of a new culture of confessionalism and self-esteem and gave her emotional stature

to raise important issues. But *Oprah* has also lent a platform to dubious causes like vaccine denialism. And it turns out to be easier to give your audience members cars, cruises, and iPads than to provide them a clear path to Live Your Best Life, the show's long-term mantra.

### Orman, Suze (1951–)

Financial adviser. Because sometimes all you really need in a self-help guru is a nice midwestern lesbian in a brightly hued leather blazer with the tanorexia of Angelo Mozilo and the balls to break the news about how it might actually be a dumb idea to: go back to school, buy a house, invest in stocks, start a business, pay your mortgage, go to school in the first place, etc. In her twenties, Orman worked as a waitress until the day one of her regulars helped collect nearly $50,000 in donations from customers to help her dreams "come true."

Orman promptly handed the money over to a shady Merrill Lynch broker who found a way to lose it all buying options, or something. In revenge, she got hired at Merrill Lynch and honed her rare genius for couching really boring actuarial advice in New Age touchy-feely rhetoric into a weirdly mesmerizing CNBC show on which callers repeatedly beg for her permission to spend money on stupid things and are usually denied.

### Ormes, Jackie (1911–1985)

African American cartoonist best known for her Patty-Jo 'n' Ginger series, which spawned a line of Patty-Jo dolls, as well as a strong, independent Torchy Brown. She designed both characters with an eye to exploding stereotypes about what black women looked like and how they behaved. Her heyday was the 1940s and 1950s, before the civil rights movement.

### other woman

**1.** Mistress. **2.** Object of scorn when women can't deal with the fact that it's actually their partners who betrayed them. **3.** My life was fine till she blew my mind. *Awwww, shucks.* Still, in the twenty-first century, believed to be the number one cause of marriages going sour. A category error, as the actual cause is that some people (many of them male, but not all) are irredeemable assholes. (*See also* MISTRESS)

### Ouija board

Occult parlor game popularized in the late 1800s (now trademarked by Hasbro) that either performs Satan's bidding

through paranormal influence or else spells out the name of the boy you're going to marry, depending.

### Our Bodies, Ourselves

The "women's health bible" and a symbol of the 1970s' women's rights movement. First published in 1970 by the Boston Women's Health Book Collective, *OBOS* was sparked by anger at the male-dominated medical establishment, which the original authors believed was just another way to control women's bodies. If women were to be truly free, they would have to understand how their own bodies worked, and so

a small group of feminist activists wrote a short pamphlet on women's health topics—abortion, pregnancy, postpartum depression—that was by women and for women. It was a runaway success, and out of that pamphlet grew the book, which has sold over four million copies and, in its latest edition, is over eight hundred pages long.

### overreacting

The same thing as reacting, just when a woman does it about something a man wishes she would just let go.

### overshare

TMI, dude.

### overweight

Faux medical term for a person who (a) has a BMI between twenty-five and thirty and/or (b) is heavier than the speaker thinks is attractive. (*See also* FAT; FAT ACCEPTANCE; FAT SHAMING)

### Page, Bettie (1923–2008)

Plucky and determined pinup model, who after a terrible, abusive childhood was discovered by Coney Island photographers straight from central casting and ended up gracing decks of cards and early bondage photographs. The price of fame was, sadly, madness, and she ended up bouncing around between marriages, mental institutions, and Billy Graham revivals. Largely refused to be photographed for the last forty years of her life, but the few photos that *do* exist indicate she kept the bangs.

### Page, Ellen (1987–)

Pro-choice environmentalist Canadian actress who has snapped up many of the decade's best roles for women—in films about pregnant teenagers, roller derby teams, and a fourteen-year-old pedophile hunter—and identifies as a feminist as a matter of course: "You know you're working in a patriarchal society when the word feminist has a weird connotation." (*See also* Juno)

### pageant

Competition that focuses on the physical appearance of its typically female contestants and requires them to perform a talent or answer questions about current events. While wearing high heels and often swimsuits. (*See also* Miss America)

### Paglia, Camille (1947–)

Author, columnist, and polarizing feminist figure with controversial theories about rape, sexuality, and prostitution. In 1992, she told *TIME* magazine, "There is something in my book [*Sexual Personae*] to offend absolutely everybody. I am proabortion, pro the legal use of drugs, propornography, child pornography, snuff films. And I am going after these things until Gloria Steinem screams."

Sometime in the following decade, Paglia evidently heard that scream—even if no one else did—because in 2005, asked about her "battle with the feminist establishment," she proudly declared: "It's over. It's completely over. I won that war!" OK, then.

### Palin, Bristol (1990–)

Eldest daughter of Sarah Palin, former governor of Alaska and the first woman to be nominated to a Republican vice presidential ticket, who became a household name overnight when it was announced, within days of her mother's nomination as John McCain's running mate, that she was pregnant at seventeen by her boyfriend Levi Johnston. The McCain-Palin ticket made a "pro-life" example of Bristol and Johnston, assuring voters that they were now engaged. The wedding never happened, and Bristol, after giving birth to a son they named Tripp, became a teen pregnancy prevention advocate. (Interestingly, she claimed that preaching premarital abstinence is "not realistic at all.") Has appeared in *Dancing with the Stars*, her own reality show, *Life's a Tripp*, and public service announcements warning that teen motherhood is not nearly as glamorous as dancing competition shows and reality TV make it look. Or something. (*See also* ABSTINENCE; PALIN, SARAH)

### Palin, Sarah (1964–)

Former governor of Alaska who became internationally infamous when she was nominated for vice president on the Republican ticket in 2008. After losing the election, she became a professional reality star, Fox News talking head, and bestselling author. Also known for her prodigious brood and their well-publicized antics. (*See also* FEY, TINA; PALIN, BRISTOL)

### Palmer, Amanda (1976–)

Singer and lead performer for the Dresden Dolls. Courted controversy for singing openly, honestly, and comedically about rape, abortion, and slut shaming—and for imitating and exploiting disability as a part of her Siamese-twin-themed side project, Evelyn Evelyn.

### Paltrow, Gwyneth (1972–)

Handy tips for being like Gwyneth:

**MAKE:** Apple, Moses, GOOP, pronouncements about better living.

**GO:** Manhattan, London, Spain... on the Road Again.

**GET:** 1 Oscar, 1 Golden Globe, 1 Emmy, 1 number 1 hit single?

**Do:** Yoga, Chris Martin, Ben Affleck, Brad Pitt

**BE:** Lifestyle guru with a shitton of money and a love of making pronouncements.

**SEE:** *Seven, Emma, Sliding Doors, Shakespeare in Love, The Royal Tenenbaums, Iron Man.* **Probably not** *Country Strong.*

### panties

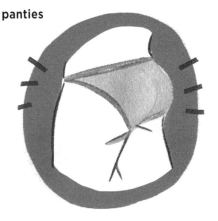

# A BRIEF HISTORY OF PANTS

Feminism and pants have been inextricably linked in Western culture.
Pants mean freedom! Here, some important moments in the history of women in pants.

## 1770s–'80s

The Queen of France, **Marie Antoinette**, an enthusiastic equestrienne, commissions several portraits depicting her in slim breeches astride a horse. She continues riding despite remonstrances from her mother and courtiers, who feared the activity would impair her ability to have children. (She had four.)

## 1851

Activist **Amelia Bloomer** begins appearing in divided trousers worn with a shortened skirt. She was introduced to the look by Elizabeth Smith Miller, who was part of the rational dress movement, made up of women in the US and England who advocated for wardrobe reform and more clothing options for women, like pants. (Dress reformers also raged against corsets.)

## 1890s

The popularity of bicycling begins to transform the perception of women in pants, making what was once seen as politically radical and socially suicidal into something modern and functional. The Lady Cyclists Association and the Rational Dress Society, both based in England, believed that cycling and pants would help women gain freedom.

## 1911

Parisian designer **Paul Poiret** debuted Middle Eastern–influenced harem pants in his collection. The look was denounced by the Vatican.

## 1914–1919

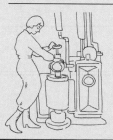

As WWI caused labor shortages, more women began working in factories and wearing pants for functionality and safety. Members of the Women's Land Army, a civilian force in Britain, were issued trousers as part of their uniform.

## 1930

Marlene Dietrich wears several pairs of pants, including as part of a tuxedo, in her American film debut, *Morocco*.

## 1968

Socialite **Nan Kempner**, denied entry to Manhattan restaurant La Côte Basque because she was wearing a YSL "Le Smoking" tuxedo, took off her pants and dined clad only in the jacket.

## 1969

Representative **Charlotte T. Reid** (R-Ill) appeared on the floor of the United States Congress in a "black wool, bell-bottomed pantsuit," according to a *Washington Post* story the next day. There was a media frenzy, and Reid decided against wearing the look again, telling the *Post*, "I am really quite serious about my service in the Congress and I wouldn't want to do anything that seemed facetious. Neither would I want to do anything to take away from the femininity of the women in the House, even though I think pants are feminine-looking."

## 1980

Fifteen-year-old **Brooke Shields** appears in a controversial commercial for Calvin Klein jeans, telling the world, "Nothing comes between me and my Calvins." CBS refused to air it; feminists denounced it; in 2010 Shields said, "I look at these pictures now and I still am sort of shocked that they became so legendary. For me, it was just a huge job I went to after school at 3 o'clock. The one with my leg up, I just remember my arm hurting. You can't plan on being iconic."

## 1992

**Vivienne Westwood**, the London designer who brought punk and fashion together with creations like bondage pants, is received by Queen Elizabeth at Buckingham Palace. Upon her departure from the palace, Westwood posed and did a turn for the assembled paparazzi, revealing she was *not* wearing pants, causing a scandal, and bringing us full circle.

**pantyhose**

Leg accessory usually made of sheer nylon, worn to demonstrate modesty, make a fashion statement, or help a woman's legs appear even-toned. Apparently, Kate Middleton brought them back into fashion. (*See also* CONTROL TOP)

**Pap smear**

Horribly named screening test invented by Greek doctor Georgios Papanikolaou and used to detect changes in the cells of the human cervix. Pap smears can help determine if a woman has an infection, abnormal cells, or cervical cancer, which, when caught early, has a high chance of being effectively treated.

**Parker, Dorothy (1893–1967)**

American poet, satirist, screenwriter, and critic famed for her witty quips and bon mots. Wrote for the *New Yorker* and was a founding member of the Algonquin Round Table, the famed group of artists and intellectuals that would meet daily at the Algonquin Hotel. One of many named on the Hollywood blacklist during the Red Scare of the 1950s. Left her estate to Dr. Martin Luther King Jr.

**Parker, Sarah Jessica (1965–)**

Actress most famous for her portrayal of Carrie Bradshaw, *Sex and the City*'s Cosmopolitan-swilling, Manolo-wearing sex columnist who "couldn't help but wonder" about love and lust in pre-9/11 Manhattan. The role turned Parker into a fashion icon; after the series ended, she became the face of global brands such as Garnier and the Gap and launched her own clothing and perfume lines. Also single-handedly started the "gigantic fucking corsage" trend. (*See also* BRADSHAW, CARRIE; SEX AND THE CITY)

**Parks, Rosa (1913–2005)**

Activist, American hero, cofounder of the Rosa and Raymond Parks Institute for Self Development, and onetime aide to Representative John J. Conyers. You probably learned about her in elementary school, through the kind of story Americans love to tell their kids: one day, after years of mistreatment, an unassuming nobody spontaneously stood up for

herself and changed the course of history with that one brave act. It is true that in Montgomery, Alabama, in 1955, Parks, an African American seamstress, refused to give up her bus seat to a white person when ordered to by the driver. And it's true that this was the catalyst for a yearlong bus boycott by Montgomery's black community, which would be led by Martin Luther King Jr. and become a major milestone in civil rights history. It's not true, however, that she was just some random middle-aged woman with tired feet and a child's sense of fairness. Parks had attempted public transit boycotts before— "My resisting being mistreated on the bus did not begin with that particular arrest. I did a lot of walking in Montgomery," she said in a 1988 interview—and had been active in the burgeoning civil rights movement for more than a decade, serving as secretary of the Montgomery chapter of the NAACP. As a result of her act of civil disobedience on December 1, Parks was not only arrested and fined but targeted socially and economically. She and her husband were both forced out of their jobs in Montgomery and went north to look for work, eventually settling in Detroit, where Parks would live until her death at the age of ninety-two.

### Parks, Suzan-Lori (1963–)

Pulitzer Prize–winning playwright.

> "I've said I write plays because I love black people. I just figured it out fairly recently. Not that I had any other reason before that, but I realized why I want black people on stage—because I love them. And it probably sounds very vague, but it's true."
>
> —to *Bomb*, 1994

### Parton, Dolly (1946–)

American singer-songwriter, actor, author, theme park owner, and national treasure. On her way up, Parton deftly avoided making everything all about her looks by…making everything all about her looks. Specifically, her enormous fake breasts—and later, fake damn near everything. Her signature look has always been so over-the-top—and she's been so candid about the amount of surgery required to achieve it—that there's really no point in belaboring the issue, which frees folks up to notice how smart, funny, and talented she is. Forget the music, the business sense, the charm, the *twenty-six* number 1 country hits, the Kennedy Center honors, Truvy Jones, Doralee Rhodes, and Dollywood: we'd be happy if we could even write one lyric as good as "pour myself a cup of ambition."

### party girl

"Can I have a falafel with hot sauce, a side order of baba ghanoush, and a seltzer, please?"

### paternalism

Fancy name for father knows best.

### paternity test

Blood test to prove or deny a man's fatherhood of a child. Dramatic device that launched a thousand celebratory dances on *The Maury Povich Show*.

### patriarchy

Smash it.

### Pattinson, Robert (1986–)

English actor. Played sullen sparkle vampire Edward Cullen in the Hollywood blockbuster series *Twilight* and quickly became the object of much frenzied girl fantasy—his face screen-printed across black panties, his supposed member molded into a cold shimmery vampire dildo. Has mixed feelings about this. "When you read the book…

it's like, 'Edward Cullen was so beautiful I creamed myself.' I mean, *every line* is like that," Pattinson said about playing the vampire. "He's the most ridiculous person who's so amazing at everything…the more I read the script, the more I hated this guy, so that's how I played him, as a manic-depressive who hates himself."

### Paul, Alice (1885–1977)

American suffragist who played an integral role in securing women's right to vote. Highly educated for a woman of her era—she had three law degrees at a time when few women even had undergraduate degrees—she organized a march on Washington in favor of women's suffrage on the day before President Woodrow Wilson's inauguration, demanding a constitutional amendment that would allow women to vote. This was a break from the state-by-state method favored by earlier suffragettes like Elizabeth Cady Stanton and Susan B. Anthony, and it caused disagreement and tension within the movement, though Paul's vision would eventually come to fruition. In 1917, Paul and other suffragettes picketed the White House and were arrested. In jail, Paul went on a hunger strike and was force-fed. The resulting media attention and political pressure caused President Wilson to prioritize the passage of a constitutional amendment, and in 1920, thanks to the Nineteenth Amendment, American women finally won the right to vote. (*See also* SUFFRAGETTE)

### PC

A type of computer and operating system. (*See also* POLITICALLY CORRECT)

### pedicure

A manicure for the feet. (*See also* MANICURE)

**peep toe**
Open-toed shoes, which are considered scandalous in some offices.

### Peete, Holly Robinson (1964–)

Actress. Now and forever, Officer Judy Hoffs. (*See also* HOFFS, JUDY)

### Pelosi, Nancy (1940–)

First female Speaker of the House and, at press time, one of the highest-ranking female politicians in American history. As the congressional representative for most of San Francisco and a woman with a great deal of power, she would tie Hillary Clinton and Michelle Obama in a contest to see who can make the most right-wing nutjobs fall apart completely. And she has more than once threatened members of Congress with her "mother-of-five voice"! What's not to love?

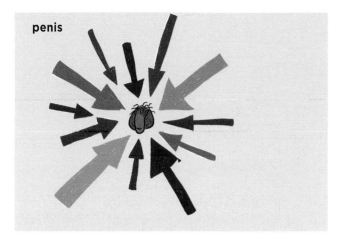

penis

### *Penthouse* letters

Fictional "letters" that appear in *Penthouse* magazine. In a generation of texting shorthand and internet emoticons, these letters and Harry Potter books are the only things keeping us literate.

### people pleaser

Person who puts others' lives before her own, raises others up while beating herself down, and wants others to like her more than she likes herself. A particularly feminine affliction, as women are encouraged to cultivate their maternal and social instincts over their personal identities and successes.

### Peppermint Patty

*Peanuts* character deliberately intended by creator Charles M. Schulz to represent the women's movement, which doesn't quite jibe with her habit of doing poorly in school and not being able to tell a dog from a person. That said, she certainly doesn't throw like a girl, and her dedication to Birkenstock-like

footwear through the changing mores of fashion is admirable. We wish, all these years later, she'd finally realize she's too good for Charlie Brown, but, hey, we've all been there.

### perfectionism

Affliction of a new breed of privileged young women who are, as journalist Courtney Martin catalogued in her 2007 book *Perfect Girls, Starving Daughters*, "relentless, judgmental with ourselves, and forgiving to others. We never want to be as passive-aggressive as our mothers, never want to marry men as uninspired as our fathers. We carry the world of guilt—center of families, keeper of relationships, caretaker of friends—with a new world of control/ambition—rich, independent, powerful, We are the daughters of feminists who said, 'You can be anything' and we heard 'You have to be everything.'"

### period

The time, or period, during which a woman is menstruating. A period lasts for between three and five days. And it happens every month. For about forty years of your life. Welcome to womanhood! (*See also* CHANGE OF LIFE; MAXI PADS; MENSTRUATION; TAMPONS)

### Perkins, Frances (1880–1965)

First woman in the US Cabinet (as secretary of labor) and major architect of the New Deal. Personally witnessed the 1911 Triangle Shirtwaist Factory fire in New York City, where over a hundred women died, many leaping to their deaths, and after that couldn't shut up for a second about workers' rights. Kept a big red envelope in which she filed away her "Notes on Male Minds," a coping strategy that led her to conclude, among other things, that men respected mothers and thus she should dress like one. By and large, that seemed to work, though she found herself nicknamed Ma Perkins at the ripe old age of thirty-three as a result. It was, in her calculation, a small price to pay for such policy innovations as, you know, Social Security.

### perky

Feminine descriptor to describe a woman's positive demeanor, and, inextricably, her breasts.

# The Periodic Table

## An Elementary Table of Terms

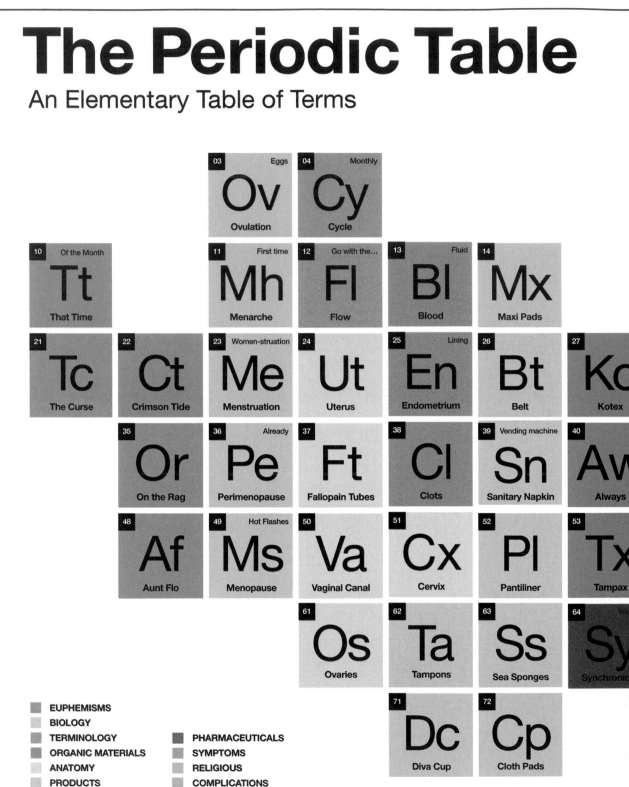

| | |
|---|---|
| 03 Eggs **Ov** Ovulation | 04 Monthly **Cy** Cycle |

| | | | | |
|---|---|---|---|---|
| 10 Of the Month **Tt** That Time | 11 First time **Mh** Menarche | 12 Go with the... **Fl** Flow | 13 Fluid **Bl** Blood | 14 **Mx** Maxi Pads |
| 21 **Tc** The Curse | 22 **Ct** Crimson Tide | 23 Women-struation **Me** Menstruation | 24 **Ut** Uterus | 25 Lining **En** Endometrium |

Other elements:
- 26 **Bt** Belt
- 27 **Ko** Kotex
- 35 **Or** On the Rag
- 36 Already **Pe** Perimenopause
- 37 **Ft** Fallopain Tubes
- 38 **Cl** Clots
- 39 Vending machine **Sn** Sanitary Napkin
- 40 **Aw** Always
- 48 **Af** Aunt Flo
- 49 Hot Flashes **Ms** Menopause
- 50 **Va** Vaginal Canal
- 51 **Cx** Cervix
- 52 **Pl** Pantiliner
- 53 **Tx** Tampax
- 61 **Os** Ovaries
- 62 **Ta** Tampons
- 63 **Ss** Sea Sponges
- 64 You t **Sy** Synchronicit
- 71 **Dc** Diva Cup
- 72 **Cp** Cloth Pads

Legend:
- EUPHEMISMS
- BIOLOGY
- TERMINOLOGY
- ORGANIC MATERIALS
- ANATOMY
- PRODUCTS
- BRANDS
- PRODUCT CATEGORIES
- PHARMACEUTICALS
- SYMPTOMS
- RELIGIOUS
- COMPLICATIONS
- MESSES
- OTHER

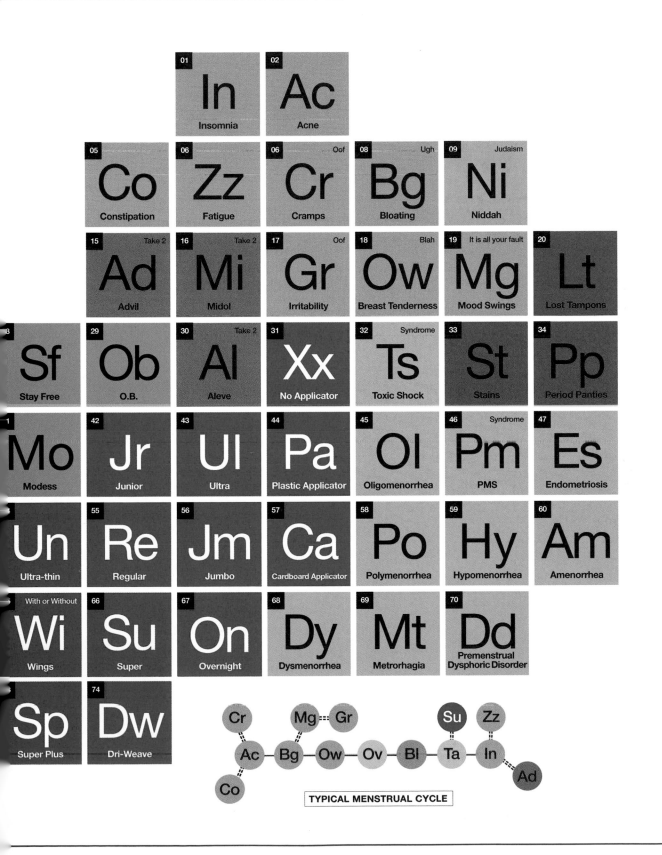

| | | 01 **In** Insomnia | 02 **Ac** Acne | | | |
|---|---|---|---|---|---|---|
| | 05 **Co** Constipation | 06 **Zz** Fatigue | 06 Oof **Cr** Cramps | 08 Ugh **Bg** Bloating | 09 Judaism **Ni** Niddah | |
| | 15 Take 2 **Ad** Advil | 16 Take 2 **Mi** Midol | 17 Oof **Gr** Irritability | 18 Blah **Ow** Breast Tenderness | 19 It is all your fault **Mg** Mood Swings | 20 **Lt** Lost Tampons |
| 8 **Sf** Stay Free | 29 **Ob** O.B. | 30 Take 2 **Al** Aleve | 31 **Xx** No Applicator | 32 Syndrome **Ts** Toxic Shock | 33 **St** Stains | 34 **Pp** Period Panties |
| 1 **Mo** Modess | 42 **Jr** Junior | 43 **Ul** Ultra | 44 **Pa** Plastic Applicator | 45 **Ol** Oligomenorrhea | 46 Syndrome **Pm** PMS | 47 **Es** Endometriosis |
| **Un** Ultra-thin | 55 **Re** Regular | 56 **Jm** Jumbo | 57 **Ca** Cardboard Applicator | 58 **Po** Polymenorrhea | 59 **Hy** Hypomenorrhea | 60 **Am** Amenorrhea |
| With or Without **Wi** Wings | 66 **Su** Super | 67 **On** Overnight | 68 **Dy** Dysmenorrhea | 69 **Mt** Metrorrhagia | 70 **Dd** Premenstrual Dysphoric Disorder | |
| **Sp** Super Plus | 74 **Dw** Dri-Weave | | | | | |

**TYPICAL MENSTRUAL CYCLE**

## perm

Chemical treatment of the hair to make it curly. For the younger generation, "the permanent wave" was first introduced in the movie *Legally Blonde*, when protagonist Elle Woods used the fact that one would not immediately dampen hair that has just been permed in order to prove a crazed curly-haired girl guilty of murder, and her client innocent. For everyone else, an unfortunate, hours-long, smelly process that is currently out of fashion.

## Perón, Eva (1919–1952)

Argentine icon and first lady from 1946 until her death in 1952. Thought by some to be a revolutionary saint who fought tirelessly for her *descamisados*; by others to be a selfish, fascist prima donna. Played by Madonna in a 1996 biopic based on Andrew Lloyd Webber's late 1970s musical *Evita*.

## Perry, Anne (1938–)

Author of historical crime novels, born Juliet Hulme, who was convicted of murdering a friend's mother at age fifteen. Kate Winslet played her in the Oscar-nominated film about the murder, *Heavenly Creatures*.

## Perry, Katy (1984–)

Christian gospel singer, born Katheryn Hudson, changed her name to Katy Perry, released a lezploitational single, began making public appearances dressed as a cartoon character,  excreted frosting from her nipples, lampooned her pop star status by donning glasses and headgear in a video about getting blackout drunk, then documented the entire fame cycle in a 3D feature film in which she thanks fans for "believing in my weirdness!" Perry embodies a new model for the modern pop star, in which the public image machine of the record, film, and television industries that churns young women into marketable pop products is presented as a winking commentary on fame instead of its product. (*See also* GAGA, LADY)

## Perry, Linda (1965–)

Lead singer of 4 Non Blondes. Partner of Sara Gilbert.

## personally, taking things

(*See* OVERREACTING)

## personhood

Ideology that strives to legally define embryos as people from the moment of fertilization, bringing a whole new meaning to antichoice claims that abortion is "murder." Though it might sound like a bad joke from an *SNL* sketch, the movement has many supporters, some of whom hold high office. (Take Kentucky senator Rand Paul, who sneakily tried to insert a personhood clause into a bill about flood insurance. Smooth!) And despite the best efforts of pro-choice activists, they're not giving up. Over the past few years, Keith Mason, founder of faith-based activist group Personhood USA, helped introduce twenty-two personhood bills and ballot initiatives. None passed, though the margin of defeat is declining. In November 2012, Republican lawmakers in Michigan went so far as to propose an amendment to the state's tax code that would allow pregnant women to claim twelve-week or older fetuses as dependents. (As for whether the GOP's benevolence would continue following birth, history suggests the answer is no.)

## PETA

Animal rights organization whose slogan is "Animals are not ours to eat, wear, experiment on, use for entertainment, or abuse in any way." Does some good work increasing awareness of animal cruelty but has a maddening tendency to objectify women by using the naked female form as a way to protest fur and meat consumption. (*See also* NEWKIRK, INGRID)

## Phair, Liz (1967–)

Musician, singer, and friendly neighborhood "blow-job queen" who made it okay for a generation of girls to be raunchy and blunt and flawed and self-conscious about their bikini lines. Her 1993 lo-fi rock album *Exile in Guyville* was a massive hit that has sold more than half a million copies to date and still

shows up on lists of the greatest albums of all time. "As a female, I don't think you're supposed to say the kind of things I wanted to say," said Phair of *Guyville*. "I think I felt like I had been listening for ten years to records where guys talked explicitly about sex and…women were sort of shunted to the area of emotion. But I've always been pissed off, frankly, that that whole myth that women aren't interested in sex…And as tough as I come across trying to be on the record, that's really the beauty of *Guyville*, is that it's really such a portrait of a vulnerable young woman trying to establish some kind of power for herself."

### Phalle, Niki de Saint (1930–2002)
French artist and sculptor and onetime fashion model celebrated for her pieces involving women and their roles in society. Her work includes life-size dolls of brides and female figures known as Nanas, which explore and comment on female archetypes and celebrate womanhood and motherhood. After purchasing land in Tuscany in 1979, she worked for twenty years to create The Tarot Garden, a sculpture garden filled with giant, colorful creations based on figures and symbols from the Tarot. (*See also* TAROT)

### phallic
The Washington Monument. Nuclear missiles. Hot dogs. Look around, and you'll notice that pretty much everything in this world is shaped like a penis.

### Photoshop
Adobe computer program for editing photographs, text, and graphics. Colloquial use: when a photograph has been markedly and recognizably digitally altered. "That looks so Photoshopped."

### Photoshop of Horrors
Digital alteration of a photo to render it unrecognizable or terrifying. Seen most often on female models in advertising campaigns and on magazine covers. Symptoms include: severed or contorted limbs, missing ribs, waists too narrow to actually contain organs, frighteningly pore-less skin, and breast reductions and/or enlargements. The cumulative effect of this Frankensteinian airbrushing can cause the average magazine reader to develop a false or unrealistic idea of what an actual human woman looks like.

## Pickford, Mary (1892–1979)

Actress and stealth Canadian, born Gladys Smith, who became "America's Sweetheart." The critic Delmore Schwartz noted that the title more or less amounted to "America's spiritual jailbait," because Pickford always pretended to be younger than she actually was. Despite a sweet public face was known to be anxious and sharp; she'd fought her way out of poverty to her huge, half-million-dollar contract. Her marriage to Douglas Fairbanks began in scandal and ended in drink. Had her career ruined when she began to talk; she called the advent of talkies "putting lipstick on a Venus de Milo."

## picky

Derogatory adjective describing unmarried women over the age of twenty-eight.

## pie

Better than cake.

## pillow fight

Childhood game that, when engaged in by adult women, is converted into an erotic symbol to infantilize them.

## pink

On the color wheel, a subhue of red (*roseus* in Latin) first named in the seventeenth century after a flowering plant. We can blame the French for the association of pink with girlhood, according to Louisa May Alcott in *Little Women*: "Amy put a blue ribbon on the boy and a pink on the girl, French fashion, so you can always tell [them apart]." However, as recently as 1918, the American publication *Earnshaw's Infants' Department* suggested that pink, "the stronger color," was better suited to boys. The pairing of baby girls and a cotton candy hue began to solidify around the 1950s, when, as fashion historian Jo Paoletti found, the color was "strongly associated with femininity." Since that time, feminist causes such as breast cancer charities have reclaimed the color for their own use, but it is still rigidly tied to gender reinforcement (and limitation) in young children from an early age and can thus be dangerous. In her book *Cinderella Ate My Daughter*, Peggy Orenstein argues that pink "firmly fuses girls' identity to appearance…and that innocent pink pretty quickly turns into something else, a kind of diva, self-absorbed pink and ultimately a sexualized pink." (*See also* BREAST CANCER)

## pinkwasher

"Pinkwasher: (pink-wah-sher) noun. A company or organization that claims to care about breast cancer by promoting a pink ribbon product, but at the same time produces, manufactures and/or sells products that are linked to the disease."

—Breast Cancer Action, the organization that coined the term

## Piper, Adrian Margaret Smith (1948–)

Artist, philosopher, and yoga teacher. Harvard philosophy PhD noted for her work on metaphysics, Kant, and metaethics. As a conceptual artist, Piper focuses on race and gender and explores the dynamics of racial profiling, notably in her interactive piece *Calling Card,* in which she handed out a card admonishing a person for their racism whenever she saw it in evidence.

## placenta

Organ that develops in the female uterus during pregnancy and assists with the exchange of nutrients and the disposal of waste in a developing human being. Expelled during labor and called "afterbirth." Many animals eat their placentas, which are full of nutrients. Some humans do, too.

## Planned Parenthood

Nonprofit reproductive health-care provider and advocate. The organization, founded in 1916 as the American Birth Control League, has been a lightning rod from the time Margaret Sanger landed in jail for distributing information about birth control to the near shutdown of the federal government almost a century later, over funding for the organization Sanger created. It's less controversial, though, to the one in five American women who has, at one point in her life, relied on a Planned Parenthood health center. There was a brief moment when women controlling their fertility, including with access to abortion, wasn't so controversial, even if it was couched in terms less terrifying to the status quo, like *family planning* and *population control*. It was the time when Richard Nixon put birth control on the national agenda and said there should be access to contraceptive services for "all those who want them but cannot afford them," and when then congressman George H. W. Bush earned the nickname Rubbers for his passion for family planning. But by the 2012 Republican presidential primaries, the antichoice fringe's obsession with taking down Planned Parenthood, starting with stripping it of government funding, had become a baseline position. It wasn't just flamethrowers like Congresswoman Michele Bachmann (who called Planned Parenthood "corrupt" and "criminal," despite the nonresults of every witch hunt); it was Mitt Romney saying "Planned Parenthood, we're going to get rid of that." But if that election politicized Planned Parenthood as never before, it also galvanized and grew support among people who wanted women's health care to be not a cause of controversy but rather an essential human right. (*See also* BACHMANN, MICHELE; BIRTH CONTROL; SANGER, MARGARET)

## *Planned Parenthood v. Casey*

Profoundly divided 1992 Supreme Court decision that didn't overturn *Roe v. Wade* (as many pro-choice observers feared it would), thanks to eleventh-hour persuasions of Republican-appointed justices. But *Casey* did essentially say that the state could put any hurdle in a woman's way to an abortion except banning it outright. It opened the door to hundreds of state-level abortion restrictions intended to impede access, as long as they didn't present an "undue burden." The only thing the Court thought was an "undue burden" was the requirement that a woman notify her husband ahead of time. It retained everything else intended to talk women out of having abortions or make them really, really hard to access, and still does to this day. (*See also* ABORTION; PLANNED PARENTHOOD; PRO-LIFE; ROE V. WADE)

### Plath, Sylvia (1932–1963)

Poet and writer. In her pseudonymously published fictionalized account of her life, 1963's *The Bell Jar*, Plath introduced readers to a young woman in New York City who, disillusioned with her lackluster career and romantic prospects, falls into depression and finds hope in the form of a diaphragm. A month after its publication, Plath sealed the door to her kitchen with a wet cloth and stuck her head in the oven while the two children she had with estranged husband Ted Hughes slept in the next room.

## *Playboy*

Hugh Hefner's gentleman's magazine that claimed to stage a revolution against the repressive sexual mores of the 1950s—but only for the silk pajama–loving men who love women caged in sad bunny costumes, injected with saline, and laid prone on the floor under some soft lighting. "The interesting thing

is how one guy, through living out his own fantasies, is living out the fantasies of so many other people," Hefner once said, falsely. (*See also* HEFNER, HUGH)

### plus-sized models

Not to be confused with plus-sized women, plus-sized models are women who model plus-size clothing, but generally wear a size 12: larger than most straight-size models, but still smaller than the average American woman (a size 14). In recent years, Ralph Lauren and Jean Paul Gaultier have both used plus-sized models in print campaigns and on the runway, which is A Good Thing. Baby steps.

### plus sizes

In stores, size 14 and up. In modeling, size 6 and up.

## PMS

A cluster of mildly unpleasant (at least if you're lucky) symptoms, sometimes including irritability and weepiness, which means men have turned it into the reason why the wimminz is bugfuck crazy and dangerous. All month.

### Pocahontas (1595–1617)

Native American woman who, we're told, palled around with English colonizers at Jamestown and maybe even saved the life of a guy named John Smith by telling her father he had to go through her if he wanted to cut off Smith's head. English people repaid the favor in 1613 by capturing her and keeping her prisoner long enough for Stockholm syndrome to set in, so when she got a chance to return to her people, she took a pass (along with a new name, Rebecca, and a husband, John Rolfe, with whom she had a son named Thomas). In 1995, she was run through the Disney Princess filter and given an adorable raccoon sidekick about which Kent A. Ono and Derek T. Buescher (authors of the academic article "*Deciphering Pocahontas: Unpackaging the Commod-ification of a Native American Woman*") wrote: "By telling the story of Pocahontas, and directing its appeals not to Native American audiences but to those outside the Native American community…Disney effectively appropriates Native American culture and Native American history and transforms them into commodities, [constructing] Pocahontas as a feminine, postfeminist, Native American woman—the strong athletic type who understands nature, animals, colonial relationships, and love, but who, above all, ultimately wants the freedom to choose to be in a heterosexual romantic relationship and then to give that relationship up to serve her community, all as expressions of her newly found liberated independence."

### Poehler, Amy (1971–)

Actress, producer, comedienne, activist, and everything that is good and right in the world. First garnered notoriety as one of the early members of the improv/sketch group-turned-comedy nerd paradise the Upright Citizens Brigade. Cast member on *Saturday Night Live* from 2001 to 2008, before she left to star as feminist political hero Leslie Knope in NBC's hit sitcom *Parks and Recreation*. Poehler has since starred in several movies and formed Smart Girls at the Party, a web series that cele-brates young girls working in science, sports, and the arts and meant to foster positivity, individu-alism, intelligence, and creativity. There is a rumor (started right now, by us) that Mariah Carey's 1993 hit "Hero" was written about Poehler. This rumor is probably a lie.

### Pogrebin, Letty Cottin (1939–)

Second-wave feminist cofounder of *Ms.* and the National Women's Political Caucus. Her children—Abigail, Robin, and David Pogrebin—were on the original cover of *Free to Be… You and Me*. (*See also* FREE TO BE…YOU AND ME; MS. MAGAZINE)

### politically correct

Pejorative term—employed self-deprecatingly by progressives and accusatorially by conservatives—for being mindful of racism, sexism, and a host of whole other isms.

### politically incorrect

**1.** Synonym for "I'm about to say something grossly racist/sexist/homophobic/transphobic and pretend I'm being edgy." **2.** When italicized, old Bill Maher show that could have been called "I'm about to say something grossly racist/sexist/homophobic/transphobic in the guise of being edgy."

### Pollitt, Katha (1949–)

Award-winning poet, feminist, and columnist. Her collection of personal essays, *Learning to Drive*, caused a tiny brouhaha because Pollitt admitted to such cardinal (and eminently relatable) sins as cyberstalking an ex-boyfriend and being a terrible driver. She was convicted in the press for Thoughts Unbecoming a Feminist, or something, and responded, in a *Guardian* interview:

"I just keep going back to the fact that feminism is about women telling the truth of their experiences. I mean, it's not about puffing yourself up in the world to look like you've got everything all figured out. You can look at the life of just about any historical feminist and they did not have these lives of quiet domestic order. They were very tempestuous people."

### polyamory

Relationship system that eschews one-on-one partnerships and encourages its participants to explore their physical and emotional attractions to other people and even develop multiple romantic attachments.

### pom-pom

(*See also* CHEERLEADERS)

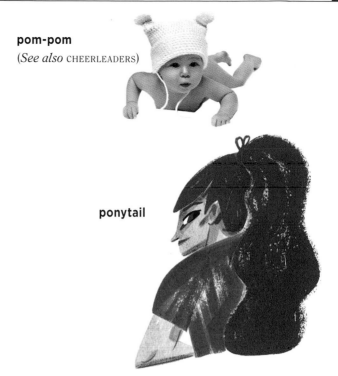

ponytail

### pooch

Often-nonexistent abdominal fat.

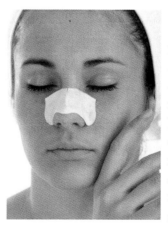

### pores

Openings on the surface skin from which hair, sebum, and other biological material emanate. Have you ever freaked out about your pores being too big or clogged or oily? If not, you're probably not an American woman, because we're conditioned to feel horrible about pores as soon as we hit puberty. Helpful tip: no expensive face cream will ever make your pores disappear so your face looks Photoshop-smooth. Sorry! (*See also* ACNE; ZITS)

### pornography

Print, online, or multimedia that depicts at least one, and usually more than one, person engaging in sexual or semisexual acts for the purposes of arousing the viewer. Usually distinguished from soft-core pornography or erotica by visibly aroused genitals and/or anuses.

### Posey, Parker (1968–)

Indie queen who clocked over thirty independent films in the nineties, of which *Party Girl* was the best. (*See also* PARTY GIRL)

### postfeminist

Postfeminists are these total dicks who are trying to trick you into thinking that feminism won (!) and gender equality has been achieved (!) in hopes that you'll do a little less complaining and a little more blow-jobbing. The patriarchy is really beneficial and comfortable for a lot of people, and now that the cat's out of the bag and it's too late to pretend that patriarchy never existed, it's easier to pretend that it's been defeated. Well, it hasn't. Do not listen to these people, for they are manipulative goobers.

### postpartum depression

Type of clinical mood disorder with a usual onset of within one year of the birth of a child. "At my lowest points, I thought of swallowing a bottle of pills or jumping out the window of my apartment," wrote Brooke Shields of her struggle to be happy after her daughter was born. After noted man of science Tom Cruise criticized her use of antidepressants to conquer her feelings of sadness, Shields wrote an awesome *New York Times* op-ed smackdown.

### postracist

(*See* POSTFEMINIST. *Extrapolate.*)

### Potter, Beatrix (1866–1943)

English author and illustrator who collected fossils and painted fungi before bringing Flopsy, Mopsy, Cottontail, and Peter to life in the early 1900s. A conservationist, Potter used her beloved countryside as inspiration for such childhood classics as *The Tale of Peter Rabbit*, *The Tale of Squirrel Nutkin*, and *The Tale of Mrs. Tiggy-Winkle.*

### Power, Samantha (1970–)

Dublin-born scholar of human rights and genocide who ended up working in the Obama administration. Rumored to also kick many a male staffer's ass at basketball. Won the Pulitzer Prize for her very first book, *A Problem from Hell*. Got herself in trouble by calling Hillary Clinton a "monster"—"off the record"—during the 2008 primaries. She had to resign from the Obama campaign briefly but made up with Hillary by the time the swearing-in rolled around.

### *Powerpuff Girls*

Animated crimefighters. The Cartoon Network's Blossom, Bubbles, and Buttercup were the late 1990s' and early 2000s' answer to *Charlie's Angels*. Apparently created in a lab experiment gone awry, they were, according to the show's theme song, made out of "Sugar, spice, and everything nice / These were the ingredients chosen / To create the perfect little girls." (They were actually created in 1991 by animator Craig McCracken while he was a student at CalArts.) "To their loyal fans and amused admirers, these kindergarten rabble-rousers represent something bigger than the next Hello Kitty," wrote Heather Havrilesky for *Salon* in 2002. "For hyper-analytical adults and avid third-wave feminists, they're animated proof that strong female characters can kick ass and take names without compromising their femininity." Havrilesky also pointed out that "it could be argued that their popularity may not reflect a dramatic shift in our society's view of gender roles, but rather our inability to stomach female anger unless it's sugarcoated in cuteness and scored with a pervasively chirpy, nonthreatening tone." (*See also* SUGAR AND SPICE)

## Prada, Miuccia (1949–)

Creative director of Prada, the fashion company established in 1913 by her grandfather Mario, who had insisted that women are unfit to run any business. Pre-Prada, was a Communist and activist for women's rights, a doctoral student in political science, and a mime apprentice at the Piccolo Teatro in Milan. The designer is often called a proponent of the "pretty-ugly" aesthetic through her use of unfashionable materials and "ugly" colors and shapes in unexpected and avant-garde ways.

## Pratt, Jane (1962–)

Editor in chief of the amazing *Sassy* magazine, the pretty good *Jane* magazine, and the tragically train-wrecky website xoJane. (*See also* JANE MAGAZINE; SASSY)

## *Precious*

2009 Lee Daniels film based on the novel *Push* by Sapphire, which chronicles the life of Claireece "Precious" Jones, an illiterate and obese inner-city teenager who is pregnant with her second child. Gabourey Sidibe, in her first major role, portrayed Precious in the film adaptation.

## pregnancy

Time during which a female with a uterus plays host to a developing fetus.

## pretty

Physically attractive. Girls and women are expected to be pretty. But not *too* pretty; otherwise, no one will take them seriously. They should try as hard as they can to be pretty, but that effort should never be visible to anyone. Does this sound like an impossibly fine line to walk? Stop complaining; complaining's not pretty.

## prima donna

(*See* DIVA)

## princess

**1.** Per Merriam-Webster, "a female member of a royal family; *especially*: a daughter or granddaughter of a sovereign." **2.** A spoiled young girl or tiny dog. **3.** One of Disney's questionably royal heroines, who are like crack to your six-year-old niece, even if her feminist parents have bent over backward to raise her in a gender-neutral environment. (We're with US Supreme Court Justice Sonia Sotomayor, who spelled it out for incipient fairy Muppet Abby Cadabby on *Sesame Street*: "Abby, pretending to be a princess is fun, but it is definitely not a career.") (*See also* DISNEY PRINCESSES; JASMINE; POCAHONTAS; PRINCESS DIANA; SOTOMAYOR, SONIA)

## Princess Diana (1961–1997)

Aristocrat, mother, activist, tabloid prey. Born Diana Spencer, she married Prince Charles in a 1981 wedding that triggered interest in royalty for a whole new generation. Gen Xers weaned on Disney princesses watched in awe as she emerged from a carriage in an enormous floofy dress; she walked in a Lady and walked out a Princess. As the years passed, we came to know her as fashionable, charitable, shy, classy, and slightly mismatched for her odd royal life, which involved constantly being in the public eye, a dorky husband, and an oppressive palace full of rules. By the 1990s, the fairy-tale marriage was over, but Princess Di emerged from the stale cocoon of royal life as a fabulous social butterfly, continuing her charity work—famously holding children with HIV at a time when AIDS-phobia was rampant—but also hitting international galas dressed to the nines. She struck up a friendship with Liz Tilberis, who worked at British *Vogue* for twenty years before becoming the editor in chief of *Harper's BAZAAR*. Once she was separated from the prince, Diana admitted that there had been three people in her marriage—herself, Prince Charles, and his mistress, Camilla Parker-Bowles—garnering even more sympathy and love, though she was already fairly universally adored. Princess Di's divorce was finalized in August 1996; she dated a heart surgeon and the Harrods heir Dodi Fayed before her untimely death in August 1997. The gruesome car crash that fatally injured the princess was blamed on the paparazzi, the palace, and the driver's drinking, but in the end, she never truly left us: Princess Di has become a symbol of the positive qualities of the monarchy—charity, elegance, compassion, beauty—as well as the negative: closed/oppressive/restrictive living, conspiracies, outdated traditions, princes who ought to be charming but are actually frogs. (*See also* AIDS; Diana; Disney princesses)

### privacy

Unwritten constitutional right to do what you want to your own body in your own home, as laid out in cases like 1965's *Griswold v. Connecticut*, which legalized contraception, 1973's *Roe v. Wade*, which legalized abortion across the country, and 2003's *Lawrence v. Texas*, which legalized sodomy.

### privilege

Among certain academics and the feminist blogosphere, a word that references unearned advantages usually conferred upon one at birth and matching one or more aspects of our culture's ideal human being: white, heterosexual, cisgender, nondisabled, nonfat, wealthy, Christian, highly educated, strong-jawed, male. If you still don't get it, start by reading Peggy McIntosh's "White Privilege: Unpacking the Invisible Knapsack," and then read the rest of the fucking internet. (*See also* CISGENDER)

### pro-ana

One of those things that, if you're not the market for it, you can hardly believe it exists. Short for "pro-anorexia," it's a movement (sort of) of mostly teenage girls who tell themselves and each other that their potentially deadly mental illness is a lifestyle choice. Every time one pro-ana website gets shut down, ten more pop up in its place. Heartbreaking.

### pro-choice

Descriptor pro–abortion rights individuals use to describe their viewpoint with respect to the legality of pregnancy termination. Often mischaracterized as "pro-abortion" by individuals opposed to abortion rights, pro-choice individuals are in favor of allowing women the legal option to terminate their pregnancies.

### pro-life

Word antiabortion-rights individuals use to describe their viewpoint with respect to the legality or morality of pregnancy termination. "Life" in this case refers to the potential life of the gestating fetus, not the life of the mother or her family. Pro-life groups often spread their message using propaganda containing the phrase "choose life"—ironic, because the "choosing" is what they aim to outlaw. In recent years, the term pro-life has been adopted by groups who believe that human life begins at the moment of conception, and that therefore certain kinds of birth control and the morning-after pill are akin to murder. (See also PERSONHOOD)

### progesterone

Female hormone necessary for a healthy pregnancy and the cause of indigestion, heartburn, constipation, and the dense, eye-stinging, tear-inducing, hot-bus-exhaust-like, suffocating flatulence known as "mom farts."

### progressive

1. Political movement that on the one hand supports women's rights with regard to voting, birth control, abortion, workforce participation, and equal pay, and on the other, has incubated a long series of sexist leaders—from *Hardball*'s Chris Matthews, who called Hillary Clinton a "witchy" "stripteaser" who only scored a Senate seat because her husband cheated, to Arianna Huffington, whose *Huffington Post* has trafficked

off the nonconsensual sexual displays of women's "nipple slips" and announced that the "next feminist issue is sleep." **2.** Car insurance company.

**promiscuous**

(*See* SLUT)

**proposal**

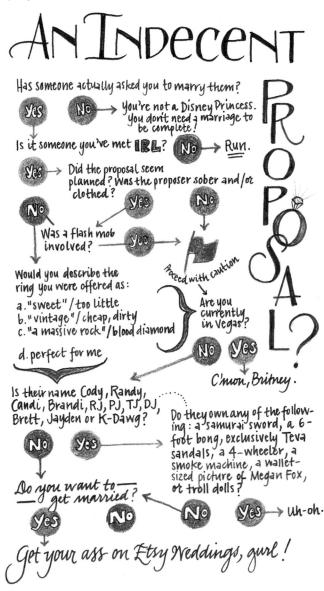

**prostitute**

A person who provides sexual services in exchange for financial compensation. Although often referred to as "the world's oldest profession," prostitution is illegal in many countries, including nearly everywhere in the United States.

**puberty**

Is fucking horrible.

**puppy**

Happiness is a warm one.

**purity ball**

Primarily Evangelical Christian event in which young women who have taken a virginity pledge attend a formal dance with their fathers, who have in turn pledged to protect their daughters' sexual and spiritual "purity." (Ew.) Also known as a father-daughter purity ball, the event is meant to promote abstinence until marriage and strong father-daughter bonds.

**pushy**

Derogatory term for a confident woman who gets what she wants.

**pussy**

**1.** A cat. **2.** Profane slang for "vagina." **3.** Another word for "wimp," usually directed to a man, e.g., "Don't be such a pussy, Mike, and prove your manhood to us, your alleged friends, by doing this incredibly dangerous and stupid thing."

**Pussy Riot**

Russian anti-Kremlin protest art collective that became the cause célèbre of 2012 after three female members were imprisoned for interrupting services at Moscow's Cathedral of Christ the Savior to deliver a ninety-second "punk prayer" entreating the Virgin Mary to deliver Russia from Vladimir Putin. Sentenced to two years in a prison colony largely out of spite for the outpouring of support the group received from Madonna, Chloë Sevigny, Paul McCartney, and others.

## queen

**1.** Female monarch. **2.** British rock band fronted by the late Freddie Mercury. **3.** Occasionally derogatory term for a flamboyant gay man. **4.** Name beleaguered women give themselves when their shitty husbands and ungrateful kids fail to appreciate their inner royalty.

### *Queen Christina*

Greta Garbo in a lesbian classic.

### Queen Elizabeth I (1533–1603)

Queen of England from 1558 until her death and possessor of the nickname Gloriana, which sure beats what we call our leaders these days. Daughter of the infamous King Henry VIII and his second wife, Anne Boleyn, Elizabeth was declared illegitimate when she was two and her dad had her mother beheaded. Elizabeth spent nearly a year imprisoned by her own half sister, Mary, but when Mary died, Elizabeth became queen and stayed on the throne for forty-four years. It was assumed she'd get married and produce an heir, but despite numerous courtships she did neither and became known as the Virgin Queen. Maybe she was too busy defeating the Spanish Armada and trying to put down Irish rebellions and overseeing the golden age of English theater. Or maybe her own family's tendency to have spouses imprisoned, banished, and killed had put her off the whole institution.

### Queen Elizabeth II (1926–)

The current and second-longest-reigning British monarch. Elizabeth came to power when she was twenty-five years old, after the sudden and unexpected death of her father, Colin Firth—er, King George VI. Elizabeth married Philip, Duke of Edinburgh, notorious for putting his xenophobic foot in his racist mouth, and they had four children: Charles, Anne, Andrew, and Edward. Elizabeth is an infamously private monarch, but in recent decades her desire to keep her personal business personal has been thwarted by her children's very public marital troubles and her grandchildren's—okay, Harry's—habit of getting publicly drunk and naked and sometimes both at once. Over the course of Elizabeth's six-decade-long reign, the British Empire has shrunk as more and more countries declare their independence from the Crown. (Although sovereign states, Australia, Canada, New Zealand, South Africa, and a bunch of other little countries are still loyal to the Crown.) They even have their own mini-Olympics, the Commonwealth Games. It's way cooler than it sounds, okay? (*See also* MIRREN, HELEN)

### Queen Latifah (1970–)

Rapper turned actress who makes excellent lady anthems ("U.N.I.T.Y.") and infinitely watchable rom-coms. (If you do not own a DVD of *Beauty Shop*, you don't know what you're missing.)

### queer
Once derogatory, now reclaimed term for having a sexuality other than hetero.

### quiche
Real men have always eaten it, but also, who cares?

### Quimby, Ramona
Title character of Beverly Cleary's beloved children's book series. Ramona, star of books like *Ramona Quimby, Age 8*,

*Ramona the Pest*, and *Ramona the Brave*, is the younger of two sisters, though in later books her parents add a third daughter to the mix. Ramona is a plucky and talkative kid, prone to missteps and embarrassment: once, at school, she tried to crack a hard-boiled egg on her head, but the egg wasn't hard-boiled, and she literally ended up with egg on her face. Ramona also has an active imagination, which some people, namely her teachers and her sister Beatrice ("Beezus"), find annoying. The Ramona books also tackle tough issues like unemployment and economic insecurity—in *Ramona and Her Father*, Mr. Quimby loses his job—and the sometimes fraught relationship between sisters, in a way that makes sense to kids who are themselves Ramona's age. The first Ramona book was written in 1955 and the most recent one in 1999, suggesting that Americans will never tire of this lovable, short-haired little weirdo. (*See also* CLEARY, BEVERLY)

### Quindlen, Anna (1952–)

Novelist, columnist, feminist who once said that "all of the qualities that you need to be a good opinion columnist tend to be qualities that aren't valued in women." Quindlen was famously given the chance to speak her mind on the op-ed pages of the *New York Times*, an opportunity she attributes to the class-action suit that seven female journalists brought against the paper in 1974, alleging gender discrimination in hiring and forcing the paper to recruit more women. "I am an affirmative action hire," Quindlen says. "And that is only a problem if you don't cut the mustard." She could, and won a Pulitzer Prize in 1992.

### Quiverfull
Conservative fundamentalist movement, its name derived from Psalm 127, whose followers reject birth control and embrace homeschooling and a return to biblical patriarchy. The most famous Quiverfull family is the Duggars, stars of the TLC reality show *19 Kids & Counting*; mom Michelle gave birth almost every year from 1988 to 2009.

## R

### race

A socially constructed classification of human beings that groups people by physical appearance, ancestry, language, and social status. It's pretty much bullshit at this point, seeing as all human beings share a common ancestor, all human beings have been feverishly boning each other for millennia, and the boundaries between "races" are vague to the point of meaninglessness. There are people who like to see the world as a big game of Risk between black, white, red, and yellow, but those people are big dummies who should be ignored.

### racism

This thing where a person looks at another person and goes, "Oh, that guy's Asian, he must be exactly the same as EVERY OTHER ASIAN PERSON ON EARTH." Which obviously makes no sense, because people are people, not groups. Some racism is violent and blatant, while other racism is subtle. The fact that the subtle racism seems to be gaining ground on the blatant racism these days *does not mean* that racism itself is going extinct. It's just adapting. Whatever "race" has the political and financial upper hand tends to be the worst offenders—thinking of themselves as the default and all other people as the "other." That assumption is one of the foundations of "privilege," and it causes a whole lot of tension and shittiness and inequality and systemic oppression and hand-wringing about "them" taking "our" stuff. A handy way to think about racism is that it's "prejudice plus power"—which means that there is no such thing as "reverse racism." Oh, also, it's not funny to call your Japanese friend "Kenny the Jap" ironically, just to show how totally not-racist you are. Don't do that. Even if Kenny swears it's okay, you should want to be better than that for your own sake. Because it makes you kind of callous and gross. Stop.

### rack

Slang for breasts. As if mounted.

### radical

In feminism, the idea that patriarchal systems of thought rule all.

### Radner, Gilda (1946–1989)

Exhibit A in the age-old debate, "Are women funny?" Not only the first woman but the first performer, *period*, to be cast on *Saturday Night Live* in 1975. Featured on the *National Lampoon Radio Hour*, alongside John Belushi, Chevy Chase, and Bill Murray (with whom she had a torrid affair, and who made her laugh "till I peed in my pants and tears rolled out of my eyes"). Created legendary *SNL* characters including bushy-haired Roseanne Roseannadanna (catchphrase: "It's always something—if it ain't one thing, it's another") and hearing-impaired eldercrone Emily Litella. Stunning Baba Wawa impersonator. Struggled with bulimia during her run on the show (as chronicled in her bestselling memoir) and later told a reporter she had "thrown up in every toilet in Rockefeller Center." Fell into deep love with Gene Wilder when filming *Hanky Panky* and fulfilled many a woman's dream of marrying Willy Wonka. Diagnosed with ovarian cancer in 1986 and bravely wrote her way through chemotherapy, finding the funny in illness even on the eve of her death. When she died on May 20, 1989, Steve Martin was rehearsing to host *SNL* and replaced his monologue with a clip of him and Radner dancing goofily all over the set. (We dare you to watch it without tearing up.) Lena Dunham, one of Radner's many spiritual descendants, has said that if she ever has a "headquarters," she wants it to be on the downtown New York street Gilda Radner Way. (*See also* DUNHAM, LENA)

## Rand, Ayn (1905–1982)

Tireless crusader against the tyranny of altruism and author of inexplicably bestselling rape-positive novels about society's oppression of plutocrats. Led regular meetings of a small group of sycophants known for accessorizing in the style of her heroes/heroines with capes, long cigarette holders, and gold dollar-sign brooches. (Future Federal Reserve chairman Alan Greenspan was one participant.) Rand's "philosophy" of "objectivism" despised emotion's influence over reason, rejected humor, and is probably best summarized by her reported dressing-down of a libertarian in the group over his refusal to smoke, wherein she argued that "to be against tobacco on the grounds that it was destroying your lungs was to be against the creative efforts of industrialists who had gone through all their trouble for consumers who didn't ap-

preciate what was being done for them." Died in 1982 following a decadelong battle with lung cancer that reduced her to collecting the Social Security benefits she had fought so hard to eradicate, but her immortal philosophy has proven entirely too dumb to fail. (*See also* DIRTY DANCING)

### rape

Performing a penetrative sex act on another person without his or her consent. According to the January 2012 revision of the FBI's Uniform Crime Report: "Penetration, no matter how slight, of the vagina or anus with any body part or object, or oral penetration by a sex organ of another person, without the consent of the victim." (Before that, the agency was still using the 1927 definition, "carnal knowledge of a female *forcibly and against her will*," which left out male victims and anyone who wasn't "forcibly" subjected to nonconsensual penetration.)

### rape culture

"What is rape culture? It is a complex of beliefs that encourages male sexual aggression and supports violence against women. It occurs in a society where violence is seen as sexy and sexuality as violent. In a rape culture, women perceive a continuum of threatened violence that ranges from sexual remarks to sexual touching to rape itself. A rape culture condones physical and emotional terrorism against women as the *norm*. In rape culture, both men and women assume that sexual violence is a fact of life, as inevitable as death or taxes."

—EMILIE BUCHWALD, PAMELA FLETCHER, AND MARTHA ROTH, *Transforming a Rape Culture*

### "rape-rape"

Term invented by *The View* host Whoopi Goldberg in an apparent effort to prove that liberals can be just as bad as conservatives when kicking a rape victim when she's down. Goldberg, defending director Roman Polanski's refusal to be turned over to US authorities for sentencing on a 1977 statutory rape charge, said, "I know it wasn't rape-rape. It was something else but I don't believe it was rape-rape." In truth, Polanski had pled down to statutory rape but was initially charged with just plain ol' rape because it was alleged that the victim refused him and he drugged her into submission. (*See also* LEGITIMATE RAPE)

### rational

(*See* LOGICAL)

### Real Housewives

Bravo's super-successful reality TV franchise, which, in 2006, started following the lives of a group of women living in a gated community in Orange County, California. At the time, the housing bubble had not yet burst and the economy was still booming…along with the egos of the females who were featured. Since then, the premise of the show has evolved from chronicling the lives of affluent women in various cities to tutting and tsking at their excess: at least ten cast members have filed for bankruptcy in recent years, which only augments the soap opera–like drama of the shows. But more important, perhaps, is the series' portrayal of the ways in which women balance society's Madonna/whore complex (trying to be sexy, while at the same time being wives and mothers), and how they interact with one another. As Camille Paglia has said, "What you're seeing is the primal battles going on among women. Men are marginalized on these shows—they're eye candy…on the borderlines of the ferocity of female sexuality." (*See also* BOTOX; FASHIONISTA; PAGLIA, CAMILLE)

### Red Hat Society

Social club inspired by 1961 poem "Warning" by English poet Jenny Joseph. Joseph's poem, which begins "When I am an old woman I shall wear purple / With a red hat which doesn't go and doesn't suit me," is a meditation on the various social pressures faced by young women to be traditionally attractive and socially appropriate. The society was eventually—and unfortunately—turned into a profit-making enterprise by California artist Sue Ellen Cooper.

### red-light district

Area within a city housing a large concentration of sex-related businesses, including gentlemen's clubs, brothels, peep shows, shops where groups of giggling bridesmaids can purchase comically oversize vibrators for their friend who is about to get married, and other related endeavors. The name's origins lie with sex-related business proprietors' propensity to entice customers with red lights.

### red ribbon

A quiet symbol of support for AIDS awareness in a time when it was still thought to be a disease that affected only already marginalized people.

### red roses

Floral symbols of love supposedly craved by American women like weddings, babies, and sex-replacement chocolate.

**Reddy, Helen (1941–)**
"I am woman, hear me roar."

## Redstockings

Radical feminist group founded in 1969 by music critic Ellen Willis and author Shulamith Firestone, who, along with the rest of their collective, wrote a manifesto (or two) that's required reading in all Gender Studies classes. ("Our chief task at present is to develop female class consciousness through sharing experience and publicly exposing the sexist foundation of all our institutions.") Redstockings controversially believed that "all men have oppressed women" but emphasized a focus on female unity across color and sexual orientation.

## rejection

**1.** The inevitable consequence of participating in a society. **2.** To Nice Guys and MRAs, a vicious crime against male entitlement. (*See also* NICE GUYS)

## religious right

Folks who want government so small, it can fit in a uterus.

## Reno, Janet (1938–)

First female and second-longest-serving attorney general in US history. Attended Cornell and Harvard and served as a state's attorney in Florida. Celebrated by all-female Miami hip-hop group Anquette, who named a 1988 song after her for her work cracking down on men who don't pay child support. Reno presided over a Justice Department that apprehended the Unabomber, the Oklahoma City bomber, and the individuals responsible for the first World Trade Center bombing. Post-Washington, she unsuccessfully ran for governor of Florida in 2002 and has since retired from public service. Once appeared on *Saturday Night Live* as herself alongside Will Ferrell, who portrayed her during a recurring sketch called "Janet Reno's Dance Party."

## Republican Party

**1.** One of only two viable political parties in the US. **2.** The party of Abraham Lincoln. A long time ago. **3.** *See also* RELIGIOUS RIGHT.

## reputation

**1.** A lingering impression of the quality of an individual's character that impacts the way others perceive that individual. **2.** Shorthand for "bad reputation," and often bestowed upon women who are sexually gregarious or give the impression of sexual promiscuity through dress, speech patterns, drug or alcohol use, or close friendships with men.

## "Respect"

Otis Redding song about a man who wants sex that Aretha Franklin turned into a plea to a no-good boyfriend living off the singer's largesse to contribute *something* to the goddamned household, "or you might walk in and find out I'm gone." (*See also* FRANKLIN, ARETHA; SELF-RESPECT)

## retro

Throwback style; a simplification of the past, where motifs and styles can be taken into account without the baggage of cultural racism, sexism, ethnocentrism, and gender conformity that accompanied the fashions. (*See* MAD MEN)

## *Rhoda*

American TV sitcom (1974–1978) and spin-off of *The Mary Tyler Moore Show*, focusing on Mary's BFF. Starred Valerie

Harper as a sassy single Jewish working woman known for her brassy New York attitude and quick-witted jokes about her weight. In the first episode, Rhoda name-drops Sara Lee frozen cheesecake ("an old friend") and *Ms. Magazine*, jokes about the great sex she's had, and patiently endures her mother's chastisement of her for not wearing a bra. The show was so successful that its ratings often topped *MTM*'s, one of the rare cases in which a program's "sidekick" became as (or more) popular than the original star. (If only it had happened to Karen on *Will and Grace!*) *Rhoda, That Girl, The Mary Tyler Moore Show, Laverne and Shirley,* and *Murphy Brown* were the single-in-the-city precursors to *Sex and the City, 30 Rock,* and *Girls.* (*See also* BROWN, MURPHY; GIRLS; MOORE, MARY TYLER; MS. MAGAZINE; ; SEX AND THE CITY)

## rhythm method

Supposed way to avoid pregnancy. Or, in many cases, to cause pregnancy.

## Rice, Anne (1941–)

Author of gothic supernatural tales incorporating philosophy, religion, and history. Rice's first bestseller, *Interview with the Vampire*, was published in 1976 while Rice grieved the loss of her young daughter to leukemia. Renouncer of organized religion but not Jesus: "In the name of Christ, I refuse to be anti-gay. I refuse to be anti-feminist. I refuse to be anti-artificial birth control. I refuse to be anti-Democrat…In the name of Christ, I quit Christianity and being Christian. Amen."

## Rice, Condoleezza (1954–)

First black woman to serve as secretary of state. National security adviser to President Bush during the September 11 attacks, Stanford professor and provost, and bestselling memoirist. When Piers Morgan landed a high-profile post-Bush-administration interview with Rice, he asked hard-hitting questions like "Do you dream of a fairy-tale wedding?" "You're quite a catch, aren't you?" and "If I was going to woo you, which isn't, you know, completely crazy, but if I was going to, how would I?" (*See also* SPINSTER)

## Rice, Susan (1964–)

DC-born African American who played three sports in high school, joined Phi Beta Kappa at Stanford, went to Oxford as a Rhodes Scholar, and went on to become an international relations rock star. Rice wore several fancy hats during the Clinton administration, including assistant secretary of state for African affairs; she spent some time after that as a senior fellow at the Brookings Institution and served as foreign policy adviser to both John Kerry's and Barack Obama's presidential campaigns. After Obama was elected in 2008, he nominated Rice to be the US ambassador to the UN. In fall 2012, Rice's name was floated as a possible replacement for US Secretary of State Hillary Clinton, which triggered exactly the response you'd expect from Republicans. (Senator John McCain, apparently honing his Grandpa Simpson impression, led the charge of GOP politicians trying to disqualify Rice before she was even nominated, insisting that she willfully misled the public about a September 11, 2012, terrorist attack in Benghazi, Libya, that killed four Americans.) She eventually withdrew her name from consideration.

## Rich, Adrienne (1929–2012)

Poet. Sylvia Plath was horrifically jealous of her. Started writing her best poetry after an early marriage to a Harvard economist fell apart and she came out. Was, of course, accused of being too angry at first. Where others might have accepted awards and accolades when people realized their talent, Rich always resisted them. Brought Alice Walker and Audre Lorde onstage with her to accept a National Book Award; refused a National Medal for the Arts from Bill Clinton, calling him "cowardly and spineless"; in a 1997 interview with *Democracy Now!* earlier that same year said,

**"Responsibility to yourself means refusing to let others do your thinking, talking, and naming for you… it means that you do not treat your body as a commodity with which to purchase superficial intimacy or economic security; for our bodies to be treated as objects, our minds are in mortal danger."**

## Richards, Ann (1933–2006)

## Richards, Cecile (1958-)

President of the Planned Parenthood Federation of America and Planned Parenthood Action Fund. Founded the progressive Texas Freedom Network and America Votes organizations; onetime deputy chief of staff to Representative Nancy Pelosi. Daughter of former Texas governor Ann Richards.

## Richards, Mary

(*See* MOORE, MARY TYLER; RHODA)

## Richards, Renée (1934-)

Trans woman and tennis ace who was prohibited from playing as a woman in the 1976 US Open, a year after she transitioned. A year later, the New York Supreme Court ruled that the US Tennis Association could piss off and that Richards could play women's tennis without passing the chromosomal testing the latter had proposed.

## Richardson, Terry (1965-)

Fashion and celebrity photographer known for often explicit subject matter and allegations of creepy behavior leveled by some of his models. Numerous models have accused Richardson of inappropriate sexual behavior on set, including Danish supermodel Rie Rasmussen, who confronted Richardson at a party and later spoke to the press. Model Jamie Peck has also written of her experiences posing for Richardson—during one session, he allegedly coerced her into giving him a handjob. Despite these claims, Richardson continues to work with top brands and clients including *Vogue*, *Vogue Paris*, *Vogue Italia*, *GQ*, and *W*.

## Ride, Sally (1951-2012)

American physicist and astronaut who at the age of thirty-two became the first American woman to blast into space. Also cowrote five children's science books with her female life partner of twenty-seven years.

## Rigg, Diana (1938-)

Emma fucking Peel.

Onetime social studies teacher, county commissioner, state treasurer, and feisty forty-fifth governor of Texas, Richards came to national prominence thanks to her keynote address at the 1988 National Democratic Convention, where she remarked of then vice president George H. W. Bush, "Poor George, he can't help it. He was born with a silver foot in his mouth." While running for governor in 1990, she promised a "new Texas," and during her tenure she added minorities and women to the Texas Rangers, reformed the prison system, and created the state lottery to help fund schools. Defeated by George W. Bush in 1994, but she went on to advise Democratic politicians and help create the Ann Richards School for Young Women Leaders in Austin.

## Rihanna (1988-)

Barbadian pop singer born Robyn Rihanna Fenty. When then boyfriend Chris Brown assaulted her before the Grammys in 2009, her personal life was ripped open and flayed for public consumption, and Robyn-the-domestic-violence-survivor was whipped up into the tornado of Rihanna-the-pop-star. The incident inspired fans and haters to debate the Social Implications of every Eminem collab, Chris Brown rendezvous, defensive tweet, sexually explicit lyric, barbed-wire-wrapped cover shot—assigning her the Top 40 test case for How Victims Should or Should Not Be, then layering it over her like everything else. "I always felt like there was a big disconnect between me and my fans," Rihanna said once. "They knew my name, what I looked like, what I dressed like, what I sounded like. But they were never connected to my personality. They never knew if I was a nice person, if I was a bitch. They never knew me."

## ring

Primary life goal of all single women, obviously. (*See* DIAMONDS; ENGAGEMENT; PATRIARCHY; WEDDING)

## Ringgold, Faith (1930–)

Painter, writer, activist, and sculptor best known for her Story Quilts, which depict narratives of family, feminism, race, and history. As a quilter-storyteller, Ringgold has used patchwork, paint, and narrative technique to tell the story of black America, erasing the distinction between craft and art in the process. As a feminist activist, she's favored raw eggs and maxi pads—which she once littered around the Whitney Museum of American Art to protest the dearth of female artists recognized in the Whitney Annual.

## riot grrrl

Early nineties DIY feminist movement that presented itself as a raw, hyperpersonal form of feminism and focused much of its attention on calling out casual misogyny in punk scenes, protesting sexual violence, rejecting male control of popular media, promoting better body image and female solidarity, and communicating its message through underground means such as Xerox-fashioned zines, punk rock songs, and temporary body modification (like Bikini Kill singer Kathleen Hanna reclaiming a word like *slut* by scrawling it on her bare stomach in red lipstick). A reaction to the "We are tired of boy band after boy band, boy zine after boy zine, boy punk after boy punk after boy," one zine explained. "BECAUSE in every form of media we see us/myself slapped, decapitated, laughed at, objectified, raped, trivialized, pushed, ignored, stereotyped, kicked, scorned, molested, silenced, invalidated, knifed, shot, choked and killed." (*See also* BIKINI KILL; BROWNSTEIN, CARRIE; HANNA, KATHLEEN; HOLE; LOVE, COURTNEY; SLEATER-KINNEY)

## Rivera, Chita (1933–)

Actress who originated the role of Anita in *West Side Story*, Velma in *Chicago*, as well as the titular *Kiss of the Spiderwoman*. Danced professionally from the age of eleven, even after a car accident broke her leg in twelve places. Recipient of a Presidential Medal of Freedom.

## Rivers, Joan (1935–)

Talk-show host, writer, plastic surgery aficionado. Bulimic, widow. Tries to find all of it funny; mostly succeeds. Kind of hard to dislike. "I blame my mother for my poor sex life," she once said. "All she told me was 'the man goes on top and the woman underneath.' For three years my husband and I slept in bunk beds."

## Roaring Twenties

Appellation referencing the 1920s in the United States and parts of Europe, an era defined by rapid political, cultural, and social changes. Artistically defined primarily by modernism—in music (jazz), visual art, and literature—with Louis Armstrong, Duke Ellington, Pablo Picasso, Gertrude Stein, H. D., and F. Scott Fitzgerald all producing major works at the time. Also responsible for the flapper, a new and liberated breed of woman known as much for her love of debauchery as for her short hair and short skirts.

## Robinson, Mary (1944-)

First female president of Ireland.

## Roe v. Wade

Landmark 1973 Supreme Court case that barred states from outlawing abortion by decreeing that the Fourteenth Amendment's due process clause guarantees American women a right to privacy and bars the state from interfering in their health-care decisions. The ruling also states that as a pregnancy progresses, the state's interest in preserving the fetus increases and thus the state has the right to heavily regulate abortions that occur after the point of viability; that is, the point at which a fetus can survive outside the woman's body.

## Roiphe, Katie (1968-)

Writer and academic who has been producing linkbait since before that term existed, needling the feminist movement with treatises on how college date rape is blown out of proportion, how juggling motherhood and career isn't that hard, why men shouldn't have to pay child support, and why powerful women really just want to be spanked.

## romance novels

Sexier and more transparent version of so-called chick lit. A genre that ranges from historical "bodice rippers" to worldwide sensation *Fifty Shades of Grey* to Jackie Collins. (*See also* CHICK LIT; FIFTY SHADES OF GREY)

## romantic, romance

Things that stir up ladies' emotions and juices, such as red roses, candlelight, diamonds, mortifying public gestures, showing up at her home or workplace unannounced, refusing to take no for an answer, talking shit about her to her boyfriend, ingratiating yourself with her friends, and sitting in the bushes outside her window. At least if you ask Hollywood comedies.

## *Rookie*

Online magazine for teenage girls actually run by a teenage girl, and so endlessly fascinating to aging adult women—

## roller derby

"Sexy, anti-corporate, amazingly fast and incredibly violent" is how Steven Wells described contemporary roller derby—an all-female, feminist-flavored resurrection of the co-ed sport that died in the seventies—in the *Guardian* in 2005. The rules of the game are somewhat baffling and almost beside the point; the new derby is a chance for women to come together in a spirit of camp, sisterhood, and punk rock and beat the shit out of each other. On roller skates. In the space of a decade, what started as a few friends in Austin, Texas, hitting the rink with helmets, kneepads, and pseudonyms like Ultra Violent, Cheap Trixie, and Kitty Kitty Bang Bang has become a worldwide phenomenon that inspired (among other things) the 2009 Drew Barrymore film *Whip It*. Shauna Cross, the L.A. Derby Doll ("Maggie Mayhem") who wrote the screenplay, told *USA Today* before its release: "I'm actually very sweet and girly off the track but utterly relentless on the track—a bit of a bruiser, really…But that's half the fun of derby: You get to be someone else. It's better than therapy."

particularly as creator Tavi Gevinson draws her inspiration from said adults' own teen years, in the form of nostalgia for nineties riot grrrl zines, xeroxed *Sassy*s, open declarations of feminist allegiance, and ritual refs to *The Craft*, *Clueless*, and Kurt and Courtney. (*See also* CLUELESS; GEVINSON, TAVI; SASSY)

### roommates

Fun to have when you first get to college and don't know anybody. Much less fun when you're in your thirties and still can't afford a decent apartment.

### Roosevelt, Eleanor (1884–1962)

"No one can make you feel inferior without your consent."
—ELEANOR ROOSEVELT, COMPLETE BOSS

1956 DEMOCRATIC NATIONAL CONVENTION

### *Roseanne*

The classic blue-collar sitcom calls for a fat man on a couch and a harpy at his feet. In 1988, Roseanne Barr took a seat on the sofa and brought working-class feminism to prime time—in the pilot of *Roseanne*, she eviscerates a donut she dubs "the male ego." When Barr's Domestic Goddess shtick fell out of favor, her sitcom perch fell to comic slobs like Kevin James, Jim Belushi, and Donal Logue, and female sitcom stars crawled back into the role of the hot and capable sidekick-wife. The TV industry wouldn't get another powerhouse figure of Barr's stature and influence until *SNL* agreed to put a certain slimmed-down head writer on the air. (*See also* FEY, TINA)

### Rosie the Riveter

Symbol of female factory workers who worked during World War II. Started life, as so many propaganda icons do, as a song: "While other girls attend their fav'rite cocktail bar / Sipping Martinis, munching caviar / There's a girl who's really putting them to shame / Rosie is her name." Norman Rockwell heard the big-band song and put a painting of a woman, with a lunch box that read "Rosie," on the cover of the *Sat-*

*urday Evening Post*. The image caught on. Even Marilyn Monroe, then still Norma Jean Dougherty, worked at an airplane factory. Though Rosie the Riveter was always depicted as white, African American women also flooded the factories and appeared in photo spreads and magazine articles pressuring women to work. (*See also* LABOR)

### Rowling, J. K. (1965–)

British author of the multibillion-dollar Harry Potter fantasy series, which Rowling dreamed up when she was a single mother living paycheck to paycheck. (*See also* GRANGER, HERMIONE)

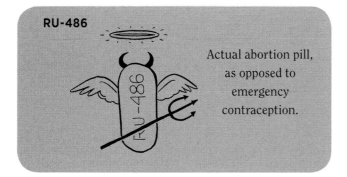

**RU-486**

Actual abortion pill, as opposed to emergency contraception.

### The Rules

Bestselling 1995 guide to female behavior that promised to find a woman a husband within a year—a year of smiling in public while holding a club soda, never calling a man, timing phone calls to end after ten minutes, delaying sex for months of dating, never accepting a weekend date after Wednesday, rarely accepting a weekday date, faking plans, and only speaking when spoken to—a romantic strategy predicated on projecting an image of—but not actually embodying—confidence, independence, and self-respect. Written by Sherrie Schneider and Ellen Fein.

### rumor

**1.** An unconfirmed bit of information typically spread through word of mouth (gossip), often salacious in nature. Truthfulness can range from 0 percent (Jennifer Aniston is finally REVENGE PREGNANT) to 100 percent (Anderson Cooper is gay). **2.** Common misspelling of the name of Bruce Willis and Demi Moore's daughter Rumer.

### Ryder, Winona (1971–)

Generation X's answer to Zelda Fitzgerald, with Johnny Depp standing in for F. Scott, complete with late-in-life meltdown that luckily, so far, hasn't led to an institution—but also no role in her thirties and forties better than that of Spock's tragic mom. (*See also* HEATHERS)

# S

### Sacagawea (1788–1812-ish)

Interpreter, guide, and diplomat who accompanied Lewis and Clark on their expedition from what is now North Dakota to the Pacific Ocean, carrying her two-month-old son with her. In 2000, the US Mint began production of a one dollar copper-and-brass coin on which she is honored.

### safe sex

Use a condom, okay?

### safety tips for women

Guides to female behavior promoted by law enforcement agencies, college campuses, and e-mail forwards that ostensibly prevent women from becoming victims of violent crimes but in fact put the burden on women to prevent rape and domestic violence at the hands of shadow-lurking strangers—don't walk alone at night, let a friend know where you are, lock your doors, don't get drunk, never park next to a van, keep a can of mace at the ready and a pair of keys lodged between your fingers—instead of targeting the friends, acquaintances, family members, classmates, and neighbors most likely to assault and rape women.

### *St. Elmo's Fire*

Sole "Brat Pack" classic not directed by John Hughes that concerns a bunch of recent college graduates moping about how shitty real life is. Rob Lowe wears a dangly earring and plays jazzy saxophone. Andrew McCarthy thinks that "love is just an illusion." Judd Nelson has not yet grown into his nostrils. Mare Winningham gives her virginity away as a "present." Demi Moore loves cocaine and requires incessant rescuing. Emilio Estevez and Ally Sheedy are there, too. An actual quote: "Please…I'm with these Arabs and they've been forcing me to do coke all night. And I only understand a little Arabic, but I'm sure I heard the words for 'gang bang' and 'white slavery.' Please get me out of here."

### Salander, Lisbeth

Titular heroine of Stieg Larsson's *The Girl with the Dragon Tattoo* and the two books that came after that, a pretty good Swedish movie trilogy, and a pretty bad American version. Lisbeth is a

tiny, furious, punk-rock genius hacker who is basically a so-ciopath, but since she saves all the torturing and murder for really bad dudes, you love her anyway. One friend of Jezebel described the Lisbeth of the books as "the most one-dimensional heroine of all time. Entirely a creepy male fantasy brought to life," adding, "and the torture porn makes it way worse."

### "sanctity of marriage"

Something politicians bloviate about to deny civil rights to same-sex couples.

### Sand, George (1804–1876)

Pseudonym of Armandine-Aurore Dupin Dudevant, a French writer and baroness who became famous for her books but also for dressing like a man, smoking in public, and having a ton of affairs, most notably with Frédéric Chopin and maybe a lady or two. (*See also* Davis, Judy)

### Sandberg, Sheryl (1969–)

Businesswoman and Facebook COO. Author. (Of the bestselling working woman's manifesto *Lean In*.) Largely thought to be the individual responsible for Facebook founder Mark Zuckerberg's transformation from sweaty, awkward child to confident, multimillionaire awkward child and the first woman to serve on the board of the company. Sandberg is generally regarded as a trailblazer for women in business and tech and a professional badass.

### Sanger, Margaret (1879–1966)

Nurse, activist, and founder of what eventually became Planned Parenthood. Watched several patients die in botched abortions before becoming a polemicist and pamphleteer on behalf of women's reproductive freedoms. Was never much of a proponent of abortion itself; preferred contraception. Repeatedly threatened with jail. Republicans rail on about her devotion to eugenics, which she did indeed endorse,

though in general she did not believe in racial hierarchies and worked rather fervently with the African American community.

### Sapphire

American author and poet best known for her novel *Push*, which was adapted for screen in 2009 with the title *Precious: Based on the Novel Push by Sapphire*.

### Sappho (ca. 610–570 BC)

Greek poetess who survives mostly in fragments and whose connection to lesbianism is disputed. Baudelaire was a big fan, and Anne Carson, too.

### Sarandon, Susan (1946–)

Actress and activist. Dashed the collective hopes of a generation of women by splitting from longtime not-spouse Tim Robbins in 2009. Is now dating a younger man, which you can do when you're a Hollywood actress with that powerful, low-register voice. (*See also* Bull Durham; Thelma & Louise)

### Sassy

Best magazine for teen girls ever, at least as remembered by women who are now in their thirties and haven't seen a copy in twenty years. Founded in 1988, *Sassy* introduced a generation of young ladies to Sonic Youth, Chloë Sevigny, and Jane Pratt, who was just a wee baby editor. The intrastaff banter and conversational tone undoubtedly influenced a lot of bloggers who came up in the first decade of the twenty-first century. After a long, dark period with no real *Sassy* analog out there, *Rookie* magazine—a project of teen lifestyle phenom Tavi Gevinson, with early support from Pratt—took up the mantle in 2011. (*See also* GEVINSON, TAVI; PRATT, JANE; ROOKIE)

---

## *SASSY*: 10 MOST MEMORABLE COVERS

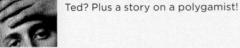

**Kurt and Courtney,**
**April 1992**

The only cover that Kurt Cobain and Courtney Love ever appeared on together. As the cover line says, ain't love grand?

**Mayim Bialik,**
**November 1992**

*Blossom* star Mayim Bialik—in all her awkward teen glory—celebrates America by wearing a flag on her head.

**Bill and Ted (Keanu Reeves and Alex Winter),**
**August 1991**

What's more nineties than Bill and Ted? Plus a story on a polygamist!

**Juliana Hatfield,**
**September 1992**

Indie star Juliana Hatfield poses with a guitar and in Dr. Martens. Inside there are eleven uses for an ex-boyfriend.

**Milla Jovovich,**
**July 1991**

Model (at the time) Milla Jovovich looking mighty witchy. And a cover line instructing us to "pout more."

**Amy Smart as Axl Rose,**
**October 1992**

Sure, why not put a female model dressed as Axl Rose on the cover of your magazine?

**February 1992**

A model holding flowers, plus girl drummers, hating on celebrities, and teens with schizophrenia. You know, the usual.

**Johnny Depp,**
**May 1990**

Why clutter a brooding photo of Johnny Depp with anything besides a line about hanging out with him?

**March 1992**

Model with a white tulle skirt and black, satiny top. (Grunge prom!) "Smells like prom spirit" is maybe the best line to grace the cover of a magazine, ever.

**Jason Priestley,**
**November 1991**

*Sassy* offered two covers of Jason Priestley, the *90210* hunk, one in which he's soaking wet and another bone-dry.

### Saunders, Jennifer (1958–)

British actress and comedienne most famous for her role as thehilarious and drunk Edina Monsoon on *Absolutely Fabulous*, which she also wrote. (*See also* ABSOLUTELY FABULOUS; FRENCH, DAWN)

### Savage, Dan (1964–)

Sex columnist, author, playwright, and TV personality. Savage's sometimes cavalier rushes to judgment have raised hackles among fat activists, trans activists, and bisexuals, but overall he's a consistently smart and strident voice calling out hypocrisy and bullshit among the American right wing. In 2003, Savage led an online assault on Senator Rick Santorum's last name, assigning it the colloquial definition, "the frothy mixture of lube and fecal matter that is sometimes the by-product of anal sex." The definition stuck. In 2010, Savage founded the It Gets Better Project to combat bullying and suicide among LGBT youth.

### *Saved by the Bell*

Early 1990s NBC Saturday morning television show that went on to be a syndication staple, *SBTB* followed the lives of five friends in the fictional town of Bayside, California, as they navigated high school, learned life lessons, and hung out at their favorite burger joint, the Max. Led by the charismatic, self-described "blond Tom Cruise," Zack Morris, the gang (which included wrestler A. C. Slater, outspoken feminist Jessie Spano, cheerleader/homecoming queen Kelly Kapowski, fashion-obsessed Lisa Turtle, and supernerd Samuel "Screech" Powers) dealt with everything from drug abuse to homelessness to jerk bosses at a private beach club, all while finding the time to start a girl group (Hot Sundae), a band (Zack Attack), and a business or two (Friendship Forever/Buddy Bands/Love Cuffs/Zit-Off/ Screech's Secret Sauce), and terrorize their principal, the hapless but well-intentioned Mr. Belding. Sweet, silly, corny, and infinitely watchable, *Saved by the Bell* represented an idealized version of high school, where five best friends can get through (and away with) anything together, always solving their problems in thirty minutes or less. (*See also* SPANO, JESSIE)

### Saville, Jenny (1970–)

British painter who traveled to Ohio, became obsessed with the state's "big women" with their "big white flesh in shorts and T-shirts," and launched a career painting literally larger-

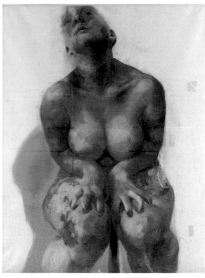

than-life portraits of the most stigmatized forms of the female body. Saville's subjects are, variously, enormous, naked, bruised, and trans, and she does not shy away from grotesque depictions of rolls of flesh, feeding tubes, genitals, or sawed-off limbs tied to the ceiling like meat. Saville's paintings evoke associations of women's bodies as medicalized, sexualized, objectified, and othered. Coming from the white, thin, socially acceptably bodied, out-of-stater Saville, it's hard to know if her bodies constitute a feminist statement, misogynist derision, or something in between.

### Sayers, Dorothy L. (1893–1957)

English crime writer and the creator of gentleman detective Lord Peter Wimsey, who, true to his name, solves crimes for his own amusement when he's not cultivating his taste for wine, male fashion, piano, cricket, or early printed broadside materials. Critics said that Sayers created Wimsey to serve as her ideal lover, but Sayers claimed otherwise: "I was particularly hard up and it gave me pleasure to spend his fortune for him," she said.

## scale

Mechanism by which a woman's worth is measured in pounds or kilograms.

## Scalia, Antonin (1936–)

Reagan-appointed Roman Catholic Supreme Court justice who believes that the Constitution does not prevent the government from executing children, denying women abortions, and discriminating against women and gays. "Sorry to tell you that," Scalia said about that last bit. "Certainly the Constitution does not require discrimination on the basis of sex. The only issue is whether it prohibits it. It doesn't."

## scandal

**1.** Word, from the Greek *skandalon*, that means a trap or a stumbling block. **2.** Basically anything that titillates celebrity gossip rags and daily tabloids, from the Penn State sex abuse case to K-Stew cheating on R-Patz to Miley Cyrus cutting off all of her hair. **3.** When italicized, Shonda Rhimes drama about a DC fixer played by Kerry Washington and based on George [H.] W. Bush's deputy press secretary Judy Smith, notable for being the first network drama with an African American female lead since 197goddamn4.

## Scarlet Letter, The

Classic 1850 story by Nathanial Hawthorne about Puritans punishing a woman for having sex. Reenacted frequently whenever Congress is in session.

## Schapiro, Miriam (1923–)

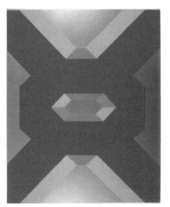

Canadian feminist artist known for her "femmages": fabric collages made using "traditional" women's textile crafts like sewing, quilting, and embroidery. Of her work, Schapiro said, "I felt that by making a large canvas magnificent in color, design, and proportion, filling it with fabrics and quilt blocks, I could raise a housewife's lowered consciousness."

## Schlafly, Phyllis (1924–)

Lawyer, author, commentator, ballistics gunner, politician, activist, publisher, and interest group president who believes a woman's place is in the home. After marrying a lawyer nobody has ever heard of, Schlafly launched a career as an activist encouraging women to do what she would not: devote her life to serving her man and children. It was a smart, squirrelly move for Schlafly and the conservative movement—only a female figure could have successfully blocked the Equal Rights Amendment that would make women equal to men, arguing that it would force women to give up their "privileges." Set the mold for socially conservative ladies like Michele Bachmann, Sarah Palin, and S. E. Cupp, who now talk themselves in circles to justify why they're in the governor's seat or on the lecture circuit instead of wifed up at home.

## schoolmarm

**1.** Old-timey lady teacher. **2.** Slur for any woman perceived as uptight and scolding.

## Scientology

To critics, an alleged cult pyramid scheme spawned by squiggly science fiction writer L. Ron Hubbard to extort closeted Hollywood gays of their fortunes, force ladies on boats into abortions, rob the mentally ill of treatment, facilitate Tom Cruise's marriages, and fleece the weak by hooking them up to some janky lie detector test administered by a dude in a *Star Trek* outfit in a church with oddly prime real estate. To devotees, a religion that draws on fifty thousand years of wisdom to logically lead man's immortal thetan soul to a state of Clear where he doesn't speak to his family, is finally freed of the bad karma that was distributed among the universe when some frozen space aliens were incinerated in a bunch of ancient volcanoes a long time ago, and is definitely NOT GAY.

## scorned woman

Hell hath no fury like one.

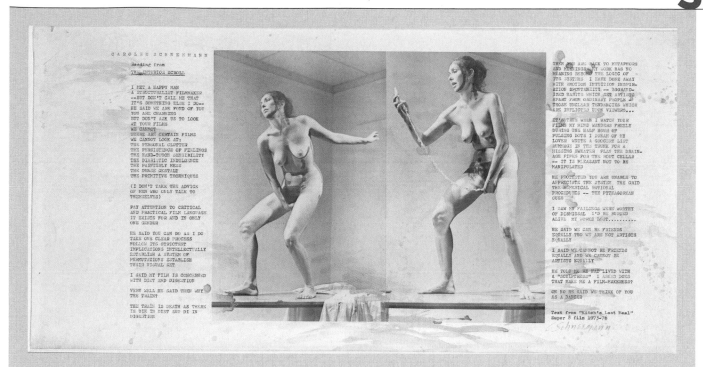

### Schneemann, Carolee (1939–)

Painter, photographer, filmmaker, and performance artist whose work has often focused on her own form. ("The life of the body is more variously expressive than a sex-negative society can admit," she once said.) Schneemann has photographed herself nude with snakes climbing up her torso, hung herself naked from the ceiling to draw and write all over the floor and walls ("I AM HUNGRY"), made a film of herself having sex as her cat watched, and spoken from the perspective of the vulva ("If the traditions of patriarchy split the feminine into debased/glamorized, sanitized/ bloody, madonna/whore…how could Vulva enter the male realm except as neutered or neutral—as castrated?") long before the *The Vagina Monologues*, inspiring decades of sex-positive artists and the Coen Brothers, who based *The Big Lebowski*'s Maude on her work. "In some sense I made a gift of my body to other women," she's said. "Giving our bodies back to ourselves." (*See also* LEBOWSKI, MAUDE)

### Scully, Dana

*X-Files* special agent played by Gillian Anderson. A brilliant forensic pathologist equally adept at discharging a firearm and exhuming a primate corpse, Scully was the tailored-suited skeptic to David Duchovny's true believer, Fox Mulder. But because this was a show about a vast government–alien conspiracy, Scully's scientific method always fell to Mulder's half-baked paranormal hunch, and Scully spent seasons spitting lines like "Time can't just disappear. It's a universal invariant!" and "What I find fantastic is any notion that there are answers beyond the realm of science!" until Mulder stepped in to rescue her from alien bounty hunters, moth people, and terminal cancer. (*See also* ANDERSON, GILLIAN)

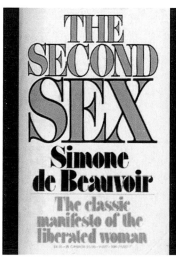

### Second Sex, The

1949 Simone de Beauvoir book on the status of women that was allegedly initially badly translated into English. Banned by the Vatican. Contains the famous line, "One is not born, but rather becomes, woman," which we're still fighting over today. (*See also* DE BEAUVOIR, SIMONE)

### Secret, The

Creepy, culty, worthless enterprise run by charlatans trying to use the "law of attraction" to attract dollars to their pockets. First gained notice as a 2006 self-help book and video that suggested that if you thought hard enough about, say, having a Lamborghini—and acted like you already had one—then a Lamborghini would literally appear in your garage. (Which means that poor people and sad people and sick people and hungry people and Lamborghini-less people COULD change their lives, but they just don't want it enough. Ha-ha—suck it, poors!) The author of *The Secret*, Rhonda Byrne, once implied that natural disaster victims are losers who could save themselves if they knew how to "attract" rescuers. Ignore, ignore, ignore.

### secretary

**1.** Administrative or executive worker who assists in the business and workplace-related tasks of an assigned superior or superiors. Although men engaged in secretarial work for hundreds of years, it began to be considered a predominantly female occupation in the beginning of the twentieth century. **2.** 2002 film that launched a raft of alt-girl sadomasochist fantasies, facilitated by noted deviant sex portrayer James Spader and indie everywoman Maggie Gyllenhaal.

### Secret Garden, The

Frances Hodgson Burnett's unforgettable 1911 novel is a portrait of Mary Lennox, a bilious brat who learns about friendship, hard work, and joy when rusticated from colonial India to a house in the English countryside by her forbidding uncle and an ailing cousin, Colin. When the children, along with cheerful neighbor Dickon, bring a dead, walled-in garden to life, so too do they come into their own.

### seductress

Vile temptress who uses her sexuality to manipulate men; often cast as an excuse for male failure. (*See also* EVE; CLEOPATRA)

### self-abuse

The consumption of Porn for Women.

### self-affirmation

You're good enough, you're smart enough, and doggone it, people like you.

### self-censorship

Biting your tongue because you know saying what you think isn't going to be worth the bullshit it will bring down on you.

### self-deprecation

Tactic employed by men to denigrate women by way of denigrating themselves, as in *Annie Hall*'s Alvy Singer's proclamation that "I would never want to belong to any club that would have someone like me for a member. That's the key joke of my adult life, in terms of my relationships with women." Since been replicated by every stand-up comedy bro looking for a wounded-puppy justification for looking down on women who have sex with him.

### self-esteem

**1.** A healthy, positive concept of your own worth. **2.** Smug justification for doing nothing to discipline your unruly children.

### selfish

Do you have a baby yet? If not, why not? If so, why are you reading this book instead of taking care of your baby?

### self-respect

To do without it, according to an appropriately titled essay from Joan Didion's 1968 book *Slouching Towards Bethlehem*,

**"is to be an unwilling audience of one to an interminable documentary that details one's failings, both real and imagined, with fresh footage spliced in for**

every screening. There's the glass you broke in anger, there's the hurt on X's face; watch now, this next scene, the night Y came back from Houston, see how you muff this one. To live without self-respect is to lie awake some night, beyond the reach of warm milk, the Phenobarbital, and the sleeping hand on the coverlet, counting up the sins of commission and omission, the trusts betrayed, the promises subtly broken, the gifts irrevocably wasted through sloth or cowardice, or carelessness. However long we postpone it, we eventually lie down alone in that notoriously uncomfortable bed, the one we make ourselves. Whether or not we sleep in it depends, of course, on whether or not we respect ourselves."

(*See also* DIDION, JOAN)

## semen

An organic emission (also known as seminal fluid) produced by the male human reproductive organs and containing, among other things, fructose, lipids, enzymes, citric acid, and sperm. Semen, which acts as a delivery system by which healthy sperm reach a female ovum for fertilization, is usually excreted during and after orgasm and ejaculation and is often white or yellowish in color. It has a distinctive taste and smell, which is sometimes compared to that of the Asia-native Callery pear tree and its descendants. It also works well as a hair-styling aid. (*See also* CONCEPTION; DAD[DY]; GEL; MORNING-AFTER PILL; SPERM)

### sensitivity chip

This guy lacks one.

### Sephora

Popular "rest stop" for urban-dwelling females en route to job interviews, dates, etc., that has become a $5 billion retail powerhouse of high-end cosmetics and toiletries. (*See also* MAKEUP)

### settling

Notion that women should attach LoJacks on mediocre men lest they find themselves unmarried and alone. Term embraced by the *Atlantic* contributor Lori Gottlieb in her cover story and eventual book *Marry Him: The Case for Settling for Mr. Good Enough*.

### Seven Sisters

Seven northeastern US women's colleges founded in the nineteenth century: Barnard, Smith, Wellesley, Mount Holyoke, Vassar, Radcliffe, and Bryn Mawr. Vassar's gone co-ed, and Radcliffe's been absorbed by Harvard, but this is still a thing.

### Sense and Sensibility

The first published novel (1811) by English author Jane Austen is the story of Marianne and Elinor, the two eldest sisters of the Dashwood family, as they struggle with issues of class, family, and romantic entanglement. Marianne, with her romantic idealism and expressive nature, is representative of sensibility, while the pragmatic and restrained Elinor embodies the qualities of sense. (*See also* AUSTEN, JANE)

### Sex and the City

Cable television show that ran from 1998 to 2004, with a movie released in 2008 and a sequel released in 2010. Originally based on Candace Bushnell's book and *New York Observer* column of the same name, the show soon took on a life of its own and became a global cultural phenomenon. Carrie Bradshaw, the show's narrator, is a sex and

relationship columnist who lives in Manhattan and spends most of her time dating various men and talking about her love life with her three friends, Samantha, Miranda, and Charlotte. Once a week, she writes a column. In later seasons, the show also had a heavy focus on fashion, emphasizing Carrie's love of expensive and impractical footwear. The show engendered both frenzied fandom and caustic criticism, and gallons of ink have been spilled debating whether or not the show is feminist, whether or not it's good for women, and whether or not anyone should care either way. But one thing is for damn sure: the two *Sex and the City* movies are terrible. Especially the second one. Just totally, irredeemably terrible. Don't say we didn't warn you. (*See also* Bradshaw, Carrie; Bushnell, Candace; cosmopolitan; cupcakes; Hobbes, Miranda)

### sex

George Michael wanted yours, Marcy Playground wanted it as well as candy, Salt-n-Pepa wanted to talk about it, James Brown felt like being an it machine, and Color Me Badd wanted to hit you up.

### sex kitten

Sexually aggressive woman; a younger iteration of the cougar. (*See also* Bardot, Brigitte)

### sex object

**1.** Someone appreciated primarily for his or her looks. **2.** What some people believe all women are, or should be. (*See also* Hefner, Hugh)

### sex offender

Someone convicted of a minor or serious sex crime—including anything from child molestation to indecent exposure to prostitution to the forwarding of underage sexts—that carries with it a lifetime sentence of a marred social standing and sometimes a blanket barring from the vicinity of schools, public parks, and swimming pools.

### sex-positive

More effective thing to shout than "fire" if you're looking to create feminist pandemonium. In its most generous interpretation, it means that one enjoys having sex, which is a wonderful thing. Also a common thing. So: everyone but asexuals are a priori sex-positive. This is usually lost on the term's most ardent adopters, who mean something more like "I'm not a prude!" by it. Or else "I'm not Andrea Dworkin!" (The term emerged during the Feminist Sex Wars of the 1980s, so fair enough.) Assume that if you have to whip this out you're veering into Bad Look territory. Of course, there is some overlap between prudes and feminists, but rarely can an issue be settled by reference to the robustness of one's sex life. The "Have You Ever…?" game is a tangent, not a principle. Best to simply argue the actual point.

### sex symbol

Like a sex object, but famous.

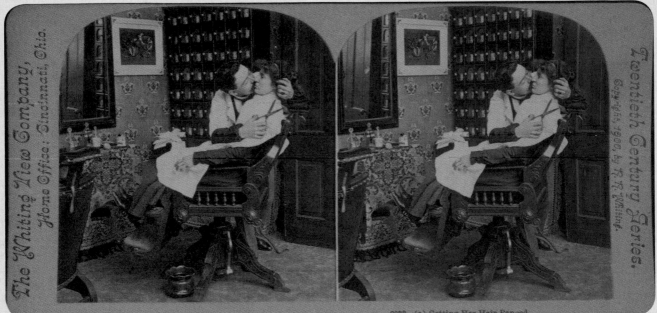

2582—(a) Getting Her Hair Banged.

## sexual harassment

A Very Bad Thing. While there is no one firm definition of sexual harassment, the understanding of the term was greatly expanded in the 1990s, thanks in part to feminist theorists like Catherine MacKinnon, who began writing about the topic in the late 1970s. Lots of things constitute sexual harassment, from discrimination based on sex to unwanted sexual contact to attempts to use sex in quid pro quo arrangements, or anything else sexual that creates a "hostile work environment." If you hear a guy complaining that he can't say what he wants to say at work for fear of running afoul of the "PC sexual harassment police," ten bucks says he's a sexual harasser.

## sexy

Person or thing that turns someone on. A short list of things and people that are sexy: George Clooney, shoes, Elizabeth Warren, baggy jeans, Stephen Colbert, bare feet, Zoe Saldana, tight jeans. Do you not find any of those things sexy? Too bad; someone somewhere does, which means they're sexy, because there's no one universally applicable rule about what is and isn't sexy. Except for Colbert, of course. Everyone wants to tap that.

## shallow

Primarily concerned with superficial, meaningless issues like fashion, makeup, child rearing, and women's place in society.

## shame

Primary means by which women are encouraged to police themselves and each other, so the patriarchy can just sit back and watch.

## shameless

To not give a fuck, particularly if you're a woman and therefore are supposed to give many. The exact terms of shamelessness change from era to era; in Edith Wharton's day, a woman was shameless if she allowed a man to escort her home after dark. Notable celebrities who've reclaimed the derogative term as an empowering cry of self-expression include Rihanna and almost every female Disney teen celeb, with the notable exception of Hilary Duff, as soon as she turns eighteen.

## Shange, Ntozake (1948–)

Author of the polyphonic *For Colored Girls Who Have Considered Suicide/ When the Rainbow Is Enuf* and a huge body of poetry. Changed her name from Paulette Williams in part because, she told the *New York Times Magazine* in 1994, "as a feminist

I thought it was ridiculous to be named after a boy." As part of Tyler Perry's option deal for the rights to her play, she required that Madea appear nowhere in his adaptation.

### Shark Week

**1.** Annual Discovery Channel orgy of shark-based programming. **2.** That time of the month.

### "She Bop"

Tame Cyndi Lauper song about masturbation that landed on Tipper Gore's PMRC (Parents' Music Resource Center) Filthy Fifteen list, earning it a Parental Advisory sticker, which was quickly becoming a badge of honor for many recording artists. Went to number 3 on the Billboard Hot 100 Chart in June of 1984. Good job, Tipper! (*See also* LAUPER, CYNDI)

### Sheen, Charlie (1965–)

American actor and train wreck famed for his substance abuse issues, domestic disputes with women, and frequent public meltdowns. Sheen seemed to get his start as a domestic abuser in 1990, after shooting his then fiancée, actress Kelly Preston, in the arm. In 1995, when he was married to a different woman, madam Heidi Fleiss named him as one of her most frequent clients. (He divorced soon after.) Several other women have accused Sheen of threatening them with violence. In 2011, Sheen underwent a very public meltdown, leading to his firing from the highly successful yet critically panned sitcom *Two and a Half Men*. Following his dismissal, the actor embarked on a nationwide tour where he proceeded to completely fall apart, all while popularizing the Twitter hashtag #winning, an online annoyance that has yet to go away.

### Sheindlin, Judge Judy (1942–)

One of the wisest women to ever work in the New York family court system or on reality court television. A no-nonsense woman who doesn't like baloney or when people think "um" qualifies as an answer, she issues swift justice as a strict adjudicator. Watched by 10 million viewers daily—and most popular with women age eighteen to fifty-four—Judge Judy

surpassed the *Oprah Winfrey Show* in the latter's final years on the air. If there's one thing that she has taught young people in her years of syndication, it's never to cosign on a loan for anyone.

### shenis

Trunklike apparatus that allows females to pee standing up. Useful for camping trips, long car rides, rooftop shenanigans.

### Sherman, Cindy (1954–)

American photographer whose stagey self-"portraits" exploded ideas of traditional femininity, commented on the role of women in the media, and made her an art world star in the early 1980s. Now just as well known for photographing fashion campaigns for Marc Jacobs, among others, though she most often works alone. Credited with having given photography the status of "true art." Her aesthetic is dramatic and gamine, but with the spotlight on artifice. Ultimately, it may go a little too much for the depersonalized grotesque for some tastes.

### Shields, Brooke (1965–)

Actress and model known for her horrible stage mother, Calvin Klein ad campaign, eyebrows, friendship with Michael Jackson, marriage to Andre Agassi, *The Blue Lagoon* and *Pretty Baby* sexy-child roles (though she remained a virgin until age twenty-two!), and tiff with Tom Cruise over postpartum depression. Oh, and also: *Suddenly Susan*. (*See also* POSTPARTUM DEPRESSION)

### shit

Happens.

### shopaholic

Obsessive consumer. In a world where a person can never have too many clothes or purses or too much jewelry or credit card debt, the shopaholic is queen, a devoted and ravenous shopper who is a slave to consumer culture. While men can exhibit signs of shopaholism, the addiction is primarily associated with women, thanks to popular novels and books that help to reinforce the fact that women are mall-roving wildebeests who can never have too many shoes.

### show choir

We'd all happily forgotten about it until *Glee* came along.

### shrill

Misogynist for "a woman just said something."

### shoes
(OMG SHOEZ.)

### Sidibe, Gabourey (1983–)

Actress whose debut role in *Precious* won her an Academy Award nomination for best actress. Critics doubted that Sidibe—dark of skin and full of figure—would work beyond her film debut, but she went on to land other film roles and a major part in the Showtime series *The Big C*.

### silicone

Canonical building material of fake boobs; dangerous when it leaks inside you.

### Silverman, Sarah (1970–)

Comedienne with a talent for satire and an interest in social politics and taboo subjects that have earned her the descriptor "controversial."

### Simpson, Carole (1941–)

First black woman to anchor a major newscast (NBC News in 1974). Almost twenty years later, she was the first woman of color to moderate a presidential debate when she took the stage with Clinton, Bush, and Perot in 1992.

MATT GROENING

### Simpson, Lisa

Perpetual eight-year-old and one of the most visible feminists in mainstream culture. Loves hobbies, books, cartoons, and animals and has a complicated relationship with a Malibu Stacy doll.

### Simpson, Lorna (1960–)

Street photographer turned studio artist whose photographic installations comment on the intersection of race and sex in society, sometimes directly—like when she paired images of a black woman's neck with the vocabulary of lynching ("noose," "collar," "loop") and feminization ("ring," "aereole," "halo"). But just because she creates representations of black women doesn't mean that Simpson's work is

### Simone, Nina (1933–2003)

Juilliard-trained singer, classical pianist, and provocateur who was discouraged from a career in classical music because she was black.

> "Did you know that the human voice is the only pure instrument? That it has notes no other instrument has? It's like being between the keys of a piano. The notes are there, you can sing them, but they can't be found on any instrument. That's like me. I live in between this. I live in both worlds, the black and white world. I am Nina Simone, the star, and I am not here. I'm a woman. My secret self is between these worlds."
> —from a letter to one of her brothers, quoted in *Princess Noire: The Tumultuous Reign of Nina Simone* (2010)

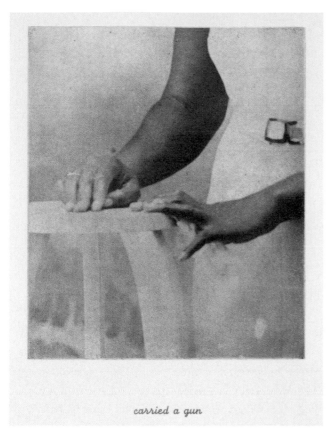

*carried a gun*

all about her. "I do not appear in any of my work," she's said. Her own experience isn't as interesting as "the way we interpret experience."

### Sims, J. Marion (1813–1883)

Surgeon considered the "father of American gynecology" for his pioneering work on the repair of vaginal fistulas. Less celebrated for the fact that he honed his surgical techniques on seven black Alabamian slave women—without anesthesia.

### sin

Religious for "everything human beings would spend all day doing if society didn't frown upon it."

### sinful

Like "indulgence," religious language frequently applied to the consumption of dessert, as though God might actually smite you for ordering the chocolate lava cake and three forks.

### single

Person who is not romantically attached.

### singleton

Person who is not married or in a long-term romantic relationship that is headed toward marriage. Popularized by Helen Fielding's hit 1996 book *Bridget Jones's Diary*, in which Bridget, a singleton, feels immense pressure from all sides (including the inside) to get married. The term she coins for the opposite of a singleton is a *smug married*. In the 2001 film adaptation, asked by one such specimen why there are so many unmarried women in their thirties these days, Bridget, the only singleton at a table of smug marrieds, says, "Suppose it doesn't help that under our clothes our entire bodies are covered in scales." Yep, some days it can feel that way. (*See also* Bridget Jones's Diary; Fielding, Helen)

### sirens

Beautiful, birdlike creatures of Greek mythology who lured sailors to their death.

### sister

**1.** Female sibling. **2.** Supercool ideological ally, peer, or friend.

### skinny

Conventional, messed-up wisdom suggests that in matters of one's physical appearance, thin is desirable, but skinny is best. Commonly heard in phrases such as "omigod you're so *skinny*," spoken and/or squealed with a hint of envy. Not to be confused with "thin," which is certainly desirable in popular culture but may bear the connotation of being underweight, which veers into the realm of medical concern. Being skinny could never kill you! Doctors might say you're too thin, but they'd never use the word *skinny*, because skinny is cute and fun, like the cheerful little sister of slender and lithe. As Kate Moss once reportedly said, "Nothing tastes as good as skinny feels." Ugh. (*See also* pro-ana)

### Skipper (1964–)

Bratty little sister of Barbie, created in order to give her internationally famous blonde sibling the appearance of family and appease concerns that she was too "sexy" and/or should have children. Originally designed as a short freckled redhead around eight to ten years of age, within just a few years Skipper had became taller, blonder, older-looking, and even somewhat scandalous: in 1975, Mattel introduced the Growing Up

Skipper doll, who was able, with the twist of an arm, to grow three quarters of an inch, narrow her waist, and develop little rubber breasts. (Just like puberty!) Oddly enough, the idea of a doll "maturing" with its owner did not go over so well with the parents of America, and Growing Up Skipper—"Two Dolls in One, Twice as Much Fun"—was pulled from the shelves.

## skirt

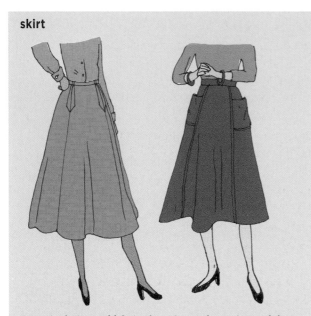

A conical piece of fabric that sits at the waist and drapes downward to cover the legs. Because of the skirt's simplicity, even cavemen—whose brains weren't yet big enough to invent pants—wore them. A straw skirt dating back to 3900 BC was reportedly discovered in an Armenian cave, and skirts have been a staple in humans' closets ever since. While there are many rulebooks in which skirts figure—work-appropriate hemlines and Catholic schoolgirl dress codes come to mind—there are no explicit rules to skirts themselves. There is, however, one very *implicit* rule: skirts are for girls, for women, for ladies—but never, ever for males. If you are a man of ancient history or a Scottish Highlander, you supposedly wear kilts. But let's be real: at the end of the day, that kilt is just a skirt. (*See also* MINISKIRT; PANTS)

## Sleater-Kinney

Olympia, Washington–based band that grew out of the riot grrrl and queercore scenes of the West Coast and put out a string of innovative records from 1995 to 2005 that ranged

from "superb" to "sublime," proving that not only can women play as well as the boys, they can even best them. (And without a bass guitar.) Helmed by Carrie Brownstein of Excuse 17 and Corin Tucker of Heavens to Betsy, who met while playing gigs together; the two were eventually joined by drummer Janet Weiss of Quasi. While they really took off after the riot grrrl movement petered out, Sleater-Kinney members continued to promote its feminist and leftist ideals in their lyrics and garnered the kind of mainstream critical attention that eluded riot grrrl bands, with rock critic Greil Marcus calling them the best band of the world in 2001. After their most straightforwardly rock album *The Woods* came out in 2005, the band went on an indefinite hiatus. Weiss went on to put out more records with Quasi. Tucker started her own band, called the The Corin Tucker Band. Brownstein went on to make a name for herself as a comedic actress, creating and starring in the sketch comedy show *Portlandia*, which is beloved for its sharp satire of organic-loving liberal yuppies. (*See also* BROWNSTEIN, CARRIE; RIOT GRRRL)

## slut

Once a slur aimed at women who have sex outside of marriage, and a lot of it.

## SlutWalk

Series of marches organized by Sonya Barnett and Heather Jarvis after a Canadian police officer stated that, in order to prevent being raped, "women should avoid dressing like sluts." The first SlutWalk, held in Toronto in April of 2011, drew three thousand people, who

listened to speeches and then made their way to police head-quarters. The idea spread from there. Some critics say the word *slut* can't be redeemed, an idea Jarvis rejects. "I come from a frame of mind that language is powerful, and you can also change language," she said.

## smarts

Modern woman's secret weapon. The Swiss Army knife of skills, being smart will serve any female well, particularly when cultivated alongside skills like wit and thoughtfulness. Society discourages women from being *too* smart (giving preference to thin, attractive, and nice), but that is only because a smart woman will fight for her fair share.

### Smith, Kiki (1954–)

American feminist artist and sculptor with a fascination with the human body and the occult. Smith's works combine fairy-tale imagery, domestic objects, body fluids, and the body itself to show the universality of the female form, as opposed to its usual erotic depiction in art. "In making work that's about the body, playing with the indestructibility of life, where life is this ferocious force that keeps propelling us; at the same time, it's also about how you can just pierce it and it dies. I'm always playing between these two extremes about life."

### Smith, Patti (1946–)

Singer, songwriter, and God-mother of Punk who has been making insightful, subversive, uncompromising music and po-etry since 1975. Her 2010 mem-oir of her friendship with Robert Mapplethorpe, *Just Kids*, won a National Book Award. In 1979, Mick Jagger called her "a useless guitar player, a bad singer, not attractive." Fuck Mick Jagger.

### Smith, Zadie (1975–)

British novelist and essayist with an interest in multiculturalism. *White Teeth* (2000), her debut novel, is in-deed a thing of beauty; her subsequent work has not quite lived up to it.

**"When your personal multiplicity is printed on your face, in an almost too obviously thematic manner, in your DNA, in your hair and in the neither this nor that beige of your skin—well, anyone can see you come from Dream City. In Dream City everything is doubled, everything is various. You have no choice but to cross borders and speak in tongues."**

—from "Speaking in Tongues," a lecture she gave at the New York Public Library in 2008

### Solanas, Valerie (1936–1988)

American writer and feminist. Solanas's best-known work, 1967's *The SCUM Manifesto*, was a radical call to arms for "dominant, secure, self-confident, nasty, violent, selfish, in-dependent, proud, thrill-seeking, free-wheeling, arrogant females, who consider themselves fit to rule the universe" to "take over the country within a year by systematically fuck-ing up the system, selectively destroying property, and mur-der." Despite being visionary, funny, and totally badass, Solanas's work has long been misunderstood and misrepre-sented. (A male publisher started the persistent rumor that SCUM was an acronym of Society for Cutting Up Men, a phrase that never appears in Solanas's text.) Solanas also struggled with mental illness, and in 1968 she shot and in-

jured artist Andy Warhol and art critic Mario Amaya because she believed that Warhol was trying to steal her work. (The 1996 Mary Harron film *I Shot Andy Warhol* focused on Solanas's life and acquaintance with the artist, with whom she briefly collaborated.) She turned herself in and, after a year in a psychiatric ward, was convicted of reckless assault with intent to harm and served two more years in prison. Since her death, both the manifesto and one of her plays, *Up Your Ass*, have been republished and produced several times. (*See also* HARRON, MARY)

### Sontag, Susan (1933–2004)

Intellectual and critic. Told the *Paris Review* that she thought of herself as Jo in *Little Women*, just like the rest of us. *Notes on Camp* and *On Photography* are her most famous works, which would annoy her if she was here to know it because what she really wanted to be was a novelist. Known for a serious, haranguing tone in her prose, but in person was apparently less dour. Got in lots of public quarrels. Has been subject to a posthumous boom in complain-y memoirs by friends and associates. Terry Castle referred to her as "flat-chested" and prone to fits of jealousy and curiosity about Adrienne Rich's girlfriend. Sigrid Nunez, who dated Sontag's son, detailed the sex advice the mother doled out in liberal quantities. Somehow all that makes us like her more, not less.

### Sorkin, Aaron (1961–)

Professional blowhard, Oscar-winning screenwriter, and creator of countless TV shows and movies about manly men with male occupations only men can do. (Sports journalism, politics, comedy writing, inventing Facebook, major league baseball.) Condescending to young female reporters and generally disappointing with regard to female characters. (On two different shows, a major plot point involved women passing their own underwear around like baseball cards or something.) Despite unremitting obnoxiousness, has written some damn great films (*A Few Good Men*, *Moneyball*) and TV shows (*Sports Night*, *The West Wing*). (*See also* CREGG, C. J.)

### sorority

To some: a club where women are subjected to humiliation, judgment, and the idea that one has to "pay for friends." To others: an organization that provides opportunities for friendship and networking while fostering a lifelong commitment to community service and sisterhood. Naturally, the lines may cross at times, depending on a sister's experiences within her sorority/campus/Greek system, so perhaps the best way to gain an informed perspective is to talk to a few of them to see what the deal is. Or you can avoid the Greek system completely, say something snarky about sorority sisters in the presence of someone who is one, and then spend twenty minutes backtracking as she makes an ass out of u and me, know what I mean?

### Sotomayor, Sonia (1954–)

The first Hispanic justice on the US Supreme Court, she drew fire during her confirmation hearings for remarks she'd made years earlier about the need for more diverse voices within the judicial system. "I would hope that a wise Latina woman with the richness of her experiences would more often than not reach a better conclusion than a white male who hasn't lived that life," she said. "No shit," replied most of us. "That's racist!" replied Rush Limbaugh and his minions. (*See also* LATINA, WISE)

### soul mate

Idea that an ideal romantic partner can be located with enough heart, gumption, and hope. Functions to affirm both marriages (they knew they had found "the one") and divorces (she had married the "wrong" person).

### Spano, Jessie

As played by Elizabeth Berkley, TV character and outspoken feminist and environmental activist who never hesitated to share her opinion on the 1990s sitcom *Saved by the Bell*.

Jessica Myrtle "Jessie" Spano was often mocked by her friends (and her occasional boyfriend, A.C. Slater) for her militant stance against sexism and her tendency to call out misogynist behavior as "macho pigism." Intelligent, driven—and, on one occasion, addicted to caffeine pills in an attempt to fit in studying for midterms with rehearsing with her girl group, Hot Sundae—Spano filled the spaces between the stereotypical prom queens and supernerds, creating an archetype that was confrontational, inspirational, and, at times, annoying in its piety. Spano's rigidity made her feminism come across as a weakness at times, but overall she stands as a rare example of a teen television character who wasn't afraid to both date the football captain and call him out on his sexist garbage when necessary. And she could rock the hell out of a denim jacket, it has to be said.

**Spanx**
Billion-dollar empire of female restraining devices.

**Spears, Britney (1981–)**
Singer and dancer who induces major depression in those who have been following along. Has been sporting a dead-eyed, defeated look for going on ten years now, ever since she broke up with Justin Timberlake. At this point, no one is holding out for a major recovery, but it would be nice if she was not reportedly still legally bound to her father and never-ending string of odd-looking fiancés and hangers-on. Sure that first song was about wanting someone to…hit her, and also sometimes she runs, sometimes she hides, sometimes she's scared of you. But few eras get the pop stars they need; they get the pop stars they deserve. Our age, apparently, deserves to linger on in smeared mascara and flip-flop misery. Oh, well.

**speculum**
Device that allows a doctor performing a pelvic exam to examine a woman's cervix. Makes a scary plastic cranking sound as it winches a vagina open like a car getting a tire changed. Described in *The Vagina Monologues* as "mean cold duck lips," the speculum has been around since ancient Rome, which means that any joke you've ever made about it has already been made hundreds, if not thousands, of times. (*See also* OB-GYN)

**sperm**
Male reproductive cell. If only it could come out of hair as easily as it does penises. (*See also* SEMEN)

**spinster**
Female bachelor, except horribly denigrated instead of culturally exalted.

# FAMOUS SPINSTERS, PAST AND PRESENT

A spinster's work has always come first, and it's time for modern career ladies to take back the term.

In the Middle Ages, spinning thread was a young girl's job, typically one she vacated upon marriage. Women who didn't marry kept spinning for life. Those who have attempted to malign old maids throughout history could barely conceal their fear of the women who refused to fulfill their central societal expectation. In 1855, *Harper's Monthly* described an "Old Maid" as a woman with the mouth of a succubus, lizard feet, and a personality that is "fierce," "untamable," and "remarkably tenacious of life," despite her "most implacable enmity to man." In 1857, *Harper's Weekly* worried that educating girls would guarantee them a spinster's life. Sounds sort of marvelous!

## Queen Elizabeth I (1533–1603)

When Elizabeth ascended to the throne as the Virgin Queen, she promised Parliament she'd marry. But she wasn't eager to surrender her power, in the kingdom or her bedroom, to a man. If she chose poorly, she risked being deposed; if wisely, she'd still be considered inferior to her consort. "If I follow the inclination of my nature, it is this," she said, "beggarwoman and single, far rather than queen and married." In speeches, she equated her strength and resilience to that of a king and claimed that she was married to all of her subjects. She died single, refusing to even name a successor.

## Jane Austen (1775–1817)

"Anything is to be preferred or endured rather than marrying without Affection," Austen wrote in a letter to her niece in 1814. "Do not be in a hurry, the right man will come at last; you will in the course of the next two or three years meet with somebody more generally unexceptionable than anyone you have yet known." It never happened for Austen, who died three years later, at forty-one. While other women were birthing and nursing endless successors, Austen's old maid status gave her the time to write some of the most beloved novels in the English language.

## Susan B. Anthony (1820–1906)

America's most dedicated suffragette was a spinster at heart from age eighteen, when she wrote, "I think any female would rather live and die an old maid." She believed that women who have "a special call for special work" should not take on the "divided duty" of marriage and rejected the idea that a "true woman" must be the "genial companion of man." Anthony preferred the company of women in all respects, even if it meant she had to help Elizabeth Cady Stanton manage her seven kids before the pair could "sit up far into the night preparing our ammunition and getting ready to move on the enemy."

## Florence Nightingale (1820–1910)

After a decade of courtship, Nightingale resolved at thirty, "the age at which Christ began his mission," to deal with "No more childish things. No more love, no more marriage." She pioneered modern nursing instead. Even as she denounced love, she derided women who "crave for being loved, not for loving" and preferred to identify as "a man of action."

## Coco Chanel (1883–1971)

Chanel mined the closets of her high-profile lovers, from the Duke of Westminster to poet Pierre Reverdy, to pioneer feminine casual chic: her early designs employed fabrics previously reserved for men's underwear. Then she marked her creations with her twin initials, which she never surrendered. "There have been several duchesses of Westminster," she said when turning down the duke's proposal. "There is only one Chanel."

## Diane Keaton (1946–)

Passing notes in ninth-grade algebra, Diane Keaton's crush ended their correspondence with, "You'll make a good wife someday." He was wrong. "I didn't want to be a wife. I wanted to be a hot date, someone to make out with," she wrote in her memoir, *Then Again*. She made out with Woody Allen, Warren Beatty, and Al Pacino, then adopted two kids on her own.

## Condoleezza Rice (1954–)

The Bush administration secretary of state's long-standing singledom inspired First Lady Laura Bush to doubt her presidential mettle ("You need a very supportive family and supportive friends to have this job") and CNN interviewer Piers Morgan to question her personality ("Are you high maintenance?"). "I've always said that I expected to grow up and get married like any nice Southern girl," she told Morgan. "But the fact is you don't get married in the abstract."

spirit fingers

## Sponge, The

Best known as Elaine Benes's favorite form of contraception, it's back on the market after a long hiatus. (*See also* BENES, ELAINE)

## Sprinkle, Annie (1954–)

It's impossible to describe Annie Sprinkle without using the word *sex* over and over again. She's a sex educator, sex worker (stripper, hooker, porn actress, etc.), sex film producer, sex author, "ecosexual," sexologist. She is sex. Sprinkle gained notoriety as a performance artist with her piece *Public Cervix Announcement*, in which audiences viewed her cervix with a speculum and flashlight. As a longtime supporter of sex worker rights and health care, Sprinkle helped spark the sex-positive feminist movement in the 1980s and says she was the first adult film actress to earn a PhD. (*See also* POR-NOGRAPHY; SEX-POSITIVE)

## stage mothers

Caricatures. The most charitable interpretation is that they're trying to help their kids live up to their full potential. The least charitable is that they're terrifying hairspray-wielding control freaks who are living vicariously through their kids, guaranteeing future psychotherapy sessions and the entire child pageant industry. (*See also* KNOWLES, BEYONCÉ; SHIELDS, BROOKE; GYPSY; LOHAN, LINDSAY; TODDLERS & TIARAS; *etc.*)

## Stahl, Lesley (1941–)

American journalist. Longtime *60 Minutes* correspondent. When Stahl was chosen to anchor CBS News on election night in 1974—a network first—her boss walked her around the set, where she'd be sitting between Walker Cronkite, Roger Mudd, and Mike Wallace. There was a fourth place setting just for her. It said "female." "My reaction in those days was to laugh," she said later. "We were just so thrilled that they let us in the door."

## Stairmaster

"Have we turned into gerbils, ladies and gentlemen? People are paying money to go into a health club and walk up invisible steps over and over again for an hour and a half. "Where are you going?" "I'm going up! And I paid for it, too! I can stay here as long as I want!" Folks, you want to go up and down stairs, move into a fifth-floor walk-up on the Lower East Side, okay?"

—DENIS LEARY, *No Cure for Cancer*

### Stanton, Elizabeth Cady (1815–1902)

Started out as an abolitionist and later embraced feminism, too. With Susan B. Anthony, refused to support the Fourteenth and Fifteenth Amendments because she was insulted by the idea of black men getting the vote before women did, though she claimed to support universal suffrage. Was unrepentantly racist in her rhetoric on that point, and yet she supported interracial marriage. Deeply Christian but felt the religion didn't give women enough credit, so she wrote her own Bible. Died long before women got the vote, let alone any other meaningful kind of equality. "The heyday of woman's life is the shady side of fifty," she is recorded as saying, but, of course, she got started a little earlier.

## stay-at-home mom

Term that emphasizes a nonworking woman's commitment to her children instead of that to her husband. The new word for housewife. (*See also* "soccer mom," which is career neutral and outside of the home.)

## Stefani, Gwen (1969–)

No Doubt singer-songwriter, solo performer, and cultural Godzilla whose personal style has devoured the platinum blonde hair of a Hollywood bombshell, the shirtdress of a Rockabilly, the forehead bindi of a Hindu, the pink hair of a punk rocker, the diamond-encrusted Gs of a gangster, and the Gothic Lolita style of a Japanese schoolgirl. (*See also* HARAJUKU GIRLS).

## Stein, Gertrude (1874–1946)

American poet who ran a Parisian salon. Incubated the Lost Generation writing talents of Ernest Hemingway and Ezra Pound and the artwork of Paul Cézanne and Henri de Toulouse-Lautrec. She and life partner Alice B. Toklas were the Ellen and Portia of the turn-of-the-century French avant garde, the first lesbian power couple on record.

## Steinem, Gloria (1934–)

Arguably the most famous feminist of the twentieth century. Writer and activist who shocked people by proving that feminists can have a calm demeanor, conventionally attractive looks, and a raucous attitude. Cofounder of *Ms. Magazine*. Might be remembered best in popular culture for rocking a Playboy Bunny uniform when she went undercover in one of Hugh Hefner's clubs (much to her chagrin), or for her less-than-amiable relationship with the so-called mother of feminism, Betty Friedan, who was more than a little competitive with her. Now in her seventies (!), Steinem is just as busy as she ever was and—fortunately or unfortunately for her—looks just as good.

## Stepford Wives, The

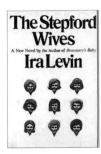

2004 movie (a remake of a 1975 version) starring Nicole Kidman's perfectly cast, immovable face, based on the 1972 book by Ira Levin about a woman who moves to Stepford, Connecticut, where every woman is a housewife, and a perfect one at that. (The term has also become a euphemism of sorts for a nip-and-tucked wealthy suburban woman.) Spoiler alert that might calm you down: in both the book and the movie, they're just robots. (*See also* FEMBOT)

### Stewart, Jon (1962–)

Witty, menschy, much-lauded straight man of *The Daily Show*, as its host, writer, and coexecutive producer. A stand-up comic turned political truth-teller, Stewart became an object lesson in the blind sides of progressive men when his main public comment on a Jezebel piece reporting on systemic sexism at his show was, "Jezebel thinks I'm a sexist prick!" (*See also* DAILY SHOW, THE; MUNN, OLIVIA)

### Stewart, Kristen (1990–)

*Twilight* actress tasked with quietly staring at cute boys, obsessively managing her suite of vampire and wolf boyfriends, and shrinking to a grayed skeleton in order to incubate her vampire progeny. As a celebrity presence, Stewart smokes weed, talks to the ground, and doesn't smile when told to. "I get some serious shit about it," she told *Vanity Fair*. "I'm not embarrassed about it. I'm proud of it." (*See also* CULLEN, EDWARD; MEYER, STEPHENIE)

### Stewart, Martha (1941–)

Former teen model turned kitchen-and-wicker-basket Fascist. Has a reputation for being controlling and difficult, which means that she is just like any woman who enjoys a modicum of success in business. When she was prosecuted for obstruction of justice and lying to investigators, the press coverage consisted of three parts schadenfreude mixed with one part glee. To fellow inmates she was M. Diddy, which doesn't make a ton of sense as a nickname because there is no letter D in her name nor is she a "Daddy" but: okay. Enjoys biting each of her new kittens on the face to show them she's their mother. No word on whether she did this to her daughter, Alexis, too. (*See also* CRAFTS, CRAFTING; KITTENS)

### stickers

1980s craze among elementary and middle school girls. Scratch 'n' sniffs, smiley faces, glittery rainbows, and unicorns (many the work of Lisa Frank, who is still selling stickers to this day), raised plastic creatures with googly eyes—the best of the best were compiled in sticker albums, or swapped with friends, until a perfect collection was created (and then forgotten, as soon as the next fad came along). Though stickers aren't quite the craze they used to be, the love for them lives on: as Jamie Keiles wrote in a piece titled "Literally the Best Thing Ever: Stickers" for *Rookie*: "A new sheet of alphabet stickers can make my day. A package of playful velour cats can make my week. Something about stupid adhesive pictures gets me really amped." (*See also* FAD; FRANK, LISA)

### stilettos

Type of high-heeled shoes, so named because the heels resemble a stiletto dagger. Or possibly for the sharp, stabbing pain one feels after wearing them for longer than five minutes.

### stirrups

Often found at the bottom of leggings. (Can also be found on equestrian saddles and, most unpleasantly, at the gynecologist's.) Leggings, for those who are confused or unsure, are not pants. They are, however, 85.3 percent more comfortable than pants. (*See also* PANTS)

### Stone, Lucy (1818–1893)

Abolitionist, suffragette, and feminist during an era when none of those paths was an easy one. The oldest of old-school feminists, her written and spoken work mirrored Susan B. Anthony's activism. In addition to her other accomplishments, Stone was the first woman from Massachusetts to graduate from college and is thought to be the first American woman to keep her maiden name upon marriage. (*See also* ANTHONY, SUSAN B.; SUFFRAGETTE)

### straight

Not gay and/or not high. (When put like that, it kind of sounds miserable, doesn't it?)

### strapless

Called "the naked look" when it was first introduced after World War II, a neckline that has become so closely associated with the concept of "formal," it's almost impossible to find a fancy dress with straps or sleeves.

### Streep, Meryl (1949–)

Multi-Oscar winner and million-time Oscar nominee. *Kramer vs. Kramer, The Iron Lady, Sophie's Choice, The Devil Wears Prada, Heartburn, Doubt*. Despite the fact that she is a white lady in her sixties, everyone—even black teenage boys—wants Meryl Streep to play them in the movie of their life. Can't sing, as *Mamma Mia!* quite clearly demonstrated, but no one cares because she is Meryl freaking Streep, and her dramatic talent and skill are such that she could have no other redeeming qualities and still be an above-average human being. Luckily, she does have other redeeming qualities. An outspoken supporter of women's rights, Streep once said that it's her "secret agenda" to inject feminism into every role she plays, and in the run-up to the 2012 election, she joined the Center for Reproductive Rights in their Draw the Line campaign urging Americans to sign a Bill of Reproductive Rights in response to attacks on access to women's health care.

### street harassment

STOP TELLING **WOMEN** TO SMILE

Hey, baby! You so beautiful. Can I get fries with that shake? Sound familiar? That's street harassment. It's sometimes known as catcalling, but it often goes beyond words shouted from stoops, construction sites, and moving cars and escalates to threats, stalking, and physical harassment. It's also a fact of life in many cities around the world. And it might sound like compliments, but really, it's a power play. Street harassment is about reminding women and other minorities—particularly gays, lesbians, and people who don't perform gender the way they're "supposed" to—who's in charge of public space.

### Streisand, Barbra (1942–)

The voice. The cat eyes. The epic nose. The lilting notes of "Papa Can You Hear Me?" from *Yentl*. Nobody rains on her parade. Ever.

### strip clubs

Venues where dancers and performers take off their clothes for an adoring public. (And money.) Iceland became an international hub for radical feminism when it banned them in 2010.

### Struthers, Sally (1948–)

Actress beloved as Archie Bunker's hippie feminist daughter, Gloria, and the *Gilmore Girls'* daffy neighbor Babette. Probably best known for her "help a starving child for just the price of a cup of coffee" ads in the 1980s. (*See also* Gilmore Girls)

### submissive

Word that can summon either fun or terror, depending on the context. On the one hand, a particular role to play in Sexy Times Theater, in which a person gets bossed around by a partner and is "forced" to have all kinds of satisfying foreplay and hot sex and orgasms, oh no. Can also signify a role in the far less fun and consensual Traditional Gender Roles Theater, in which a person, usually a woman, is expected to just sort of sit there with a stupid look on her face and cater to the needs and/or ego of any male in the vicinity. One of these is a fun, optional activity; the other is a soul-destroying trap. Those who need tips on how to distinguish the two should remember that the one with handcuffs and spanking is actually *less* humiliating, in the long run. (*See also* Fifty Shades of Grey)

### suffragette

Woman who adamantly, dramatically protested for her right to vote in early-twentieth-century Great Britain. Law-abiding citizens who supported the movement were referred to as suffragists. Suffragettes, on the other hand, embraced civil disobedience as a tactic and were fond of chaining themselves to fences. One woman died during a protest, and many suffragettes were force-fed in prison after embarking on a hunger strike. The UK granted women over thirty the right to vote in 1918 if they met certain requirements, and all women over twenty-one the right to vote in 1928. (American women were able to vote for the first time at the national level in 1920.)

### suffragist

(*See* suffragette)

**sugar and spice**

According to the popular nineteenth-century nursery rhyme "What Are Little Boys Made Of?," two of the ingredients that go into making a little girl. The poem demonstrates the complete lack of anatomical knowledge held by the scientific community in the nineteenth century. In fact, it wasn't until 2003 that the sciences discovered that little girls were made out of DNA, muscles, bones, and skin, just like everybody else.

### SuicideGirls

Soft-core porn site featuring punk, pierced, goth, tattooed, and otherwise alterna amateur models in various state of undress, which shows that getting "alternative" girls naked doesn't necessarily bring an alternative view on looking at naked women. The site has been criticized for censoring models' blog posts that criticize management, requiring exclusivity in its modeling contracts, and claiming to be "women-owned," despite being overseen and operated by Portland neoconservative dude Sean Suhl. "If SuicideGirls portrayed themselves as *Hustler*, or *Playboy*, that would be fine, whatever—people have the right to make their own choices," one former model said, after some staged a mass exodus from the site. "But don't pretend to be alternative and punk rock. There's nothing punk rock about that website."

### Summers, Buffy

Ass-kicking, vamp-stabbing, teen protagonist of *Buffy the Vampire Slayer*, created by Joss Whedon, who longed to flip the script on the cliché of the helpless blonde chick who gets killed in every horror movie. On the TV show, high school is hell (it's literally situated on the Hellmouth), and Buffy's responsible for keeping the supernatural at bay while also acing her classes. As she tells her mom: "Do you think I chose to be like this? Do you have any idea how lonely it is? How dangerous? I would love to be up-

stairs watching TV or gossiping about boys or…God, even studying! But I have to save the world. Again." (*See also* Buffy the Vampire Slayer; Whedon, Joss)

### superficial

(*See* shallow)

### supermodel

Not to be confused with a regular model who, in the shadow of one of these exalted beings, is nothing more than a tall person, the supermodel has successfully become a household brand and recipient of gazillions of dollars. Supermodels secure lucrative contracts with blue-chip brands and are often found gliding down the runway of a Victoria's Secret fashion show, posing on the cover of *Sports Illustrated*'s swimsuit issue, hosting television shows with varying degrees of success, and/or in the arms of Leonardo DiCaprio. They also

make bank by slapping their name on products (see: Gisele Bundchen's line of unremarkable flip-flops). While some supermodels are canny businesswomen, others just have really good managers. In contrast to runway models, whose looks are comparatively unique, supermodels are traditionally considered super fucking hot by the red-blooded male population. Notable supermodels include Cindy Crawford, Heidi Klum, Tyra Banks, Kate Moss, and Naomi Campbell, who in her heyday famously said that she would never get out of bed for less than $10,000. (Last we heard, Campbell was gorgeously swanning around the yacht of some Russian oligarch, as supermodels are wont to do.) (*See also* BANKS, TYRA; FASHION; FASHION MODEL)

### Superwoman
Contemporary mythological creature who maintains a professional career, cleans her own house, schedules and chauffeurs her own kids, and still remains sexy for her husband, who evidently can't be bothered to help with any of it. ("Supergirl" is the name of the actual comic book hero.)

### supportive
Good friends and good foundation garments.

### sweat
Fluid excreted by glands in the body to aid in cooling. Women are not supposed to sweat, or even perspire, which kind of makes it hard to play sports, leave the house on hot days, or even work out enough to maintain a patriarchally approved figure.

### Sweet Valley High
Series of terrible young adult novels about impossibly beautiful teenagers—chiefly the blonde, blue-eyed, California-girl twins Jessica and Elizabeth Wakefield. Jess was the impulsive, selfish, mildly sexy perpetual cautionary tale, and Liz was the boring, upstanding bookworm you're supposed to root for. They were both canonically "a perfect size 6" until 6 became the new 14. (The Wakefields became a "perfect size 4" sometime in 2008.) The story lines were pure 1980s teen-angst melodrama, with lots of new love, rivalry, breakups, parental divorce, and the occasional death from a cocaine overdose or car crash. Everything you need to know about the fucked-up messages this series sent can be found in a 2012 interview with creator Francine Pascal. Specifically, in answer to the question "Who would you consider the best catch: [rich, handsome, arrogant prick] Bruce Patman, [not-rich, handsome, mostly decent at first] Todd Wilkins, [rich, handsome, down-to-earth] Nicholas Morrow, or [not-rich, not-handsome class clown] Winston Eggbert?" Pascal replies, "Bruce Patman, absolutely."

### sweetie
Term of endearment that can be uttered by anyone from a significant other to an older waitress, but which is frequently bastardized into an infantilizing, sexist slur.

### swimsuit
**1.** What you wear to go swimming. **2.** Emotional torture device women are expected to stress about "fitting into" all year, because people without culturally approved thin, hairless bodies have no business swimming in public. (Wearing a comfortable T-shirt and shorts or even a skirted tankini is giving up.)

### Swinton, Tilda (1960–)
Weird, smart, talented, prolific, uncompromising, androgynous actress who refuses to conform to conventional beauty standards and messes with gender. Won an Oscar for *Michael Clayton*.

# T

### T&A

Abbreviation for tits and ass, used by the laziest of sexual objectifiers. "Tits and ass can change your life / they sure changed mine."—Val, *A Chorus Line* (*See also* ASS; TITS, TITTIES)

### Taming of the Shrew, The

Sexist Shakespearean play that was turned into an actually excellent Cole Porter musical, *Kiss Me, Kate*, *TTOTS* has spawned numerous pop culture iterations, including the ice-skating romance *The Cutting Edge* and the classic teen movie *10 Things I Hate About You*. (RIP Heath.)

### tampons

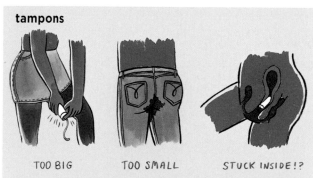

TOO BIG      TOO SMALL      STUCK INSIDE!?

Cylindrical-shaped bits of cotton inserted into the vagina to collect menstrual blood that have inspired a vigorous advertising market as companies compete for dollars by presenting images of joyous women wearing white clothing and engaging in various physical activities.

### Tan, Amy (1952–)

Chinese American novelist who has authored *The Joy Luck Club*, *The Kitchen God's Wife*, and *The Bonesetter's Daughter*, among others and surely deserves some blame for the rash of "Noun's Female Relative"–titled books in the past ten years.

### tanning

Darkening of the complexion through exposure to light, natural or artificial. In various contexts, has been associated with lower-class manual labor, upper-class lives of leisure, sexual attractiveness, or gauche vanity.

### tart

Loose woman; a tangy, sour flavor; or a delicious (usually fruit) pastry.

### Taylor, Elizabeth (1932–2011)

Golden-age film star who clung to the trappings of glamour through eight failed marriages, five broken backs, two hip replacements, a hysterectomy, thirty-five years of painkiller addictions, and a sixty-pound weight gain: "Big girls need big diamonds," she said once. (*See also* CLEOPATRA)

### tears

Salty drops of water that flow freely from your eyes when you are sad, upset, in pain, laughing, very very happy

**tarot**

or pretty much anytime you are overcome with emotion. Sometimes, tears can come out of nowhere and feel very embarrassing, but other times, tears can be cathartic and cleansing.

### teen, teenager

Person between the ages of thirteen and nineteen. In the West, the teenage years are considered a tumultuous period: puberty hits, with all its attendant bulges, urges, and follicular development. By eighteen, teens are allowed to drive a car, vote, and go to war. The first recorded use of "teenage" dates back only to the 1920s, because the concept of a period between childhood and full adulthood is relatively new. Just as the concept of childhood as a pure and innocent time in a human's life is a more recent cultural construct, so is the idea that you get almost a whole decade to be an oily, hormonal mess with very few responsibilities and regrettable taste in music.

### Teena, Brandon (1972–1993)

Nebraskan trans man born Teena Brandon who forged a small-town romance with a nineteen-year-old girl and became an international symbol for antitrans violence after his friends forcibly stripped, raped, and killed him after discovering he was not born male. His life and death were dramatized in the Oscar-winning film *Boys Don't Cry*.

### television

Medium through which to watch recorded or live programming. A hundred years ago, if you wanted to watch a story acted out in your living room, you had to get the kids to put on a play. Today, you can watch virtually any TV show, at any time, on a tiny pocket computer that can connect to a global network everywhere you go. Progress.

### termagant

One of the more humorous synonyms for "scold" or "shrew."

### terrorist

A person who utilizes terror to commit violent acts, usually to fulfill a religious or political purpose. It's also the right wing's go-to term for anyone who opposes their ideology and/or seems vaguely Muslim. (Or brown!) Not surprisingly, wingnuts are less fond of using the word to describe people who harass and gun down abortion providers.

### thalidomide

Drug prescribed by doctors in the midtwentieth century to ease morning sickness that also caused devastating birth defects. Oops. This discovery occasioned the world's collective "Ohhhhh!" moment that fetuses can't handle everything adults can, and since then, pregnant women have been encouraged to give up everything from sushi to Advil, just in case.

### Thatcher, Margaret (1925–2013)

British politician and onetime prime minister. The original Sarah Palin, complete with the lakes of hairspray sacrificed to bring you That Hair. Whatever else you can say about her, she certainly proved that a woman was a man's equal in one respect: just as cruel and reactionary if the circumstances dictated it. Thatcher cut most social programs in Britain, was unrepentantly racist toward immigrants, and befriended Ronald Reagan. She did, however, make one lasting contribution to society: before she was a barrister and a prime minister, she was a research chemist working on emulsifiers for ice cream.

### Thelma & Louise

1991 Callie Khouri–penned classic about two female friends, played by Susan Sarandon and Geena Davis, who kill an attempted rapist and have no choice but to go on the lam. Introduced the world, in a serious way, to William Bradley Pitt. Caused an unusually high degree of twitching in certain male backsides. One worried, in print, about the rise of "Killer Bimbos." By more contemporary standards, it's harmless fun. (*See also* Davis, Geena; Sarandon, Susan)

### therapy

Emotional work with a trained medical doctor, psychologist, or social worker. Or masseur, aesthetician, psychic medium, Reiki healer, crystals expert, Ayurvedic consultant, or shopping buddy.

### thin-skinned

Accusation regularly leveled by offensive people in order to excuse away their own offensiveness and turn the criticism onto their target.

### Thomas, Betty (1948–)

Actress who won an Emmy as steely, bitchy (in a good way) Sergeant Bates on *Hill Street Blues*. Now the director of such cinematic classics as *John Tucker Must Die* and *Alvin and the Chipmunks: The Squeakwel*. (Coming of age as a strong, powerful career woman in a male-dominated profession does have its downsides.) Though surely the champagne fountain in the backyard helps.

### Thomas, Clarence (1948–)

Ultraconservative Supreme Court justice who at least makes the judiciary a bit less white, if only in appearance. (He went seven years without making any sort of public statement while on the Court.) Confession: we're still confused about the pubic hair on the soda can. What was it for, other than signaling extreme boorishness? Had that maneuver worked for him, or someone he knew of? What kind of person thinks of that as a "joke"? (*See also* HILL, ANITA)

### Thomas, Marlo (1937–)

*That Girl*. Emmy, Grammy, and Golden Globe award–winning actress who taught little kids that it was totally cool for boys to cry and play with dolls and for girls to choose their own non-Prince in Shining Armor futures. Seriously, *Free to Be… You and Me* was incredibly progressive; consider this line: "everyone's born with a clean shave. It's just that girls keep theirs, and boys don't." Genius. Thomas also helped Gloria Steinem found the country's first women's fund, the Ms. Foundation for Women. (*See also* FREE TO BE…YOU AND ME)

### Thompson, Emma (1959–)

In the seventies, she was palling around with Stephen Fry and Hugh Laurie (and banging the latter) as a member of the Footlights comedy troupe at Cambridge University, where she earned an English degree. In the eighties, she became a star of British TV, winning a BAFTA for her performance in *Fortunes of War*. In the nineties, she became a full-blown movie star, winning Oscars for *Howards End* and *Sense and Sensibility*, but was frequently overshadowed in the US press by then husband Kenneth Branagh, whom a lot of people foolishly took to be the more talented half of the couple. In the aughts, she raised a daughter and took in a

### Thomas, Helen (1920–2013)

Legendary journalist who covered the White House from the last years of the Eisenhower administration to the first years of the Obama administration. Thomas, who had served as both the first female member and first female president of the White House Press Correspondents' Association, resigned from her post with Hearst Newspapers after suggesting that Israeli Jews should "go home" to Europe or wherever during a videotaped interview in 2010.

teenage Rwandan refugee with her second husband, Greg Wise, and embodied Nanny McPhee, Sybill Trelawney in the *Harry Potter* movies, and Agent O in *Men in Black 3* on the big screen. It's too soon to say what the theme of the teens will be for her, but we'll go out on a limb and predict it will involve kicking a lot of ass. (*See also* SENSE AND SENSIBILITY)

**thong**

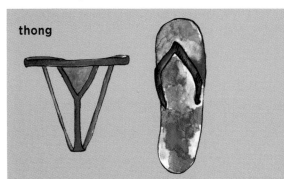

Undergarment with a thin strip of fabric that sits between the buttock cheeks, like a string of dental floss and just as comfortably. Immortalized in the 1999 musical masterpiece "Thong Song" by R&B artist Sisqó, in which the singer tells a woman he has just met on the dance floor that she has "dumps like a truck" and beseeches her to "let me see that thong." Though this might have worked for Mr. Sisqó (doubt it!), is not recommended as a pickup technique. In Australia and other parts of the world, "thongs" are what Americans call flip-flops. Social mortification can easily ensue.

**threesome**

Sex act involving any three people, but most often depicted as the heterosexual male fantasy of two girls and a guy.

**tiger mom**

Creation of midtier public intellectual Amy Chua, whose experience with strict Chinese upbringing inspired a lurid memoir-slash-exposé—titled *Battle Hymn of the Tiger Mother*—of what her fellow Confucians really think of our rotting empire and the shameful parenting practices that got us here. Within weeks of the 2011 publication of her screed against sleepovers and self-esteem, Chua was publicly debating Larry Summers at the World Economic Forum.

**tights**

Accessories worn fitted on the legs for fashion, warmth, or both. Whatever the reason, tights are a gift from the fashion gods. Typically made from cotton or nylon, they come in a multitude of colors, weaves, and designs and can be anything from practical to playful to sexy.

**Titanic**

James Cameron's turgid, two-VHS-tape ode to literary irony, Kate Winslet's breasts, wistful class war, synthy wind instruments, diamond-hoarding old ladies, and (spoiler!) freezy water deaths that ballooned wildly out of budget to $200 million, then *totally encouraged him* when the film (and the Celine Dion–led sound track, and the fifteenth anniversary 3D theatrical rerelease) made it all back by the billions. Enabled *Avatar*. (*See also* WINSLET, KATE)

**tits, titties**

Commonly, slang for "breasts," but we prefer it as a synonym for "the best." "This crème brûlée is tits."

**TMI**

Acronym for too much information of a personal, superintimate nature, information that is often readily available on the internet. Likely destined to be examined with regret in retrospect. Examples: stories you decided to write *and publish* about the color, odor, texture, and/or taste of (a) your pee, (b) your feces, (c) your ejaculate, (d) your placenta, or (e) the tampon you accidentally left inside your body for two weeks. Alternate interpretation: an act of personal and political bravery and truth telling. Fundamental to honest exchanges about physical and emotional realities that must be acknowledged squarely and without prejudice before we can be free. (*See also* OVERSHARE)

**TMZ**

Shameless celebrity news website run by former lawyer Harvey Levin. Within the first thirty seconds after a celebrity overdoses, you can bet that TMZ has contracted with every person in a ten-mile radius and has a report up detailing the number of pills said celeb consumed. The website has come under fire for colluding with (aka paying off) aggressive paparazzi, but it will most likely continue to exist until we get tired of Kim Kardashian, which will be never.

### Toddlers & Tiaras

Reality show on the TLC network that explores the American subculture of child beauty pageants. People tend to criticize TLC for betraying its original name (The Learning Channel) by airing such trash. But were it not for *T&T*, we would not have learned that dentures for a five-year-old are called "flippers," that it's okay (or at least legal) to spray tan an eighteen-month-old, and that you can't get reported to Child Protective Services for dressing your three-year-old up as a hooker and filming it, as long as it's done in the name of the "talent" portion of a beauty pageant. (*See also* PAGEANT)

### tomboy

Female who likes to do "boy" things like wear jeans, play sports, run around outside, or discuss politics.

### Tomlin, Lily (1939–)

Actress and comedienne who made her name on *Laugh-In* and is now a guest star staple of hourlong network dramas.

Has a tendency to appear late in a series' run, a bit like an angel of death, which is a shame because she really should be headlining a show. Was once nominated for an Oscar for her performance in Robert Altman's *Nashville*; it's a shame she didn't get the same courtesy for her work opposite Jane Fonda and Dolly Parton in 1980's *Nine to Five*. Out lesbian. Went on an amazing rant against David O. Russell on the set of *I Heart Huckabees*. "I'm not as brilliant as you, I can't keep up with you," in a fantastic bit of underminery. He began throwing things. A YouTube classic was born.

### touchy

Some people are touchy because they're overemotional and defensive and they think everything is about them and they have their shoelaces caught in the Escalator of Perpetual Outrage. Some people are touchy because you're being a dick and trying to trivialize their concerns and make them think they're crazy for standing up for themselves (see gaslighting). Some people—mainly creeps and hippies—are touchy because they won't stop touching you. Those people need to step off. (*See also* OVERREACTING)

### tramp

Term initially meaning a street person or vagabond. Now a colloquial word used to describe a promiscuous or provocatively dressed woman. While it's a pejorative term, those who use it are generally just jealous of a woman's hustle.

### tramp stamp

Tattoo commonly associated with being sexually promiscuous and/or of a poorer economic class—and sported by celebrities considered as such, like Pamela Anderson and Britney Spears—this lower back–located design typically features astrological characters or ocean residents like dolphins.

### transgender

Blanket term for people who feel, believe, or know that there is a disconnect between their gender identity and/or gender expression and the gender they were assigned at birth. It's a huge category, one that encompasses everyone from the androgynous to the genderqueer to the intersexed. In other words: a category for people who know that categories are necessarily limiting.

### trauma

Getting your period in school while wearing white jeans, per teen magazines.

### trend

Fashion craze that will be over before you can afford to participate in it.

### troll

**1.** A mythological being with an unattractive appearance. Usually lives under a bridge or in a cave. **2.** An internet commenter who purposely posts inflammatory messages on internet forums or blogs with the intent of angering readers and derailing the conversation.

### trollop

Old-fashioned word for slut. (Particularly a bedraggled, low-class, or discourteous one.) Came back into fashion after liberal activist-writer Cliff Schecter's *The Real McCain: Why Conservatives Don't Trust Him and Independents Shouldn't* reported that anonymous sources claimed to have heard Senator John McCain (R-AZ) tell his wife Cindy, "At least I don't plaster on the makeup like a trollop, you cunt."

### trousseau

Term for all the accoutrements that go along with women being traded and/or sold to their husbands like frilly virginal cattle. Can refer to (1) the dowry, which is the money and goods that a new bride brings along to her husband's household; or (2) the hope chest, which is a fancy box full of linens 'n' things that the new bride will use to pretty up her husband's cave; or (3) the bride's pretty dress/virgin uniform. Brides used to work for years sewing their trousseaus, to make sure that the brides were worth their husbands' hard-earned cash and/or goats. Fun fact: in the UK and Australia, the trousseau is also known as the "bottom drawer" or the "glory box," which is obviously hilarious because VAGINA.

### true love

May or may not exist. (Sorry.) (*See also* SOUL MATE)

### Truth, Sojourner (1797–1883)

Abolitionist and feminist best known for her speech "Ain't I a Woman?," which in an act of supreme arrogance may have been doctored by the white man who put the speech into print. (He made her sound Southern, though she lived in the North.) Truth escaped slavery in 1826 with her smallest daughter and took her owners to court to recover her son from them, too. She only became a preacher and a speaker in her late forties, but at that point she put out a memoir and gave the series of rousing speeches that would make her famous. "Man is so selfish that he has got women's rights and his own too, and yet he won't give women their rights. He keeps them all to himself."—from a speech at the first meeting of the Equal Rights Association, an organization formed in 1867 to join efforts to achieve gender equality and racial equality

### tube top

In theory, a strapless shirt. In practice, a highly effective biceps workout, because 40 percent of all time spent wearing it will be devoted to hiking it up.

### Tubman, Harriet (1820–1913)

Abolitionist who escaped from slavery and made several return trips to Maryland to help hundreds of others gain

freedom. Also served as a nurse and scout for Union forces during the Civil War. A devout Christian, Tubman used the North Star to guide her escapes and earned the nickname Moses. "I was the conductor of the Underground Railroad for eight years, and I can say what most conductors can't say; I never ran my train off the track and I never lost a passenger," she said.

### Turner, Kathleen (1954–)

The Voice. Came into our lives in a pulpy thriller called *Body Heat*, worked her way up to *Peggy Sue Got Married* and *Romancing the Stone*, then disappeared for a while. Reproductive rights activist. Felled before her time, careerwise, by a bad case of arthritis, and plagued by intermittent bouts of alcoholism ever since. Children today might know her only as Chandler Bing's mother, a terrible shame.

### Turner, Tina (1939–)

Singer born Anna Mae Bullock and known for such hits as "Private Dancer," "Better Be Good to Me," and "We Don't Need Another Hero." Met future husband and singing partner Ike Turner in the clubs of St. Louis, where she was rechristened Tina. The rest is a sad history of drugs, infidelity, beatings, and suicide attempts until she left him in the late 1970s, a story recounted in *What's Love Got to Do with It*, a movie she participated in making in the early 1990s. When Ike finally died in 2007, her only statement was that she hadn't spoken to him in over thirty years.

### tutu

### Twilight

Pop culture phenomenon unleashed by writer Stephenie Meyer in 2005 with the release of her first novel in a four-part series that followed the life of teenager Bella Swan as she moved to Forks, Washington, and did normal teenage girl stuff, like, you know, deciding whether her heart belonged to a vampire or a werewolf. Fans of the series (known as Twihards) were split into two camps: Team Edward (the vampire) or Team Jacob (the werewolf). Meyer's Edward Cullen, the vampire who drives a Volvo and sparkles in the sun, drew criticism from some bloggers, including pamgutz at Divine Chaos, who pointed out that Cullen is "controlling, stalkerish, obsessive, mentally unstable and is a false standard for relationships," and that his behavior fits several descriptors typically used to identify domestic abusers. This argument hasn't stopped the story from growing in the public eye—a series of five films, starring Kristen Stewart, Robert Pattinson, and Taylor Lautner, has grossed over a *billion* dollars at the box office. (*See also* CULLEN, EDWARD; MEYER, STEPHENIE; STEWART, KRISTEN; VAMPIRES)

### twilight sleep

Professionally administered fugue state—thanks to a chemical cocktail made up of the painkiller Demerol and amnesia-causing antinausea drug scopolamine—famously depicted in the *Mad Men* episode "The Fog" and dreamed up by Dr. Carl Gauss as a way to replace the use of chloroform as an anesthetic during pregnancy. The idea was that women would drift off into a pain-free sleep and awake with a beautiful bundle of joy. That was not the case. The drugs didn't take away pain; they took away the mother's entire memory of the birth, as well as her self-control. Women under twilight sleep would scream and thrash around because of the pain, often leading them to be tied down and their heads wrapped in gauze so as not to injure themselves. The drugs would often render the babies drowsy or unresponsive.

A 1958 *Ladies' Home Journal* article addressing the "tortures that go on in modern delivery rooms" had an overwhelming response from readers, with one nurse reporting that she had "seen patients with no skin on their wrist from fighting the straps." The procedure became less common until it dropped out of favor altogether.

# U

## ugly

Someone not considered conventionally attractive. Or: someone who judges people by their looks.

## Ullman, Tracey (1959–)

Comedienne who starred in a handful of eponymous television programs, won seven Emmys, spawned the *Simpsons*, and is regularly shunted into a category of people who are "not actually funny" (women). (*See also* COMEDIENNE)

## ultrasound

High-frequency wave above the threshold of human hearing that, when applied to the belly of a pregnant woman with a bunch of squicky gel, can show the magnified vision of a fetus. Mandated before abortion in several states.

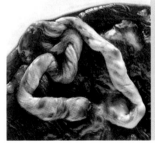

## umbilical cord

Connection between an embryo or fetus and a placenta in a developing mammal. Average length at full term is twenty inches, or fifty centimeters. (*See also* PLACENTA)

## un-American

1950s euphemism for Communist. Modern euphemism for not white.

## unchaste

Woman who is lewd, obscene, and most horrifyingly, not a virgin. In other words: the GOP's worst nightmare.

## underage

(*See* JAILBAIT)

## underwear

(*See* PANTIES)

## unfriend

Harsh sentence for someone who has wronged you and a necessary protective strike in the healing period after a bad breakup. (The longer you wait, the more photos you'll have to overanalyze of your ex doing body shots with someone in a tube top.) (*See also* TUBE TOP)

## unicorn

## unpopular

Natural state of any teenager with a brain. (Promise!)

## unsightly

Unappealing, unpleasant, or not to be seen in polite company. Adjective that often accompanies a mention of wrinkles, cellulite, body hair, or any other aspect of the normal aging process.

## unsupportive

**1.** Lacking the physical stiffness or formidability to properly hold the weight of something in place. **2.** Lacking care for or faith in the goals of another person. **3.** Those triangle-shaped bras that don't have underwire in them.

## uppity

Racially not-so-coded term for a person, especially a woman, who acts entitled to the same respect, dignity, and opportunities as someone who was born rich, white, and male.

## urban myth

For fuck's sake, you guys, tampons do not contain asbestos, Coke does not kill sperm, and you can't get pregnant in a hot tub without having sex. Snopes.com is your friend. Alarmist forwarded e-mails are not.

### vagina

Technically, the tubular tract that makes up the interior of the female genitalia. Colloquially, among women who feel too clinical or hippie to call the outside the "vulva," the whole shebang—from clit to labia to vaginal tube. (*See also* VULVA)

## VAGINAL EUPHEMISMS

You have five minutes to list as many slang terms for female genitalia as you possibly can. What words will you choose? If you're a man, you're far more likely to spitball vaginal slang that frames the organ as an **"abjection"**: a **"dirty," "smelly," "leaky," "uncontained" "wound."** According to a 2001 study in the *Journal of Sex Research*, men favor terms like **"gash," "gaping ax wound," "black cat with its throat cut,"** or **"sliced stomach"** for female genitalia, but see their own organs as **"an attacking danger"** like a **"heat-seeking missile,"** a **"torpedo,"** or the **ax** itself. Concluded researchers: "we have a scenario where **women's genitalia are wounds**, and **male genitalia inflict wounds.**"

### vagina dentata

Name for a variety of bizarre folk horror myths in which the labia around a woman's vagina sprout teeth. The myth feeds into a whole mess of male fears about women—the strange popular view of the vagina as an unfeminine, beastly organ; the male fear of literal and figurative castration when he enters into a relationship with a woman; the idea of women as succubi who rob men of their power. The concept has inspired innovations both technological and artistic—from the antirape devices inserted into the vagina to attack a penis on insertion to the indie film *Teeth*, starring a teenage girl with a mouth between her legs.

### vajazzling

Don't ask. (*See also* HEWITT, JENNIFER LOVE)

### Valenti, Jessica (1978–)

Author of accessible feminist lit like *The Purity Myth* and *Full Frontal Feminism*—and advanced-placement blog Feministing—who introduced a new genera-  tion of girls to pop feminist thinking and so became a target of both radical feminists, who criticized the immense attention paid to a feminist writing for a popular audience, and conservative ones, who once loudly scolded her for wearing a shirt near former president Bill Clinton.

### Valentine's Day

Hallmark holiday designed to raise the stakes of human relationships and push love's players to prove themselves through commerce. A perfect storm of antifeminist and procapitalist sentiment—albeit one that sometimes succeeds in producing authentic declarations of love and friendship. Tina Fey skewered the ire the holiday inspires among progressives when *30 Rock*'s Liz Lemon insisted on instead celebrating "Anna Howard Shaw Day," the namesake of a women's suffrage advocate born on February 14, 1847.

### Valentine, Emily

*Beverly Hills, 90210* character with short bleached hair, a leather jacket, and a motorcycle who caught the eye of both Brandon Walsh and Dylan McKay. After going on dates with both and earning the wrath of Brenda Walsh, she eventually wound up with Brandon and an uneasy friendship with the rest of the gang. After drugging and then stalking Brandon, she ended up institutionalized but was seen again during the college years, when he visited her in San Francisco, and later, when they kissed during a layover in Los Angeles. (*See also* BEVERLY HILLS, 90210)

### Valium

Mother's little helper.

### Valley of the Dolls

1966 Jacqueline Susann novel and relic of a more civilized age in which you couldn't simply blog about the bizarre self-destructiveness of celebrities but had to work all of their thinly veiled identities into one novel. And what a novel it is! There's Neely O'Hara, a clear Judy-Garland-a-like, descending from adorable child stardom into nonstop barbiturate popping (these pills being the "dolls" of the title) and madness. There's Jennifer North, an odd hybrid of Marilyn Monroe and Brigitte Bardot, with tragic secret abortions and tragic naked appearances in French art films. Someone goes after Helen Lawson (Ethel Merman) and *rips her wig off.* Tony Polar (Dean Martin) has a *brain disease that makes him rape people.* Aside from informing you, the reader, that at some point in our history people really wanted to know the hidden dirt on Ethel Merman, its sheer balls-out anti-PC inappropriateness makes it a solidly compelling read. Also: there is a film adaptation. It must be seen to be believed. For, oh, yes: it is worse than you can even imagine.

### vamp

**1.** Femme fatale known for her sexual prowess. **2.** Chanel's iconic nail color, a dark red and black shade resembling dried blood, which flew off the shelves in the midnineties.

### vampires

Go-to crush/boyfriend for modern ladies. From *Dracula* to *Buffy* to *Twilight, The Vampire Diaries* and *True Blood,* vampires are dangerously sexy seducers, and a fictional heroine is a *nobody* unless she's got at least one lusting after her. Newfangled vampires hardly ever bite anyone for fun, and the whole "bloodlust" aspect is generally just a thinly veiled metaphor for lust. Sex—penetration, blood, pleasure, pain—is what vamps are really all about, and why women love them. For some reason, when you dress one up as a pale emo dude who practices restraint, ladies like him even more.

### Vanity Fair

Condé Nast–published magazine by, for, and about the filthily rich. Occasionally has a nice, long, gossipy article suitable for a short flight; otherwise not really much of a cut above *Us Weekly.*

### Van Pelt, Lucy

Small of stature, blue of dress, and indomitable of spirit. Seems to be the one character in *Peanuts* with the least amount of tolerance for Charlie Brown's sad-sackery. (When you consider that even his dog gets sick of listening to the guy, that's saying something.) Best known for her many, many attempts to convince Charlie that she will not pull the football away when he tries to kick it (she will) and similarly numerous attempts to convince piano-playing Schroeder that theirs is a precious, pure, and destined love he should return wholeheartedly (he won't). Kind of a jerk, but prone to talking about how ladies should be presidents, and seemingly capable of running every single thing in town,

from a drive-by therapy clinic to a Christmas pageant. In twenty years, her precocious little brother, Linus, will be contributing essays to *n+1,* Charlie Brown will be talking about how he could contribute essays to *n+1* if the world valued sensitive guys like him, and Schroeder will be writing tunes for Katy Perry. Meanwhile, Lucy will be working at a Planned Parenthood and planning her mayoral run. She's got a power of will, that one. Watch out.

## vasectomy
Besides condoms, the only form of birth control controlled by men.

## Vatican, The
Governing body of the Catholic Church that resides in a walled, landlocked city-state (population 800) ruled by a spiritual authority who is secretly elected on ballots that are burned into white smoke, wears gold shield-hats, travels in a glass case on the back of a Mercedes-Benz SUV, and decrees whether billions of women should be forced to carry children against their will, if gay prostitutes should die of AIDS, how to resolve the energy crisis, etc.

## Vega, Suzanne (1959–)
Folksinger-poet. In 1981, Vega spent a morning watching the rain, reading a newspaper, drinking a cup of coffee, and writing a song about pretending not to notice that she was surrounded by people—and totally alone—in the middle of New York City. Vega called her song "Tom's Diner" and recorded it a cappella; a decade later, the song became an international hit, inspiring artists from 2Pac to "Weird Al" Yankovic.

## Venus
Second planet from the sun and one named after the Roman goddess of love and beauty. According to one popular self-help book from the early nineties, women are from there.

## venereal disease
Your grandfather's sexually transmitted disease, back when the scariest by-product of casual sex (besides pregnancy) was picking up some syphilis and gonorrhea from a "good-time girl." Abbreviated as VD. (*See also* CHLAMYDIA)

## vibrator
Mechanical device applied to one's clitoris, G-spot, taint, or prostate for the purposes of arousal and/or orgasm.

## victim blaming
In his 1971 book *Blaming the Victim*, sociologist William Ryan defined it as "justifying inequality by finding defects in the victims of inequality." Ryan's focus was on urban African American families and the systemic social forces that kept so

many of them in poverty, while most of white America saw "the negro problem" as an epidemic of laziness and weak character. Just as racism fueled (and still fuels) that sort of victim blaming, sexism is the chief driver of the type that holds rape survivors responsible for failing to prevent their own attacks, female employees responsible for keeping their bosses' hands off their asses, and domestic violence victims responsible for all the years they stayed with abusers who threatened to kill them if they left.

## victim mentality

What people are accused of having when they complain about oppression, as though what's really holding them back is not a racist, sexist, homophobic, ableist system, but their own pathetic negativity.

## Victorian

When we think of the Victorian Era, we think of: wigs, powder, uncomfortable chairs, Charles Dickens, prudishness, Oscar Wilde, Gothic revivalism, high collars, Charles Darwin, parasols, morality, and—obviously—Queen Victoria, who reigned from 1837 until her death in 1901.

---

### virgin

Social construction of sexual inexperience that defines the avoidance of vaginal penetration before marriage as a worthy goal. (*See also* PURITY BALL; VALENTI, JESSICA)

---

## virginity

Condition of a person who has not yet had sex. Irrelevant to pretty much everything, but highly valued in many cultures, at least in women.

## Virgin Mary

Physical mother of Jesus Christ and proud winner of the Miss Impossible Female Standards of Virtue contest for the past two thousand years running. According to the Catholic Church, Mary of Nazareth was a virgin when God placed a fetus in her uterus. Was accused of promiscuity—most notably by her husband, Joseph—after she showed up pregnant, at which point God had to intervene. The point being: if even the Virgin Mary got slut-shamed, there's no way you're getting through life without receiving some of the same. Sorry.

## Vogue

Condé Nast magazine founded in 1892 that has evolved into the preeminent fashion magazine on the planet. Helmed since 1988 by editor Anna Wintour, who has created a glossy juggernaut of fashion, celebrity, style, and lifestyle. Wintour calls her use of elite photographers to shoot ridiculously priced couture on underweight models "aspirational"; but the exclusivity of the magazine's subjects—mostly white, mostly thin, mostly wealthy—could also be called offensive, exclusionary, disdainful, snobbish, discriminatory, and closed minded. Still,  *Vogue*, as a name and brand, holds serious cachet, worldwide—there are nineteen different editions in countries and regions, including China, Russia, Korea, and India. (*See also* FASHION; VREELAND, DIANA; WINTOUR, ANNA)

## voluptuous

**1.** Stacked. **2.** Euphemism for anything from "chubby" to "really fat."

## Vreeland, Diana (1903–1989)

Influential editor who worked for magazines like *Harper's BAZAAR* and *Vogue* (where she was editor in chief from 1963 to 1971) and is remembered for many fashion milestones, including her proclamation that the bikini was "the most important thing since the atom bomb," discovering Edie Sedgwick, and advising First Lady Jacqueline Kennedy in matters of style.

### vulva

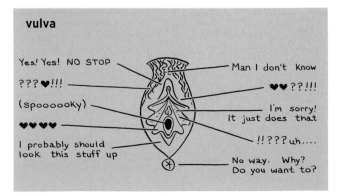

## W

**waistline**

**1.** Part of a dress that nips in between the bust and the skirt. **2.** What we were all supposed to be "watching" in the 1970s, before all-new body image anxiety zones like "cankles" and "muffin top" were invented. (*See also* CANKLES; MUFFIN TOP)

### Waiting to Exhale

Novel by Terry McMillan published in 1992; later, a movie directed by Forest Whitaker and starring Angela Bassett and Whitney Houston that was called "a social phenomenon" by the *L.A. Times* because of its predominantly black and female cast. "Despite themselves, the four black women whose turbulent love lives are explored with a salty good humor…all subscribe to the myth of a knight in shining armor," wrote Stephen Holden for the *New York Times*. "By the end of the film…one of the four actually finds her Prince Charming, and another has established a long-distance correspondence with someone who shows distinct Mr. Right potential." However, notes Holden, "these princely paragons are shining exceptions" in a story that portrays men as dogs. Oh, and the soundtrack! A tour de force with all of the biggest divas of the time, including Houston herself, as well as Toni Braxton, TLC, and Mary J. Blige. (*See also* HOUSTON, WHITNEY)

**waitress**

**1.** Diminutive term for a female server at a restaurant. **2.** A single member of the experimental New Wave band The Waitresses. (*See also* CASTLEBERRY, FLORENCE JEAN)

### Walker, Alice (1944–)

Revolutionary black feminist author whose masterpiece *The Color Purple* became an Oscar-bait vehicle for Oprah Winfrey. Apparent bad mother. (*See also* COLOR PURPLE, THE; WALKER, REBECCA)

### Walker, Kara (1969–)

Contemporary artist who explores the black female American experience through larger-than-life cut-paper silhouettes. Walker draws on images of African Americans from the past, specifically the antebellum South, as well as stories and folktales, to explore slavery, desire, and violence. She was one of the youngest recipients of a MacArthur "genius" grant. Walker's work remains highly controversial, both for its graphic and often grotesque imagery and for her use of African American stereotypes. Walker notably likened the aftermath of Hurricane Katrina to the conditions on slave ships: "I was seeing images that were all too familiar. It was black people in a state of life-or-death desperation, and everything corporeal was coming to the surface: water, excrement, sewage. It was a re-inscription of all the stereotypes about the black body."

### Walker, Rebecca (1969–)

Third-wave feminist who called her mother, Alice, both a bad feminist and a bad parent: "I meet women in their 40s who are devastated because they spent two decades working on a PhD or becoming a partner in a law firm, and they missed out on having a family," she wrote in her 2008 book *Baby Love: Choosing Motherhood after a Lifetime of Ambivalence.*

**"Thanks to the feminist movement, they discounted their biological clocks. They've missed the opportunity and they're bereft. Feminism has betrayed an entire generation of women into childlessness. It is devastating. But far from taking responsibility for any of this, the leaders of the women's movement close ranks against anyone who dares to question them—as I have learned to my cost."**

(*See also* BIOLOGICAL CLOCK; WALKER, ALICE)

### Walters, Barbara (1929–)

Journalist, television interviewer, and producer. Once a trailblazer, now chiefly known for extensive collection of studded, embroidered, and otherwise bedazzled blouses and the small army of lighting technicians who follow her around with a backlight. Seriously, this woman once moderated presidential debates and now spends most of her time trading bon mots with Elisabeth Hasselbeck. Famously asked actress Katharine Hepburn what kind of tree she'd be.

### Wann, Marilyn (1966–)

Fat acceptance activist—or, as she'd put it, "fat liberation" activist—before most of us knew there was such a thing. In 1993, at twenty-seven years old, five feet four, and approximately 245 pounds, Wann was denied health insurance coverage because of her weight. That outrage kicked off a career in which she'd publish a popular zine, book, and website called *Fat!So?*, perform with groups of fat dancers, cheerleaders, and synchronized swimmers, invent a "Yay! scale" that offered compliments instead of numbers, and fight for weight discrimination legislation in several cities and states—including San Francisco, where the law was changed in 2000 to protect fat people. An avid exerciser and cook, Wann is a strong proponent of a "Healthy at Every Size" approach to wellness. "In my political worldview, the intention of eating to produce weight loss is counterproductive and does more harm than good," she told the magazine of her alma mater, Stanford, in 2003. "Honoring one's own appetite, not denying the body's reality, with food that is nourishing—now *that* is health-enhancing." (*See also* FAT; FAT ACCEPTANCE; FAT SHAMING)

## wannabe

**1.** Slang for "want to be," an adjective or noun describing someone pretending to be something they're not. **2.** The 1996 song by the Spice Girls that helped propel the British girl group to stardom.

## war on women

Phrase to describe a decades—centuries!—long assault on women's rights, opportunities, and autonomy. "The Association had never declared 'war on women'; the firebrand had been 'forced' on it. The war had been declared from the other side," went one speech at the twenty-second meeting of the American Medical Association when it declared itself opposed to the admission of women to the Association in…1871. *Plus ça change.* Now refers primarily to Republican attacks on women's reproductive rights and, to a lesser extent, other civil rights like fair pay and rape statutes. Conservatives occasionally whine about the term, claiming it's incorrect to call it a "war." (Sure, if in your view that whole Vietnam thing in the 1960s was just an "armed conflict.") Low-intensity effort whose tactics include eschewing an outright ban of abortion in favor of just regulating it out of existence, or airing one's repugnant views about "legitimate rape" to the press instead of just adding "In favor of rape" to the party platform. In other words, the tactics of cowards, and, mercifully, losers. (*See also* ABORTION; LEGITIMATE RAPE; PRO-CHOICE; PRO-LIFE; RAPE-RAPE)

### Warren, Elizabeth (1949–)

Harvard professor turned public policy advocate who rose to national prominence as the US economy fell apart. Appointed in 2008 to oversee government bailouts under the Obama administration, she worked to create the new Consumer Financial Protection Bureau, and, in 2012, she was elected first female senator from Massachusetts, following one of the more surreal (and expensive) political races in modern history against Republican and former *Cosmo* centerfold model Scott Brown, whose campaign smeared her as everything from a socialist welfare queen to a "Fauxcahontas" for identifying her heritage in multiple cookbook entries and one academic directory as part Cherokee. Since entering the political spotlight, Warren has encountered the absurdity of society's physical expectations for female politicians: she is an attractive woman who doesn't look typically "sexy." "Elizabeth Warren has got that very short bob, little or no makeup, and little glasses," Washington, DC, hostess and resident ditz Sally Quinn has said. "What would she look like with long hair? With her glasses off? She would be a real babe. But would people take a babe seriously as a consumer czar?…That's a little depressing, that she can't look more like the babe that she is."

### Wasserstein, Wendy (1950–2006)

Tony- and Pulitzer-winning playwright of *The Heidi Chronicles* and numerous other stage dramas. The Brooklyn-born Wasserstein broke more barriers than you'd expect given that she was born in the second half of the twentieth century. At the Yale School of Drama in the 1970s, "she studied no plays by women, nor did she meet a single woman director," according to her Jewish Women's Archive biography. After that, "Wasserstein was determined to prove that a woman need not be insane, desperate or weird in order to be stageworthy. Consequently, she devoted her entire playwriting career to exploring the lives of intelligent, talented women." The wit and heart that defined Wasserstein's writing earned her frequent comparisons to Neil Simon, not to mention the distinction of being the first woman to win a Tony Award for Best Play. After her untimely death of lymphoma in 2006, Broadway theaters dimmed their lights in her honor. Her first and only novel, *Elements of Style*, was published posthumously to critical acclaim.

### waxing

Perhaps the most painful of the hair removal processes for women (and some men), this particular form of torture can be applied just about anywhere on the body, and in fun patterns, too. (*See also* VAJAZZLING)

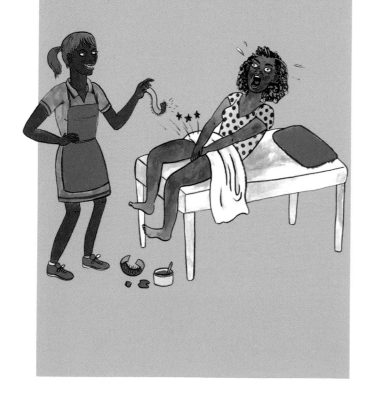

### Weaver, Sigourney (1949–)

Arguably best known for playing Ellen Ripley in the four *Alien* films, but also wowed moviegoers in *Working Girl*, the underrated *Heartbreakers*, and *Avatar* with an unflinching stare that manages to intimidate and charm at the very same time.

### wedding

Ceremony in which a couple is married. Traditionally, marriage is an institution that subjugates women, signifying the legal transference of a woman's ownership from father to husband, at which point—in different periods of time—she could then be controlled through rape, beating, or purse strings. Marriage has improved in recent years—the letter of the law no longer condones rape, and in some US states even gay people can do it—but weddings still enact the campy musical theater version of the traditional marriage contract, with the bride as its top-billed star. An engagement ring and transferred last name mark the husband's claim to her body as his territory. A white dress symbolizes the bride's offering of virginity. His ritualistic public removal of her garter symbolizes its loss. And the tossing of the bouquet trains single women to aspire to join her ranks. (It gives other guests the chance to hightail it to the open bar.)

## weight

When used to describe a personality, a cultural positive—a person of heft, substance, influence, and power. In physicality, a liability, at least among women. You can't help but wonder if the two are aligned—that women who take up both physical and cultural space constitute a threat.

## Weight Watchers

Commercial diet program that recently used the tagline "Diets Don't Work" in an ad campaign, evidence in favor of the adage that if you listen, people will tell you the truth about themselves.

## Wells, Ida B. (1862–1931)

One of the first African American woman journalists. Born before the Emancipation Proclamation, but free by the age of one. In 1884, almost thirty years before the birth of Rosa Parks, Wells refused to give up her seat on a train to a white man—then sued the railroad. Writing about that case kicked off her journalism career; five years later, she would go full-time, as a partner in the Memphis-based *Free Speech and Headlight* newspaper. Her investigation into the 1892 lynching of three of her peers, however, led angry white men to destroy the paper's office and effectively run Wells out of town. She eventually settled in Chicago, where she continued writing and organizing against lynching in the South and segregated schools. She also marched for women's suffrage, helped in founding the NAACP, and ran for the Illinois State Legislature before her death in 1931. Badass.

## Welty, Eudora (1909–2001)

American writer who never really moved out of her parents' house and maybe never had sex. An accomplished author of odd, lovely short stories and novels about the intersections of identity and community, the tension between passion and security, and the way that relationships are complicated but also important. Oh, and the South. The South was big. Welty was on staff at the *New York Times Book Review*, earned a graduate degree in business from Columbia, and contributed to the *Atlantic Monthly* and the *New Yorker*. Won a Pulitzer Prize for her novel *The Optimist's Daughter*.

## wench

Colloquial and antiquated British term that refers to either a lower-class woman, a black woman, or a promiscuous woman, conveniently collapsing Western civilization's offensive class, gender, and racial positions into one perfect syllable.

## West, Mae (1893–1980)

Actress and so much else. The famously misquoted line, "Why don't you come up sometime, and see me?" is what the Brooklyn native purrs in the 1933 Academy Award–winning film *She Done Him Wrong* as she attempts to seduce Cary Grant. But West didn't just drawl the line—she wrote it. The movie was based on her Broadway show *Diamond Lil*; she also wrote *I'm No Angel*, another flick in which she starred (with Grant) as an irresistible, sexually charged charmer with an endless stream of handsome suitors—and the diamonds to prove it. West's bawdy, brazen sexuality was her trademark; her first starring role on Broadway was in a play called *Sex*, which she wrote, produced, and directed. The titles of her projects alone (*The Wicked Age, The Constant Sinner, It Ain't No Sin*) indicated her enthusiasm for depicting strong, confident, shameless women who were quick with a quip. Unfortunately, her racy dialogue and love 'em and leave 'em plots were racy enough to draw the attention of the moral police—and worse, the censors. The Hays Code of 1934—which banned the depiction of women and men in bed together and "excessive or lustful kissing"—had a huge impact on West's career. Her screenplays were edited such that it became difficult for her to stay true to her brand of entertainment. So much is summed up in her first line on film: after a hat-check girl says, "Goodness, what beautiful diamonds," West replies, "Goodness had nothing to do with it, dearie." (*Goodness Had Nothing to Do with It* would later be the title of West's bestselling autobiography.)

## Westheimer, Dr. Ruth (1928–)

German-born author and sex therapist and educator who went from being a Holocaust survivor to a cultural icon. If you came of age in the 1980s, then you probably pronounce "masturbation" with a German accent.

## Wharton, Edith (1862–1937)

Author of thirty-eight novels, including *Ethan Frome, The House of Mirth*, and *The Age of Innocence*, which made her the first woman to win a Pulitzer Prize. "But," says Wharton's  *New York Times* obituary, "her reputation rested mostly upon her achievement as the chronicler of Fifth Avenue, when the brownstone front hid wealth and dignity at its ease upon the antimacassar-covered plush chairs of the Brown Decade." A child of privilege—one branch of her family was the Joneses of "keeping up with" fame—Wharton grew up to be a devastating critic of her own class. "The only way not to think about money," she wrote in *The House of Mirth*, "is to have a great deal of it."

## Wheatley, Phillis (1753–1784)

Poet and slave. Her owners taught her to read and write and then paraded her poetic talents about as a sort of party trick. Her work was good enough that white men naturally accused her of forging it. Once wrote a poem about George Washington, for which he personally thanked her, but she still had to wait until her owner's death to be released from forced servitude. Abolitionists adored her example, but she died as a free domestic servant at thirty-one, along with her third child. From "On Being Brought from Africa to America": "Remember, Christians, Negros, black as Cain, / May be refin'd, and join th' angelic train."

### Whedon, Joss (1964–)

Creator of *Buffy the Vampire Slayer* and *Angel*, director of *The Avengers*, and the living embodiment of the *Revenge of the Nerds*. Third-generation Hollywood writer whose work has been deeply engaged with pop cultural tropes, particularly those that involve women, Whedon began his journey into the canon when he turned to genre fiction, writing scripts for such films as *Alien: Resurrection*, and a campy take on horror movies called *Buffy the Vampire Slayer*, which hit screens in 1992. It was that last movie and the idea behind it—that the so-called Final Girl to survive the predations of horror movie monsters could be a hero and a figure of expectations-defying strength rather than simply of purity and innocence—that made Whedon both a feminist and a nerd hero. (*See also* Buffy the Vampire Slayer)

### When Chickenheads Come Home to Roost

Founding text of hip-hop feminism. Writer Joan Morgan's spirited 1999 memoir sparked a new movement by pioneering a vision of feminism that "fuck[ed] with the grays"— namely, a feminism that looked at the complications and complexity of race, gender, and pop culture through a decidedly hip-hop lens.

> **wife**
>
> *"Wife.* Four letters. One syllable. Simple, or so it seems. Yet this common word has become one of the most complex signifiers in the English language, weighted by past definitions, blurred by personal biases. The associations it elicits are bipolar in their scope: by the beginning of the twenty-first century, wife was variously presented as the source of female damnation or salvation, enchantment or disenchantment, captivity or rescue. Take your pick. Evidence can be marshaled to support either case. The truth exists in neither."
>
> —ANNE KINGSTON, *The Meaning of Wife*

### Wifey

Published in 1978, an adult novel by Judy Blume about open marriages in the swinging seventies. Blume never shied away from taboo topics—masturbation (*Deenie*), menstruation

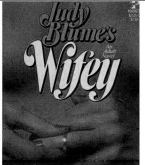

(*Are You There God? It's Me, Margaret*), and wet dreams (*Then Again, Maybe I Won't*)— and *Wifey*, her first foray into adult fiction, was no exception. (*See also* Blume, Judy)

### whiny

An anxious and annoying tone of voice or type of speech that is typically attributed to women (as an insult) and small children (as a fact). I don't *want* to do that. I don't *want* to go there. I don't *like* her, why are you making me hang out with her? Pleaaaase buy me this random thing. Whyyyy won't you call me? I'm too tired. I want to go home. I haaaate this place.

### White, Betty (1922–)

Veteran actress and national treasure. In an industry that discards many female stars at puberty, White stretched her career into its seventh decade by marketing her sassy-old-lady shtick to multiple generations of whippersnappers. After an  illustrious career in radio (!) and television, White debuted as elderly in 1985's *Golden Girls* (playing sweet, naive widow Rose), then rebooted her career as a deeply elderly television parodist, mining old people humor for *SNL* viewers who weren't even born when *Golden Girls* hit the air.

### whore

Extraderogatory term for a sex worker. (*See also* prostitute)

### Wilder, Laura Ingalls (1867–1957)

Author of the autobiographical Little House series, written for children, which follows a pioneer family traveling and settling the United States of the 1900s. In later years, controversy emerged as to whether the series had in fact been penned by Rose Wilder Lane, Laura's daughter, and embroidered for readers, though this has never bothered fans, who still flock to one of the Ingalls and Wilder homes in De Smet, South Dakota, and Mansfield, Missouri, respectively. (*See also* Little House on the Prairie)

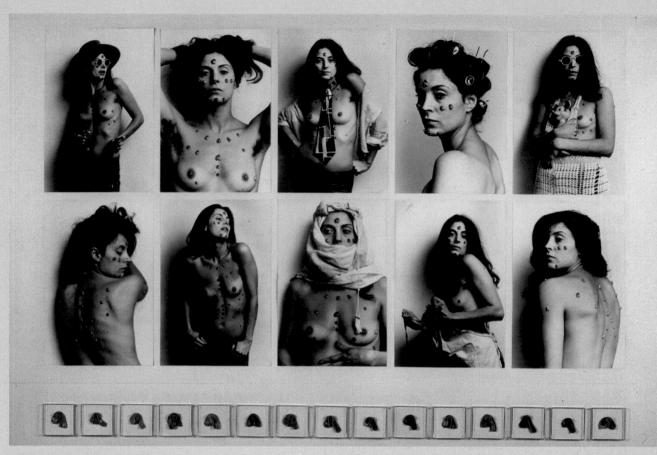

### Wilke, Hannah (1940-1993)

Artist and sculptor of the kind of thing people long mocked feminist art for, which is to say the vagina, or vulva, or whichever part happened to inspire her in the moment. Wilke's chosen medium in her most famous work was chewing gum, which…isn't half-strange, actually. Of course then she stuck it to her naked body and took pictures of herself in said condition. It works for us.

### Williams, Vanessa L. (1963-)

First African American to earn the title of Miss America; resigned after nude photos taken years before were published. Went on to release several albums, star on Broadway, and have notable roles on shows like *Ugly Betty* and *Desperate Housewives*.

### Williams, Venus (1980-) and Serena (1981-)

Tennis. Sisters. Tennis. Sisters. Tennis. Sisters. Tennis Sisters. *Tennis* Sisters. It must get really exhausting for one never to be mentioned without the other, though that's just a guess. Jehovah's Witnesses (both of them). Brought up in Compton, California, and trained with their father on local public tennis courts, which is mentioned at the head of every profile, too. Their excellence in the face of that upbringing leads to some odd backhanded compliments. Even noted literary figure John Jeremiah Sullivan had to get a word in about this in the *New York Times Magazine*, in 2012, calling it "dramatic" and "strange" that "this African-American family [is] organizing itself, as a unit, in order to lay siege to perhaps the whitest sport in the world and pulling it off somehow." Which sounds like a plausible statement until you learn that the siblings, who have twenty-two Grand Slam titles between them, have long boycotted one tournament where people shouted the N-word at them. (Which also raises the question: why does that tournament still exist at all?)

### Willis, Ellen (1941–2006)

Writer and feminist who covered the feminist movement first, and best, with thorough, stylish early essays on rape trials and prosex feminism and abortion rights, her involvement in in-person protest groups like Redstockings and No More Nice Girls, and later works on pop culture, teshuva, aging radicals, and war. (*See also* REDSTOCKINGS)

### Wilson, Ann (1950–) and Nancy (1954–)

Brunette lead vocalist and blonde lead guitarist of the now-classic rock band Heart. Ann's the one who spent her whole

career being shamed about her weight and finally had gastric banding surgery in 2002. Nancy's the one who was married to Cameron Crowe for a while and composed music for a bunch of his movies. Together, they were among the first female rockers to write their own songs and play their own instruments, which earned them all the respect typically afforded beautiful, ambitious women, especially in the sixties and seventies: pats on the head, seminaked photo shoots, and rumors of scandalous sexual activity. (Some asshole's attempt to get attention by claiming Ann and Nancy were having an incestuous affair led to their hit "Barracuda.") The Wilsons have sold over 35 million albums (so far), paved the way for every lady rock star of the last forty years, and publicly told Sarah Palin—who attempted to use "Barracuda" as her theme song during the 2008 presidential campaign—to go fuck herself (albeit not in so many words). The best. Plus, you can never go wrong putting "Crazy on You" on the jukebox.

### Winfrey, Oprah (1954–)

Billionaire former talk show host, magazine publisher, actress, philanthropist, perpetually hounded for her weight (fluctuating) and relationship status (unmarried). (*See also* OPRAH)

### wings

Curved adhesive accessory on maxi pads designed to prevent leaks but that in reality stick to you, the pad, or pretty much anything except your underwear.

### Winslet, Kate (1975–)

English actress, multiple Oscar nominee. (She won for 2008's *The Reader.*) Since her breakout role as a murderous, lovesick teenager in *Heavenly Creatures*, she's consistently made interesting choices and delivered terrific performances, which would be reason enough to adore her, but why stop there? She's almost as well known for refusing to take shit about her weight—which fluctuates, but normally lands her in the category "thin among average women, a little chubby among Hollywood actresses." Not even when she was young, not even when she was naked on camera, not even when she became the star of the highest-grossing film of all time and the whole world was staring at her, did she take any shit. In 2003, when *GQ* gave her unrecognizably long, thin legs in a cover photo, she pitched a righteous fit and made them apologize for misleading the public. "I just don't worry about my weight anymore," she told *Good Housekeeping* in 2007. "I notice it…but I don't avoid anything, and I'm not a fanatic. I think that's a miserable, terrible way to live your life." Then she got naked on screen again and won that Oscar, so there you go. (*See also* TITANIC)

### Wintour, Anna (1949–)

Editor of American *Vogue* and arguably the most powerful individual in the entire fashion industry. (Disagree, and you may never work in this town again.) Wintour, who is very British, is the daughter of Charles Wintour, the former editor of London's *Evening Standard*. She has said that her father "really decided for me that I should work in fashion," which is a bit sad, but Wintour excelled at her predetermined profession, working her way up to the *Vogue* mother ship through fashion editor stints at magazines like *Harper's BAZAAR*. Wintour also worked at *Viva*, a ladies' companion to *Penthouse*, but she doesn't really talk about that. She also reportedly dated Bob Marley, but she doesn't really talk about that, either. Damn shame. Wintour and her trademark bob have helmed *Vogue* since 1988; in that time she has turned the fashion and lifestyle magazine into a many-tentacled beast of branding and influence. Her interest in a given young designer will make a star out of him (and it usually is a "him"). The clothes she features in *Vogue* will dictate what a department store puts on its shelves and, in turn, what you will buy and wear, be it the high-priced designer original or the trickle-down knockoff that'll be on the racks at Forever 21 in three months. Wintour is a front-row fixture at fashion shows, as are the guests who accompany her (tennis champion Roger Federer is an inexplicable favorite), and they are

closely watched during every Fashion Week. Sometimes, she has been known to smile. In 2003, a former assistant of Wintour's, Lauren Weisberger, published *The Devil Wears Prada*, a thinly veiled roman à clef about her time working in the *Vogue* offices. The bestselling "novel" portrays Wintour as a sadistic and inhumane boss with little regard for the mental or emotional health of her minions; whether or not this is a wholly accurate portrayal of Wintour has been subject to debate, though everyone seems to agree that there's more than a shred of truth in it. (One popular nickname: Nuclear Wintour.) The book was eventually made into a hit movie starring Anne Hathaway and Meryl Streep, and now it can be occasionally enjoyed on basic cable. (*See also* FASHION; VOGUE)

**witch**
**1.** Wiccan.
**2.** Common villain of children's media.
**3.** Cop-out Halloween costume.
**4.** Euphemism for "bitch" among people who think of that as "the B-word."
(*See also* CACKLE OF RADS; COVEN; CRAFT, THE)

### The Witch of Blackbird Pond

Young adult novel by Elizabeth George Speare that tells, through heroine Kit, the story of the witch trials that erupted in a stern Connecticut colony. Kit arrives into her extended family's New England home from Barbados like a bird of paradise amidst a flock of drab sparrows. Fleeing an unwanted marriage and a debt-ridden plantation, Kit distinguishes herself immediately by diving into the cold Atlantic to save a child's toy, then further incites the tight-laced community with her beautiful slashed-sleeve silk dresses, unconventional teaching methods, and spirited tongue. Though she tries heartily to stir gruel with the best of them, a friendship with an elderly Quaker woman, Hannah, leads them both to be accused of witchcraft. Thank heaven for that fiery love interest, sailor Nat.

## WNBA

Women's basketball league founded in 1996. It's never quite caught on the way the NBA has, but its popularity in the 1990s inspired a generation of girls to join their high school sports teams and made Sheryl Swoopes and Lisa Leslie famous.

### Wolf, Naomi (1962–)

Writer and activist who never lived up to the expectations set in her best-selling 1991 book *The Beauty Myth*, which detailed the ways in which women are suffocated by the visual demands of society. Since then, she's been a bit of a troll, clashing with her peers by supporting noted woman-izer and alleged rapist Julian Assange and releasing the astonishingly bad *Vagina: A New Biography*, which was instantly met with a noisy public feminist what-the-fucking. (*See also* VAGINA)

### woman

Technically, the term for a female human. Subjectively, a lot more.

### womanly

Silly term used to silence "unconventional" women and enforce traditionalist conformity. In actual fact, *literally anything* that a woman does is "womanly." Driving a truck. Digging a hole. Repairing a fridge. Putting on lipstick. Squishing a bug. Eating a croissant. Also: belching.

### women's lib

Term for the feminist movement popularized in the 1960s and '70s until hateful jerks had made it such a scornful, mocking phrase, it needed to be replaced.

### women's work

Never done.

### womyn

Alternative spelling of the word *woman* to defeat the implicit patriarchalist phallic invasion of the letter *a*. Further proof that at least some of 1970s' radical feminist theory was invented while all involved were high on weed. Not recommended for current use except among those who live on communes, wear organic hempen garments, and have only eaten bean sprouts for the last three years, in which case, they should do whatever they need to do because they are proud warrior moon goddesses, and we don't want to get in their way.

### Wonder Woman

Most underrated superhero in history. An American icon, her fortunes rose and fell with the current state of feminism in the United States—she's been every-thing from a prosisterhood equality warrior to a swooning romance novel–style heroine. Despite her enduring popularity, Won-der Woman has been rele-gated to straight-to-DVD movies and comic anthologies while her comrades Batman and Superman receive the blockbuster treatment every few years. Required viewing: Lynda Carter's definitive show; the YouTube Wonder Woman Mix; the gender and superheroes documentary *Wonder Women!*

## Wong, Anna May (1905–1961)

Asian American actress and star of Hollywood films (silent and talkie), Broadway shows, and television. Criticized by the Chinese and Chinese American communities for accepting "Dragon Lady" or "Butterfly" roles and perpetuating Chinese stereotypes, Wong struggled against this type of casting and fought to win the roles her enormous talent deserved. Considered one of the most beautiful actresses of her day as well as one of the most talented, Wong, much like Josephine Baker, left for Europe and found huge success and better roles, though she returned to the United States eventually. Never the leading lady she should have been, Wong could still proudly sing in her cabaret shows: "I'm Anna May Wong / I come from old Hong Kong / But now I'm a Hollywood star."

## Woodman, Francesca (1958–1981)

Photographer whose pieces usually involved her own body, often naked, melting into the floor, or the wall, or hanging from a doorway. Committed suicide, which adds to the haunting impression that she simply wanted to disappear.

## Words with Friends

One evolutionary step up from Facebook Scrabble.

**work**

**workout**

## wrinkles

Natural result of aging skin, which ostensibly look worse on a woman than plastic surgery or injected fillers do. We're not convinced.

## Wurtzel, Elizabeth (1967–)

Manic Pixie Dream author who became the poster girl for affluent angst when her beautifully written memoir of drug-addiction-in-a-party-dress, *Prozac Nation*, made her famous in her early twenties.

## Wyman, Jane (1917–2007)

Actress. America's first and only ex-wife of a president, Wyman costarred with Ronald Reagan in 1938, married him in 1940, had three children with him, won an Academy Award, then divorced him in 1948—a split rumored to revolve around the premature death of their third child, or else political differences. "I've always been a registered Republican," Wyman said later. "But it's bad taste to talk about ex-husbands and ex-wives, that's all. Also, I don't know a damn thing about politics."

## Xanax

Yes, please.

## *Xena, Warrior Princess*

Ambiguously lesbian supernatural fantasy *Hercules* spin-off that toyed with an are-they-just-a-couple-of-experimenting-girlfriends-or-are-they-just-platonic-girlfriends dynamic between Xena and traveling companion Gabrielle. The two traversed epochs of mythological world history to battle warlords for six seasons in syndication (and reams of fan-written slash fiction) before consummating their relationship in an eroticized mouth-to-mouth resuscitation.

## xenophobia

Fear of foreigners, i.e., the right wing's favorite fund-raising tool after antiabortion propaganda.

## X-rated

In the early years of film, Hollywood was ruled by a Production Code that cracked down on the shooting of films featuring such scandalous visuals as "scenes of passion," "pointed profanity," dancing with "indecent movements," and "white slavery." In 1968, the MPAA replaced the Code with a voluntary post-production rating system that codified X as a highly restricted designation—and therefore an instant marker of anti-establishment cool. The MPAA slapped an X on *A Clockwork Orange* for its simulated rape scenes, *The Evil Dead* for its gruesome violence, and *Midnight Cowboy* for its "homosexual frame of reference"; *Cowboy* nevertheless scooped up the Oscar for Best Picture in 1970. Keying into the cool factor, porn producers in the 1970s started stamping an X (or three) on their own films to draw in clients seeking out those "scenes of passion." In 1990, the MPPA changed the X rating to NC-17—and trademarked it—to avoid conflating explicit mainstream fare with hardcore smut.

## XXX

According to *Brewer's Dictionary of Phrase & Fable*, an X scrawled on a beer cask used to indicate that the brewer had surrendered the sufficient duty to the government for selling the stuff. Tripling the boozy signal evolved into shorthand for all things extreme—scrawled on a jug, it's a stiff alcoholic drink (maybe moonshine); a winning line in the game of tic tac toe; shorthand for kisses (or is it hugs?); relayed over a radio signal, it's a distress call just short of SOS; affixed to film, it's hardcore porn.

## xylophone

Because every reference book worth its salt needs to mention this percussion instrument beloved by toddlers.

# Y

### yeast infection

An explosive, sensitive, clumpy mess that is all but unavoidable in the endless seesaw of vulvar distress. To wit: the antibiotics for a UTI can cause a yeast infection, antiyeast meds can irritate a UTI, and so on and so forth. The search for a miracle cure has led to many home therapies: yogurt, garlic cloves, olive oil, frozen yogurt tampons, secret scratching, and prayer among the most popular.

### "Yellow Wallpaper, The"

Short story written in 1892 by Charlotte Perkins Gilman, based on her own experience of postpartum depression, for which a doctor advised her to "live as domestic a life as far as possible," to "have but two hours' intellectual life a day," and "never to touch pen, brush, or pencil as long as you live." Narrates the protagonist's obsession with the wallpaper in her room, and a presence—a familiar presence—she detects behind it. Gilman gave up on this "treatment" after three months. The story, she explained, "was not intended to drive people crazy, but to save people from being driven crazy, and it worked." (*See also* DEPRESSION; GILMAN, CHARLOTTE PERKINS; POSTPARTUM DEPRESSION)

### "yes means yes"

Sex-positive version of the 1970s slogan "no means no" and a new battle cry promoting enthusiastic consent—as opposed to the absence of a negative—as the standard for moving forward with a sexual encounter. Also the title of a 2008 feminist anthology edited by Jaclyn Friedman and Jessica Valenti. (*See also* VALENTI, JESSICA)

### yoga

Spiritual and physical discipline originating in India. Though technically referring to a certain school of Hindu philosophy, yoga has, in the Western world, come to mean a series of movements that mix stretching, balance, strength, and meditation. In previous eras, the practice was mostly practiced by men, but it has been enthusiastically embraced by women, particularly in the past few decades. In the United States, yoga is so popular that a very profitable ($6 billion in revenues a year) industry of videos, equipment, classes, and exercises has sprung up, and yoga apparel retailers like Lululemon are known to charge up to $120 for a pair of stretch pants. Spiritual indeed!

### yogurt

According to comedienne Sarah Haskins, "the official food of women."

### "you're just jealous"

Infantile, intellectually dishonest statement made to derail a conversation and reject legitimate criticism of yourself or something you admire.

### youth

Expected of women throughout their life cycle.

### yummy mummy

British slang for a young, attractive mother. (*See also* MILF)

### YWCA

Probably where you had swimming practice after school, or stayed when you couldn't afford a hotel room on some lackluster trip.

# Z

### Zaharias, Babe Didrikson (1911–1956)

Texas-born athlete who was good at everything—baseball, diving, roller-skating, bowling, and basketball. She sewed her own uniforms. She won Olympic gold in track and field. But she dominated at golf, becoming the sport's first female star, before the second wave hit, women athletes gained social legitimacy, and Billie Jean King altered the landscape forever. By the time she died in 1956, Babe had won every golf title she possibly could.

### zines

Self-published publications with a circulation of less than 1,000, often a labor of love that does not produce a profit. While that definition could technically apply to numerous publications throughout the whole of human history, the DIY aesthetic of zines is associated with the 1990s, when the medium hit its stride and gained mainstream recognition, thanks in part to its roots in the riot grrrl movement, which utilized zines to spread political messages. While a handful of zines, like *BUST*, *Bitch*, and *Dazed and Confused*, have gone on to become established periodicals with larger circulations, the internet has all but made the medium obsolete. (*See also* BITCH; BUST MAGAZINE; HANNA, KATHLEEN; RIOT GRRRL)

### zipless fuck

Perfect one-night stand—sex free of guilt, shame, and, commitment— a concept introduced in Erica Jong's 1973 bestseller *Fear of Flying*. (*See also* JONG, ERICA)

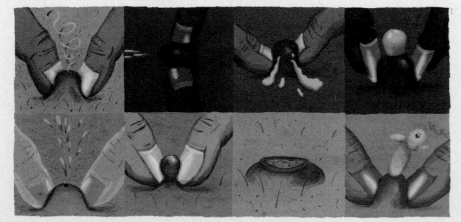

### zits

**1.** Acne. **2.** Device in the classic, oh-my-fucking-God, how-did-no-adult-ever-stop-me-from-playing-this-with-all-of-my-friends-at-age-nine, it-is-so-hilariously-deeply-misogynist teen parlor game Girl Talk, wherein a player would be forced to place a small red dot sticker on her face in order to register her lack of worth as a romantic partner, creative talent, or friend.

### zombies

**1.** Undead creatures who consume the brains of the living in movies. Often call for "braaaains."
**2.** Something very distressing to members of The Cranberries.
**3.** Figure in Haitian folk religion; a being literally raised from the dead via mystical means, or under the control of a spell.

### zygote

Too young to be a slut, so way more entitled to civil rights than you are.

# ACKNOWLEDGMENTS

**T**he editor wishes to thank the following individuals: Daniel Greenberg, Gaby Darbyshire, Emily Griffin, Nicole Page, Nick Denton, Jessica Coen, Scott Kidder, Erica Warren. Much gratitude to the Holmes and Armstrong families, numerous friends and confidants, and a pair of felines named Frog and Toshi. A special shoutout is in order to the loyal, loud-mouthed writers and readers—past and present—of Jezebel, the little ladyblog that could. You are my favorite lesbian shitasses.

# CONTRIBUTORS

**Anna Holmes** is a writer and editor who has worked with such publications as *Glamour, InStyle*, the *New York Times, Newsweek*, and the *New Yorker* online. She is the author of the 2002 book *Hell Hath No Fury: Women's Letters from the End of the Affair*. In 2007 she founded the popular website Jezebel, which she oversaw until her departure in 2010. You can follow her on Twitter and Instagram at @annaholmes.

**Kate Harding** is the author of *Asking for It*, co-author of *Lessons from the Fat-o-sphere*, and founder of the now-retired body acceptance website Shapely Prose. She occasionally updates kateharding.info and tweets as @kateharding.

**Amanda Hess** is a freelance writer and editor who writes about youth, sexuality, and technology. She lives in Los Angeles. You can reach her on Twitter at @amandahess or on her website, sexwithamandahess.com.

**Chloe Angyal** is an editor at Feministing.com and a regular Jezebel contributor, and she writes about politics and pop culture for a range of other publications. She was born and raised in Sydney, Australia, and now lives in New York City. You can read more of her work at chloesangyal.com and follow her on Twitter at twitter.com/chloeangyal.

**Katie J. M. Baker** is a Jezebel staff writer who enjoys making people uncomfortable at parties by telling them her beat is "mostly abortion and rape." (And she wouldn't have it any other way.) She has also written for publications such as the *New York Times* and the *San Francisco Chronicle*. You can find her online at katiejmbaker.com and @katiejmbaker.

**Gabrielle Birkner** is a New York–based writer, editor, and digital strategist. She has served as director of digital media at The Forward, where she founded and edited the women's-issues blog The Sisterhood, and as a religion reporter and features editor at the *New York Sun*. Follow her on Twitter at @gabibirkner.

**Susie Cagle** is a writer and illustrator in Oakland, California, who's been called "the angrier version" of other writers and illustrators. She's covered crisis pregnancy centers, anarchist riots, building occupations, and more for the *Atlantic*, the *Guardian*, the *Boston Review*, and other fun places. She tweets at @susie_c, sometimes in drawings.

**Irin Carmon** is a reporter at MSNBC and a former staff writer at *Salon*. From 2009 to 2011 she was a staff writer at Jezebel, where she (separately) earned the ire of Scott Baio and certain *Daily Show* staffers, and covered the Republicans' reproductive rights onslaught. In 2011, she was named one of *Forbes* 30 under 30 in Media and has been honored by the Hillman Foundation, the New York Abortion Access Fund, and NARAL-NY for her reporting on reproductive rights. You can follow her on Twitter at @irincarmon.

**Megan Carpentier** is a writer and editor whose tenure at Jezebel from 2007 to 2009 was followed by stints at Air America, Talking Points Memo, and Raw Story (where she never wrote about her period again). Her non-menstruation-related work has also been seen in the *Guardian*, the *Washington Post, Bitch, BUST, Glamour, Women's eNews*, and *RH Reality Check*. In 2009, she became the only person you know to be simultaneously published in *Foreign Policy* and *Us Weekly*. She can be found cursing on Twitter at @megancarpentier.

**Pixie Casey** (not her real name) spent two years as Jezebel's first weekend editor and is now a staff writer for *Rookie*. She is, was, and always will be Team Cake.

**Alexis Chaney** lives in Chicago but refuses to change her DC residency on principle. She is the director of development for First Floor Theatre, and a proud graduate of the University of Chicago in a major that has fifteen syllables. If you are interested in her thoughts on Reasonable Shorts, pop culture, Henry Rollins, and her continuing adventures as a Professional Intern, you may follow her on Tumblr and Twitter at @notalexus.

**Jessica Coen** is the editor in chief of Jezebel. A Michigan native, she has worked at *New York Magazine*, *Vanity Fair*, and Gawker; her writing has also appeared in the *New York Times* and *Glamour*. She splits her time between New York and Chicago and can fit two weeks' worth of clothes in a single carry-on bag.

**Domitille Collardey** is a Brooklyn-based cartoonist and illustrator from Paris. Her work has appeared in the *New York Times*, the *Believer*, *McSweeney's*, *Nobrow Magazine*, and others. She is currently working on the webcomic Wreckhall Abbey at http://www.wreckhallabbey.com. Check out http://www.domitille-collardey.com for more!

**Molly Crabapple** is an artist whose published books include *Discordia* (with Laurie Penny), *Devil in the Details*, *Saints and Sinners*, *Week in Hell*, *Puppet Makers*, and the forthcoming *Straw House*. Called "equal parts Hieronymus Bosch, William S. Burroughs, and Cirque du Soleil" by the *Guardian*, "a downtown phenomenon" by the *New York Times*, and "a brilliant and principled artist" by BoingBoing, her clients as an illustrator include the *New York Times*, the *Wall Street Journal*, the *Box*, and Red Bull.

**Madeleine Davies** is a Wisconsin-born writer and performer living in New York and a staffer at Jezebel.

**Eleanor Davis** is a cartoonist and illustrator living in Athens, Georgia. Check out her work at doing-fine.com.

**Vanessa Davis** is a cartoonist and illustrator living in Los Angeles. Her most recent book, *Make Me a Woman*, was published by Drawn and Quarterly in 2010. See more of her work at www.spanielrage.com.

**Michelle Dean's** writing has appeared at the *New Yorker*, the *Nation*, *Slate*, and many other fine publications. She was once a disgruntled lawyer who commented far too much on Jezebel.

**Sady Doyle** is the founder of the blog Tiger Beatdown. She cares about lady things almost as much as she cares about reading the internet. Almost.

**Kate Dries** is a staffer at Jezebel and founder of the website Smart Girls Who Do Stupid Things. Currently a fellow at BuzzFeed, she was formerly a web producer for WBEZ. She has written for *Thought Catalog*, the *Billfold*, *Zelda Lily*, and *PopMatters*, and produces The Guy Friends Podcast, a sex- and dating-advice show for anyone who is not a straight man.

**Hilary Elkins** is a writer living in New York City. She has written for *GQ*, *Elle*, *Marie Clare*, and the *New Republic*, among others. Originally from Louisiana, she loves Sazaracs, marathons, and (most of) the American South.

**Rana Emerson** has written about media and popular culture for *Gender & Society*, *xoJane*, *Pop Matters*, and other publications. When not at her day job at the City University of New York, she can be found basking in the rays of her TV, trying to be like Leslie Knope and Brienne of Tarth but actually living more like the Grandma's House Simon Amstell and Lucy Van Pelt.

**Tatyana Fazlalizadeh** is a Brooklyn-based oil painter and illustrator whose work focuses on portraiture and social/political themes. An Oklahoma City native, she exhibits her paintings in galleries nationally while completing illustration commissions for magazines, films, and books. Also working in public art, her latest project addresses street harassment through a series of street-art posters. You can view her work at http://tlynnfaz.com, and follow her at http://twitter.com/fazlalizadeh.

**Ann Friedman** is a magazine journalist who loves the internet. The former executive editor of *GOOD* magazine, she's now a columnist for *New York Magazine*'s website and for the *Columbia Journalism Review*. She's into GIFs, pie charts, and #realtalk. Find her at www.annfriedman.com.

**Catherine Garcia** is a Southern California–based writer, reporter, and editor. Her work has appeared in *Entertainment Weekly* and EW.com, the *New York Times*, and other publications, but the highlight of her professional career remains being considered an expert on Hello Kitty wines by MSNBC (sadly, she accidentally erased the DVR recording to prove it). You can see her work at catherinegarcia.word-press.com.

**Sarah Glidden's** first full-length book, a graphic memoir entitled *How to Understand Israel in 60 Days or Less*, was published in 2010 by DC Vertigo. She is currently working on her second book, *Rolling Blackouts*, a work of graphic journal-ism following reporters into Iraqi Kurdistan, Lebanon, and Syria, which will be published in 2014 by Drawn and Quarterly. Her short pieces of graphic journalism have been published in *Cartoon Movement*, *Ha'aretz*, and *the Jewish Quarterly*. You can find more of her work at sarahglidden.com.

**Jessica Grose** is a writer, editor, and grizzly-bear enthu-siast. She was formerly on staff at *Slate* and Jezebel, and she is the coauthor of the book *Love, Mom: Poignant, Goofy, Brilliant Messages from Home*, and the author of the novel *Sad Desk Salad*. Follow her on Twitter at @JessGrose or at her website.

**Katie Halper** is a comedienne, writer, filmmaker, and former history teacher. She performs around the country and her writing and videos have been published by the *New York Times*, Comedy Central, the *Nation* magazine, Gawker, *Nerve*, Jezebel, the *Huffington Post*, *Alternet*, *Raw Story*, and *Fem-inisting*. She is also the director of *Kinderland*, a documentary about the social-justice summer camp she, as well as her mother and grandmother, attended. Find her at @kthalps and katiehalper.com.

**Mikki Halpin** is a writer and the author of three books. She is currently editing a new edition of *The SCUM Manifesto*.

**Lisa Hanawalt** is an illustrator whose work has appeared in the *New York Times*, *Vanity Fair*, *McSweeney's*, *Vice Maga-zine*, *Lucky Peach*, *Chronicle Books*, *Bloomberg Business-Week*, and *Glamour*. *My Dirty Dumb Eyes*, a collection of her comics and artwork, is being published by Drawn and Quar-terly in 2013. Lisa's website is www.lisahanawalt.com.

**Margaret Hartmann** is a writer and former staffer at Jezebel.

**Rachel Herrick** is an artist whose Obeast Project, a pseudo-scientific satire of cultural anxiety and fat bias, uses the tropes of natural history to educate viewers about the endan-gered North American Obeast, a muumuu-clad animal per-formed by the artist herself. Herrick's detailed Museum for Obeast Conservation Studies (MOCS) installations enact the stigma and dehumanization of obesity literally; the *Obeast Project* can be experienced online at the MOCS website (obeasts.org), rachelherrick.com, and in her two-volume bookset *A Guide to the North American Obeast*, published by Publication Studio in 2013.

**Kyla Jones** is a writer and teacher living in Philadelphia, Pennslyvania. Prior to becoming a high school English teacher and reading specialist, she worked at *GQ* maga-zine. She likes crossword puzzles, crime novels, and bourbon.

**Elisa Kreisinger** is a remix artist known as Pop Culture Pirate. Her work involves mashing up TV to make *Mad Men* into feminists and *The Real Housewives* into lesbians. See her work at PopCulturePirate.com.

**Wendy MacNaughton** is an illustrator. She lives in San Francisco with her partner and their cats, and yes, her con-tribution is autobiographical.

**Amanda Marcotte** is a freelance feminist writer and journal-ist who blogs for *RH Reality Check*, *Slate*'s XX Factor, and her own site, Pandagon. She loves punk rock, cats, and pre-tending she knows how to DJ. She's a prolific Twitter villain who can be followed at @amandamarcotte.

**Marisa Meltzer** is the coauthor of *How Sassy Changed My Life*.

**Tracie Egan Morrissey** is senior writer at Jezebel, and has been with the site since its launch in 2007. She has authored several terrifying educational books for children like *Weapons of Mass Destruction and North Korea and Skin Cancer*, as well as the stoner advice book *Pot Psychology's How to Be*. Her work has appeared in the *New York Times*, *Newsweek*, *Vice*, *BUST*, *Playgirl*, VH1, and Gawker. She is somebody's wife and somebody else's mother.

**Kris Mukai** is an illustrator working in Brooklyn, New York. Her work can be found at www.krismukai.com.

**Anna North's** writing has appeared in the *Atlantic Monthly*; *Glimmer Train*; the *San Francisco Chronicle*; the *Paris Review Daily*; on Jezebel, where she was a staff writer and editor; and on BuzzFeed and at *Salon*, where she is now a senior editor. Her first novel, *America Pacifica*, was published by Reagan Arthur Books/Little, Brown in 2011, and you can follow her on Twitter at @annanorthtweets.

**Latoya Peterson** spent way too much time reading as a child. Luckily, she became a writer, which is a return on the investment. She used to write for Jezebel, runs Racialicious .com, and occasionally does some work when not reading paranormal romance novels at 3 a.m.

**Kartina Richardson** is a filmmaker and writer. She is the author of Mirrorfilm.org and a contributing critic for the PBS show *Ebert Presents at the Movies*.

**Alyssa Rosenberg** is the critic at *ThinkProgress* and a columnist at *Slate*'s XX Factor blog. Her work has appeared in the *Atlantic*, *Esquire*, the *Daily Beast*, the *New Republic*, and many other publications. She lives in Washington, DC.

**Erin Ryan** is a former writer for VH1's *Best Week Ever* and a current staffer of Jezebel. A Midwestern native, she currently resides in Brooklyn, along with everybody else. She's not available for children's parties.

**Jenna Sauers** is a New York–based freelance writer and a frequent contributor to Jezebel, *Bookforum*, the *New York Observer*, and the *Village Voice*.

**Becky Sharper** is a Southern-born incorrigibly feminist New Yorker. She one of the founders of *The Pursuit of Harpyness* blog.

**Lizzie Skurnick** is the author of *Shelf Discovery*, an essay collection on the best teen books of all time, and the editor in chief of Lizzie Skurnick Books. She contributes to the *New York Times Magazine*, NPR, Jezebel, the *Awl*, and many other outlets. She lives in Jersey City.

**Elizabeth Carey Smith** is a graphic designer, letterer, illustrator, and type designer in Brooklyn. With tattoos of all twenty-six letters of the alphabet, it is unlikely you will ever meet a bigger type nerd. Her studio is theletteroffice.com. She tweets real talk at @theoriginalecs.

**Jen Sorensen's** comics and illustrations have appeared in a variety of publications, including NPR.org, *Ms. Magazine*, the *Progressive*, *Daily Kos*, *Alternet*, the *Los Angeles Times*, *Bitch Magazine*, the *Village Voice*, and *MAD*. She has won several awards from the Association of Alternative Newsweeklies and an Aronson Award, and was the 2012 Herblock Prize Finalist. You can read her weekly political cartoons at jensorensen.com and her tweets at @SorensenJen.

**Sadie Stein** was a contributing editor at Jezebel from 2008 to 2011. She is deputy editor of the *Paris Review*.

**Dodai Stewart** is the deputy editor of Jezebel and has been with the site since 2007. Raised in New York, she's written for various publications, including *Glamour*, *New York Magazine* and the *New York Times*. She shares an apartment in Manhattan with her antisocial chihuahua.

**Rachel Syme** grew up among the dusty tumbleweeds in New Mexico and was blown eastward to New York City, where she now writes for NPR, the *New Yorker*, *New York Magazine*, and elsewhere. She is writing a new biography of F. Scott Fitzgerald for Random House and spends far too much time doing "research" by wearing feather headdresses and drinking gin martinis. She runs the On Biography series at the 92Y in New York and hangs out on Twitter more than she should. Find her at @rachsyme.

**Julie Teninbaum** is a graphic designer, illustrator, and cheese lover whose work has appeared in *TIME* magazine, the *Wall Street Journal*, *Fast Company*, and *Glamour*, among other publications. Her projects have included The Weather Report (theweatherreport.tumblr.com), Side View Mirrors (www.julieteninbaum.com), and the infamous Schmooklyn t-shirt (shmattah.com).

**Moe Tkacik,** a freelance investigative journalist and essayist, was one of the original Jezebel staffers. You can follow her work at daskrap.com and her periodic little spurts of fury directed at libertarians, "fiscal conservatives," and certain ex-boyfriends at @moetkacik. She is proud to report having completed, at age thirty-four, her first successful home highlighting procedure.

**Rebecca Traister** writes about women, media, and politics for *Salon*, the *Nation*, *Elle*, the *New York Times Magazine*, the *Washington Post*, and elsewhere. She is the author of *Big Girls Don't Cry: The Election That Changed Everything for American Women* and a forthcoming book about single women.

**Jennifer Gerson Uffalussy** was one of the original staffers at Jezebel. She currently consults on brand strategy and creative direction for retailers working in the e-commerce space and is finishing her first novel.

**Alysha Webb** was born and raised in Sonoma County, California, before moving to Manhattan. A major advocate for women's empowerment, she has worked with publications like *Real Simple* magazine and currently manages her own blog: *Winc* magazine. When her head isn't buried in a book she can be found dancing or with paintbrush in hand.

**Esther C. Werdiger** makes comics, illustrates, writes, and podcasts. Based in New York, but originally from Melbourne, Esther plans on writing a graphic novel in the near future, very slowly. More work, links, and contact details can be found at www.estherwerdiger.com.

**Lindy West** is a staff writer at Jezebel, where her main beats are fat people, dickheads, and celebrity fetuses. Her work has also been published in the *Guardian*, the *Stranger*, *GQ*, *Slate*, *Vulture*, the *Daily Telegraph*, and others. She lives in Seattle.

**Elizabeth Whitman** is a journalist focusing on the Middle East and mental health. She has written for the *Nation* and has also been a reporter at the United Nations in New York.

**Christie Young** is an artist and illustrator from Texas. She splits her time between drawing comics for *PLEASUREZONE* (www.pleasurezone.me), working on an etiquette book for the modern woman (Random House, 2014), and cruising the Craigslist free section. She currently lives and works in Brooklyn.

**Ping Zhu** is a freelance illustrator and Los Angeles native based in London. She dearly misses the experience of cutting open a perfectly ripe avocado. Her work has been published in the *New York Times*, the *New Yorker, O Magazine*, and the *Wall Street Journal*. Her first book, *Swan Lake*, is a concertina published by Nobrow Press.

**Jess Zimmerman** is in charge of cute animals, dick jokes, and *Futurama* references for Grist.org. Before that she did actual journalism for FactCheck.org, and somewhere in there she wrote alternately embarrassing, feminist, and embarrassing/feminist essays for *xoJane*. Also she's on Twitter a lot at @j_zimms. Like, a lot.

**Claire Zulkey** is the author of *An Off Year*, published by Dutton in 2009 and selected by Indie Booksellers for the Autumn 2009 Kids' Indie Next List and nominated as one of the ALA's 2010 Best Books for Young Adults. Since 2003 Claire has run the blog Zulkey.com, which is now produced by NPR affiliate WBEZ. She is a television critic and contributor to the *Los Angeles Times* and AV Club.

# PHOTO AND ILLUSTRATION CREDITS

Paramount: Floozy: Kris Mukai. Sandra Fluke: Getty Images. Jane Fonda: WireImage/Getty Images. Betty Ford: MCT via Getty Images. Jodie Foster: Gamma-Keystone via Getty Images. Anne Frank: Getty Images. Helen Frankenthaler: Helen Frankenthaler (American, born 1928), Lorelei, 1957, oil on untreated cotton duck, frame: 75 x 91⁷/₈ x 2½ in. (190.5 x 233.4 x 6.4 cm), Brooklyn Museum, purchase gift of Allan D. Emil, 58.39. © 2013 Estate of Helen Frankenthaler / Artists Rights Society (ARS), New York. Aretha Franklin: Getty Images. French kissing: Susie Cagle. Betty Friedan: Getty Images. Female friendship: Sarah Glidden. Margaret Fuller: Getty Images. Diane von Furstenberg: WireImage. **G** Lady Gaga: BuzzFoto/FilmMagic. Indira Gandhi: India Today Group/Getty Images. Greta Garbo: Getty Images. Gardasil: Courtesy Merck Laboratories. Geisha: Frank Carter/Getty Images. Gerber baby: Associated Press. Tavi Gevinson: Getty Images. Julia Gillard: Getty Images. Gilmore Girls: AllStar/Warner Brothers. Ruth Bader Ginsburg: Getty Images. Girdle: Roger Viollet/Getty Images. Girls: AllStar/HBO. Girl Scout: Domitille Collardey. Girls Gone Wild: PR Newswire/Associated Press. Glitter: Shutterstock. Gluck: Getty Images. Golden Girls: ABC Studios via Getty Images. Natalia Goncharova: © 2013 Artists Rights Society (ARS), New York/ADAGP, Paris/Scala/Art Resource, NY. Jane Goodall: Getty Images. Kim Gordon: AFP/Getty Images. "Feminist Ryan Gosling," courtesy Running Press and ©Think Film/courtesy Everett Collection. Betty Grable: Associated Press. Martha Graham: Time & Life Pictures/Getty Images. Temple Grandin: WireImage/Getty Images. Hermione Granger: AllStar/Warner Brothers. Germaine Greer: Time & Life Pictures/Getty Images. Pam Grier: Getty Images. G-spot: Susie Cagle. G-string: Shutterstock. Guerrilla Girls: Associated Press. **H** Zaha Hadid: Evan Agostini/Invision/AP. Hair: Ping Zhu. Fannie Lou Hamer: Associated Press. Mia Hamm/soccer ball: Shutterstock. Chelsea Handler: FilmMagic/Getty Images. Kathleen Hanna: Getty Images. Lorraine Hansberry: Getty Images. Happiness: Elizabeth Carey Smith. Harlot: Eleanor Davis. Harpy: Eleanor Davis. Emmylou Harris: Getty Images. Debbie Harry: Getty Images. Nina Hartley: WireImage/Getty Images. Goldie Hawn: Getty Images. Salma Hayek: Getty Images. Health of the Mother: Associated Press. Hello Kitty: Courtesy Sanrio. Audrey Hepburn: Moviepix/Getty Images. Katharine Hepburn: Sarah Glidden. Eva Hesse: © Estate of Eva Hesse. Untitled, 1965, drawing on paper, 45.9 x 61.0 cm. Tate, London / Art Resource, NY. Anita Hill: Associated Press. Paris Hilton: Getty Images. Hannah Hoch: Bridgeman-Giraudon/Art Resource, NY. Billie Holiday: Redferns/Getty Images. Joan Holloway: Associated Press. Jenny Holzer: Lustmord, 1993, ink on skin; Cibachrome print, 13 x 20 in.; 33 x 50.8 cm, courtesy Jenny Holzer/Art Resource, NY. Lena Horne: NBCU Photo Bank via Getty Images. Whitney Houston: Redferns/Getty Images. Arianna Huffington: FilmMagic/Getty Images. John Hughes/Breakfast Club: AllStar/Universal Pictures. Clair Huxtable: NBC-TV/Kobal/Art Resource. Hysteria: Lisa Hanawalt. **I** Ice Cream: Ping Zhu. I Love Lucy: Getty Images. Iman: Getty Images. Indigo Girls: Getty Images. Ingrown hair: Eleanor Davis. Insatiable: Jen Sorensen. Ironing: Shutterstock. Graciela Iturbide: Cuatro pescaditos (Four Fishes), Juchitán, Oaxaca, 1986, gelatin silver photograph, image: 12 x 8 in. (30.5 x 20.3 cm), Brooklyn Museum, gift of Marcuse Pfeifer, 1990.119.38, © Graciela Iturbide, courtesy Brooklyn Museum and Graciela Iturbide. Molly Ivins: MCT via Getty Images. **J** Janet Jackson: WireImage/Getty Images. Judith Jamision: WireImage/Getty Imges. Jasmine: AllStar/Disney. Mae Jemison: Sarah Glidden. Jersey Shore: MTV/Kobal/Art Resource. Joan Jett: Getty Images. Jezebel: Warner Bros. Pictures/PhotoFest. Angelina Jolie: AFP/Getty Images. Grace Jones: WireImage/Getty Images. Erica Jong: Getty Images. Barbara Jordan: Getty Images. Florence Griffith Joyner: AFP/Getty Images. Juicy Couture: Courtesy Juicy Couture. Juno: AllStar/20th Century Fox. **K** Pauline Kael: Time & Life Pictures/Getty Images. Elena Kagan: Getty Images. Frida Kahlo: My Birth, 1932 (oil on copper), private collection/photo: Jorge Contreras Chacel/The Bridgeman Art Library, © 2013 Banco de México Diego Rivera Frida Kahlo Museums Trust, Mexico, D.F. / Artists Rights Society

(ARS), New York. Mindy Kaling: WireImage/Getty Images. Kate & Allie: Getty Images. Keds: Courtesy Keds. Flo Kennedy: Getty Images. Kewpie: Courtesy Bonniebrook Historical Society. Billie Jean King: Popperfoto/Getty Images. Kiss: Shutterstock. Kittens: Shutterstock. Knitting: Shutterstock. Knocked Up: AllStar/Universal Pictures. Beyonce Knowles: Getty Images. Lee Krasner: Mysteries, 1972, oil on cotton duck, 69½ x 89½ in. (176.5 x 227.3 cm), Brooklyn Museum, Dick S. Ramsay Fund, 73.100. © 2013 The Pollock-Krasner Foundation / Artists Rights Society (ARS), New York. Barbara Kruger: Untitled, 1985 (litho & screenprint printed in colour on wove paper), Kruger, Barbara/Detroit Institute of Arts, USA/Founders Society Purchase, John S. Newberry Fund/The Bridgeman Art Library. Aung San Suu Kyi: AFP/Getty Images. **L** Labia: Susie Cagle. Labor: Jen Sorensen. k.d. lang: Getty Images. Laptop: Shutterstock. Lassie: Time & Life Pictures/Getty Images. Wise Latina: Getty Images. Laundry: Shutterstock. Cyndi Lauper: Getty Images. Maude Lebowski: AllStar/Gramercy Pictures/Universal Pictures. Nikki S. Lee: The Hip Hop Project (2), 2001, color photograph, courtesy Sikkema Jenkins & Co. Pave 161. Leg warmers: Vanessa Davis. Annie Leibovitz: FilmMagic. Liz Lemon: Eric Liebowitz, NBC/Photofest. Annie Lennox: WireImage/Getty Images. Lettuce: Shutterstock. Edmonia Lewis: Schomburg Center, NYPL/Art Resource, NY. Librarian: Jen Sorensen. Maya Lin: Getty Images. Mary Todd Lincoln: Associated Press. Lingerie: Shutterstock. Lipstick: AMC/PhotoFest. Liquid Courage: Shutterstock. Locket: Sarah Glidden. Lara Logan: Getty Images. Lindsay Lohan: Getty Images. Lolita: Getty Images. Loofah: Shutterstock. Jennifer Lopez: WireImage/Getty Images. Audre Lorde: Getty Images. Courtney Love: Redferns/Getty Images. Luxury: Elizabeth Carey Smith. Jane Lynch: Getty Images. **M** Machismo: Shutterstock. Shirley MacLaine: Time & Life Pictures/Getty Images. Mad Men: AllStar/LionsGate. Rachel Maddow: Getty Images. Madonna: Getty Images. Makeup: Domitille Collardey. Male chauvinist pig: Jen Sorensen. Mama: Jen Sorensen. Manic Pixie Dream Girl: Camelot Pictures/Kobal/Art Resource/Bailey, KC. Wilma Mankiller: Getty Images. Sally Mann: The Washington Post/Getty Images. Mannequin: Shutterstock. Veronica Mars: The CW/PhotoFest. Penny Marshall: ABC via Getty Images. M.A.S.H.: Lisa Hanawalt. Mata Hari: Gamma-Keystone via Getty Images. Maude: CBS via Getty Images. Maxi pads: Eleanor Davis. Marissa Mayer: Bloomberg/Getty Images. Jenny McCarthy: NBCU Photo Bank via Getty Images. Melissa McCarthy: WireImage/Getty Images. Hattie McDaniel: Getty Images. Cleopatra: SSPL via Getty Images. Wu Zetian: British Library/Robana via Getty Images. Isabel I: Getty Images. Mean Girls: Paramount Pictures/PhotoFest. Julie Mehretu: WireImage/Getty Images. Rigoberta Menchu: AFP/Getty Images. Menstruation: Susie Cagle. Angela Merkel: Getty Images. M.I.A.: Getty Images. Bette Midler: Redferns/Getty Images. MILF: Elizabeth Carey Smith. Edna St. Vincent Millay: Getty Images. Kate Millett: Getty Images. Miniskirt: Vanessa Davis. Helen Mirren: Getty Images. Aristotle: Getty Images. Norman Mailer: Time & Life Pictures/Getty Images. Miss America: Getty Images. Rush Limbaugh: Associated Press. Donald Trump: Getty Images. Missionary position: Susie Cagle. Miss Piggy: Associated Press. Joan Mitchell: Time & Life Pictures/Getty Images. Joni Mitchell: Getty Images. Marilyn Monroe: Getty Images. Mary Tyler Moore: WireImage/Getty Images. Rita Moreno: WireImage/Getty Images. Robin Morgan: WireImage. Alanis Morissette: Getty Images. Morning-after Pill: Courtesy Teva Pharmaceuticals. Toni Morrison: FilmMagic/Getty Images. Kate Moss: Time & Life Pictures/Getty Images. Constance Baker Motley: Associated Press. Mr. Big: New Line Cinema/PhotoFest. Ms. Magazine: REPRINTED BY PERMISSION OF MS. MAGAZINE, © 1981, © 1982. Olivia Munn: Getty Images. Alice Munro: AFP/Getty Images. My Little Pony: Courtesy Hasbro. **N** Nachos: Shutterstock. Nanny: Walt Disney Pictures/Kobal/Art Resource. National Organization for Women: Getty Images. National Woman's Party: Bettmann/Corbis/AP Images. Nesting: Shutterstock. Louise Nevelson: Portrait, 1953-1955, etching on paper, sheet: 24⁵/₈ x 18¾ in. (62.5 x 47.6 cm), © 2013 Estate of Louise

Nevelson / Artists Rights Society (ARS), New York, courtesy Brooklyn Museum. Ingrid Newkirk: Getty Images. Nice Guys: Susie Cagle. Nichelle Nichols: Getty Images. Stevie Nicks: Ping Zhu. Florence Nightingale: Getty Images. Anais Nin: Gamma-Rapho via Getty Images. Cynthia Nixon: WireImage/Getty Images. Laura Nyro: Getty Images. **O** Annie Oakley: Bettmann/Corbis/AP Images. Joyce Carol Oates: Getty Images. Ob-gyn: Susie Cagle. Michelle Obama: Getty Images. Flannery O'Connor: Associated Press. Sandra Day O'Connor: Time & Life Pictures/Getty Images. Sinead O'Connor: Redferns/Getty Images. Odetta: Getty Images. Rosie O'Donnell: Getty Images. Sandra Oh: FilmMagic/Getty Images. Georgia O'Keeffe: Time & Life Pictures/Getty Images. Peggy Olson: AllStar/LionsGate. Yoko Ono: WireImage/Getty Images. Catherine Opie: Self-Portrait/Cutting 1993, C-print, 40 x 30 inches (101.6 x 76.2 cm) CO 164, courtesy Regen Projects. Oprah: Harpo/Kingworld/Courtesy Neal Peters Collection. Suze Orman: AFP/Getty Images. Ouija board: Shutterstock. **P** Bettie Page: Getty Images. Pageant: Kris Mukai. Camille Paglia: Time & Life Pictures/Getty Images. Sarah Palin: Getty Images. Amanda Palmer: Associated Press. Panties: Ping Zhu. Pants: Sarah Glidden. Pantyhose: Ping Zhu. Dorothy Parker: Getty Images. Sarah Jessica Parker: Getty Images. Rosa Parks: Getty Images. Dolly Parton: Getty Images. Party Girl: First Look Pictures/PhotoFest. Robert Pattinson: Getty Images. Alice Paul: Getty Images. Peep toe: Lisa Hanawalt. Nancy Pelosi: Roll Call/Getty Images. Penis: Susie Cagle. Peppermint Patty: AllStar/CBS. Period: Shutterstock. Periodic Table: Julie Teninbaum. Perm: Jen Sorenson. Eva Peron: Getty Images. Katy Perry: FilmMagic/Getty Images. Liz Phair: Redferns/Getty Images. Niki de Saint Phalle: Associated Press. Phallic: Shutterstock. Mary Pickford: Getty Images. Pie: Sarah Glidden. Sylvia Plath: Bettmann/Corbis/AP Images. PMS: Elizabeth Carey Smith. Pocahontas: Ping Zhu. Amy Poehler: Getty Images. Katha Pollitt: Courtesy Katha Pollitt. Ponytail: Ping Zhu. Pores: Shutterstock. Parker Posey: Getty Images. Beatrix Potter: Popperfoto/Getty Images. Powerpuff Girls: AllStar/Warner Bros./Cartoon Network. Jane Pratt: Associated Press. Princess: Shutterstock. Princess Diana: Ping Zhu. Marriage Proposal: Elizabeth Carey Smith. Puppy: Shutterstock. Pussy Riot: AFP/Getty Images. **Q** Queen Christina: AllStar/MGM. Queen Elizabeth: Getty Images. Queen Latifah: Associated Press. Anna Quindlen: Getty Images. **R** Gilda Radner: NBCU Photo Bank via Getty Images. Ayn Rand: Time & Life Pictures/Getty Images. Real Housewives: Bravo/PhotoFest. Red Hat Society: Elizabeth Carey Smith. Helen Reddy: Redferns/Getty Images. Rhoda: Getty Images. Condoleezza Rice: FilmMagic/Getty Images. Adrienne Rich: Getty Images. Ann Richards: Getty Images. Terry Richardson: WireImage/Getty Images. Sally Ride: Time & Life Pictures/Getty Images. Rihanna: Getty Images. Faith Ringgold: Associated Press. Riot Grrrl: Linda Rosier. Chita Rivera: Getty Images. Joan Rivers: NBCU Photo Bank via Getty Images. Roller Derby: Lisa Hanawalt. Eleanor Roosevelt: Getty Images. Roseanne: Esther Werdiger. Rosie the Riveter: Time & Life Pictures/Getty Images. J. K. Rowling: Getty Images. RU-486: Eleanor Davis. Winona Ryder: Time & Life Pictures/Getty Images. **S** Sacagawea: Getty Images. Lisbeth Salander: AllStar/Sony Pictures Releasing. Sheryl Sandberg: Bloomberg via Getty Images. Margaret Sanger: Getty Images. Sappho: Susie Cagle. Susan Sarandon: Getty Images. Jenny Saville: Self Portrait, 1992 (oil, oil pastel & paper collage on paper), private collection/photo © Christie's Images/The Bridgeman Art Library. Dorothy L. Sayers: Popperfoto/Getty Images. Miriam Schapiro: Ox, 1968 (collage, 23½ x 29³/₈ in.) collection of The Newark Museum, Gift of Ruth Bowman, Newark Museum/Art Resource, NY. Phyllis Schlafly: Associated Press. Carolee Schneemann: Interior Scroll. 1975, Screenprint with handwriting in beet juice, coffee and urine on paper, print; image and support: 90.5 x 183.0 cm, Tate, London/Art Resource, NY. Secretary: AllStar/LionsGate. Semen: Jen Sorenson. Sense and Sensibility: AllStar/Columbia. Sensitivity chip: WireImage/Getty Images. Sex and the City: HBO/PhotoFest. Sexual harassment: Library of Congress/FSA-OWI collection. Ntozake Shange: Getty Images. Charlie Sheen: WireImage. Judge Judy Sheindlin: Fox/PhotoFest. Cindy Sherman: Untitled Film Still #53, 1980, courtesy Cindy Sherman and Metro Pictures. Brooke Shields: Getty Images. Shoes: Vanessa Davis. Gabourey Sidibe: Getty Images. Sarah Silverman: FilmMagic/Getty Images. Nina Simone: Redferns/Getty Images. Lisa Simpson: Fox/PhotoFest. Lorna Simpson: Details, 1996. 21 photogravures. Digital Image © 2013 Museum Associates/LACMA. Licensed by Art Resource, NY. Skirt: Esther Werdiger. SlutWalk: Getty Images. Kiki Smith: Born, 2002 (colour litho), Brooklyn Museum of Art, New York, USA/Emily Winthrop Miles Fund/The Bridgeman Art Library. Patti Smith: Redferns/Getty Images. Zadie Smith: Getty Images. Valerie Solanas: Bettmann/Corbis/AP Images. Susan Sontag: AFP/Getty Images. Jessie Spano: NBC/Courtesy Neal Peters Collection. Spanx: Zuma. Britney Spears: Getty Images for City of Hope. Speculum: Shutterstock. Sperm: Jen Sorensen. Spinsters: Esther Werdiger. Spirit Fingers: Jen Sorensen. Elizabeth Cady Stanton: Getty Images. Gertrude Stein: Time & Life Pictures/Getty Images. Gloria Steinem: Getty Images. Jon Stewart: Getty Images. Kristen Stewart: Getty Images. Martha Stewart: FilmMagic. Stilettos: Christie Young. Stirrups: Susie Cagle. Lucy Stone: Getty Images. Meryl Streep: Getty Images. Street harassment: Tatyana Fazlalizadeh. Barbra Streisand: Time & Life Pictures/Getty Images. Suffragette: Elizabeth Carey Smith. Sugar and Spice: Domitille Collardey. Buffy the Vampire Slayer: The WB/PhotoFest. Supermodel: NY Daily News via Getty Images. Tilda Swinton: Getty Images. **T** Tampons: Lisa Hanawalt. Amy Tan: Getty Images. Elizabeth Taylor: WireImage/Getty Images. Tears: Esther Werdiger. Tarot: Molly Crabapple. Brandon Teena: Associated Press. Margaret Thatcher: Bob Thomas/Getty Images. Thelma & Louise: Getty Images. Betty Thomas: NBCU Photo Bank via Getty Images. Helen Thomas: Getty Images. Marlo Thomas: ABC via Getty Images. Emma Thompson: WireImage/Getty Images. Thong: Christie Young. Tiger mom: Getty Images for Time Warner. Toddlers & Tiaras: ZUMA Press, Inc./Alamy. Tomboy: Jen Sorensen. Lily Tomlin: Time & Life Pictures/Getty Images. Tramp Stamp: Susie Cagle. Tube top: Domitille Collardey. Harriet Tubman: Getty Images. Tina Turner: Redferns/Getty Images. Tutu: Shutterstock. **U** Tracey Ullman: Getty Images. Umbilical cord: Shutterstock. Unicorn: Esther Werdiger. **V** Vagina dentata: Domitille Collardey. Jessica Valenti: Courtesy Jessica Valenti. Valentine's Day: Getty Images. Valium: Christie Young. Lucy Van Pelt: PhotoFest. Venus: Jen Sorensen. Vibrator: Shutterstock. Diana Vreeland: Getty Images. Vulva: Eleanor Davis. **W** Waiting to Exhale: United Archives GmbH/Alamy. Waitress: Christie Young. Alice Walker: Getty Images. Kara Walker: A Work on Progress, 1998, cut paper on wall, approx. 69 x 80 inches, 175.3 x 203.2 cm, courtesy Sikkema Jenkins Co. Barbara Walters: Getty Images. Elizabeth Warren: Boston Globe via Getty Images. Waxing: Lisa Hanawalt. Sigourney Weaver: Getty Images. Ida B. Wells: Getty Images. Eudora Welty: Getty Images. Wench: Susie Cagle. Mae West: Getty Images. Edith Wharton: Getty Images. Phillis Wheatley: British Library/Robana via Getty Images. Betty White: Getty Images. Hannah Wilke: S.O.S. Starification Object Series, 1974–82 (10 b & w gelatin silver prints with 15 chewing gum sculptures mounted on board 41 x 58 inches, framed.) Collection of the Museum of Modern Art, New York. © Marsie, Emmy, Damon, and Andrew Scharlatt/ Licensed by VAGA, New York, NY. Vanessa L. Williams: Associated Press. Venus and Serena Williams: AFP/Getty Images. Ann and Nancy Wilson: Getty Images. Oprah Winfrey: Getty Images. Wings: Shutterstock. Kate Winslet: Getty Images. Anna Wintour: Sarah Glidden. Witch: Molly Crabapple. WNBA: NBAE/Getty Images. Naomi Wolf: The Washington Post/Getty Images. Wonder Woman: ABC/PhotoFest. Anna May Wong: Getty Images. Work: Shutterstock. Workout: Shutterstock. Elizabeth Wurtzel: Getty Images. **X** Xena, Warrior Princess: AFP/Getty Images. XXX: Shutterstock. **Y** Yogurt: Shutterstock. Yoga: Lisa Hanawalt. **Z** Babe Didrikson Zaharias: NY Daily News via Getty Images: Zits: Domitille Collardey. Zombies: Eleanor Davis. Zygote: Eleanor Davis. Mombies: Jen Sorensen. **ACKNOWLEDGEMENTS:** Eleanor Davis.